Key Concepts in Critical Theory

ALIENATION AND SOCIAL CRITICISM

EDITED BY

Richard Schmitt
and Thomas E. Moody

HUMANITIES PRESS

NEW JERSEY

D0209461

This collection first published in 1994 by Humanities Press International, Inc.,
Atlantic Highlands, New Jersey 07716.

© 1994 by Humanities Press

Library of Congress Cataloging-in-Publication Data

Alienation and social criticism / edited by Richard Schmitt, Thomas E. Moody.
p.   cm.   — (Key concepts in critical theory)
Includes bibliographical references and index.
ISBN 0–391–03797–8
1. Alienation (Social psychology)   I. Schmitt, Richard, 1927–   .
II. Moody, Thomas E.   III. Series.
HM291.A45   1994
302.5'44—dc20   93–12416
                                   CIP

A catalog record for this book is available from the British Library.

Printed in the United States of America

ALIENATION
AND
SOCIAL CRITICISM

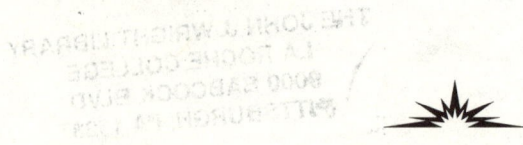

Key Concepts in Critical Theory

Series Editor
Roger S. Gottlieb

Published

JUSTICE
Edited by Milton Fisk

DEMOCRACY
Edited by Philip Green

ALIENATION AND SOCIAL CRITICISM
Edited by Richard Schmitt and Thomas E. Moody

Forthcoming

GENDER
Edited by Carol Gould

RACISM
Edited by Leonard Harris

DECONSTRUCTION AND SOCIAL THEORY
Edited by Bill Martin

ECOLOGY
Edited by Carolyn Merchant

EXPLOITATION
Edited by Kai Nielsen and Robert Ware

IMPERIALISM AND GLOBAL CAPITALISM
Edited by Robert Ross

ALIENATION AND SOCIAL CRITICISM

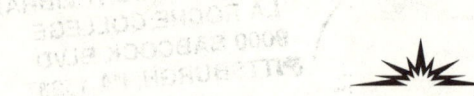

Key Concepts in Critical Theory

Series Editor
Roger S. Gottlieb

Published

JUSTICE
Edited by Milton Fisk

DEMOCRACY
Edited by Philip Green

ALIENATION AND SOCIAL CRITICISM
Edited by Richard Schmitt and Thomas E. Moody

Forthcoming

GENDER
Edited by Carol Gould

RACISM
Edited by Leonard Harris

DECONSTRUCTION AND SOCIAL THEORY
Edited by Bill Martin

ECOLOGY
Edited by Carolyn Merchant

EXPLOITATION
Edited by Kai Nielsen and Robert Ware

IMPERIALISM AND GLOBAL CAPITALISM
Edited by Robert Ross

CONTENTS

PART IV: DISABILITY

PART V: OLD AGE

PART VI: NATURE

PART VII: WHAT IS TO BE DONE?

SERIES EDITOR'S PREFACE

THE VISION OF A rational, just, and fulfilling social life, present in Western thought from the time of the Judaic prophets and Plato's *Republic*, has since the French Revolution been embodied in systematic *critical theories* whose adherents seek a fundamental political, economic, and cultural transformation of society.

These critical theories—varieties of Marxism, socialism, anarchism, feminism, gay/lesbian liberation, ecological perspectives, discourses by antiracist, anti-imperialist, and national liberation movements, and utopian/critical strains of religious communities—have a common bond that separates them from liberal and conservative thought. They are joined by the goal of sweeping social change; the rejection of existing patterns of authority, power, and privilege; and a desire to include within the realms of recognition and respect the previously marginalized and oppressed.

Yet each tradition of critical theory also has its distinct features: specific concerns, programs, and locations within a geometry of difference and critique. Because of their intellectual specificity and the conflicts among the different social groups they represent, these theories have often been at odds with one another, differing over basic questions concerning the ultimate cause and best response to injustice, the dynamics of social change, the optimum structure of a liberated society, the identity of the social agent who will direct the revolutionary change, and in whose interests the revolutionary change will be made.

In struggling against what is to some extent a common enemy, in overlapping and (at times) allying in the pursuit of radical social change, critical theories to a great extent share a common conceptual vocabulary. It is the purpose of this series to explore that vocabulary, revealing what is common and what is distinct, in the broad spectrum of radical perspectives.

For instance, although both Marxists and feminists may use the word "exploitation," it is not clear that they really are describing the same phenomenon. In the Marxist paradigm the concept identifies the surplus labor appropriated by the capitalist as a result of the wage-labor relation. Feminists have used the same term to refer as well to the unequal amounts of housework, emotional nurturance, and child raising performed by women in the nuclear family. We see some similarity in the notion of group inequality (capitalists/workers, husbands/wives) and of unequal exchange. But we also see critical differences: a previously "public" concept extended to the private realm; one first centered in the economy of goods now moved into the life of emotional relations. Or, for another example, when deep ecologists speak of "alienation" they may be exposing the contradictory and destructive relations of humans *to* nature. For socialists and anarchists, by contrast, "alienation" basically refers only to relations among human beings. Here we find a profound contrast between what is and is not included in the basic arena of politically significant relationships.

What can we learn from exploring the various ways different radical perspectives utilize the same terminology?

Most important, we see that these key concepts have histories and that the theories of which they are a part and the social movements whose spirit they embody take shape through a process of political struggle as well as of intellectual reflection. As a corollary, we can note that the creative tension and dissonance among the different uses of these concepts stem not only from the endless play of textual interpretation (the different understandings of classic texts, attempts to refute counterexamples or remove inconsistencies, rereadings of history, reactions to new theories), but also from the continual movement of social groups. Oppression, domination, resistance, passion, and hope are crystallized here. The feminist expansion of the concept of exploitation could only grow out of the women's movement. The rejection of a purely anthropocentric (human-centered, solely humanistic) interpretation of alienation is a fruit of people's resistance to civilization's lethal treatment of the biosphere.

Finally, in my own view at least, surveys of the differing applications of these key concepts of critical theory provide compelling reasons to see how complementary, rather than exclusive, the many radical perspectives are. Shaped by history and embodying the spirit of the radical movements that created them, these varying applications each have in them some of the truth we need in order to face the darkness of the current social world and the ominous threats to the earth.

ROGER S. GOTTLIEB

ACKNOWLEDGMENTS

THE EDITORS ARE GRATEFUL to the following publishers and authors for permission to reprint their articles:

Pantheon Books, a division of Random House, for permission to reprint two interviews from *Working* (1974) by Studs Terkel.

University of Notre Dame Press for permission to reprint "A Proposal" from Frithjof Bergman, *On Being Free* (1987).

Sandra Bartky for permission to include "Narcissism, Femininity and Alienation." This piece appeared originally in *Social Theory and Practice* 8(1982) and is now reprinted in Sandra Bartky, *Femininity and Domination* (New York: Routledge, 1990).

Kluwer Academic Publishers for permission to reprint Iris Marion Young, "Pregnant Embodiment: Subjectivity and Alienation," originally published in *The Journal of Medicine and Philosophy* 9(1984).

Maria Lugones for permission to reprint "Playfulness, 'World'-Travelling, and Loving Perception" originally published in *Hypatia* 2(1987).

To Grove Weidenfeld for permission to reprint "The Negro and Language" from Frantz Fanon, *Black Skin, White Masks* (New York: Grove Press, 1967).

To June Jordan for permission to reprint "Report from the Bahamas" from *On Call* (Boston: South End Press, 1985).

To Irving Zola for permission to reprint "Communications Barriers between the Worlds of 'Able-Bodiedness' and 'Disability'" and "Four Steps on the Road to Invalidity: The Denial of Sexuality, Anger, Vulnerability and Potentiality" from the *Australian Disability Review* 3(1988).

To Shevy Healey and Calyx Press, Corvallis, Oregon, for permission to reprint "Growing to be an Old Woman: Age and Ageism" from *Women and Aging: An Anthology by Women* (Corvallis: Calyx Press, 1986).

To Cynthia Rich for permission to reprint "Ageism and the Politics of Beauty" from *Sojourner* (May 1988).

To Bill McKibben for permission to reprint portions of "The End of Nature," first printed in *The New Yorker* (September 11, 1989).

To Steven Vogel and the editors of *Social Theory and Practice* for permission to reprint "Marx and Alienation from Nature" from *Social Theory and Practice* 14.

To Roger Gottlieb and Temple University Press for permission to reprint "The Dominated Self" from *History and Subjectivity* (Philadelphia: Temple University Press, 1987; paperback edition Atlantic Highlands, NJ: Humanities Press, 1993).

To Firebrand Books for permission to reprint Minnie Bruce Pratt, "Identity: Skin, Blood, Heart" from Elly Bulkin, Minnie Bruce Pratt, and Barbara Smith, eds., *Yours in Struggle: Three Feminist Perspectives on Anti-Semitism and Racism* (New York: Long Haul Press, 1984).

Why Is the Concept of Alienation Important?

RICHARD SCHMITT

ASK ANYONE ABOUT THE shortcomings of our society and they will mention injustice. Some people own many opulent mansions; others sleep in the streets. Some people receive highly sophisticated and costly health care, but many children die from lack of elementary medical attention in their first year. Some young people attend lavish schools. Others leave school without having learned to read.

You will also hear complaints about rampant corruption: the standards of probity in public life are deplorably low. Shady deals, conflict of interests, and dishonesty are so common that much of the time they do not even attract attention.

Many will talk about the unbelievable level of violence in this society—wife beating and murder are daily occurrences, as are children bringing loaded guns to school. Violence, or the threat of it, is our preferred solution for international conflict, as well for disagreements at home.

But you will only rarely find someone who talks about alienation. The concept of alienation is not in most people's vocabulary. The variety of experiences of alienation are familiar, but the vocabulary to describe those experiences is not. Hence many people find themselves suffering without being able to articulate their suffering or knowing how to deal with it. For alienation underlies much of the suffering and decay of our society. It is one of the major sources of its ills. Much that is amiss is due to alienation in its different embodiments.

It is the purpose of this book to make alienation a more familiar idea. We need to begin by clarifying the concept of alienation itself.

I. MARX'S IDEAS ABOUT ALIENATION

The discussion of alienation stands in the shadow of Marx. What has been written about alienation is, by and large, a gloss on Marx's notes in his *Economic and Philosophical Manuscripts*. But Marx did not leave us a complete theory of alienation; his notes on the subject are just that, notes that introduce a number of major themes. All of them are important, but they do not fit together into one complete and consistent theory.

One central theme focuses on the individual worker, who is said to live in order to work instead of working in order to live (Tucker 1978: 204). Work is the main purpose of the worker's life. What is most genuinely human—the free development of one's capacities, and the expression of one's personality in one's activities—is withheld from the worker whose life consists of short periods of rest between long days of work. "As a result . . . the worker no longer feels him-[or her]self to be freely active in any but his [or her] animal functions" (Tucker 1978: 74).

Another theme is the *experience* of alienation. Here is what Marx tells us about that:

> What then, constitutes the alienation of labor? First, the fact that labor is *external* to the worker, i.e. it does not belong to his essential being, that in his work, therefore, he does not affirm himself but denies himself, does not feel content but unhappy. . . . (Tucker 1978: 74)

Work is "external" to the worker; it is a mere means to staying alive, and does not contribute to enriching his or her life. In their work, workers are estranged from themselves because they do not affirm themselves in their work. They are, therefore, unhappy.

Marx introduces an additional theme, powerlessness, where the concept of alienation has a much wider scope. Workers produce only to strengthen their enemies, they do not control the process of work, or the purposes that work serves. They are capable of being free but are not, in fact, free (Schmitt 1987: 151).

But we can see that powerlessness both contributes to alienation—the politically and economically powerless have no choice but to live only in order to survive—and is a result of it—if all you can do is survive, your life is not really your own, your person remains undeveloped and most of your abilities lie fallow and so you are powerless in the sense that you cannot come anywhere near being the person you might be. Most of your powers remain undeveloped. You are powerless as a person.

Gathering together these three themes we get a fairly familiar conception of alienation: the alienated are deprived of formal rights, such as political participation, and are hence unable to ensure humane working conditions and adequate wages. They are therefore unable to live a fully human life in which they can develop as many of their capacities as they choose. The wage workers of the early industrial revolution, as well as the very oppressed in our society, exemplify alienation in that sense: they are too poor, too powerless, to become as well-developed, as personally and politically powerful, as they might, if they were given the opportunities to which they are entitled. Alienation, in that sense, is "a crippling of body and mind" (Marx 1967: 363), of being less than fully human, failing to develop fully. Persons are alienated if they lack fulfillment (Ollman 1971; Olsen 1978; Schaff 1970). This seems to imply that alienation is a universal condition for humans—surely no one is or ever could be completely fulfilled. This is true enough, but where *social criticism* enters is where alienation is the result of social features that could and should be changed. It is not a criticism of a society that people are not completely fulfilled; but it *is* a criticism of a society that people are arbitrarily and unnecessarily unfulfilled.

But there exists in Marx a further, different understanding of alienation: he observes in the same set of notes, that as a fully free and developed human being one "contemplates . . . [one]self in a world that . . . [one] has created" (Tucker 1978: 76). Here alienation is no longer powerlessness in the economic or the political realm but finding oneself in a world which one has not created, in which one not only does not recognize oneself, but is constantly reminded that one does not really belong. This is the alienation of the victims of sexism, racism, ageism, and class prejudice. This concept of alienation is considerably broader than the previous ones. Here alienation is not just the result of being deprived of rights that everyone else has, and the opportunities to avail oneself of them. What is missing, in addition, is the ability to participate in shaping one's world. But in shaping a world one defines the identities of the persons in it—their roles, their obligations, their rights. Unable to shape our world, we are unable to define our identities, but rather live out lives prescribed to us by others. We are, in that sense, not ourselves.

The existentialist tradition echoes these different aspects of alienation. Alienation is an injury to the self—alienated selves are powerless, unhappy. Neither their lives nor their persons are their own. Kierkegaard describes alienation as an inability to act or to commit oneself. Alienated selves are too indecisive, too vague and unfocused to say: This is who I am; this is what I want; this is what I am going to do (Kierkegaard 1959). Nietzsche criticizes modern men and women in very similar terms. Their desires are flaccid, their wills corrupted, they lack the courage to engage in risky projects, or to pursue their goals through difficulties and conflicts (Nietzsche 1954). Heidegger sees alienation in our unwillingness to strike out for ourselves, being anxious, instead, to follow the latest fashion, to wear, say, or do whatever everyone else wears, says, and does (Heidegger 1962). Sartre, finally, detects an inevitable distance between oneself and what one does: we are, he says, always pretending to be someone, but we never fully are that particular person because a part of us is always standing aside, observing our own performance of a role (Sartre 1956).

Different descriptions of alienation emphasize different aspects of the experience. That should not worry us; after all alienation is experienced in many different ways. It appears to different people in different guises, and they therefore describe it in somewhat different ways.[1]

II. EXAMPLES

Let's look at some examples of alienation: they will show that we need to use the broader sense of alienation. Alienation is more than being deprived of the ability to develop fully; it cannot be understood unless we acknowledge forthrightly that the alienated are not themselves, because their identities, having been imposed on them, are not their own. Hence they are always at odds with and strangers to themselves.

Here is June Jordan writing about her mother:

> No one had ever suggested to her, no one had ever shown my mother, a kind of "women's work" that might be easy or enjoyable or generally regarded as "important" or prestigious or recognizable as the invention of power. My mother had never heard of women who command militia units, or chair international committees for human rights, or piece together movements for the liberation of a people. What she knew was that even as a child, she must devise a means of survival where nothing of that sort was readily available to her. What she knew was that surviving as a Black woman meant living on her own, depending absolutely on no one other than herself. . . . What she knew was that surviving as a Black woman meant hard, endless work that left her dark hands swollen and gray from the bleach in the laundry water and cracked from the ceaseless rubbing of the clothes against the rippled surface of the scrub board. (Jordan 1985: 104–5)

At first reading, this passage seems to be a clear representative of the familiar understanding of alienation: here is a woman whose life was filled to overflowing with hard work, who never had the opportunity to which we all are entitled of finding out that there is more to life than hard work, that there are joys that only education, leisure, a certain material well-being, and meaningful work can bring. This woman is alienated, everyone will tell us, because she was denied her basic rights and access to the minimum of material well-being we should all enjoy. As a result she was unable to develop fully as a human being.

But look again: she was not only poor and forever working hard for others, but as a *Black woman* she was unable to rely on anyone else because no one could be trusted not to take advantage of her, not to turn on her unexpectedly, not to let her nurture him only to disappear, not to allow her to take care of house and children faithfully only to fire her at a moment's notice. She finds herself in a world in which the law guarantees her a long list of rights to property, to bear arms, to think and worship as she pleases, to speak her mind, and to vote and run for office. But in the same world, she *learns* from bitter experience, that she is not a person like other persons, that she does not play a role in the worlds of others as an important participant. What is more, she learns that she is banished from the human family *because she is a Black woman*. Yes, she lacks minimal material and educational opportunities. But more importantly, because she is a Black woman, she is cast out from the human race, her needs are no one's concerns, commitments to her may be broken, and she does not deserve recognition, gratitude, let alone love.

In a long lifetime of work she has learned her lesson. She has learned to be a person "living on her own, depending on absolutely no one" and with that she has learned a lesson about her self that love, sharing, trust are not for her. Did she also learn that she did not deserve any of that? June Jordan does not tell us. But we know many persons in similar conditions who learn just that, that they are seriously defective. How do they learn that lesson? Listen to another passage from June Jordan's book:

> We [viz., Blacks in America] approach our maturity inside a larger social body that will not support our efforts to become anything other than the clones of those who are neither our mothers or our fathers. We begin to grow up in a house where every true mirror shows us the face of somebody who does not belong there, whose walk and whose talk will never look or sound "right," because that house was meant to shelter a family that is hostile to us. (Jordan 1985: 123)

For similar descriptions of the black experience consult Frantz Fanon (Fanon 1967: 36). Growing up in a culture that not only does not respect the ways of black people—or of women, or of workers, or of the aged, the handicapped, homosexuals, and others—but is actively hostile to them, persons learn to be hostile to themselves and to think, like June Jordan's mother, that she did not deserve love and trust and respite under the care of friends. They begin to think of themselves, as Fanon points out, in the dominant language in which being black is being inferior, in which being female is to be of lesser value, in which being a worker is being uncouth, or in which being old is being incompetent.

Here emerges a much more profound sense of alienation, not just a lack of opportunities that results in leaving talents undeveloped, but a deep cleavage in one's very self: the hostility of the dominant opinions and dominant groups in the society becomes one's own and thus one's own self becomes loathsome or defective or insignificant to oneself. One is estranged not just from this ability or that possible life path, but from ever being oneself. Nothing illustrates that better than the experience of women who have, in fact, been able to develop their talents but who end up feeling that the work they do is not really theirs, that their lives do not belong to them, because they grew up in a world hostile to them, especially if they are intelligent and well-educated.

> I do not have the sense of having been at the center of my life, directing its course; I am not even aware of having been there at all, living it all out. Nor do I seem to myself to be the Outcome of All That Has Happened. I recognize

only a certain continuity of style, the style of a solemn owl hoping to grow up a womanly Charlie Chaplin, but not quite able to manage the juggling with the careless air it requires. (Rorty 1977: 41)

The author, an accomplished, widely published, and respected philosopher, does not lack the ordinary rights everyone has, she does not lack material well-being or access to the best that our society has to offer. But she lives in a society that still believes that

A good woman should not want work of her own; the wish for such work betrays 'neurosis' or, worse still, 'narcissism'. Above all one should be healthy and good. (Ruddick 1977: 144)

Living in a world that restricts the roles accessible to women, that regards white people as exempt from practicing the ordinary decencies in relation to Blacks, and that is too frightened of aging to see old persons for who they are—in such a world it is difficult, if not impossible, to be at one with oneself, to be the wholehearted and unquestioned author of one's work, or to trust oneself to find persons one can trust.

This is a much broader concept of alienation than the more common one of alienation as the failure to develop one's abilities fully. Here alienation consists of self-estrangement not just from what one might possibly be or accomplish, but from one's innermost self. Living in a world that does not accept one, one is unable to be fully unified because one cannot fully affirm oneself—to use Marx's phrase once more. Even when someone is able to develop fully s/he is vulnerable to alienation to the extent that s/he cannot make that development her or his own, cannot "feel at home" in the accomplishments and recognition such development brings.

The person one is becomes invisible behind the derogatory definition. Nor would one be less alienated were the stereotype that conceals one's individual uniqueness purely laudatory. There are those among us, persons of goodwill, who think that Black persons are in some way superior, enabled by racism and suffering, or that prisoners are all innocent victims of an unjust society. There are men who, genuinely, put women on a pedestal. But such stereotypes, are, in the end, no less hurtful than the negative stereotypes, because in either case the person must fit into a ready-made identity. They are robbed of the opportunity to define themselves and it is for that reason that their selves are felt to be not their own because, indeed, they are not, but are imposed from the outside.

What results is clearly alienation in a broad sense: alienation attacks the very center of one's being because one is always at one remove from oneself and one's acts. Alienation is more than being deprived of the wherewithal to develop fully; one is deprived of a more profound and important ability: to take part in defining who one is, as Black, as woman, as old person, or as worker. An alien identity is imposed from the outside.

III. Varieties of Alienation

But how is this alien self imposed? And by whom? The answers to these questions are complex. Alienation is imposed in different ways, by individuals or by groups, by others and, even, by oneself. It is avoidable in some cases, and not in others.

Marx observed that the alienated find themselves in a world not of their making, a world in which they are not active participants but the victims of impersonal forces. Hence the alienated do not feel themselves to be at the center of their lives. In order to get a clear view of that sort of alienation we need to go back into history for many centuries and look at the life of a medieval peasant.

You can imagine him getting up while it is still dark on a later winter morning. He gets out of bed and slips into the clothes he wore the day before. These are clothes he has worn for many years. At one time they were his father's Sunday best, but now after many years of hard wear, washing, and mending, they are what he wears day in, day out. He grabs a piece of black bread and goes out into the barn to milk the cow. Then, because it is time to plow, he hitches the horse to the plow and goes to prepare the field for planting. He does what he has always done, and what his father has done before him. His people have been farm tenants for many generations, as have been the other peasants in the village. His house looks like theirs. His life is like theirs, governed in small detail by customs, and by the rules the priest lays down for his flock.

It is a hard life, but in many ways not unlike the life of working people in our world—except for one thing: this peasant not only does not notice that he lives in a world not of his own making, but does not think that it is for him to make his world. His universe is God's creation; He has assigned roles and places to everyone, and everyone is expected to do his job as assigned. Sometimes that job is enjoyable; often it is hard and bitter. But there is no choice but to do well, to work hard and do one's assigned task.

In that respect, our situation is different and more complicated. While we all recognize that we live in a society which makes (sometimes) justified demands on us and assigns us certain obligations, we also think of ourselves as distinct individuals with our own life plans and values. Each person has, or should have, an identity that is self-created and self-maintained. We differ from the imaginary medieval peasant in thinking very differently about ourselves. Each of us has his or her own life to lead as s/he sees fit within the limitations imposed by others' rights to the same sort of self-determination. We have personal identities, all our own, which the medieval peasant did not have. He was content to be known as his father's son, and to do the work his father did. He did not insist that he have his own name, or choose an occupation that suited him particularly. Hence we are capable of being alienated—we can find ourselves in a world not of our own making—while that was a problem he could not and did not have. For us it is possible to live in a world that we *did* make; failing in that we are alienated. For him, world making was not a possibility, neither, therefore, was alienation.

Our sense of ourselves as deserving a life of our own, as self-determining individuals, is an important ingredient of alienation. There are very different sorts of alienation depending on the different ways in which one's self is not of one's own making, or one's self-determination is compromised by oneself, or by others, or by events not under anyone's control.

Some alienation is imposed by ordinary life changes. Aging produces bodily changes that one adjusts to only with effort. I look in the mirror and realize that I think of myself as a much younger man. My mental image of myself does not have as many wrinkles as I do. Here is a perfectly straightforward sort of alienation: it is specific, usually temporary, where I do not recognize myself in the mirror and have difficulties living with ease in my changing body. Iris Young describes those sorts of experiences in her description of being pregnant.[2]

Some alienation is imposed by naked coercion. Slaves, prisoners, whole populations moved forcibly to a new location, far away from their familiar land, where they must live under unfamiliar conditions and find new strategies for survival. They experience alienation. Examples of that are very common, from the removal of Native Americans from their tribal lands to reservations to moving people out of their houses to make way for a highway or some other edifice in the name of "urban renewal." One finds oneself in an unfamiliar place where one does not know one's way around. There are different trees and plants, and the familiar cues about impending weather, or the changing seasons are missing. One lives in an unfamiliar world, and to that extent is powerless. Here alienation is imposed from the outside by a hostile group. One is forced into a world, not of one's own making, in which one does not recognize oneself.

Other kinds of alienation are imposed from the outside in similar ways, but the imposition is not as obvious because it seems well-meaning and benign. The "gentleman" who opens the door for a woman, the man who takes a chair out of a woman's hand to carry it for her—there are many acts of apparent kindness which reinforce the lesson that women's bodies are weak, or that women forever need protection and help. Teachers advise minority students not to aim for college, or steer working-class students towards vocational training. They appear well-meaning, and perhaps they genuinely are, but the effect is to hamper the expansion of the student's power, as male politeness has the effect of restricting women to roles of weakness and dependence. These actions force people into worlds made by others. They impose definitions of the self, of what a person can do, which women or minorities had no hand in shaping.

In these different ways, alienated people find themselves living in a society which has already determined who they are: a black man, a woman, an old person. With each of these labels comes a series of harsh prejudgments: of lacking enterprise or intelligence, of lacking rationality, of being generally useless. These stereotypes are enforced in a multitude of informal and more formal ways: Men whistle at women and make sexual comments, touch them, make sexual advances. They are just being "friendly." Such established and accepted practices define a situation and the persons in it, by restricting what one, as a woman, can do. She can play along and thus be in the traditional role as sex object. If she protests, a different set of traditional responses come into play to punish or reject her as either overly emotional, frigid, or "bitchy." Thus there are a limited number of ways in which she can *act*. But one is how one acts. Restricting one's scope of actions makes one be who one is, or defines one. Many other sorts of informal practices give women a certain sort of social identity: The way they are, or are not, listened to, how men talk to them, and about what, what sorts of things one expects them to be good at, or to be interested in, etc. And each of these definitional practices has its appropriate enforcement practice: Women who insist on using their intelligence will be isolated socially, etc.

As a result large numbers of persons in our society lack autonomy. Their lives, their values and projects are not their own, because they are predefined by others, without consulting the persons whose lives and persons are thus defined. This is not merely a matter of being deprived of opportunities, but of not being oneself, of not being at one with oneself. What one would like, what one would choose is forbidden because it conflicts with the prevailing preconceptions of what is fitting for such as oneself: no, women cannot be president; no, black people cannot claim that their way of speaking English is as legitimate as that of white people, etc. More insidious even are the many cases where people are given inconsistent definitions: allowed into professions, women or people of color are made to feel out of place, and thus can never feel fully that their professional projects are theirs. We saw examples of that earlier in section II. In all these examples, particular individuals cannot say: This is who I am, this is what I do, this is what I stand for, because their particularity, their uniqueness, is concealed by the prevailing conception of what "women," "Blacks," etc., are like. Thus the socially imposed definition prevents the individual from defining who s/he is. Whatever ends up being his/her occupation, or way of life, is thus in a very profound way not their own, because it is imposed, not chosen.

This is alienation; much of it is imposed without one's noticing it at the time, often by people who are friends and whose motives are of the best. Often this becomes alienation with which one cooperates willingly. Living long enough in a world not of one's own making, one adjusts. One begins to believe that one is a weak woman, a not quite trustworthy person, not meant for great deeds, or forever condemned to be an outsider. One internalizes the identities that others have concocted for one from their own greed and interests, or from their own fears.

Everyone is, to use a different example, afraid of death, or serious impairment. We try to evade that fear; we do not want to be reminded that everyone will die; most of us will grow old and lose some of our powers; many will be seriously impaired before we die. These are facts, but they are uncomfortable and we do not want to be reminded of them. Thus we pretend that old people and people with disabilities are different. They belong to a different race. What makes them inferior will not happen to us. We transmute our fear for ourselves into derogatory stereotypes about others. But for most of us that evasive strategy will backfire. The day comes when you are old enough to retire and you will think that you are "over the hill," and the jokes you made about others are now jokes about yourself. You have become an agent in your own alienation. In the different selections of this book, you will find many examples of the different ways in which we are complicit in our own alienation.

IV. LIBERALISM AND THE AUTONOMOUS INDIVIDUAL

In our culture alienation is not a central concern. In order to understand why that is so, we need to understand the dominant outlook in our society. Liberalism dominates our thinking about politics, and, more generally, about the ways we fashion our social life.

Liberalism stresses, no doubt correctly, that persons differ widely in their needs and desires and endowments. Hence it insists that

> . . . society, being composed of a plurality of persons, each with his own aims, interests and conceptions of the good, is best arranged when it is governed by principles that do not *themselves* presuppose any particular conception of the good. (Sandel 1982: 1)

The well-organized society does not impose a conception of the good life on each of its members, but instead allows each one the maximum latitude to shape his/her own life, consistent with granting similar latitude to everyone else. To this end, liberal society guarantees to all the same set of rights to pursue goals of their own choosing and to participate in the direction of common affairs. In addition, a minimal equalization of opportunities may be necessary in order to allow each member of the society the opportunity to make use of his or her freedoms. While the extent to which the society needs to supply equal opportunities is a matter of vigorous debate, there is no doubt that some extreme conditions of poverty and degradation make a mockery of any claim to give equal freedom to all citizens.

In conditions of extreme deprivation or under repressive regimes, individuals clearly are not able to pursue the good life as they perceive it. Where bare survival is daily in question, pursuit of human fulfillment is not a possibility and work serves mere physical existence, rather than physical existence being the precondition of creative human work. Similarly, under repressive regimes, human beings, even if reasonably well-fed, housed, and schooled, do not have the freedom of choice to determine their own life paths for themselves and thus cannot aspire to genuine human fulfillment.

Liberalism insists, therefore, that each one of us must be guaranteed certain rights, as well as a minimum of material well-being in order to enable us to live the good life as we conceive of it. It insists that as long as we are free to believe what we choose, and are free to live according to our beliefs (provided we do not interfere with the similar freedoms of others), we are as free as we could be and our life is fully our own. The freedom to live according to our beliefs definitely requires some legal guarantees of the requisite rights, to free speech and conscience, freedom to own property and to move as one pleases and, more generally, certain rights to privacy.

Liberalism affirms what I said earlier, namely that in our society we take for granted that people lead different sorts of lives, that they choose what sorts of lives to lead, and that they are entitled to make such choices and to live by them. Liberalism values this diversity of life patterns, chosen by different individuals, that makes alienation possible. Only people who aspire, and believe firmly that they have a right to aspire, to live their own lives, can be prevented from doing that, in the different ways I just indicated. Only they can, therefore, be alienated.

When it talks about contemplating oneself in a world of one's own making, liberalism uses the language of rights. In order for each of us to make our lives and ourselves be who we want them to be, we need certain rights that are familiar to all: civil rights to protect us against political and social coercion, political rights in order to be able to fashion the political environment, and economic rights to private property in order to be able to provide for ourselves and ours the wherewithal needed for the life we have chosen. If our rights are respected by all others, liberalism seems to think, we can each make our own worlds, determine ourselves, and lead lives we choose for ourselves.

But it is not difficult to see in the light of the discussion of alienation in this chapter, and in the selections that follow, that rights are necessary but are not sufficient to ward off alienation. A preliminary indication of that is the fact that some groups have in this century managed to improve their rights situation. But there is little evidence that their alienation has been ameliorated. Alienation is a certainty as long as your rights are methodically violated. If they are respected, however, alienation may still prevail. The guarantee of rights does not guarantee full self-determination. But liberalism does not know what else one might need. Liberalism therefore does not understand alienation and, in fact, conceals it. Liberalism's language of rights is just not adequate for understanding alienation.

The language of rights, for instance, does not allow one to protest alienation.[3] Rights are, ultimately, always legal rights, at least insofar as they are enforceable only in courts of law. For example, women have the right not to be physically abused. Everyone has a right to have his or her person and possessions to be secure. But women's alienation is maintained not only by physical abuse but by *what* men say to women—e.g., calling grown women "girls" to suggest that they are not full adults deserving the consideration and respect of full adults—and *how* men talk to women—many men will suddenly turn a serious conversation into a flirtatious one—again to suggest that a woman is a sex object, not a serious intellectual, lawyer, or business associate.

These are just two of a large number of different ways in which male behavior maintains women's alienation, but they are interesting cases for our purposes. If we discuss these two cases in terms of rights, we are immediately faced with a conflict of rights: don't men have a right to free speech as do women? One does not want to deny that, but I think one must also see that the conflict between men and women is not a conflict of rights. Yes, we do and should have the right to free speech. But having that right does not allow you to speak in traditional ways about members of other groups—or even your own—because those traditional ways consolidate alienation. The language of rights is too limited to allow us to talk about the injuries we do to each other in promoting alienation. We need to look more closely at liberalism and its conception of human beings in order to understand that.

Liberalism is a response to the underlying conditions that make alienation possible: the acceptance that each of us is entitled and, indeed, should lead his or her life as s/he chooses. But it interprets this self-determination in such a narrow way that it cannot understand alienation and, in fact, must conceal it. Why does it do that?

Liberalism arose in opposition to and as a critique of the sort of communal society which I previously characterized in the description of the imaginary medieval peasant. That was a society where individual life choices counted for little, for life was governed by community standards, by traditions, and by the Church. In such a society the project of having a life of one's own, of living in a world one has created, is not a possibility because one's life is determined by the choices of the group as embodied in the traditions, in the ways in which "we" have always done things. In reaction to this collectivist society, liberalism adopted a very individualistic stance. What makes my life mine is that I determine it, *by myself*, that I make my choices, all by myself, that no one can tell me what to do, and I can tell anyone who tries to leave me alone. Living in a world one has created came to mean that one's world was one's own, *alone*.

Liberalism operates with a very specific concept of persons—it not only places great value on the autonomy of individuals, but defines autonomy in a very specific way. By being autonomous it means being subject only to one's own values or choices. If fully autonomous, persons are governed only by their own values or choices, which are clearly distinguishable from anyone else's, and by the rules of justice that guarantee the same freedoms to everyone else. Persons are autonomous because the rules they follow are *theirs*, because they adopted them for themselves and by themselves. The autonomous person is haunted by the specter of heteronomy, of being a conformist, of adopting moral principles from others without sufficient thought to truly make them one's own (Benn 1975/6, 1982; Frankfurt 1971; Haworth 1986; Kuflik 1984; Sandel 1982; Young 1986).

Human beings, on this view, are quite separate from one another. Each runs his or her life as s/he sees fit; each defines who s/he is. Rights specify the ways in which each of us must leave the other be: I must let you say what you have to say; I must respect your private property; I must refrain from using physical violence to prevent you from political action. You have the same obligations towards me. Each of us has a series of rights and these rights determine precise ways in which we must leave each other alone. As long as we do that, we are innocent of any problems another person may have.[4] But in the real world we are not separate, and we are not alone. Our lives are intertwined in immensely complex ways. How we talk to each other, what we say, and in what tone of voice affects who we each separately are. We each have a hand in who each of us is. Yes, we have rights to be left alone in specific ways and these rights are very important. But if you respect my rights you may still, in many other ways in which we are implicated in each others' lives, burden me with your preconceptions and co-opt me into being who you want me to be. The conflicts over those sorts of influences on each other are conflicts over alienation, but they are not conflicts over rights. For rights belong to us insofar as we are separate; alienation affects us insofar as we are not.

Everyone knows that we are shaped by our environment and are socialized into certain values. Liberals cannot and do not deny that. But they think about socialization in their own characteristic way. They maintain that, in a well-ordered society, every person, white or black, male or female, is capable of autonomy, of forming his or her goals and values independently of social pressures or deprivations. We are in a variety of ways affected by our social context but these effects are not inescapable. A person who is not defective and who makes an effort to be rational is able to recognize the influences of environment and family and then choose to allow them to continue to be influences, or to free him or herself from them (Young 1980). Who a person is, is not *necessarily* shaped by the social practices of a culture. A person can always win out to independence and self-determination to escape social pressures and demands. If there are social prejudices, they can be uncovered and rejected. Liberalism not only values autonomy highly, but believes that it is attainable for human beings of ordinary endowment and character, if only we are given the rights and minimal material prerequisites to which we are entitled.[5] This means that each person can become a separate person so that s/he can be self-determining. Overcoming social pressures is understood as going off by oneself, isolating oneself, making choices for oneself, in the spaces that are provided for us by our different sorts of rights. The claim is that we can overcome the forces of socialization by separating ourselves. Being one's own person is to be impervious to outside influences that one chooses not to be affected by.

But that isolation, that immunity to the effects of others on ourselves—either of individual others, or of groups who affect us as teachers, employers, or via the media—is purely imaginary. We are always enmeshed in complex social interactions that shape our very individualities. Insofar as liberalism overlooks that, it must ignore the effect of social forces on the individual. Liberalism overlooks alienation—the destruction of selves whose social identity is prescribed without their being allowed to participate in defining it. If persons are overwhelmed by oppression, if they bow to pressure and become complicit in their own alienation, the liberal sees this as an individual failure. There is no alienation in the liberal's view of society. But there are a lot of weak, neurotic, and conformist individuals.

V. Liberalism Produces and Maintains Alienation

But by concealing alienation, liberalism actively perpetuates alienation. If it is possible, as the liberal protests, to surmount the effects of social conditions, if I am, for instance, able to unmask the racial stereotypes for the irrational prejudices they are, then I need not let them affect me, and hence the sort of destruction of human lives, of the very core of human selves, described in the preceding section, is not only not necessary, but is the fault of the person who allows her or himself to be destroyed by that prejudice. From the liberal's point of view, June Jordan's mother is not the innocent victim of her condition that has made her into a person who is unable to trust because she thinks that she does not deserve to be trusted. On the contrary she is herself to blame for what happened to her because instead of internalizing racial prejudice she should have been able to see it for the prejudice it is and stepped out boldly into the world, knowing that she was as good and as valuable as the next person.

If that seems unduly harsh, one can always say that this woman, being very poor and having no access to education, may well have been burdened too heavily to be able to emancipate herself from prejudice. But we cannot avoid similar judgments in the case of the women who have gained access to education but who still feel that their work is not theirs, that they are impostors, not capable of doing well. Their self-estrangement is suffered while they are free citizens, living in comfortable circumstances. It must therefore be the result of personal failures. The women scholars who feel ill at ease in their role must be called "neurotic"—unless one chooses to take their experience as proof that women's "natural" fulfillment lies elsewhere and they feel out of place, because they have put themselves in a place that is not rightfully theirs. The liberal, holding on to the belief that one can insulate oneself against unwanted external influences, that the beliefs and values of others need not affect mine, has no choice but to interpret these cases as the results of personal failures, specifically failures to emancipate oneself from one's surroundings, failure to become "the captain of one's ship, and the master of one's soul."

This misrepresentation is useful for those who are powerful in this society: it allows men, who enforce alienation on women, to blame women for not being like men. Instead of seeing the existence of the stereotypical wife and mother as evidence against the liberal conception of human nature, the assumption of autonomy led to the conclusion that women were defective men. That allowed men to "help" women, it created a "woman question" that men could debate, while maintaining the underlying power relations. Thus men could conceal their responsibility for the condition of women behind the stance of the chivalrous protector of women.

More importantly, the misrepresentation made it difficult even to state women's discontent, or that of other oppressed groups, because the only kinds of causes of discontent in the individualist's vocabulary are deprivations of rights, extreme material deprivation, or personal inadequacy. The powerlessness of the oppressed groups is reinforced by blaming their condition on them themselves by defining them as inadequate. The extreme consequence of alienation, of being unable to participate in defining one's identity, is the inability to articulate one's own alienation. By excluding that concept of alienation from their vocabulary, liberal philosophers have done their part in maintaining existing power relations.

By insisting that we are separate individuals who can transcend social pressures and influences with effort, liberalism conceals alienation. For men it perpetuates the tyranny of oppressive conceptions of masculinity. For women and other groups, never admitted to the privileges of autonomy, it lays the blame for their obvious lack of autonomy on them, thus reinforcing the stereotypes of women and people of color as less able and accomplished than men.

The concept of alienation is, therefore, indispensable for describing accurately the condition of oppressed groups in our society and for pointing to their causes. Only if we use the concept of alienation can we talk about the ways in which social conditions—specifically being prevented from participating in defining one's identity—damage many lives. Only if we recognize the importance of that concept of alienation can we engage in social criticism that identifies the injuries to oppressed groups correctly. Only if we raise accurate criticisms can we ever hope to be able to make changes in the society that genuinely better lives.

The concept is, additionally, indispensable because it provides one means for unmasking the liberal's false claims about the possibility of autonomy. But that, in turn, will allow us to see more clearly how individualism keeps people oppressed because it maintains powerlessness and continues to obscure real problems by blaming the victims of an alienating society for their problems. It is a first step toward liberation to lift the burden of self-blame that the individualist ideology of the autonomous person has imposed on most of us. Once having seen that the fault is not all with us, we can turn to look very directly at our world to see the concrete ways in which we have been excluded from defining who we are.

VI. WHAT YOU WILL FIND IN THIS BOOK

All of us, in one respect or another, find ourselves saddled with social identities that we had no hand in shaping. Wherever we go we find that we are defined as women, as persons of color, Jews, handicapped, old, homosexual, as students, as middle class, etc.,[6] and that to the extent that we are defined by those characteristics, others know us by just looking at us, know what we want, what we are likely to do, what our life goals are or should be, and what we are capable of. If we depart from the stereotype imposed on us, we encounter outrage or wariness:

> Just as the Jew who spends money without thinking about it is suspect, a black man who quotes Montesquieu had better be watched. (Fanon 1967: 35)

The alienated are well-known to all without any effort on the knower's part, without anyone needing to take the trouble of listening to them.

Most discussions of alienation perpetuate alienation because they too do not take the trouble to listen to the alienated, to find out what alienation is like and what the alienated think about their condition, its origins and causes, and how it might be remedied. Discussions of alienation are excessively abstract; they seem to take for granted that alienation is the same for everyone and that its lineaments are well known. Such talk about alienation only deepens self-estrangement: no one listens to the alienated, their condition is already familiar, and needs no further exploration.

The essays in this volume break with this tradition. Our effort has been to collect writings which consider the experience of alienation of persons in different situations. What emerges is a complex picture of different experiences, different problems, and different questions about alienation that require much further thought and study. The selections in this volume take alienation seriously as a real experience of real persons—ourselves among them. They show that we are very far from understanding alienation.

Very different experiences of alienation gave rise to the essays in this volume. They are written by women and men, with color and without, heterosexual as well as lesbian, young and old. They look at alienation at work, alienation of the disabled, alienation from nature, as well as alienation according to gender, race, age, and poverty. In each case, alienation is connected with the misperception of a group maintained, often forcibly, by outsiders. But for different groups the connection between their reality and how the world construes that reality is different. Physical disability is no more a justification for stereotyping than skin color is for denigration. But physical disability is a problem in a way in which skin color is not.

> With the rise of black power, a derogatory label became a rallying cry, "Black is beautiful!" . . . But what of the chronically ill and disabled? Can we yell, "Long live cancer!" . . . (Zola, 1988: 14)

What shall we say of aging? Is it a real problem or do we only perceive it as one because we have internalized the denigrating stereotypes? That question deserves a good deal of careful discussion. The essays in this volume are designed to show that such a discussion is needed and to stimulate it.

Out of different experiences come a significant range of understandings of alienation. Healey uses this notion of alienation: the old are labeled and diminished by those labels. The ways in which stereotypes not only alienate but prevent the alienated from understanding and being solidary with one another are displayed in Jordan's essay, while Zola adds that the alienated are prevented, by the prevailing stereotypes, from being fully aware of their own condition. In a world in which the disabled are asked to overcome their handicaps, they cannot really feel of the fatigue or the pain of their condition. Rich stresses the physical distaste that the dominant groups have for those they stereotype, for the old, for homosexuals, people of color, the disabled. Both Young and Bartky speak of alienation as "objectification." The very general perception of alienation in these essays is the same, the details vary enormously. In response to many of these ideas, McGary reminds us that Black people, at least—and the same is true of many other groups—have resisted alienation very successfully by building their own communities in which they defined who they were.

In all of these instances, persons are alienated from themselves because others do not allow them to form their own self-definitions. But that also alienates them from others: women, or blacks, or the old are objectified—a bodily characteristic is taken to stand for the whole person—and thus are known immediately. No effort is needed to find out who that woman, that black person, that old man are. They are just that: female, black, old; and that is all they are. Such disinterest in other persons distances people from one another. The presumed transparency of some makes any real contact impossible, and therefore alienates persons from themselves and from others.

In analogous ways, human beings are alienated from nature insofar as they take nature as already known and familiar either as "raw materials" or "resources" to be exploited, or as "wilderness" to be preserved. In either view, nature is completely other from human beings, and it has a clear function and role in human existence. But such preconceptions are open to question: are we not also part of nature? If nature is there to be exploited or to be preserved, is that true also of human beings? After all our origins are not that different from those of bears or wolves. We are as dependent on weather and plants as are our animal cousins, and our social organization shows signs of our ancestry in the bands of monkeys, or even in the complexities of the beehive. Once we remember these, and many other connections to trees and mountains and oceans and their varied inhabitants, we see that talk about "nature" as completely different from us is itself a manifestation of our alienation from nature.

Considering our alienation from nature we are forced to ask ourselves once more, who we are, as human beings, and in what ways we are and in what ways we are not part of nature.

Alienation is the result of social processes. In explaining my alienation, I need to point to a particular group of people who do particular things that result in my alienation and, having done that, I will be asked why I think these people are doing to me what they are doing. Do they know what they are doing, are they acting on consciously formed intentions? We find that these selections pick out very different groups as the originators of alienation—white men, colonialism, middle-class men and women, the "Fashion-Beauty Complex," organized Western medicine—and ascribe very different motives to them. The disabled, Zola suggests, are hidden because they remind us of our own vulnerability. Minnie Bruce Pratt thinks that a good deal of stereotyping is the result of fear that those one has harmed will come back to take their revenge, or that those of us who mean well, nevertheless, retain our prejudices for fear that, in order to surrender them, we would have to change ourselves, and change is frightening. The question, Why is there alienation? receives very different answers. None of them is obviously final. The question of causation needs a good deal more work and reflection.

In most discussions, alienation is treated as monolithic; the alienated hence appear as a unified group. Various authors in this anthology point out that, in fact, no one is simply alienated, but persons are alienated in specific respects and may thus be suffering alienation in some contexts of their lives and be inflicting alienation in other contexts. Lugones and Jordan are particularly eloquent in tracing some of the extremely complex interconnections between the alienation of different kinds of people.

It is not true, it turns out, that one either alienates or is alienated. Most of us are involved in both. But we are, moreover, complicit in many ways in our own alienation, sometimes reluctantly, happily and even wholeheartedly at other times. That insight, stressed repeatedly and in different ways, in these essays, complicates our understanding of alienation.

Not surprisingly, finally, these essays present us with a wide range of suggestions of what we need to do in order to reduce, if not remove, all traces of alienation from the world. There is a good deal of talk about self-examination in order to become more aware of one's own biases that serve to alienate others as well as to perpetuate one's own. But there are also suggestions for social change in order to diminish alienation at work, or of the old. There is no complete theory of social or internal change here: no one says this is what alienation is, this is what we need to do. But the partial suggestions made all deserve being taken very seriously.

These essays tell us much about alienation; they also raise many problems and questions for further study. They thus open the way to future work on the topic and stimulate thinking.

Notes

This essay has profited a good deal from comments by Tom Moody. Much of it—both insights and errors—derives from conversations with Lucy Candib.

1. I have provided a much more elaborate description of alienation in my book *Alienation and Class* (Schmitt 1983). For another explanation of the concept of alienation, from a somewhat different perspective, see the following essay, "Alienation and Poverty: The View from Comalapa."

2. She denies that those are instances of alienation, because she restricts the term alienation to self-estrangements that are socially imposed. One can obviously use the term "alienation" in wider and narrower senses, as long as one is clear what one is doing. Clearly it is only socially-imposed alienation that can be *criticized*.

3. See Howard McGary's essay, "Alienation and the African-American Experience" (reprinted in this book) which disagrees with this view.

4. Some may object to this account of liberalism's neglect of alienation. Rights, they may say, are concepts that belong in the political sphere. Of course, there are other, private moral obligations we have to each other, which go beyond the rights each of us has. But that defense of liberalism would make alienation a matter of the private interactions of individuals. But it is not that at all. Alienation is a social phenomenon, and a political one. It cannot be understood if political relations are limited to mutual rights.

5. Why liberalism minimizes the effect of social forces on us and thereby conceals alienation is a difficult and complex question which I cannot answer here. I have provided the beginning of an answer in my "Autonomy and Alienation" (Schmitt 1988).

6. At the same time, it is very important not to conclude from the pervasiveness of alienation that we are all equally oppressed, or that one person's alienation is as hurtful as another's. For that is clearly not true.

References

Benn, S. I. (1975). "Freedom, Autonomy and the Concept of a Person." *Proceedings Aristotelian Society* (NS) 76: 109–30.

————. (1982). "Individuality, Autonomy and Community." In *Community as Social Value*, edited by E. Kamenka, 43–62. New York: St. Martin's Press.

Fanon, F. (1967). *Black Skin, White Masks*. New York: Grove Press.

Frankfurt, H. (1971). "Freedom of the Will and the Concept of a Person." *The Journal of Philosophy* 68.

Haworth, L. (1986). *Autonomy: An Essay in Philosophical Psychology and Ethics*. New Haven: Yale University Press.

Heidegger, M. (1962). *Being and Time*. New York: Harper and Brothers.

Jordan, J. (1985). *One Call: Political Essays*. Boston: South End Press.

Kierkegaard, S. (1959). *Either/Or*. Princeton: Princeton University Press.

Kuflik, A. (1984). "The Inalienability of Autonomy." *Philosophy and Public Affairs* 13: 271–98.

Marx, K. (1967). *Capital, Vol. I*. New York: International Publishers.

Nietsche, F. (1954). *Thus Spoke Zarathustra*. In *The Viking Portable Nietzsche*, edited by Walter Kaufmann. New York: Viking.

Ollman, B. (1971). *Alienation: Marx's Conception of Man in Capitalist Society*. London: Cambridge University Press.

Olsen, R. (1978). *Karl Marx*. Boston: Twayne.

Rorty, R. (1977). "Dependency, Individuality and Work." In *Working It Out*, edited by S. Ruddick and P. Daniels, 38–54. New York: Pantheon.

Ruddick, S. (1977). "A Work of One's Own." In Ruddick and Daniels, eds., *Working It Out*, 129–46.

Sandel, M. (1982). *Liberalism and the Limits of Justice*. Cambridge: Cambridge University Press.

Sartre, J. P. (1956). *Being and Nothingness*. New York: Philosophical Library.

Schaff, A. (1970). *Marxism and the Human Individual*. New York: McGraw-Hill.

Schmitt, R. (1983). *Alienation and Class*. Cambridge: Schenkman Publishing Co.

————. (1987). *Introduction to Marx and Engels*. Boulder, Colo.: Westview.

————. (1988). "Autonomy and Alienation." *Praxis International* 8: 222–36.

Tucker, R., ed. (1978). *The Marx-Engels Reader*. New York: Norton.

Young, I. (1980). "Socialist Feminism and the Limits of Dual Systems Theory." *Socialist Review* 10: 169–88.

Young, R. (1986). *Personal Autonomy: Beyond Negative and Positive Liberty*. The Hague: Croom Helm.

Zola, Irving K. (1988). "The Language of Disability: Problems of Politics and Practice." *Australian Disability Review* 1, no. 3: 13–21.

PART I

Work

You say, "quickly tell me
Before the robots came,
What was it like to work the line?"

I close my eyes.
Onslaughts of noise split the air
Filth drives deep into my pores.
Smells. Fumes. Foremen scream.
Clothes glue to flesh and stink
of mindnumbing exhaustion.
Muscles melt. Eyes sting.

No time to do things right.
They don't want it right
They just want it
Now
Fast
Jobs roll to me
by me

past me.
Turn. Run. Grab. Reach. Slam.
Rivet. Fumble. Ache. Next job. . . .

What was it like? It was my life.
I cannot tell you all my life
quickly. I can tell you only this.

Robots
always
worked the line. *

THE MOST COMMON UNDERSTANDING of work alienation takes assembly line work, manual work in factories, as its example. Such work is tedious, exhausting; it provides no scope for ingenuity or creativity; it does not give the worker any pride. It is alienating in the most ordinary sense of that term insofar as it is unpleasant. It is alienating in the same sense in which we find standing in line unpleasant, or dealing with unfriendly bureaucrats.

But the experiences chronicled in the selections in this section exemplify alienation in a much more complex and devastating form. The unpleasantness of the work is a part of it, but only a part. Barbara Herrick's work is not actually unpleasant; she enjoys parts of it. It gives her some pride and satisfaction because she is good at it. But she hates selling stuff that is worthless—that's "quackery"—and she hates being forever on her guard against sexual innuendo, sexual offers, or worse. On top of that, she always has to be nice. She can't tell men that they insult her, that she hates or despises them, that she gets paid more than they. Mike Lefevre, in comparable ways, can't tell the foreman what he really thinks of him; he can't punch him out as he would like to.

These two do work which, for different reasons, they do not want to be doing. Both, in different ways, feel insulted by their jobs. They feel that they are not taken seriously, are not valued for who they are. In their work, they find themselves defined as persons they not only are not, but as persons who do not deserve respect. Their work is alienating because others define who they are. It is additionally alienating because the definitions imposed on them are derogatory.

Notice here that each works within definite limits; their options are set by others and they cannot change them. Yes, in one way they make their own lives by choosing their jobs and staying in them. But in another way, they are bound because some obvious options are not open. Mike Lefevre has nowhere to take his grievances about his job or his foreman; his union is no more on his side than his employer. No one wants to know about his ideas about his job and, if they did know they wouldn't want to do anything about it. Saying that Mike shapes his own life overlooks the fact that he has very little power in his world. The same is true for Barbara: can she talk to anyone about fairly constant sexual harassment? There is no one in the firm who wants to deal with that. So her choices are limited precisely when it comes to making her job better. She is a lot

---

*Doris Delaney, "Before the Robots," UAW Solidarity (December 16–31, 1981): 10, quoted in Kathy E. Ferguson, *The Feminist Case against Bureaucracy* (Philadelphia: Temple University Press, 1984), 86.

richer than Mike but, in the end, just as powerless. Essential to their alienation is lack of power.

To the extent that they accept the prevailing beliefs about individual autonomy they take responsibility for their lives, and thus think of themselves as the ones who make their lives as destructive and insulting as they are. Thus they are the agents of their own degradation and *that* is alienating because they both believe that their life is theirs, in some way, but feel, at the same time, that it is not theirs. They "do not feel at home in their work"—work is constant insult and pretense. But somehow that life is also theirs, and is of their own making. In that conflict arises another form of alienation.

But Mike holds on to his rebelliousness and his pride in knowing that he hates his job. So does Barbara save herself by being secretly in opposition. Anne Bogan does not even have that private refuge from alienation. She is happy to associate with "persons of quality"—men who are high up in the executive hierarchy. But she will never be a man, or an executive. Her alienation is complete: in the same breath she brags about her accomplishments and acknowledges that she is only a woman, only a secretary. She has accepted without question that she is second rate and second class. Her pride in her relative success depends on her accepting that fact about herself.

Alienated Labor

KARL MARX

SO FAR WE HAVE considered the alienation of the worker only from one aspect; namely, *his relationship with the products of his labor*. However, alienation appears not merely in the result but also in the *process of production*, within *productive activity* itself. How could the worker stand in an alien relationship to the product of his activity if he did not alienate himself in the act of production itself? The product is indeed only the *resumé* of activity, of production. Consequently, if the product of labor is alienation, production itself must be active alienation—the alienation of activity and the activity of alienation. The alienation of the object of labor merely summarizes the alienation in the work activity itself.

What constitutes the alienation of labor? First, that the work is *external* to the worker, that it is not part of his nature; and that, consequently, he does not fulfill himself in his work but denies himself, has a feeling of misery rather than well-being, does not develop freely his mental and physical energies but is physically exhausted and mentally debased. The worker, therefore, feels himself at home only during his leisure time, whereas at work he feels homeless. His work is not voluntary but imposed, *forced labor*. It is not the satisfaction of a need, but only a *means* for satisfying other needs. Its alien character is clearly shown by the fact that as soon as there is no physical or other compulsion it is avoided like the plague. External labor, labor in which man alienates himself, is a labor of self-sacrifice, of mortification. Finally, the external character of work for the worker is shown by the fact that it is not his own work but work for someone else, that in work he does not belong to himself but to another person.

Just as in religion the spontaneous activity of human fantasy, of the human brain and heart, reacts independently as an alien activity of gods or devils upon the individual, so the activity of the worker is not his own spontaneous activity. It is another's activity and a loss of his own spontaneity.

We arrive at the result that man (the worker) feels himself to be freely active only in his animal functions—eating, drinking, and procreating, or at most also in his dwelling and in personal adornment—while in his human functions he is reduced to an animal. The animal becomes human and the human becomes animal.

Eating, drinking, and procreating are of course also genuine human functions. But abstractly considered, apart from the environment of human activities, and turned into final and sole ends, they are animal functions.

We have now considered the act of alienation of practical human activity, labor, from two aspects: (1) the relationship of the worker to the *product of labor* as an alien object which dominates him. This relationship is at the same time the relationship to the sensuous external world, to natural objects, as an alien and hostile world; (2) the relationship of labor to the act of production within labor. This is the relationship of the worker to his own activity as something alien and not belonging to him, activity as suffering (passivity), strength as powerlessness, creation as emasculation, the *personal* physical and mental energy of the worker, his personal life (for what is life but activity?), as an activity which is directed against himself, independent of him and not belonging to him. This is *self-alienation* as against the above-mentioned alienation of the *thing*.

We have now to infer a third characteristic of *alienated labor* from the two we have considered.

Man is a species-being not only in the sense that he makes the community (his own as well as those of other things) his object both practically and theoretically, but also (and this is simply another expression for the same thing) in the sense that he treats himself as the present, living species, as a universal and consequently free being.

Species-life, for man as for animals, has its physical basis in the fact that man (like animals) lives from inorganic nature, and since man is more universal than an animal so the range of inorganic nature from which he lives is more universal. Plants, animals, minerals, air, light, etc., constitute, from the theoretical aspect, a part of human consciousness as objects of natural science and art; they are man's spiritual inorganic nature, his intellectual means of life, which he must first prepare for enjoyment and perpetuation. So also, from the practical aspect, they form a part of human life and activity. In practice man lives only from these natural products, whether in the form of food, heating, clothing, housing, etc. The universality of man appears in practice in the universality which makes the whole of nature into his inorganic body: (1) as a direct means of life; and equally (2) as the material object and instrument of his life activity. Nature is the inorganic body of man; that is to say nature, excluding the human body itself. To say that man lives from nature means that nature is his body with which he must remain in a continuous interchange in order not to die. The statement that the physical and mental life of man, and nature, are interdependent means simply that nature is interdependent with itself, for man is a part of nature.

Since alienated labor: (1) alienates nature from man; and (2) alienates man from himself, from his own active function, his life activity; so it alienates him from the species. It makes *species-life* into a means of individual life. In the first place it alienates species-life and individual life, and secondly, it turns the latter, as an abstraction, into the purpose of the former, also in its abstract and alienated form.

For labor, *life activity*, *productive* life, now appear to man only as *means* for the satisfaction of a need, the need to maintain his physical existence. Productive life is, however, species-life. It is life creating life. In the type of life activity resides the whole character of a species, its species-character; and free, conscious activity is the species-character of human beings. Life itself appears only as a *means of life*.

The animal is one with its life activity. It does not distinguish the activity from itself. It is *its activity*. But man makes his life activity itself an object of his will and consciousness. He has a conscious life activity. It is not a determination with which he is completely identified. Conscious life activity distinguishes man from the life activity of animals. Only for this reason is he a species-being. Or rather, he is only a self-conscious being, i.e. his own life is an object for him, because he is a species-being. Only for this reason is his activity free activity. Alienated labor reverses the relationship, in that man because he is a self-conscious being makes his life activity, his *being*, only a means for his existence.

The practical constructions of an *objective world*, the *manipulation* of inorganic nature, is the confirmation of man as a conscious species-being, i.e. a being who treats the species as his own being or himself as a species-being. Of course, animals also produce. They construct nests, dwellings, as in the case of bees, beavers, ants, etc. But they only produce what is strictly necessary for themselves or their young. They produce only in a single direction, while man produces universally. They produce only under the compulsion of direct physical needs, while man produces when he is free from physical need and only truly produces in freedom from such need. Animals produce only themselves, while man reproduces the whole of nature. The products of animal production belong directly to their physical bodies, while man is free in face of his product. Animals construct only in accordance with the standards and needs of the species to which they belong, while man knows how to produce in accordance with the standards of every species and knows how to apply the appropriate standard to the object. Thus man constructs also in accordance with the laws of beauty.

It is just in his work upon the objective world that man really proves himself as a *species-being*. This production is his active species-life. By means of it nature appears as his work and his reality. The object of labor is, therefore, the *objectification of man's species-life*; for he no longer reproduces himself merely intellectually, as in consciousness, but actively and in a real sense, and he sees his own reflection in a world which he has constructed. While, therefore, alienated labor takes away the object of production from man, it also takes away his *species-life*, his real objectivity as a species-being, and changes his advantage over animals into a disadvantage in so far as his inorganic body, nature, is taken from him.

Just as alienated labor transforms free and self-directed activity into a means, so it transforms the species-life of man into a means of physical existence.

Consciousness, which man has from his species, is transformed through alienation so that species-life becomes only a means for him. (3) Thus, alienated labor turns the *species-life of man*, and also nature as his mental species-property, into an *alien* being and into a *means* for his *individual existence*. It alienates from man his own body, external nature, his mental life and his *human life*. (4) A direct consequence of the alienation of man from the product of his labor, from his life activity and from his species-life, is that *man* is alienated from other *men*. When man confronts himself he also confronts *other* men. What is true of man's relationship to his work, to the product of his work and to himself, is also true of his relationship to other men, to their labor, and to the objects of their labor.

Interviews from *Working*

STUDS TERKEL

MIKE LEFEVRE

IT IS A TWO-FLAT *dwelling, somewhere in Cicero, on the outskirts of Chicago. He is thirty-seven. He works in a steel mill. On occasion, his wife Carol works as a waitress in a neighborhood restaurant; otherwise, she is at home, caring for their two small children, a girl and a boy.*

At the time of my first visit, a sculpted statuette of Mother and Child was on the floor, head severed from body. He laughed softly as he indicated his three-year-old daughter: "She Doctor Spock'd it."

I'm a dying breed. A laborer. Strictly muscle work . . . pick it up, put it down, pick it up, put it down. We handle between forty and fifty thousand pounds of steel a day. (Laughs.) I know this is hard to believe—from four hundred pounds to three- and four-pound pieces. It's dying.

You can't take pride any more. You remember when a guy could point to a house he built, how many logs he stacked. He built it and he was proud of it. I don't really think I could be proud if a contractor built a home for me. I would be tempted to get in there and kick the carpenter in the ass (laughs), and take the saw away from him. 'Cause I would have to be part of it, you know.

It's hard to take pride in a bridge you're never gonna cross, in a door you're never gonna open. You're mass-producing things and you never see the end result of it. (Muses.) I worked for a trucker one time. And I got this tiny satisfaction when I loaded a truck. At least I could see the truck depart loaded. In a steel mill, forget it. You don't see where nothing goes.

I got chewed out by my foreman once. He said, "Mike, you're a good worker but you have a bad attitude." My attitude is that I don't get excited about my job. I do my work but I don't say whoopee-doo. The day I get excited about my job is the day I go to a head shrinker. How are you gonna get excited about pullin' steel? How are you gonna get excited when you're tired and want to sit down?

It's not just the work. Somebody built the pyramids. Somebody's gonna build something. Pyramids, Empire State Building—these things just don't happen. There's hard work behind it. I would like to see a building, say, the Empire State, I would like to see on one side of it a foot-wide strip from top to bottom with the name of every bricklayer, the name of every electrician, with all the names. So when a guy walked by, he could take his son and say, "See, that's me over there on the forty-fifth floor. I put the steel beam in." Picasso can point to a painting. What can I point to? A writer can point to a book. Everybody should have something to point to.

It's the not-recognition by other people. To say that a woman is *just* a housewife is degrading, right? Okay. *Just* a housewife. It's also degrading to say *just* a laborer. The difference is that a man goes out and maybe gets smashed.

When I was single, I could quit, just split. I wandered all over the country. You worked just enough to get a poke, money in your pocket. Now I'm married and I got two kids. . . . (Trails off.) I worked on a truck dock one time and I was single. The foreman came over and he grabbed my shoulder, kind of gave me a shove. I punched him and knocked him off the dock. I said, "Leave me alone. I doing my work, just stay away from me, just don't give me the with-the-hands business."

Hell, if you whip a damn mule he might kick you. Stay out of my way, that's all. Working is bad enough, don't butt me. I would rather work my ass off for eight hours a day with nobody watching me than five minutes with a guy watching me. Who you gonna sock? You can't sock General Motors; you can't sock anybody in Washington; you can't sock a system.

A mule, an old mule, that's the way I feel. Oh yeah. See. (Shows black-and-blue marks on arms and legs, burns.) You know what I heard from more than one guy at work? "If my kid wants to work in a factory, I am going to kick the hell out of him." I want my kid to be an effete snob. Yeah, mm-hmm. (Laughs.) I want him to be able to quote Walt Whitman, to be proud of it.

If you can't improve yourself, you improve your posterity. Otherwise life isn't worth nothing. You might as well go back to the cave and stay there. I'm sure the first caveman who went over the hill to see what was on the other side—I don't think he went there wholly out of curiosity. He went there because he wanted to get his son out of the cave. Just the same way I want to send my kid to college.

I work so damn hard and want to come home and sit down and lay around. *But I gotta get it out.* I want to be able to turn around to somebody and say, "Hey, fuck you." You know? (Laughs.) The guy sitting next to me on the bus too. 'Cause all day I wanted to tell the foreman to go fuck himself, but I can't.

So I find a guy in a tavern. To tell him that. And he tells me too. I've been in brawls. He's punching me and I'm punching him, because we actually want to punch somebody else. The most that'll happen is the bartender will bar us from the tavern. But at work, you lose your job.

This one foreman I've got, he's a kid. He's a college graduate. He thinks he's better than everybody else. He was chewing me out and I was saying, "Yeah, yeah, yeah." He said, "What do you mean, yeah, yeah, yeah. Yes, sir." I told him, "Who the hell are you, Hitler? What is this *Yes, sir* bullshit? I came here to work, I didn't come here to crawl. There's a fuckin' difference." One word led to another and I lost.

I got broke down to a lower grade and lost twenty-five cents an hour, which is a hell of a lot. It amounts to about ten dollars a week. He came over—after breaking me down. The guy comes over smiles at me. I blew up. He didn't know it, but he was about two seconds and two feet away from a hospital. I said, "Stay the fuck away from me." He was just about to say something and was pointing his finger. I just reached my hand up and just grabbed his finger and I just put it back in his pocket. He walked away. I grabbed his finger because I'm married. If I'd been single, I'd a grabbed his head. That's the difference.

You're doing this manual labor and you know that technology can do it. (Laughs.) Let's face it, a machine can do the work of a man; otherwise they wouldn't have space probes. Why can we send a rocket ship that's unmanned and yet send a man in a steel mill to do a mule's work?

Automation? Depends on how it's applied. If frightens me if it puts me out on the street. It doesn't frighten me if it shortens my workweek. You read that little thing: what are you going to do when this computer replaces you? Blow up computers. (Laughs.) Really. Blow up computers. I'll be goddamned if a computer is gonna eat before I do! I want milk for my kids and beer for me. Machines can either liberate man or enslave 'im, because they're pretty neutral. It's a man who has the bias to put the thing one place or another.

If I had a twenty-hour workweek, I'd get to know my kids better, my wife better. Some kid invited me to go on a college campus. On a Saturday. It was summertime. Hell, if I had a choice of taking my wife and kids to a picnic or going to a college campus, it's gonna be the picnic. But if I worked a twenty-hour week, I could go do both. Don't you think with that extra twenty hours people could really expand? Who's to say? There are some people in factories just by force of circumstance. I'm just like the colored people. Potential Einsteins don't have to be white. They could be in cotton fields, they could be in factories.

The twenty-hour week is a possibility today. The intellectuals, they always say there are potential Lord Byrons, Walt Whitmans, Roosevelts, Picassos working in construction or steel mills or factories. But I don't think they believe it. I think what they're afraid of is the potential Hitlers and Stalins that are there too. The people in power fear the leisure man. Not just the United States. Russia's the same way.

What do you think would happen in this country if, for one year, they experimented and gave everybody a twenty-hour week? How do they know that the guy who digs Wallace today doesn't try to resurrect Hitler tomorrow? Or the guy who is mildly disturbed at pollution doesn't decide to go to General Motors and shit on the guy's desk? You can become a fanatic if you had the time. The whole thing is time. That is, I think, one reason rich kids tend to be fanatic about politics: they have time. Time, that's the important thing.

It isn't that the average working guy is dumb. He's tired, that's all. I picked up a book on chess one time. That thing laid in the drawer for two or three weeks; you're too tired. During the weekends you want to take your kids out. You don't want to sit there and the kid comes up: "Daddy, can I go to the park?" You got your nose in a book? Forget it.

I know a guy fifty-seven years old. Know what he tells me? "Mike, I'm old and tired *all* the time." The first thing happens at work: When the arms start moving, the brain stops. I punch in about ten minutes to seven in the morning. I say hello to a couple of guys I like, I kid around with them. One guy says good morning to you and you say good morning. To another guy you say fuck you. The guy you say fuck you to is your friend.

I put on my hard hat, change into my safety shoes, put on my safety glasses, go to the bonderizer. It's the thing I work on. They rake the metal; they wash it; they dip it in a paint solution and we take it off. Put it on, take it off, put it on, take it off, put it on, take it off. . . .

I say hello to everybody but my boss. At seven it starts. My arms get tired about the first half hour. After that, they don't get tired any more until maybe the last half hour at the end of the day. I work from seven to three-thirty. My arms are tired at seven-thirty and they're tired at three o'clock. (Laughs.) 'Cause that's when there's a beginning and there's an end. That I'm not brainwashed. In between, I don't even try to think.

If I were to put you in front of a dock and I pulled up a skid in front of you with fifty hundred-pound sacks of potatoes and there are fifty more skids just like it, and this is what you're gonna do all day, what would you think about— potatoes? Unless a guy's a nut, he never thinks about work or talks about it. Maybe about baseball or about getting drunk the other night or he got laid or he didn't get laid. I'd say one out of a hundred will actually get excited about work.

Why is it that the communists always say they're for the workingman, and as soon as they set up a country, you got guys singing to tractors? They're singing about how they love the factory. That's where I couldn't buy communism. It's the intellectuals' utopia, not mine. I cannot picture myself singing to a tractor, I just can't. (Laughs.) Or singing to steel. (Singsongs.) Oh whoop-dee-doo, I'm at the bonderizer, oh how I love this heavy steel. No thanks. Never happen.

Oh yeah, I daydream. I fantasize about a sexy blonde in Miami who's got my union dues. (Laughs.) I think about the head of the union the way I think of the head of my company. Living it up. I think of February in Miami. Warm weather, a place to lay in. When I hear a college kid say, "I'm oppressed," I don't believe him. You know what I'd like to do for one year? Live like a college kid. Just for one year. I'd love to. Wow! Sports car! Marijuana! Wild sexy broads. I'd love that, hell yes, I would.

Somebody has to do this work. If my kid ever goes to college, I just want him to have a little respect, to realize that his dad is one of those somebodies. This is why even on—(muses) yeah, I guess, sure—on the black thing. . . . (Sighs heavily.) I can't really hate the colored fella that's working with me all day. The black intellectual I got no respect for. The white intellectual I got no use for. I got no use for the black militant who's gonna scream three hundred years of slavery to me while I'm busting my ass. You know what I mean? (Laughs.) I have one answer for that guy: Go see Rockefeller. See Harriman. Don't bother me. (Laughs.)

After work I usually stop off at a tavern. Cold beer. Cold beer right away. When I was single, I used to go into hillbilly bars, get in a lot of brawls. Just to explode. I got a thing on my arm here. (Indicates scar.) I got slapped with a bicycle chain. Oh, wow! (Softly) Mmm. I'm getting older. (Laughs.) I don't explode as much. You might say I'm broken in. (Quickly) No, I'll never be broken in. (Sighs.) When you get a little older, you exchange the words. When you're younger, you exchange the blows.

When I get home, I argue with my wife a little bit. Turn on TV, get mad at the news. (Laughs.) I don't even watch the news that much. I watch Jackie Gleason. I look for any alternative to the ten o'clock news. I don't want to go to bed angry. Don't hit a man with anything heavy at five o'clock. He just can't be bothered. This is his time to relax. The heaviest thing he wants is what his wife has to tell him.

When I come home, know what I do for the first twenty minutes? Fake it. I put on a smile. I got a kid three years old. Sometimes she says, "Daddy, where've you been?" I say, "Work." I could have told her I'd been in Disneyland. What's work to a three-year-old kid? If I feel bad, I can't take it out on the kids. Kids are born innocent of everything but birth. You can't take it out on your wife either. This is why you go to a tavern. You want to release it there rather than do it at home. What does an actor do when he's got a bad movie? I got a bad movie every day.

I don't even need the alarm clock to get up in the morning. I can go out drinking all night, fall asleep at four, and bam! I'm up at six—no matter what I do. (Laughs.) It's a pseudodeath, more or less. Your whole system is paralyzed and you give all the appearance of death. It's an ingrown clock. It's a thing you just get used to. The hours differ. It depends. Sometimes my wife wants to do something crazy like play five hundred rummy or put a puzzle together. It could be midnight, could be ten o'clock, could be nine-thirty.

What do you do weekends?

Drink beer, read a book. See that one? *Violence in America.* It's one of them studies from Washington. One of them committees they're always appointing. A thing like that I read on a weekend. But during the weekdays, gee . . . I just thought about it. I don't do that much reading from Monday through Friday. Unless it's a horny book. I'll read it at work and go home and do my homework. (Laughs.) That's what the guys at the plant call it—homework. (Laughs.) Sometimes my wife works on Saturday and I drink beer at the tavern.

I went out drinking with one guy, oh, a long time ago. A college boy. He was working where I work now. Always preaching to me about how you need violence to change the system and all that garbage. We went into a hillbilly joint. Some guy there, I didn't know him from Adam, he said, "You think you're smart." I said, "What's your pleasure?" (Laughs.) He said, "My pleasure's to kick your ass." I told him I really can't be bothered. He said. "What're you, chicken?" I said, "No, I just don't want to be bothered." He came over and said something to me again. I said, "I don't beat women, drunks, or fools. Now leave me alone."

The guy called his brother over. This college boy that was with me, he came nudging my arm. "Mike, let's get out of here." I said, "What are you worried about?" (Laughs.) This isn't unusual. People will bug you. You fend it off as much as you can and when you can't, you punch the guy out.

It was close to closing time and we stayed. We could have left, but when you go into a place to have a beer and a guy challenges you—if you expect to go in that place again, you don't leave. If you have to fight the guy, you fight.

I got just outside the door and one of these guys jumped on me and grabbed me around the neck. I grabbed his arm and flung him against the wall. I grabbed him here (indicates throat), and jiggled his head against the wall quite a few times. He kind of slid down a little bit. This guy who said he was his brother took a swing at me with a garrison belt. He just missed and hit the wall. I'm looking around for my junior Stalin (laughs), who loves violence and everything. He's gone. Split. (Laughs.) Next day I see him at work. I couldn't get mad at him, he's a baby.

He saw a book in my back pocket one time and he was amazed. He walked up to me and he said, "You read?" I said, "What do you mean, I read?" He said, "All these dummies read the sports pages around here. What are you doing with a book?" I got pissed off at the kid right away. I said, "What do you mean all these dummies? Don't knock a man who's paying somebody else's way through college." He was a nineteen-year-old effete snob.

Yet you want your kid to be an effete snob?

Yes. I want my kid to look at me and say, "Dad, you're nice guy, but you're a fuckin' dummy." Hell yes, I want my kid to tell me that he's not gonna be like me. . . .

If I were hiring people to work, I'd try naturally to pay them a decent wage. I'd try to find out their first names, their last names, keep the company as small as possible, so I could personalize the whole thing. All I would ask a man is a handshake, see you in the morning. No applications, nothing. I wouldn't be interested in the guy's past. Nobody ever checks the pedigree on a mule, do they? But they do on a man. Can you picture walking up to a mule and saying, "I'd like to know who his granddaddy was?"

I'd like to run a combination bookstore and tavern. (Laughs.) I would like to have a place where college kids came and a steelworker could sit down and talk. Where a workingman could not be ashamed of Walt Whitman and where a college professor could not be ashamed that he painted his house over the weekend.

If a carpenter built a cabin for poets, I think the least the poets owe the carpenter is just three or four one-liners on the wall. A little plaque: Though we labor with our minds, this place we can relax in was built by someone who can work with his hands. And his work is as noble as ours. I think the poet owes something to the guy who builds the cabin for him.

I don't think of Monday. You know what I'm thinking about on Sunday night? Next Sunday. If you work real hard, you think of a perpetual vacation. Not perpetual sleep. . . . What do I think of on a Sunday night? Lord, I wish the fuck I could do something else for a living.

I don't know who the guy is who said there is nothing sweeter than an unfinished symphony. Like an unfinished painting and an unfinished poem. If he creates this thing one day—let's say, Michelangelo's Sistine chapel. It took him a long time to do this, this beautiful work of art. But what if he had to create this Sistine chapel a thousand times a year? Or if da Vinci had to draw his anatomical charts thirty, forty, fifty, sixty, eighty, ninety, a hundred times a day? Don't you think that would even bore da Vinci?

Way back, you spoke of the guys who built the pyramids, not the pharoahs, the unknowns. You put yourself in their category?

Yes. I want my signature on 'em, too. Sometimes, out of pure meanness, when I make something, I put a little dent in it. I like to do something to make it really unique. Hit it with a hammer. I deliberately fuck it up to see if it'll get by, just so I can say I did it. It could be anything. Let me put it this way: I think God invented the dodo bird just so when we get up there we could tell Him,

"Don't you ever make mistakes?" And He'd say, "Sure, look." (Laughs.) I'd like to make my imprint. My dodo bird. A mistake, mine. Let's say the whole building is nothing but red bricks. I'd like to have just the black one or the white one or the purple one. Deliberately fuck up.

This is gonna sound square, but my kid is my imprint. He's my freedom. There's a line in one of Hemingway's books. I think it's from *For Whom the Bell Tolls*. They're behind the enemy lines, somewhere in Spain, and she's pregnant. She wants to stay with him. He tells her no. He says, "If you die, I die," knowing he's gonna die. But if you go, I go. Know what I mean? The mystics call it the brass bowl. Continuum. You know what I mean? This is why I work. Every time I see a young guy walk by with a shirt and tie and dressed up real sharp, I'm looking for my kid, you know? That's it.

ANNE BOGAN

We're on the thirty-second floor of a skyscraper, the office of a corporation president. She is his private secretary. The view of the river, railroad yards, bridges, and the city's skyline is astonishing.

"I've been an executive secretary for eight years. However, this is the first time I've been on the corporate end of things, working for the president. I found it a new experience. I love it and I feel I'm learning a lot."

I become very impatient with dreamers. I respect the doers more than the dreamers. So many people, it seems to me, talk about all the things they want to do. They only talk without accomplishing anything. The drifters are worse than the dreamers. Ones who really have no goals, no aspirations at all, just live from day to day. . . .

I enjoy one thing more than anything else on this job. That's the association I have with the other executives, not only my boss. There's a tremendous difference in the way they treat me than what I've known before. They treat me more as . . . on the executive level. They consult me on things, and I enjoy this. It stimulates me.

I know myself well enough to know that I've always enjoyed men more than women. Usually I can judge them very quickly when I meet a woman. I can't judge men that quickly. I seek out the few women I think I will enjoy. The others, I get along with all right. But I feel no basic interest. I don't really enjoy having lunch with them and so on.

You can tell just from conversation what they talk about. It's quite easy. It's also very easy to tell which girls are going to last around the office and which one's aren't. Interest in their work. Many of them aren't, they just don't dig in. They're more interested in chatting in the washroom. I don't know if that's a change from other years. There's always been some who are really not especially

career-minded, but they have to give a little bit and try a little harder. The
others get by on as little as possible.

I feel like I'm sharing somewhat of the business life of the men. So I think I'm
much happier as the secretary to an executive than I would be in some woman's
field, where I could perhaps make more money. But it would be an extension of a
successful executive. I'm perfectly happy in my status.

*She came from a small town in Indiana and married at eighteen. She had graduated
from high school and began working immediately for the town's large company. "My
husband was a construction worker. We lived in a trailer, we moved around a lot.
There's a lot of community living in that situation and I grew pretty tired of it. You can
get involved; you can become too friendly with people when you live too close. A lot of
time can be wasted. It was years before I started doing this."*

I have dinner with businessmen and enjoy this very much. I like the background music in some of these restaurants. It's soothing and it also adds a little
warmth and doesn't disturb the conversation. I like that atmosphere and the
caliber of people that usually you see and run into. People who have made it.

I think if I've been at all successful with men, it's because I'm a good listener
and interested in their world. I enjoy it, I don't become bored with it. They tell
me about their personal life too. Family problems, financial, and the problems of
raising children. Most of the ones I'm referring to are divorced. In looking
through the years they were married, I can see this is what probably happened. I
know if I were the wife, I would be interested in their work. I feel the wife of an
executive would be a better wife had she been a secretary first. As a secretary,
you learn to adjust to the boss's moods. Many marriages would be happier if the
wife would do that.

BARBARA HERRICK

*She is thirty; single. Her title is script supervisor/producer at a large advertising agency,
working out of its Los Angeles office. She is also a vice president. Her accounts are
primarily in food and cosmetics. "There's a myth: a woman is expected to be a food
writer because she is assumed to know those things and a man doesn't. However, some
of the best copy on razors and Volkswagens has been written by women."*

*She has won several awards and considerable recognition for her commercials. "You
have to be absolutely on target, dramatic, and fast. You have to be aware of legal
restrictions. The FTC gets tougher and tougher. You must understand budgetary
matters: will it cost a million or can it be shot in a studio in one day?"*

*She came off a Kansas farm, one of four daughters. "During high school, I worked
as a typist and was an extremely good one. I was compulsive about doing every tiny job*

very well." She graduated from the University of Missouri. According to Department of Labor statistics, she is in the upper one percent bracket of working women.

In her Beverly Hills apartment are paintings, sculpted works, recordings (classic, folk, jazz, and rock), and many books, most of them obviously well thumbed.

Men in my office doing similar work were being promoted, given raises and titles. Since I had done the bulk of the work, I made a stand and was promoted too. I needed the title, because clients figured that I'm just a faceman.

A faceman is a person who looks good, speaks well, and presents the work. I look well, I speak well, and I'm pleasant to have around after the business is over with—if they acknowledge me in business. We go to the lounge and have drinks. I can drink with the men but remain a lady. (Laughs.)

That's sort of my tacit business responsibility, although this has never been said to me directly. I know this is why I travel alone for the company a great deal. They don't anticipate any problems with my behavior. I equate it with being the good nigger.

On first meeting, I'm frequently taken for the secretary, you know, traveling with the boss. I'm here to keep somebody happy. Then I'm introduced as the writer. One said to me after the meeting was over and the drinking had started, "When I first saw you, I figured you were a—you know. I never knew you were the person writing all this time." (Laughs.) Is it a married woman working for extra money? Is it a lesbian? Is it some higher-up's mistress?

I'm probably one of the ten highest paid people in the agency. It would cause tremendous hard feelings if, say, I work with a man who's paid less. If a remark is made at a bar—"You make so much money, you could buy and sell me"—I toss it off, right? He's trying to find out. He can't equate me as a rival. They wonder where to put me, they wonder what my salary is.

Buy and sell me—yeah, there are a lot of phrases that show the reversal of roles. What comes to mind is swearing at a meeting. New clients are often very uptight. They feel they can't make any innuendoes that might be suggestive. They don't know how to treat me. They don't know whether to acknowledge me as a woman or as another neuter person who's doing a job for them.

The first time, they don't look at me. At the first three meetings of this one client, if I would ask a direct question, they would answer and look at my boss or another man in the room. Even around the conference table. I don't attempt to be—the glasses, the bun, and totally asexual. That isn't the way I am. It's obvious that I'm a woman and enjoy being a woman. I'm not overly provocative either. It's the thin, good nigger line that I have to toe.

I've developed a sixth sense about this. If a client will say, "Are you married?" I will often say yes, because that's the easiest way to deal with him if he needs that category for me. If it's more acceptable to him to have a young, attractive, married woman in a business position comparable to his, terrific. It makes me safer. He'll never be challenged. He can say, "She'd be sensational. I'd love to get her. I could show her what a real man is, but she's married." It's a way out for him.

Or there's the mistress thing: well, she's sleeping with the boss. That's acceptable to them. Or she's a frustrated, compulsive castrator. That's a category. Or lesbian. If I had short hair, wore suits, and talked in a gruff voice, that would be more acceptable than I am. It's when I transcend their labels, they don't know what to do. If someone wants a quick label and says, "I'll bet you're a big women's libber, aren't you?" I say, "Yeah, yeah." They have to place me.

I travel a lot. That's what gets very funny. We had a meeting in Montreal. It was one of those bride's magazines, honeymoon-type resorts, with heart-shaped beds and the heated pool. I was there for three days with nine men. All day long we were enclosed in this conference room. The agency account man went with me. I was to talk about the new products, using slides and movies. There were about sixty men in the conference room. I had to leave in such a hurry, I still had my gaucho pants and boots on.

The presentation went on for an hour and a half. There was tittering and giggling for about forty minutes. Then you'd hear the shift in the audience. They got interested in what I was saying. Afterwards they had lunch sent up. Some of them never did talk to me. Others were interested in my life. They would say things like, "Have you read *The Sensuous Woman?*" (Laughs.) They didn't really want to know. If they were even more obvious, they probably would have said, "Say, did you hear the one about the farmer's daughter?" I'd have replied, "Of course, I'm one myself."

The night before, there was a rehearsal. Afterwards the account man suggested we go back to the hotel, have a nightcap, and get to bed early. It was a 9:00 A.M. meeting. We were sitting at the bar and he said, "Of course, you'll be staying in my room." I said "What? I have a room." He said, "I just assumed. You're here and I'm here and we're both grown up." I said, "You assumed? You never even asked me whether I wanted to." My feelings obviously meant nothing to him. Apparently it was what you did if you're out of town and the woman is anything but a harelip and you're ready to go. His assumption was incredible.

The excuse I gave is one I've used many times. "Once when I was much younger and innocent, I slept with an account man. The guy turned out to be a bastard. I got a big reputation and he made my life miserable because he had a loose mouth. And even though you're a terrifically nice guy and I'd like to sleep with you, I feel I can't. It's my policy. I'm older and wiser now. I don't do it. You have to understand that." It worked. I could never say to him, "You don't even understand how you insulted me."

It's the always-have-to-please conditioning. I don't want to make any enemies. Only of late, because I'm getting more secure and I'm valued by the agency am I able to get mad at men and say, "Fuck off!" But I still have to keep egos unruffled, smooth things over . . . I still work with him and he never mentioned it again.

He'll occasionally touch my arm or catch my eye: We're really simpatico, aren't we baby? There may be twelve men and me sitting at the meeting and they can't call on one of the girls or the receptionist, he'd say, "Let's have some coffee, Barbara. Make mine black." I'm the waitress. I go do it because it's easier than to protest. If he'd know my salary is more than his I doubt that he'd have acted that way in Denver—or here.

Part of the resentment toward me and my salary is that I don't have a mortgage on a home in the Valley and three kids who have to go to private schools and a wife who spends at Saks, and you never know when you're going to lose your job in this business. Say we're having a convivial drink among peers and we start grousing. I'm not allowed to grouse with the best of them. They say, "Oh, you? What do you need money for? You're a single woman. You've got the world by the balls." I hear that all the time. . . .

Clients. I get calls in my hotel room: "I want to discuss something about production that didn't go right." I know what that means. I try try to fend it off. I'm on this tightrope. I don't want to get into a drunken scene ever with a client and to literally shove him away. That's not going to do me any good. The only thing I can do is avoid that sort of scene. The way I avoid it is by suggesting an early morning breakfast meeting. I always have to make excuses: "I drank too much and my stomach is really upset, so I couldn't do it right now. We'll do it in the morning." Sometimes I'd like to say, "Fuck off, I know what you really want."

"I've had a secretary for the last three years. I hesitate to use her . . . I won't ask her to do typing. It's hard for me to use her as I was used. She's bright and could be much more than a secretary. So I give her research assignments, things to look up, which might be fun for her. Rather than just say, 'Here, type this.'

"I'm an interesting figure to her. She says, 'When I think of Women's Lib I don't think of Germaine Greer or Kate Millett. I think of you.' She sees my life as a lot more glamorous than it really is. She admires the externals. She admires the apartment, the traveling. We shot two commercials just recently, one in Mexico, one in Nassau. Then I was in New York to edit them. That's three weeks. She takes care of all my travel details. She knows the company gave me an advance of well over a thousand dollars. I'm up in the fine hotels, travel first-class. I can spend ninety dollars on a dinner for two or three. I suppose it is something—little Barbara from a Kansas farm and Christ! look where I am. But I don't think of it, which is a funny thing.

It used to be the token black at a big agency was very safe because he always had to be there. Now I'm definitely the token woman. In the current economic climate, I'm one of the few writers at my salary level getting job offers. Unemployment is high right now among people who do what I do. Yet I get calls: "Will you come and write on feminine hygiene products?" Another, involving a food account: "We need you, we'll pay you thirty grand and a contract. Be the answer for Such an' Such Foods." I'm ideal because I'm young enough to have four or five solid years of experience behind me. I know how to handle myself or I wouldn't be where I am.

I'm very secure right now. But when someone says to me, "You don't have to worry," he's wrong. In a profession where I absolutely cannot age, I cannot be doing this at thirty-eight. For the next years, until I get too old, my future's secure in a very insecure business. It's like a racehorse or a show horse. Although I'm holding the job on talent and responsibility, I got here partly because I'm attractive and it's a big kick for a client to know that for three days in Montreal there's going to be this young brunette, who's very good, mind you. I don't know how they talk about me, but I'd guess: "She's very good, but to look at her you'd never know it. She's a knockout."

I have a fear of hanging on past my usefulness. I've seen desperate women out of jobs, who come around with their samples, which is the way all of us get jobs. A lot of women have been cut. Women who had soft jobs in an agency for years and are making maybe fifteen thousand. In the current slump, this person is cut and some bright young kid from a college, who'll work for seven grand a year, comes in and works late every night.

Talk about gaps. In a room with a twenty-two-year-old there are areas in which I'm altogether lost. But not being a status quo type person, I've always thought ahead enough to keep pace with what's new. I certainly don't feel my usefulness as a writer is coming to an end. I'm talking strictly in terms of physical aging. (Laughs.) It's such a young business, not just the consumer part. It's young in terms of appearances. The client expects agency people, especially on the creative end, to dress a certain way, to be very fashionable. I haven't seen many women in any executive capacity age gracefully. . . .

The part I hate—it's funny. (Pause.) Most people in the business are delighted to present their work and get praise for it—and the credit and the laughter and everything in the commercial. I always hate that part. Deep down, I feel demeaned. Don't question the adjectives, don't argue, if it's a cologne or a shampoo. I know, 'cause I buy 'em myself. I'm the biggest sucker for buying an expensively packaged hoax thing. Face cream for eight dollars. And I sell and convince.

I used Erik Satie music for a cologne thing. The clients didn't know Satie from Roger Williams. I'm very good at what I do, dilettantism. I go into my act: we call it dog and pony time, show time, tap dance. We laugh about it. He says,

"Oh, that's beautiful, exactly right. How much will it cost us?" I say, "The music will cost you three grand. Those two commercials you want to do in Mexico and Nassau, that's forty grand. There's no way I can bring it in for less." I'm this young woman, saying "Give me forty thousand dollars of your money and I will go away to Mexico and Nassau and bring you back a commercial and you'll love it." It's blind faith.

Do I ever question what I'm selling? (A soft laugh.) All the time. I know a writer who quit a job equivalent to mine. She was making a lot of money, well thought of. She was working on a consumer finance account. It's blue collar and black. She made this big stand. I said to her, in private, "I agree with you, but why is this your test case? You've been selling a cosmetic for years that is nothing but mineral oil and women are paying eight dollars for it. You've been selling a cake mix that you know is so full of preservatives that it would kill every rat in the lab. Why all of a sudden . . .?"

If you're in the business, you're in the business, the fucking business! You're a hustler. But because you're witty and glib . . . I've never pretended this is the best writing I can do. Every advertising writer has a novel in his drawer. Few of them ever do it.

I don't think what I do is necessary or that it performs a service. If it's a very fine product—and I've worked on some of those—I love it. It's when you get into that awful area of hope, cosmetics—you're just selling image and hope. It's like the arthritis cure or cancer—quackery. You're saying to a lady, "Because this oil comes from the algae at the bottom of the sea, you're going to have a timeless face." It's a crock of shit! I know it's part of my job, I do it. If I made the big stand my friend made, I'd lose my job. Can't do it. I'm expected to write whatever assignment I'm given. It's whorish. I haven't written enough to know what kind of writer I am. I suspect, rather than a writer, I'm a good reader. I think I'd make a good editor. I have read so many short stories that I bet you I could turn out a better anthology than anybody's done yet, in certain categories. I remember, I appreciate, I have a feeling I could. . . .

Alienation and Poverty:
The View from Comalapa

RICHARD SCHMITT

THE CONCEPT OF ALIENATION is a part of a particular conception of human life: unlike animals, human beings determine what it means to be a human being. The outline of a human existence is not drawn by biology; within the limits of our biology, different cultures have defined humanity in very different ways. What it means to be human is determined by human beings themselves. As Nietzsche said *der Mensch ist das noch nicht festgestellte Tier* (human beings are animals which are not fixed and whose nature has not been established). Alienation occurs when persons are limited in their ability to determine what their life should be like. Persons are alienated insofar as their person is defined by others, without their participating in the process of definition. To the extent that the members of a given society are alienated, they are therefore not free.

I had written a paper about all this before I went on a visit to Nicaragua where I stayed in a small country town, called Comalapa. Whatever else one may see there, the overwhelming impression is one of stark poverty—a poverty that appears to reframe the central issues of human life. Not fulfillment but getting by, not being one's own person but staying alive, finding food and shelter, and medical care, seem to be the pressing issues. Days are very long, it is a great effort to get anything done—to collect the firewood that one cooks on, to get to work in cities with faltering public transportation, to keep clean in a city where there is no water two days a week, and to get food where food supplies are scarce and unpredictable.

As I watched people patiently stand in line, cook their meals over smoking open fires, watched a little girl as she scrubbed a chair with water and a few leaves, or a boy carefully sweeping the sandy lot in front of his family's shack, that was pieced together from boards, tree branches, and corrugated iron, my

thinking about alienation seemed not only totally out of place but deeply mistaken. It seemed decadent, self-pitying, and self-indulgent.

What follows is an attempt to think through that experience. The issues raised do not apply only to underdeveloped societies at war. Poverty is not foreign to the United States; extreme deprivation is familiar also in our country. The general question is therefore whether the theory of alienation applies to some of us, but not to others, not to the poor.

That question gives rise to a second, more serious one, namely whether the conception of human life that gives rise to all this talk of alienation does not imply that the lives of the poor are, in some way, less than human because conditions of extreme deprivation leave no room for self-definition, and for making oneself into one's own person; for the poor, life's main problem is more basic and less philosophical, namely to stay alive. But if being properly human is to define oneself and thereby to define what it means to be human, the lives of the poor are less than human. Dare we affirm that?

In the course of the attempt to find answers to these questions we will clarify the concept of alienation.

I. ALIENATION

Thinking about alienation goes back, at least, to Hegel. Since then alienation has played a significant role in the thought of Kierkegaard (Kierkegaard 1954), Marx (Schmitt 1987), Nietzsche (Nietzsche 1955), Heidegger (Schmitt 1969), and Sartre (Sartre 1956). All these thinkers share certain common views about human life and what it means to be a human being. The concept of alienation is one important element in that shared conception of human life.

The concept of alienation makes sense only in relation to a web of assumptions that define what it means to be a human being. These assumptions are:

1. There is a human essence, just as there is an essence—a defining set of characteristics—of all other kinds of things. But the essence of humans is not only different in its content from, say, the essence of animals, but it is a different *kind* of essence. The essence of animals determines what it means to a dog, or a cow, or a rooster. That essence is an objective fact in the world that human thought can discover but not alter. The human essence, on the other hand, is not, in that sense, an objective given: human beings are what they believe themselves to be, and what they make themselves be by virtue of their everyday activities.

This thesis obviously requires important qualifications.

2. Our biological nature is very little affected by our beliefs about it, or by our daily actions. Aristotle's beliefs about human reproduction were mistaken, as was Descartes' conception of the nervous system as a set of strings through which the mind manipulated the body, as if it were a marionette. Their beliefs about reproduction or the nervous system did not alter human physiology, but human

physiology proved their beliefs erroneous. Faith healing is not impossible, but some diseases that prove impervious to psychoanalysis are cured by surgery. Thus there is a biological substrate to human existence over which thought has very limited power.

3. Human beings lead their lives in very different ways, not only because they are subject to different geographical, economic, and social conditions but because they have different beliefs about what is properly human. In our society, we believe that competition is the way to distribute scarce resources. Places in what are thought to be the best schools go to winners in academic competition. Wealth and power go to the winners in economic and in political competition. The upshot of that is that certain sorts of persons, persons who are, as we say, "good competitors," who function well under the stress of competition, who are good at taking exams, who are quick and aggressive—such persons are successful in our society. As a consequence they are the people whom we learn to look up to as children. They exemplify the sort of personality that we try to emulate as we grow up. A successful competitor is an important example of what it means to be human in our society.

Contrast this with the practice of the American Plains Indians among whom generosity, helping those less fortunate than oneself, was a major virtue:

> The Plains Indians were indeed intensely individualistic in matters of prestige, but economically they were often the reverse, sharing food freely with anyone, and other chattels at least with kinfolk. A potentially successful farmer would thus be held back in his economic progress by a host of needy spongers if he clung to tribal ethics. (Lowie 1954: 221)

These Plains Indians needed to change quite fundamentally what they regarded as the correct way for persons to own and to share property, before they could function successfully in the white man's economic system. They had to redefine what it means to be a human being. In these ways human beings, in their different cultures, determine what it means to be human.

4. It is, of course, not true that any given individual can be whoever she would like to be simply by virtue of believing she is that sort of person. My firm belief that I am a brilliant thinker does not make me one. My equally firm confidence in my own wisdom does not make me into a sage that anyone listens to profitably. What determines the sorts of persons each of us are, are not the individual beliefs of individual persons as much as the beliefs that are shared widely in the society. We are born into a given society and as we grow up we absorb its preconceptions long before we develop an independent critical stance toward those beliefs, so much so that the critical stances we take as adults are always formulated in the vocabulary that is dominant in the society in which we live and whose definitions of being a person are also ours.

5. The meaning of being human in our society is defined by our beliefs. But

the term "belief" is used in two very different senses which need to be distinguished if we are to understand the conception of being human that forms the background for the theory of alienation. For purposes of understanding the concept of alienation we need to distinguish between beliefs that are merely verbal and frequently are quite different from what we do—for instance our beliefs about Christian charity, which we rarely act on—and beliefs that are embodied in practices. These beliefs need not be put in words at all. If we do express them, they only put into words what we do every day in many different ways. Examples are our beliefs about the value and rightness of competition. Thus human beings define themselves collectively, not individually, in their practices, and not just in what they say, but in what they practice.

6. These practices and the beliefs that articulate them are so close to us—they define after all who we are—that they are not readily available to us. It takes a good deal of thought and effort to present to ourselves who we really are, how we live our lives, what we believe to be the most human way of being.

7. Practices and beliefs are put into words most often when they appear no longer adequate or when they are confronted by practices very different from ours. Then they are stated, subjected to criticism, and changed. With the change in our practices we become different persons. The meaning of being human changes and it is we who change it.

The prolonged struggle of women in our society has involved first of all a slow, painful effort to articulate all the ways in which women are devalued, such as in the ways in which we use our language, in access to work, to education, to opportunities in business. Gender-based prejudices have been uncovered in the sciences and, finally, the prevalent conceptions of science and scientific method have been subjected to criticism for being male-identified. Here we have an example of the effort required to bring our own practices into the full light of explicit awareness. Much hard work and controversy was required for us as a society to understand more clearly how the roles of women were defined. That effort has by no means come to an end. Together with the effort at articulating practices goes an attempt to change them. We have reformed our speech in certain ways, access to work and education has broadened for women, and there are continuing efforts to criticize and rethink the results of science as it pertains to the lives of women. In the process we all change, for the definition of being human changes, however slowly.

Once, being human was clearly to be a man—women, being somehow less than full human beings, were therefore patronized by men and treated with less than full respect. Being human, being a man, was to be tough, unemotional, aggressive, and self-contained. All of this has been thrown into doubt and that means not only that we talk differently—if that is all that it meant it would not be interesting—but that we act, or try to act, differently. The definition of what it means to be a human being has changed.

8. The previous definition of what it meant to be human and what it meant to be a woman was imposed on women by the culture and those who dominated it. Women found themselves to be certain sorts of persons without having had a hand in making themselves be human beings of that sort. They were thereby *alienated* because the definition of what it meant to be female was not a definition that women had any hand in shaping. Their lives thus were not theirs to the extent that the outlines of those lives were defined by others. The changes in the meaning of being a human female, on the contrary, that women have made constitute resistance to alienation. Here women contribute powerfully to the new meaning of being a female person and thus contribute to the new definition of what it means to be a human being.

9. Alienation occurs if one is not one's own person, and one's life is not one's own. That condition occurs when groups do not participate in that process of collective definition of what it means to be a human being but, instead, have imposed on them a conception of who they are. The struggle against alienation consists of making the socially defined outlines of one's life explicit and to participate in the process of redefining who one is.

Ours is an alienating society because in the pursuit of wealth, power, and efficiency we ignore what sorts of persons we become by virtue of organizing our lives as we do. The prevailing individualism which holds that a society is best arranged if everyone, separately, arranges his or her life as suits them best, conceals the fact that the definition of what it means to be human is a *social* product. The collective definition of human nature is hidden from us and thus we cannot even ask questions about the way in which our institutions shape our humanity. Being unable even to question the social definition of our humanity, we are all the more unable to determine what it means for us to be human. Alienation is the inevitable result (Schmitt 1983, 1988a).

II. Life in Nicaragua

Picture a country where the vast majority of people, in the city as well as the country, live in wooden shacks with walls made of planks, or adobe, or just thin tree branches, ten by ten, with a dirt floor, and a corrugated tin roof. If they are well-off, they have an outhouse and running water, out in the street where fifteen to twenty families use one faucet for all their water, perhaps with electricity, perhaps not. But many get their water out of the river in which the cattle is also watered, and people bathe and wash their clothes. During the dry season, when the river runs dry, they buy water from their neighbors who are fortunate enough to have wells. Food is cooked over open fires, under some sort of jerryrigged roof in the rainy season, and outdoors the rest of the year.

These houses have no closets because people do not own anything that requires closets. A nail in the wall holds all the clothes they own. A wooden table or two suffices to store their few plates, knives, forks, pots, and pans, and serves at the same time for washing up after meals. Only the wealthy have refrigerators, and only they have radios and television sets.

Transportation is difficult. In the city, people set out to walk to work, or to stand in line for the occasional bus, at three and four in the morning, when it is still dark for another two hours. In the country, there are few roads, people travel on horseback, if they have a horse, by decrepit truck if they are fortunate to own one, or manage to hitch a ride, or they walk, carrying a little bag with food and, if they are men, their machete, or, if they are women, more likely than not, a small child. In such a world the whole day—and they are usually very long days—is taken up with getting to work, with getting the wood for the stove, fetching the water, with getting the food, cooking the rice, cooking the beans, making tortillas.

Washing clothes requires boiling them on the stove—requiring more wood—and then rubbing and rinsing them on a big stone in the yard or down by the river, when there is water in the river. Keeping the house clean requires sweeping the hard clay floor and the dusty space in front of the house with green branches.

Families are large. The bigger children take care of littler ones and do chores at an early age. Very young children are sent out to make a few pennies by selling food that has been prepared in the home, or they sell wood that they have gathered somewhere. You see quite little ones along the road, with their pushcarts fetching something, bringing something somewhere else.

Children do go to school. Some of their health needs are met, in some towns, by public health clinics. These clinics often do not have doctors, for the doctors that live in the town do not take care of patients without money, or do not practice medicine at all, because they can earn more money running the farms they inherited from their fathers.

Many children die. There is a good deal of malnutrition. Milk is hard to come by, even in the countryside because the cows are moved to the mountains in the dry season. The really poor people do not have cows, few have goats, and milk is expensive to buy.

I stayed in the house of a relatively wealthy family. They had several rooms and a little patio where the hibiscus and lemon trees were in bloom, and a vine produced large green fruits that are turned into juice. Whitewashed stone walls and tile roofs made the rooms cool in the hot hours of the day. But in the kitchen there was only an open fire, and if the wind was unfavorable woodsmoke filled the house. In the evening, the whole village was wreathed in woodsmoke. Even here, the older woman, her grey hair in two thick braids, got up around 5 A.M. and started the fire and cooked all day in the smoky kitchen. The maid started work at the same time and was still working in the evening, cleaning up the kitchen for the last time that day.

III. The Questions

As I was watching this maid go about her business tirelessly, a woman who looked to be in her fifties and who worked from before dawn to after nightfall, day in, day out, to get enough to eat, to live, but not much more than that, all kinds of questions started to rise in my mind about alienation. Did that concept make any sense in that context? How can we talk about alienation, about not being one's own person in a world where it takes all one's energy and ingenuity to meet the most pressing needs? More than that, watching this life, it suddenly seemed that my preoccupation with alienation was self-indulgent. Why whine about not defining oneself when my present life is comfortable, and it does not take all day to take care of the bare necessities, when life is relatively secure and there is leisure to enjoy? Most seriously, the theory of alienation seems to devalue the lives of the people I saw. If life is genuinely human to the extent that we define ourselves, then life in the Third World and, let us not forget, for *many* people in our own country is not genuinely human. But a theory that does not distinguish between hard and deprived lives and lives that are less than human must be rejected. It is tempting, at this point, to take a "historical" view and say that alienation, being a historical phenomenon, is possible only once economic productivity and the general standard of living have reached a certain minimal level. Alienation is therefore not an appropriate concept to apply in the Third World but it is at home in our society. While that may well be true, we would deprive ourselves of a number of important insights if we took that easy road out of these painful questions.

In trying to answer these questions, we will see a number of pitfalls in the discussion of alienation. We must be careful not to turn our reflection about the life in the Third World into a romantic glorification of the "simple life"; we must not use discussions of alienation as excuses for copious self-pity; we must not disguise our own class prejudice in descriptions of the life of the poor. All of these do not contribute to a better understanding of alienation. They are simply indications that we too are alienated.

IV. The Glorification of the Simple Life

In the perspective from Comalapa, the language of alienation seemed idle and misplaced. As I thought about the lives of the people around me, passages from the Old Testament rose up from memory:

> A man that is born of woman is of few days, and full of trouble. He cometh forth like a flower and is cut down; He fleeth also as a shadow, and continueth not. (Job 14: 1, 2) I know that there is nothing better, but for a human to rejoice and to do good in his life. (Eccles. 3: 12)

Life is short and full of work and pain. A person can do no better than to do right and to be as cheerful as possible. There is no room in that view of human life for demands for self-definition or determining the meaning and direction of one's own life. The human essence is not open to be given content by human beings themselves but is set by divine decree. Our task is to worship, enjoy, and endure. It is a short step from this memory of Old Testament views to a slightly different position, namely that the life portrayed there, the simple life of the poor, is much to be preferred to the complex, decadent, and corrupt life in our society. Away with luxury, away with intellectual sophistication, with the imaginary problems of the modern city dweller, the agonies about finding the right relationship, or work that is genuinely fulfilling, or freeing oneself from one's childhood traumas! Praise for the simple life, the life of the Nicaraguan campesino, the life of the honest poor in our country, because it is more genuine, more substantial, more human than life in our degenerate world! Complaints about alienation are part of that world, part of falling away from our human substance which the simple life, with its elemental concerns, still preserves. We must reject all thinking about alienation as only one more symptom of our decadence. This theme can be found, in slightly different permutations, throughout our intellectual tradition. It comes up over and over again in the writings of Tolstoy and his glorification of the Russian peasant: Levin and Platon in *War and Peace*. In "The Death of Ivan Ilych," Gerasim, a young peasant lad, takes care of his dying master. He is the only one who is willing to acknowledge that Ivan Ilych is dying. His direct simplicity allows Ivan Ilych to die well in a corrupt and lying culture that evades death and shirks the ultimate tasks.

The same theme recurs, in politics, in populist rhetoric that glorifies the people, meaning usually the "common man," the person without wealth, education, or sophistication. It recurs, as we shall see in a later part of this book, in discussions of our relationship to nature. Alienation from nature is often understood as a falling away from the simple harmony with nature that "less civilized" people than us still hold on to.

In Comalapa, and places like it, that sort of glorification of the poor, of the simple life, and with it a rejection of all talk about alienation is enormously attractive. But one must carefully distinguish between an attempt to rediscover the important tasks in our own life and the utter rejection of our own life in favor of a fantasy about the simple life which is no more than a projection of our own problems. On the one hand, there is a recognition that our life is immensely complex, while life in Comalapa is simpler, although no doubt not as simple as it appears to the visitor. The complexities of our life are confusing. It is easy to lose one's way, to pin one's hopes on wealth or fame, or try to dull pains by acquiring goods, or turn away from the suffering of the world and our own part in it, by taking up complex and engrossing hobbies, or working tirelessly for a business that, if one thought at all, would seem not to deserve all this energy. Is it worth a lot of energy to outsell your competitor in paper clips or Scotch tape? Or is it even worth a great deal of energy to beat your colleagues in the race to be the first to publish an important scientific discovery? The discovery may be genuinely important, but how important is it to be the one who published first?

It may be useful to return for a time to a situation where these complexities do not confuse one. It may be in the nature of a retreat to collect one's own thinking about one's life, and to enable one to recollect what is really important. But that self-recollection is quite different from the inclination to reject one's own life, and thus oneself, in favor of another way of life, to praise the unlettered because one is educated and bored with it, the poor because one is materially comfortable but not at peace, the oppressed because one has choices and a modicum of control over one's life but does not like the life one has chosen. This is not a telling criticism of alienation but, rather, a manifestation of it. The self-hatred of the alienated is here thinly disguised by praise of the Russian peasant or of the Nicaraguan campesino.

Our alienation, in fact, leads us to misread the life of the people of Comalapa. As we shall see below, their fundamental choices are no different from ours even if they take very different concrete forms for them and for us. Life in Comalapa may not be used to discredit the theory of alienation as a product of a decadent age, refuted by the elemental innocence of the poor, the peasant, the survivor. The poor, the peasants, have not chosen to be poor or to be peasants. Few soldiers remain under arms once peace has been restored. The simple goodness of the poor is no more than a self-hating fantasy of the alienated.

V. ALIENATION AND THE INTELLECTUALS

But talking about alienation did not only seem out of place, it seemed positively disagreeable, weak and self-pitying, and, to be sure, such talk often is. Thinking, writing, and talking about alienation may be a prelude to resistance, or it may just be a way of being alienated, of wallowing in one's malaise and confusions. It is true that writings about alienation easily turn into whining. One's sorrow is not far removed from self-pity—self-pity that paralyzes and turns into slightly masochistic pleasure at one's own suffering. Thus Dostoyevski's Underground Man says:

> And it is just in that cold and loathsome half-despair and half-belief . . . in that intensely perceived, but to some extent uncertain, helplessness of one's position—in all that poison of unsatisfied desires that have turned inwards— in that fever of hesitations, firmly taken decisions, and regrets that follow almost instantaneously upon them—that the essence of that delight that I have spoken of lies. (Dostoyevski n.d.: 116–17)

There is a certain voluptuousness in reciting the hopelessness and despair of one's existence. One enjoys, paradoxically, talking about one's suffering.

Sitting in Comalapa, watching the hard lives of its people showed in sharp relief that we make alienated and self-destructive uses of our understanding of alienation when we use it to gain sympathy for ourselves (from whom?—the others have the same problem). Writers about alienation make a great deal of the fact that every person is "ultimately alone" (Schmitt 1983: 80). In a town where the vast majority of families live in one room shacks that complaint seems peevish and ungrateful. Among people whose lives are narrowly circumscribed by physical hardship and deprivation, complaints about the burdens of our freedom, of the unbearable anxiety provoked by choice seem despicable. The problems of an Oblomov, whose life paralyzes him to the point where he cannot get out of his bed, seem funny, at best, in Comalapa. But the joke soon pales and revulsion at my own self-indulgence takes the place of laughter. It is difficult not to see my own thinking and writing about alienation as a perverse refusal to enjoy what I have, because pain is more pleasurable.

It is a special problem of intellectuals that thinking is easily divorced from action. Often that is for the best; often it is very destructive. Thinking about alienation that does not eventuate in action but just deplores one's inability to contribute to a definition of one's humanity only serves to perpetuate one's own powerlessness. Inactivity thus reinforces alienation because it deepens one's paralysis. Every hour of self-pity is an hour lost for making changes and overcoming alienation. The view from Comalapa makes it amply clear that thinking about alienation that does not lead to action is merely alienation reproducing itself. The passivity of alienation brings its own perverse rewards. The disgust I felt is a reaction to alienation enamored of itself that does not want to struggle for liberation. Before we saw alienation distort our view of people in Comalapa. Here alienation distorts our own life, concealing the call to action that is implicit in one's recognition of alienation behind the figure of the helpless victim.

VI. ALIENATION WITHOUT CLASS PREJUDICE

In the view from Comalapa, talk about alienation is additionally repellent because it seems to denigrate the lives of the poor. It seems to tell us that a human life is one that defines itself and, in the process, defines what it means to be human. The poor, whose trajectories are predetermined for them by the sheer deprivation of their condition, by their extreme neediness, thus do not seem to be fully human. In his most humanist phase, when Marx eloquently denounces the alienation of workers, he declares that capitalism produces

> . . . palaces—but for the worker hovels. It produces beauty, but for the worker, deformity. . . . It produces intelligence, but for the worker idiocy,

cretinism (Tucker 1978: 73). As a result . . . the worker no longer feels him[or her]self to be freely active in any but his[or her] animal functions— eating, drinking, procreating . . . and in his[or her] human functions [s/]he no longer feels him[or her]self anything but an animal. What is animal becomes human and what is human becomes animal. (Tucker 1978: 74)

Alienation deprives workers of their humanity: "what is human becomes animal." The worker is not much better than an animal. Here Marx, the great advocate of the working masses of his time, is clearly misled by his own middle-class view of what it means to do manual work.

Class prejudice takes two forms in the discussion of alienation: In Marx's view the poor are alienated, because their "higher" functions are subordinated to the demands of sheer survival. The alternative view is that poverty is so constricting that poor folks are not even capable of alienation. In both cases the central message is that "they" are utterly different from "us"—persons with a college education, who do white-collar work, and who have some money in the bank, or, at least, have a decent credit rating.

But the signs of class prejudice are palpable in both views: the poor, all lumped together into one grand class, are looked at completely from the outside and at a distance. Are there not very different sorts of poverty, and is poverty not borne in very different spirits? People who work hard for little money who live in a part of town where everyone else has similar incomes are in a very different position from the homeless person who sleeps on the subway grates in Manhattan. People who work, but make little money, have a very different life from the people who cannot find work. The reasons for not finding work make an enormous difference: whether it is race prejudice, or disability, or being "too old." The poverty in Comalapa, which is appalling to us who come from the United States on a visit, is an established fact of life for Nicaraguans. They have always lived that way. Struggle is essential to their existence. It is not news.

Poverty is a real burden, and an unjust one. But it does not define anybody. People are not fixed into a rigid mold by being poor.

VII. ALIENATION AND THE POOR

We have seen that it is tempting, when visiting Comalapa, to fantasize that the simple life is proof against alienation and promises us relief from our despair. But that thought is the outcome of our own alienation and distorts and denigrates the reality of life in Comalapa. In the same vein, our thinking about alienation seems no more than shameful delight in our own powerlessness. But this also is an error. Here our alienation misrepresents itself, showing us to ourselves as victims rather than as opponents of our alienation. We have finally seen that when middle-class persons talk about alienation, class prejudice may well distort their analyses. But all of these observations do not completely answer our initial

question: why does talk about alienation seem so out of place in Comalapa?
Alienation occurs only where two conditions are met:

1. the social and economic conditions for deliberate creation of culture and
   of humanity are present, and
2. people fail to, or are unable to define what it means to be human
   deliberately.

The first of these conditions is complex. Only a culture that values the
individual self-determination of persons can appreciate the problem of alienation. Thus certain clusters of ideas must prevail if alienation is to be a problem.
For alienation to be a real problem, there must be the material conditions for
individual self-determination. It must be possible to move to new places, to take
up different occupations, to change one's personal style, one's tastes. Thus a
certain level of material well-being must go hand in hand with individualism
before alienation can come to be a real problem (Schmitt 1983: chap. 5). Only
under those conditions is self-determination abstractly possible and can people
be alienated because, in fact, they are unable to determine who they are and
what it means to be a human being.

In Comalapa these conditions clearly obtain. At first, life there seems, to the
visitor, too circumscribed by physical want, by life at the margins of survival to
allow any choices of different ways of life. But that, I think, is the outsider's
misperception. A more careful view shows that there are clear alternatives,
however limited, for everyone. We can characterize these alternatives crudely as
between the person who takes pride in herself in keeping her house and yard
clean and perhaps nurturing a few flowers through the dry season, as opposed to
the drunkard who succumbs to the hardship of this life.[1] There are major choices
of religion, whether to attend the local Roman Catholic church regularly, or
join one of the Protestant Evangelical churches spread widely throughout
Central America. There are choices of friends and mates. There are choices
about child rearing. These are not choices between public and private school
education, but different parents talk differently and attend differently to their
children, and have different relations to them.

There is the difference between the people in the neighborhood who give of
themselves and share their meager space with others in need, or provide
leadership to the neighborhood organizations, as opposed to those who take
advantage of their neighbor's needs thereby to enrich themselves, or find an
outlet for their rage in banditry. Most Nicaraguan families have relatives living
in the United States. Such moves are possible. If they choose to remain they can
join the various political factions, jockeying for power, or reside in the grum-
bling middle section of the political spectrum.

Poverty, whether in Comalapa or in the United States, may reduce the sheer
number of choices, but not anywhere to the degree that alienation is not a fact

of life. The fundamental problems are for the Comalapans what they are for us: to resist the pressure to accept ready-made definitions of who we are and who human beings are—whether those are made by a ruling group or by an impersonal system—and to assert themselves against those definitions and the alienation they impose. The Comalapans' scope for resistance is much more limited than ours, but that may merely mean that they resist as successfully, or more so, than we do. The view from Comalapa also makes clear that insofar as we spend less energy just staying alive, we should devote more energy to resisting alienation, and to resisting those forces and groups, including ourselves, that impose it on us.

Note

1. For a description of the sorts of options at resistance open to peasants in Pinochet's Chile see Richards (1985). In community organizations, peasants draw collective conclusions which lead to a change of life. "The change of attitude that we are interested in leads the peasants to affirm themselves and their organizations as generators of their own objectives" (96).

References

Dostoyevski, F. (n.d.). "Notes from the Underground." In *Best Short Stories*, 171–240. New York: Modern Library.

Kierkegaard, S. A. (1941). *Concluding Unscientific Postscript*. Princeton: Princeton University Press.

Kierkegaard, S. A. (1954). *Sickness unto Death*. New York: Doubleday Anchor.

Lowie, R. H. (1954). *Indians of the Plains*. New York: American Museum of Natural History.

Nietzsche, F. (1955). *Beyond Good and Evil*. Chicago: Gateway.

Richards, H. (1985). *The Evaluation of Cultural Action: An Evaluative Study of the Parents and Children Program (PPH)*. London: Macmillan.

Sartre, J. P. (1956). *Being and Nothingness*. New York: Philosophical Library.

Schmitt, R. (1969). *Martin Heidegger on Being Human*. Gloucester: Peter Smith.

Schmitt, R. (1983). *Alienation and Class*. Cambridge: Schenkman Publishing Co.

Schmitt, R. (1987). *Introduction to Marx and Engels*. Boulder: Westview.

Schmitt, R. (1988). "Alienation and Autonomy." *Praxis International* 8: 222–36.

Tucker, R., ed. (1978). *The Marx-Engels Reader*. New York: Norton.

PART II

Gender

WORK ALIENATION IS OBVIOUS to most of its victims—but not to all of them as the interview with Anne Bogan shows. But much of it is imposed by straightforward coercion. The employer tells you to take orders or else. . . . The alienation of women is more complex and much more subtle. It takes many different forms.

Tom Moody's essay is the proper introduction to this section. It takes Marx's view of alienation as its starting point, and contributes to its clarification. In so doing, it also shows the connection of Marx's views to the specific alienation suffered by women.

But that alienation takes very different forms: the other essays in this section examine at least three different kinds. Major bodily changes, such as pregnancy, leave you with a body that seems alien, unmanageable. One ordinarily feels at home in one's body, it moves as one wants it to move, fits where one knows it will. But now, suddenly, that easy familiarity is interrupted. One is a stranger to oneself in one's body. It is not too difficult to think of other comparable experiences, such as old age or accidents like broken legs or loss of eyesight.

This is alienation that overcomes one from the outside, in some way, even though it is so intimately connected with one's daily experience of oneself. It is also, at least sometimes, temporary. Pregnancy lasts approximately nine months, one adjusts to some loss of powers in old age and even becomes comfortable with different work rhythms. Other impairments are temporary or are incorporated successfully into one's life and one's person.

But pregnancy threatens with alienation of a different sort once it becomes a concern of the medical profession. For now what seems to the pregnant woman a challenge to her sense of self that she is slowly integrating into her self, becomes a concern, a problem to be solved, a difficulty to be ameliorated by someone else who supposedly understands those things. Her pregnancy comes under someone else's management, who has information, for example, by means of ultrasounds, or blood tests, which count for more than the pregnant woman's experience. The pregnancy becomes "objectified." Here alienation is brought to us from the outside by other persons—as the representatives of medical practice, of the predominantly male outlook of obstetrical practice.

Bartky also talks about objectification. But Young talks about objectification of a condition—pregnancy—while Bartky talks about a *person* being objectified, when one aspect of her is taken to be the whole person. Women are objectified insofar as they are regarded as primarily, and exclusively, female bodies. A part is taken as the whole person. The whole person is treated as if she were only a female body and nothing else. No wonder that she does not recognize herself in that world!

But surprisingly, Bartky points out, she does. Here is a kind of alienation that is not only imposed from the outside, but is, in certain ways, self-inflicted. She quotes Dinah Shore as saying: "If I had just won the Nobel Peace Prize but felt my hair looked awful, I would not be glowing with self assurance. . . ." (Did Albert Einstein feel that way?) Here the male view of the person has become internalized. Alienation is, if not self-imposed from the beginning, significantly aided by the woman who sees herself primarily as a body.

Women adopt this alienating stance towards themselves under the continuing and massive influence of the "fashion-beauty complex"—the complex network of corporations who make money by selling "beauty" and who would lose many good customers, if women were no longer interested in spending so much time, energy, and money on their appearance. To the extent that women are complicit in this alienation, they are complicit with a sector of the economy that thrives on an alienating and objectifying view of women.

The Alienation of Women under Capitalism

TOM MOODY

> Women's special alienation . . . shows itself in the male domination of culture, in sexual suppression, sexual objectification, and estrangement from bodily potential. The fragmentation of the person and prohibition against expressing human creativity that these forms of estrangement express present a paradigmatic case of Marxian alienation.[1]

SOME FEMINISTS HAVE CRITICIZED Marxism for its inability to give a serious analysis of women's oppression. A Marxist analysis centers around women's exclusion from, or oppression in, the market, and concerns, for example, the need of capitalism to maintain the reserve army of labor. Such economic analysis seems to make the oppression of women a spinoff of the much more important activity of the economy, secondary to the central phenomena of worker exploitation and class struggle. Furthermore, feminists have argued that in Marx's view, women in their role as domestic workers are unalienated. Describing what she calls the traditional Marxist interpretation of alienation, Alison Jaggar says:

> those who do not participate directly in the social relations that characterize the capitalist mode of production are alienated insofar as they are excluded from capitalist relations of production: thus, not all women are alienated, and those who are do not suffer special gender-specific forms of alienation.[2]

Thus Marx's theory of alienation seems to be unhelpful in assessing the position of women under capitalism. I believe these criticisms to be mistaken. An analysis of the oppression of women centered around alienation can provide a much deeper and more satisfactory typology of the oppression of women under capitalism than such critics think. I do not wish to argue here that Marxism can provide a complete explanation of women's oppression under capitalism,[3] merely that it can give us a better description than is usually thought. What I wish to do here is to briefly explain what Marx meant by alienation, then to apply that concept to the situation of women under capitalism.

I. ALIENATION IN GENERAL

Alienation is not merely an economic phenomenon. It may have its roots in alienated labor and in private property, but Marx stresses that all sectors of society are interdependent: "everything which appears in the worker as an activity of alienation, of estrangement."[4] Alienation takes cultural, ideological, political, psychological, and of course, religious forms. So that even if some sectors of society do not participate directly in alienated labor, they still participate in an alienated culture. Marx has two notions of alienation, which he does not always keep distinct. The first is the notion of estrangement. This is what Marx has in mind when he speaks of alienation from species-being, for example. Our species-being is to be active creatures—what Marx calls *homo faber*. We are alienated from that nature when we are placed in situations that prevent us from realizing that active potential. This idea has led some to believe that Marx has an essentialist view of human nature. Ollman points out that when discussing estrangement Marx generally uses language that suggests that an essential tie has been cut. People are separated from their work, or their work and their creative natures have been separated. The alienated person has become an "abstraction," that is, one isolated from the social whole. She is such because she has lost touch with human specificity. "He has been reduced to performing undifferentiated work on humanly indistinguishable objects among people deprived of their human variety and compassion."[5] The second notion of alienation is that of facing alien powers. Marx speaks of loss of control over the products of one's activity, for example. One faces a culture, a work environment, a family situation, all of which are the products of human activity, in which one cannot recognize one's own values or contributions and which is controlled by values foreign to one's own. One creates a product and it becomes a commodity on the market. One has a baby in a hospital which treats one's pregnancy as an illness. One faces a political environment where decisions are made over one's head and do not reflect one's own values. One faces institutions that have taken on a life of their own and seem to be independent of human control: sexuality, for instance, or purely economic phenomena:

> Under private property . . . each tries to establish over the other an alien power, so as thereby to find satisfaction of his own selfish need. The increase in the quantity of objects is therefore accompanied by an extension of the realm of alien powers to which man is subjected.[6]

Two questions need to be answered:

1. Does alienation presuppose essentialism? Can we be alienated without an essential self to be alienated from?
2. What's wrong with alienation? That it causes the alienated to suffer? That it is a lie? That it retards or prevents human fulfillment?

Answered correctly, the second can help us with the first. If the problem with alienation is that the natural potential of human beings is being wrongly thwarted, then we may need to see Marx as an essentialist. Marx suggests this:

> free, conscious activity is man's species-character . . . it is only because he is a species-being that he is a conscious being, i.e., that his own life is an object for him. Only because of that is his activity free activity. Estranged labor reverses this relationship, so that it is just because man is a conscious being that he makes his life activity, his *essential being*, a mere means to his existence.[7]

The essentialism here seems to me to be minimal. Marx means that our nature in any given period is created by the interaction of our activity with the world. There is no constant Hobbesian-like content to our natures, only a constant desire to be active in the world.[8] There is what might be called a second-order human nature, but not any constant transhistorical set of moral or psychological characteristics. Calling *homo faber* a "desire" to be active is misleading insofar as it suggests a psychological trait. It is closer to a teleological end. That end can be thwarted or encouraged. Marx's complaint against capitalism is that it thwarts that human desire to be active.[9] Marxists can argue that human nature historically has been gendered, but that nonetheless female "nature" and male "nature" are but historical and social constructions. It is then open to Marxists to criticize and analyze the specific shape gender takes in a given time. The overriding metaphysical trait of being creatively active is shared by both sexes. But even if that "nature" is second-order, there is still some appeal to an essentialist human nature here. That this human nature is open-ended and ungendered is an improvement over most other human nature views, but is still metaphysically suspicious.

Suppose though that we give (2) a more utilitarian answer. In many respects Marx appears to be an ideal utilitarian, with the ideal defined in quasi-Aristotelean terms of self-realization.[10] Alienation occurs when people are prevented from reaching that ideal. Marx is graphic in his descriptions of the stultifying effects of capitalism on workers. Below we will see some equally unpleasant effects of alienation on women. This approach allows one to employ alienation for social assessment while relieving one of essentialist burdens. To be successful though, it will be necessary to be careful about how we specify the ideal. What are human goods? We must not identify them with the satisfaction of conscious wishes, desires, or feelings in the liberal fashion (though we must not ignore those wishes or feelings either), for to do so might force us to claim that subjectively happy workers are necessarily unalienated. The clear facts of domination and manipulation of people's wishes and desires requires us to insist that even those who feel happy can be alienated. Marx has an objectivist view of human goods—his scathing remarks about Bentham elevating the English shopkeeper into the prototype of humanity show that. On objectivist grounds, people can be deprived of a good without their realizing it or being bothered by it.

There is a clear and pressing need in Marxist theory for an analysis of this objective character of human goods. Marx himself usually provides an unhelpful counterfactual: objective human goods are those that people would actually want if their desires and needs were not distorted by class bias (and we must add here, by gender bias). Since such clarity can be only obtained under communism, this is unhelpful to those of us still laboring under capitalist distortions. Further, it is entirely possible that such objectivism about human needs is tantamount to having an essentialist human nature view. Put it this way: Marx does think there is something constant about human beings. They are (or ought to be) striving for self-realization through communal activity. But the nature of this activity, the moral and psychological qualities of people—all these are open-ended. The content of human nature in any given period would then be so indeterminate as to almost be purely environmentally caused. Yet Marx still has a place to stand in making moral critiques of capitalism because he can appeal to this goal of self-realization, whereas pure environmentalism has no such Archimedean point of moral criticism. If human beings can happily be anything, where is the critical edge?

But important as these issues are, they cannot be pursued here. I turn now to showing how Marx's theory of alienation illuminates the oppression of women under capitalism.

II. ALIENATION FROM SPECIES-BEING

Marx discusses four types of alienation, the first of which is *of woman from species-being*. The species-being in question is, of course, *homo faber*. Women are even more alienated here than are men since sex discrimination, the sexual division of labor, and the psychological training of most women prevents them from being even as active and creative as men. Jan Slagter suggests that capitalism replaces fulfillment of species-being with the reproduction of gender-being, that is, of two distinct types of human beings, neither allowed to reach full creative potential because both are limited to gender potential at best.[11] The supersession of the alienation of men and women from species-being then would require the elimination of gender.

Marx also speaks of alienation from nature as a case of alienation from species-being. For women, alienation from nature appears in their alienation from their bodies.

> As we are alienated from nature, so are we alienated from our animal natures. The forces of capital and patriarchy, puritanism, and a kind of consumer-hedonism (as well as the dualistic metaphysical heritage . . .) combine to estrange us from our bodily well-being.[12]

Unlike a man, whom Marx claims is "reduced to an animal," a woman is estranged from her animal nature, from her own body, which is appropriated and fetishized. Iris Young says:

> the norms of femininity suppress the body potential of women. We grow up learning that the feminine body is soft, not muscular, passive, incapable, vulnerable. . . . Developing a sense of our bodies as beautiful objects to be gazed at and decorated requires suppressing a sense of our bodies as strong, active subjects moving out to meet the world's risks.[13]

Here the dualism of mind and body becomes fragmentation of a human being, with a woman being more identified with her body than is a man, but only with her alienated body, which she sees as deficient insofar as she has internalized the messages of what Sandra Bartky calls the "fashion-beauty complex." A woman's body becomes a constant project, a constant reproach for its failure to meet the standards of the spring weight-reduction ads displaying sleek bikinied bodies and exhorting her to get ready for the beach. "The fashion-beauty complex . . . create[s] a market for products and services to counteract the ones which have brought [women] to a debilitated state in the first place."[14] Then there is what Bartky calls feminine narcissism: the sexual objectification by women of their own bodies.[15] Such phenomena are alienation in the sense of self-estrangement and of alienated needs. Then there is the pervasive objectification of women's bodies for commercial purposes. Women constantly see images of their sexuality portrayed in ways that seem alien to them—as sluts, as sex kittens, as temptresses, but always there for male pleasure and at male disposal.

Here too falls sexual alienation. Many radical and lesbian feminists have noted the oppressive character of "compulsory heterosexuality."[16] Rigid gender separation and strong prohibitions against homosexuality result in an alienating restriction of female sexuality. Such cases are sometimes seen as counter examples to Marxism. They are so only if one reads Marx as claiming that alienation is *caused* by capitalism. Since such sexual constraints clearly predate capitalism and also exist contemporaneously with it in noncapitalist cultures, if Marx claimed that capitalism creates such alienation, he was clearly wrong. I think that Marx actually held a more cautious view: alienation is not created by capitalism, but takes specific and exacerbated forms under it. Sexism and homophobia did not appear in human history with the coming of capitalism.

Rather, capitalism seized upon such preexisting forms of sexual alienation, changing and intensifying them for its own purposes. The existence of sexual constraints in European culture prior to capitalism would not be a counterexample to this Marxist claim. Thus while radical feminists are right that sexism and patriarchy are not unique to capitalism, this claim does not contradict Marx.

Characteristically Marxist is the emphasis on the social nature of sexuality: heterosexuality is not natural, but a social institution that benefits an oppressor group. Here too we might refer to Wilhelm Reich, Herbert Marcuse, and others who have argued that the restriction of sexuality to genital activity serves the interests of capitalism.[17] And we can look to Foucault for suggestions about the ways in which sexuality has been subordinated to power through its subjection to medicine and psychiatry (although Foucault does not seem to recognize that power congeals differently around female than around male sexuality). Ehrenreich and English have described the ways in which medicine and psychiatry have made women's sexuality alien to them.[18] And women's sexual activity has been restricted in kind and quantity in periods without reliable birth control, due to the demand of men to know who their biological children are for inheritance purposes. All these are concrete instances of women's alienation from nature expressing itself in their alienation from their bodies.

Alienation from species-being also lies in the fact that women under capitalism are the private property of first their fathers, later their husbands. For Marx then, women would now be the only class of humans to be the property of other humans.

> With the division of labour, . . . which in turn is based on the natural division of labor in the family . . . is given simultaneously . . . private property: the nucleus, the first form of which lies in the family, where wife and children are the slaves of the husband. This latent slavery in the family, though still very crude, is the first property, but even at this early stage it corresponds perfectly to the definition of modern economists who call it the power of disposing of the labor-power of others.[19]

As *Female Sexual Slavery* all too vividly points out, this ability of men to dispose of the labor power of women can range from the metaphorical in the case of wives in American states with liberal legislation to quite literal in cases of female slavery and prostitution.[20] Not so long ago no American woman could charge her husband with rape, because he had legal access to her body. In some states, this is still the case. A woman's body is not hers, and her labor is devoted to the service of her husband and children. Marx at one point illustrates the miserable condition of the workingman under capitalism by pointing out that he is forced to sell his wife and children, to become a slave dealer. Marx's complaint here seems to be not that the wife and children are slaves, but that the worker has to sell them. Women are mere possessions, rather than human beings. Note the importance of an analysis that Marx never provided, but which Engels tried to: if alienation and alienated labor spring into being with private property in a mutually reinforcing relationship, and if women are the first private property, then some analysis of the original appropriation of women is crucial. The subjugation of women appears as the historical origin of alienation.

The analysis can begin either with private property or with division of labor. If we begin with division of labor, we begin, Marx says, with the sexual division of labor and so find it necessary to explain how men and women came to be assigned different tasks. Here Marx seems to think it is natural, though he never really does any analysis here.

III. ALIENATION FROM ONE'S OWN ACTIVITY

Marx's second type of alienation is *alienation from one's own activity.*

> What then constitutes the alienation of labor? First, the fact that labor is external to the worker, i.e, it does not belong to his essential being; that in his work, therefore, he does not affirm himself but denies himself, does not feel content but unhappy, does not develop freely his physical and mental energy but mortifies his body and ruins his mind. The worker therefore only feels himself outside his work, and in his work feels outside himself. He is at home when he is not working, and when he is working, he is not at home. His labor is therefore not voluntary, but coerced; it's forced labor. It is therefore not the satisfaction of a need; it is merely a means to satisfy needs external to it.[21]

Some modern feminists argue that Marxism can explain the oppression that women share with men as laborers, but none of their oppression as *women* laborers. Women face wage and advancement barriers, sexual exploitation and harassment, that men do not face. So, Marx's analysis may explain some of the problems women face as workers, but leaves out everything that is gender specific.[22] To establish this point though it is not sufficient to point out that in concrete work situations Marx's claim that workers enter the market as "abstract laborers, the bearers of abstract labor-power" is insufficiently detailed. Workers do enter the market as women, as blacks, as young or old. Marx did not intend his claim to deny this. Marx is pointing out that the crucial factor for a worker is the bearing of abstract labor power. Other specific individual factors tend to be less important or to disappear altogether. Marx, remember, is contrasting the capitalist work situation with feudalism where who a worker was was crucial in determining the character of the work s/he did. Marx clearly recognized that workers enter the market as individuals, but unlike under feudalism where the inherited status of the worker was determinant, under capitalism what primarily counted was the worker's ability to work. Social position—who one was—no longer mattered much: what counted was the ability to sell labor power, to work for wages. Marx never intended this characterization to stand in place of specific concrete analyses so the fact that it does not suffice as such an analysis does not refute it. There is no crude reductionism here that suggests that *all* that counts in such situations is one's position in relation to the means of production; rather a suggestion that relative to feudalism, one's ability to work is vastly more important under capitalism than are individual factors. Is it consistent with Marxism to point out that the situations of a woman worker, a black worker, a white male worker, are quite different? Certainly it is. But what Marx insists upon here is that these differences overlie a fundamental similarity that they all have in being workers in a capitalist market. A woman worker and a male worker are still workers and as such face similar types of alienation. A woman in addition will face styles of alienation peculiar to her as a woman.

One important way that people are alienated from their own activity is by loss of control over it. Are women deprived of control over their own activity? In some ways yes, just as men are: they are unable to find meaningful and fulfilling work, or to control either the nature or the products of their labor—but there is a double alienation here since the gender division of labor ensures that women typically cannot even achieve the full range of alienated labor available to men. If women are raised not to see their bodies as "strong active subjects moving out to meet the world's risks," they are thereby disabled from at least certain kinds of heavily physical work, and depending on the extent to which this is as well a psychological handicap, may not be competitive with men in certain areas. This inaccessible labor may or may not be fulfilling: nothing general can be said here. Specific analyses of specific kinds of inaccessible work are needed. But many women who have moved into work formerly reserved for men are finding it unfulfilling. But this speaks to the issue of the nature of one's work, whereas the point here is the extent of one's control over it. Since there are labor sectors which the gender division of labor and their own training prevent women from entering, to that extent they suffer a loss of control over their labor—regardless of whether those inaccessible areas would prove to be fulfilling.

What then of domestic work, to which the gender division of labor has long relegated women who do not or cannot work for wages? Domestic women seem to have a rather high degree of labor control. On a day-to-day basis middle-class women work when they want to—they structure as they wish the tasks that have to be done. A husband does not function like a capitalist; he does not take over the mental labor of designing the work to be done, leaving the woman to carry it out. Nor does the husband have hiring and firing power over his wife, despite his economic power over her. One might thus expect that on this score at least women in the home would be less alienated than women or men in the market. Nancy Hartsock argues something very like this in *Money, Sex, and Power*.

Yet lack of control over domestic labor does occur because domestic women do work within constraints such as husbandly expectations, the kind of technology that is available to them, and cultural expectations that result in more and more housework: houses are expected to be much cleaner now than they were fifty years ago, people have more clothes to be cleaned, and so on.

> The increasing subjection of the domestic childrearing process to scientific control suggests that mothers' experience is parallel in this respect to the experience of wage laborers and provides one reason for characterizing mothers' work as alienated.[23]

One needs here a detailed analysis of the constraints under which women labor in the home and a systematic comparison of the severity of these domestic constraints with the constraints women face in the market before any general comparisons can be made between the alienation of domestic women and market women (and men). If we now move to the second kind of alienation from one's activity—alienation from meaningful self-realizing work—we see that housewives are largely confined to uninteresting and unrewarding work— the obvious exception here is childbearing and rearing. Capitalism turned middle-class women into domestic workers, while stripping them of the useful economic activities they once performed. These activities were increasingly moved into the market economy and the remaining domestic work kept out of it. Thus women became worse off than men whether they worked or stayed home. Domestic work was rendered trivial and valueless—thus it was not worth paying for. Wage work submitted women to the same market alienation as men plus sexual discrimination and harassment, and confinement to the pink-collar ghetto. Unless all labor under capitalism is so alienated that no distinctions of degree are worth making, then women are more alienated with respect to self-fulfilling labor than are men.

While many domestic tasks have this alienating quality, childbirth and childrearing seem not to. Many women find childrearing immensely fulfilling and do not in the least see it as a piece of drudgery necessary in order to get economic support. Nancy Hartsock says:

> the directly sensuous nature of much of women's work leads to a more profound unity of mental and manual labor, social and natural worlds, than is experienced by the male worker in capitalism. The unity flows from the fact that women's bodies, unlike men's can be themselves instruments of production: in pregnancy, giving birth, or lactation, arguments about a division of mental from manual labor are fundamentally foreign.[24]

Absolutely right. There is no need to dispute the point. It is not necessary that women be totally or completely alienated for alienation to be a serious persistent feature of women's lives. Childbirth and rearing obviously are meaningful and fulfilling for many women. But we should also note the limitations on this activity. If women are in charge of reproductive labor, then to the extent to which they are not allowed control over the reproductive process, they are alienated. This lack of control manifests itself in a number of ways: antiabortion laws, hierarchical medical systems that put (mostly male) doctors in charge, the difficulty in obtaining cheap safe reliable contraception. There is alienation in the fact that women are encouraged to see childbirth as an illness rather than as a natural process and thus in true Foucaultian fashion to surrender control of the birth process to experts, mostly male.

The dark side of satisfaction in childrearing is the capitalist objectification of women as natural mothers fulfilling their destiny *only* by childbearing and rearing. It is one thing to find satisfaction in freely chosen childrearing. It is another to do so as a result of training and education that leave one unable to conceive of any other options, or guilty if one is not a mother or not happy as a mother. Being unable not to choose a kind of work is very much a lack of control. Furthermore,

> Women do not control the conditions of their motherhood. . . . [I]n advanced capitalist countries, where children have become an economic burden . . . women are often unable to bear the number of children they wish: either they cannot afford to support children alone, their husbands resist more children, or they suffer involuntary sterilization.[25]

One can imagine *fully* alienated reproduction. Read *The Handmaid's Tale* of young fertile women who are exclusively vessels for reproduction, the products of their labor going to the couple for whom they are involuntary "surrogate" mothers.[26] The Baby M case suggests the fact that a woman's body can be an instrument of production can be turned against her: childbirth for Mary Beth Whitehead was a recognizable parody of *The Handmaid's Tale*. Alienation in reproduction will cease only when women gain control, through safe contraceptives and available abortion, elimination of male domination of medicine, and elimination of economic and legal conditions that make it possible and necessary for women to sell their pregnancies.

IV. ALIENATION FROM THE PRODUCTS OF ONE'S LABOR

Alienation is also *from the products of one's labor*. What one produces passes out of one's hands into the control of others. These products enter market relations and become commodities, and one has only whatever relationship to them cash will bring. Ollman suggests that this means that the products of human activity are being transformed and are moving out of human control altogether, becoming reified or fetishized (these last are the psychological counterparts of the loss of control). They take on needs of their own, which humans are then forced to satisfy. Everything is stood on its head: human productive activity, instead of serving human needs, becomes objectified in such a way that people end up serving its needs.

Women as wage workers are in this sense alienated in exactly the same way men are. Let us bypass the issue of the status of domestic labor and look at women as mothers. Does this kind of alienation pertain? Lydia Lange says:

> If children are products, it makes sense to ask who should own and control them, a question which seems to me not only morally unsavory, but also impossible to make sense of within historical materialism.[27]

Unfortunate and unsavory as it is, those questions are not only being asked but answered to the disadvantage of women. Young and poor women often face pressure to give up their children for adoption. In the recent Baby M case Mary Beth Whitehead's baby was taken from her and delivered to a man. The New Jersey court made it very clear that it was within its province to decide who should "own and control" Baby M, and it decided that the sanctity of contract ruled against the mother. It is not farfetched to speculate that if such babyselling becomes common, there will be severe pressures on poor women to sell pregnancies. It is hard to imagine a clearer case of women losing control of the products of their labor for purely economic reasons. Their babies become commodities and subject to all the appropriate economic laws.

> If it [contract motherhood] becomes a socially acceptable way for a wife to help out the family budget, how can the law protect women from being coerced into contracts by their husbands? Or their relatives? Or their creditors? It can't. . . . If contract motherhood takes hold, a woman's "right to control her body" by selling her pregnancies will become the modern equivalent of "she's sitting on a fortune." Her husband's debts, her children's unfixed teeth, the kitchen drawer full of unpaid bills, will all be her fault, the outcome of her selfish refusal to sell what nature gave her.[28]

V. ALIENATION FROM OTHERS

Marx's fourth type of alienation is *alienation from others*. Capitalism renders us unable to have genuine human relations. We become instrumental for each other, the "cash nexus" extends to the way we view other human beings as well as more literal commodities. We can purchase human qualities, so it becomes less important to really have them. We become the owners of our traits and aptitudes, "possessive individuals."

> Money's properties are my-the-possessor's-properties and essential powers. Thus what I am and am capable of is by no means determined by my individuality. I am ugly, but I can buy for myself the most beautiful of women. Therefore I am not ugly, for the effect of ugliness—its deterrent power—is nullified by money. . . .[29]

Women suffer here too: they become the objects money can purchase, tokens to prove that men are handsome, intelligent, witty. Businessmen who have made it take "trophy wives." We are separated from one another, competitive with one another in the capitalist zero-sum game. Solidarity and true self-realization in working in community with others is impossible. Here is perhaps the most trenchant of the analyses that Marx can make with respect to women. It is also familiar so I will not rehearse here the many ways in which women under advanced capitalism are prevented from having healthy human relationships with men as well as with other women. But a few comments:

Note that this separation is between groups—most notably races and genders (and of course, classes), as well as between individuals. Gender alienation in work shows up in sexual harassment and the sexual division of labor. Women not only suffer the same worker alienation as men but they also appear in the job world as women workers, dominated, segregated, and exploited by male workers, as well as by capitalists.

Second, note how difficult it is to have a healthy relationship with someone who controls your bread and butter, who sees you as a sexual object, who cannot see you at all through the haze of cultural stereotyping, or who is threatened if you reveal any intelligence or ability; or with another woman who has been trained to regard you as competition for a man, or who has internalized female self-hatred and thus regards neither you (nor herself) as worth talking to or about.

Note too the ways in which women who enter the work force are required to become pseudomen and to deny very real parts of their personalities if they wish to succeed, and the extent to which capitalist housing arrangements segregate and isolate domestic women. Alison Jaggar claims that "in the 20th century mothers have been isolated from other women in a way that is new."[30] This isolation of women from each other is alienating, and prevents the formation of community among women, a community that Marx sees as necessary to self-realization.

Another element is that the liberal ethos of capitalism raises expectations of full humanity that capitalism cannot meet. Unable to find fulfillment in work or other public activity, men turn to various kinds of privatizations, one of which is love. Love is expected to be the source of meaning and fulfillment. Capitalism creates and reinforces an extremely strong public/private split and the primary focus of privacy is the home. Women are expected, as caretakers of the home, to provide what men cannot get in their public life. Thus women become enshrined and bewhored—they must be the pure protectors of the kind of morality that men cannot afford to live by in public, yet since sex is the most accessible form of capitalist love, they must also be the living embodiments of men's erotic fantasies, sexy sluts. This means that women have a difficult time being seen for who they really are by men (and, inevitably, sometimes by themselves). And when, inevitably, men cannot find complete meaning for their lives here either, which they cannot since love and family are being asked to carry much too great a burden—the result is quite often domestic violence, a lashing out in rage and disappointment at one of the very few people over whom an ordinary man has any power.

VI. Conclusion

It appears then that Marx's theory of alienation can describe significant amounts of women's oppression under capitalism. Whether Marxism is an adequate theory of women's oppression has not been addressed. In discussing women's alienation we appealed to a number of factors—cultural, ideological, political, economic—which have not yet been shown to be reducible to Marxist units of analysis. Nothing I have said here suggests that these factors will require appeal to independent explanations such as patriarchy or that they will not.

Notes

1. Jan Slagter, "The Concept of Alienation and Feminism," *Social Theory and Practice* 8(1982): 155
2. Alison Jaggar, *Feminist Politics and Human Nature* (Totowa: Rowman and Allanheld, 1983), 307–8.
3. For extensive discussions of this issue, see Lydia Sargent, ed., *Women and Revolution: A Discussion of the Unhappy Marriage of Marxism and Feminism* (Boston: South End Press, 1981).
4. Karl Marx, *Economic and Philosophical Manuscripts of 1844* (Peking: Progress Publishers, 1974), 74.
5. Bertell Ollman, *Alienation: Marx's Conception of Man in Capitalist Society* (London: Cambridge University Press, 1976), 134.
6. Marx, *Economic and Philosophical Manuscripts*, 101.
7. Ibid., 68. Marx's italics.
8. See Alan Buchanan, *Marx and Justice* (Totowa: Rowman and Alanheld, 1982), for a persuasive defense of this position.
9. See Isidor Walliman, *Estrangement: Marx's Conception of Human Nature and the Division of Labor* (New York: Greenwood Press 1981).
10. See Alan Gilbert, "Democracy and Individuality," *Social Philosophy and Policy* 3(1986): 19–58; and Jon Elster, "Self-Realization in Work and Politics: The Marxist Conception of the Good Life," *Social Philosophy and Policy* 3(1986): 97–126.
11. Slagter, "The Concept of Alienation and Feminism."
12. Ibid., 157.
13. Iris Young, "Is There a Woman's World?" (Presented to *The Second Sex—Thirty Years Later: A Commemorative Conference on Feminist Theory* sponsored by the New York Institute for the Humanities, New York University, September 1979), quoted in Sandra Bartky, "Narcissism, Feminity, and Alienation" in this book.
14. Slagter, "The Concept of Alienation and Feminism," 158.
15. Bartky, "Narcissism, Feminity, and Alienation."
16. Adrienne Rich, "Compulsory Heterosexuality and Lesbian Existence," *Signs: Journal*

for Women in Culture and Society 5(1980). See also Ann Ferguson, Jacquelyn N. Zita, and Katherine Pyne Addelson, "On Compulsory Heterosexuality and Lesbian Experience: Defining the Issues," *Signs* 7(1981).

17. Adrienne Rich, "Compulsory Heterosexuality and Lesbian Existence." Wilhelm Reich, *Sex-Pol: Essays 1929–1934* (New York: Vintage Books, 1972); and Herbert Marcuse, *Eros and Civilization* (Boston: Beacon Press, 1955).
18. Barbara Ehrenreich and D. English, *For Her Own Good: 150 Years of the Experts' Advice to Women* (New York: Anchor Books, 1979).
19. Karl Marx, *The German Ideology* in *Karl Marx: Selected Writings*, ed. David McLellan (Oxford: Oxford University Press, 1977), 168.
20. Kathleen Berry, *Female Sexual Slavery* (New York: Prentice-Hall, 1979).
21. Karl Marx, *Economic and Philosophic Manuscripts*, 66.
22. There is a great deal of excellent literature on this topic. See Lydia Sargent, ed., *Women and Revolution*; Zillah Eisenstein, ed., *Capitalist Patriarchy and the Case for Socialist Feminism* (New York: Monthly Review Press, 1979); and Ann Foreman, *Femininity as Alienation: Women and the Family in Marxism and Psychoanalysis* (London: Pluto Press, 1977). See also the excellent bibliographical references in Jaggar, *Feminist Politics*, esp. chaps. 8 and 10.
23. Jaggar, *Feminist Politics*, 312ff.
24. Nancy Hartsock, *Money, Sex and Power* (Boston: Northeastern University Press, 1983), 243ff.
25. Jaggar, *Feminist Politics*, 310.
26. Margaret Atwood, *The Handmaid's Tale* (Boston: Houghton Mifflin, 1986).
27. Lynda Lange, "Toward a Theory of Reproductive Labor" (Unpublished manuscript), quoted in Jaggar, *Feminist Politics*.
28. Katha Pollitt, "Contracts and Apple Pie: The Strange Case of Baby M," *The Nation* (May 23, 1987), 685.
29. Marx, *Economic and Philosophic Manuscripts*, 120.
30. Jaggar, *Feminist Politics*, 312.

Narcissism, Femininity, and Alienation

SANDRA LEE BARTKY

One of the many things men don't understand about women is the extent to which our self-esteem depends on how we feel we look at any given moment—and how much we yearn for a compliment, at any age. If I had just won the Nobel Peace Prize but felt my hair looked awful, I would not be glowing with self-assurance when I entered the room.

—Dinah Shore[1]

I. "FEMININITY" AS ALIENATION

AN IMPORTANT NEW BODY of theory is being born out of what Amy Bridges and Heidi Hartmann have called "The Unhappy Marriage of Marxism and Feminism."[2] The name most commonly given to the offspring of this union is "socialist-feminism," even though many of those who are most responsible for its emergence are not agreed on what to call it.[3] Tentative, impressionistic, and clearly unfinished, socialist-feminism has nevertheless identified and in many cases transcended the limitations of both bourgeois feminism and orthodox Marxism. Socialist-feminists have dealt the traditional Marxist account of the origins of patriarchy a blow from which it is unlikely ever to recover.[4] They have exposed the fatal lack in traditional Marxism both of a theory of sexuality and of an adequate account of human psychological development, and have begun to formulate theory in these areas from a historical materialist perspective with challenging results.[5] Further, socialist-feminists have subjected several of the central categories of Marxist analysis to searching critical scrutiny, chiefly the categories of "production" and of "relations of production." They have claimed that these categories are conceived too narrowly to allow an adequate understanding either of the oppressive character of the relations between men and

71

women or of what in fact constitutes the proper economic or productive "base" of society.[6]

One of the tasks which socialist-feminists have yet to accomplish is the alteration and elaboration of Marx's theory of alienation. Marx's account of the alienation of labor is both normative and descriptive: it is at once a powerful indictment of the capitalist system and an accurate description of some of the more salient features of that system. According to Marx, the alienated or estranged worker is self-estranged, not in the sense that the self is the agent of its own alienation (though Marx sometimes seems to suggest this), but because the state of alienation consists in the prohibition of those activities which are constitutive of selfhood. For Marx, labor is the most distinctively human activity; following Hegel, he regards the product of labor as an exteriorization of the worker's being, an objectification of human powers and abilities. But under capitalism, workers are alienated from the products of their labor as well as from their own productive activity. The capitalist organization of production is such that the workers lose control of what they have produced; their products cease to be mirrors in which they are able both to affirm and to enlarge their distinctively human capacities. These products serve instead to enrich the capitalist and to augment the power of capital, an "alien force" inimical to the worker's vital interests. The loss of the product has its analogue in the worker's loss of control over his or her own productive activity. What distinguishes human "species-being" from the being of other species is our distinctive laboring activity. This Marx regards as the free, self-aware, and creative transformation of nature in accord with human needs. But under capitalism, work is degraded. Most workers lack any opportunity for artistic or intellectual development; far from allowing workers to affirm or to augment their essential human powers, work under capitalism is forced labor to which the worker goes each day like a condemned prisoner, a mere drudgery which "mortifies the body and ruins the mind."[7]

The conception of alienation employed by Marx has two core features: it refers both to a *fragmentation* of the human person, a "splintering of human nature into a number of misbegotten parts"[8] and to a *prohibition* on the exercise of typically human functions. When workers lose control of the products of their labor or of their own productive activity, they have undergone fragmentation within their own persons, a kind of inner impoverishment; parts of their being have fallen under the control of another. This fragmentation is the consequence of a form of social organization which has given to some persons the power to prohibit other persons from the full exercise of capacities the exercise of which is thought necessary to a fully human existence.

If we understand alienation in this way, it can be seen that Marx's theory of alienation, focused as it is on that fragmentation of the self which is a consequence of the organization of material production under capitalism, may well apply to women insofar as we are *workers*, but not insofar as we are women.

Women undergo a special sort of fragmentation and loss of being as women: women suffer modes of alienation which are absent from Marx's account and which can be distinguished from the ways in which all workers, men and women alike, are alienated under the prevailing system of material production.

From this perspective, then, we may regard many parts of the emerging feminist critique of patriarchy as building blocks of a new theory of alienation, a refined and comprehensive theory able to incorporate Marx's insights into the nature of the human condition under capitalism and at the same time to grasp what is specific to the experience of women in a way that orthodox Marxism has failed to do. Some examples of distinctively feminine modes of alienation may make this clearer. The cultural domination of women, for example, may be regarded as a species of alienation, for women as women are clearly alienated in cultural production. Most avenues of cultural expression—high culture, popular culture, even to some extent language—are instruments of male supremacy. Women have little control over the cultural apparatus itself and are often entirely absent from its products; to the extent that we are not excluded from it entirely, the images of ourselves we see reflected in the dominant culture are often truncated or demeaning. Human beings distinguish themselves from animals not only, as Marx says, when they start to produce their own means of subsistence, but when they begin to invent modes of cultural expression, such as myth, ritual, and art, which make possible the bestowal of meaning upon their own activity. If this is so, then the prohibition on cultural expression denies to women the right to develop and to exercise capacities which define, in part, what it means to be human.

The historic suppression and distortion of the erotic requirements of women is clearly an instance of *sexual* alienation, for just as workers can be alienated from their labor, so can women be estranged from their own sexuality. The double standard of sexual morality, still widely in force, is pertinent here, as are the now discredited but formerly influential theories of innate female sexual passivity and of the dual orgasm. Sexual alienation itself is only one manifestation of a larger alienation from the body. Iris Young has described the ways in which

> the norms of femininity suppress the body potential of women. We grow up learning that the feminine body is soft, not muscular, passive, incapable, vulnerable. Our parents, teachers and friends suppress our natural urges to run, jump, risk, by cries that we should not act so boldly and move so daringly. . . . Developing a sense of our bodies as beautiful objects to be gazed at and decorated requires suppressing a sense of our bodies as strong, active subjects moving out to meet the world's risks and confront the resistances of matter and motion.[9]

Young also argues that restrictions on feminine body comportment generate a restricted spatiality in women as well, a sense that the body is positioned with invisible spatial barriers.

If women are alienated from the body in these ways, we suffer a different form of estrangement by being too closely identified with it in others. Sexual objectification, as I have suggested elsewhere, occurs when a women's sexual parts or sexual functions are separated out from her person, reduced to the status of mere instruments or else regarded as if they were capable of representing her.[10] To be dealt with in this way is to have one's entire being identified with the body, a thing which in many religious and metaphysical systems as well as in the popular mind has been regarded as less intrinsically valuable, indeed as less inherently human, than the mind or personality. Clearly, sexual objectification is a form of fragmentation and thus an impoverishment of the objectified individual; it involves too the implicit denial to those who suffer it that they have capacities which transcend the merely sexual.

A socialist-feminist theory of the alienation of women has yet to take precise theoretical shape. All the modes of such alienation will have to be uncovered and examined both in their relationships to one another and to the modes of estrangement described by Marx. The agents and occasions of such alienation will have to be identified. The estrangements attendant not only upon class and sex but upon race as well will have to be integrated into such a theory. That structuring of the unconscious modes of existence which facilitates the reproduction of alienated modes of existence will have to be revealed.

The development of such a theory, so it seems, is an urgent and compelling task for feminist political thought. But there is one salient difference between the alienation of labor and the notion of femininity as alienation, a difference which may threaten to sabotage the project at the start. It would be odd to regard something as alienating if it were not, by and large, disagreeable. Workers may have to engage in alienated labor because they lack any other way of making a living, but they do not go enthusiastically to the assembly line. Worker dissatisfaction, as everyone knows, has been amply documented, by Marxist and non-Marxist social scientists alike. But however unwilling feminists may be to admit it, many women appear to embrace with enthusiasm what seem to be the most alienated aspects of feminine existence. There is no dearth of contenders for the title of "Miss America." Most teenage girls would rather be Bo Derek than Madame Curie. "Playmate of the Month" is an enviable status. Thousands of women have been attracted to movements like "Fascinating Womanhood" which aim both to safeguard and to promote the more objectionable norms of femininity. Women of all classes buy large numbers of books and magazines which teach them how to be better, that is, more "feminine" women. There is no comparable body of literature which teaches workers to be better workers. In fact, that sort of training is generally imposed on people against their will, first in school, later by the boss or foreman. Workers resist alienated labor, if not militantly, then at the very least in small acts of sabotage or in fantasy.

We must determine whether the gratifications of "womanliness" do indeed constitute counterexamples to the claim that much of what is held out to us as "femininity" is in fact alienation. Since it will be impossible here to examine or even to identify everything which might qualify as a pleasure of this sort, I have selected a paradigm case, the case of so-called "feminine narcissism." Sexual objectification, I argued earlier, displays the characteristic marks of alienation. Now sexual objectification typically involves two persons, one who objectifies and one who is objectified. But objectifier and objectified can be one and the same person: a woman can become a sex object for herself, taking toward her own person the attitude of the man. She will then take erotic satisfaction in her physical self, reveling in her body as a beautiful object to be gazed at and decorated. Such an attitude is commonly called "narcissism," a term which received its baptism in psychoanalysis. In the most general sense, the narcissist, says Freud, "treats his (her) body in the same way as otherwise the body of a sexual object is treated."[11] Psychoanalysis, the most influential personality theory of modern times, has held not only that women are significantly more narcissistic than men (a finding which is, for us, compatible with the pervasive sexual objectification of women) but that narcissism is a necessary feature of the normal feminine personality. But how are we to understand such a claim? How is feminine narcissism possible, that is, how is it possible for sexual objectification, which is profoundly alienating, to produce narcissistic states of consciousness, which are profoundly satisfying? We can understand the *interest* women have in conforming to the requirements of sexual objectification, given our powerlessness and dependency; less easy to explain is the *pleasure*.

In the next section, I shall examine the nature of feminine narcissism, an element of major significance in the psychic lives of women. While the term "narcissism" has come in recent years to have a very wide application. I shall restrict my use of the term to its original meaning in psychoanalytic parlance, namely to an infatuation with one's bodily being.[12] I do not intend by the use of this term to refer to any personality disorder, but to an erotic disposition psychoanalytically trained observers and laypersons alike regard as typically female, to what in an older language would have been called "feminine vanity." I shall try to show that feminine narcissism is not the rock on which the idea of femininity as alienation must founder. On the contrary, a fuller disclosure of this phenomenon can help to reveal the nature of a mode of self-estrangement which lies close to the heart of the feminine condition itself.

II. On Feminine Narcissism

Narcissism, for Freud, is our primal psychic situation, the original disposition of the libido. In the beginning, the

> ego's instincts are directed to itself and it is to some extent capable of deriving satisfaction for them on itself. This condition is known as narcissism and this potentiality for satisfaction is termed auto-erotic.[13]

Women, far more than men, are likely to remain in this "primal psychic situation," not surprisingly, since in the Freudian scheme of things, the female psyche is more archaic than the male one. The explanatory device Freud uses to account for the greater proneness of women to self-admiration and bodily display is, of course, penis envy. Lacking the penis, young girls regard themselves as physically inferior to boys; feminine preoccupation with the body is an effort to compensate for an unconscious sense of physical deficiency.[14] In "On Narcissism" Freud takes note of the fact that feminine narcissism flowers in adolescence, but he makes an uncharacteristically crude effort to account for this:

> With the development of puberty the maturing of the female sexual organs, which up till then have been in a condition of latency, seems to bring about an intensification of the original narcissism. . . .[15]

Helene Deutsch adds refinement to the favorite Freudian hypothesis. For her, feminine narcissism operates in the psyche as a counterweight to feminine masochism: The "feminine woman . . . is characterized by her struggle for a harmonious accord between the narcissistic forces of self-love and the masochistic forces of dangerous and painful giving. . . ."[16] While Deutsch does not express herself in quite this way, her meaning is clear: narcissistic *Eros* in woman binds masochistic *Thanatos*. Without the antidote of self-love, woman would be helpless before the misfortunes an inherently masochistic nature will surely bring upon itself—as if a psychic constitution composed in such large measure of masochism and narcissism were not misfortune enough.

Neither psychoanalytic explanation is convincing. Narcissism in both sexes may have its origin in infantile eroticism, but Freudians cannot account for its perpetuation in women except by reference to the generally discredited theory of penis envy, or to the even more questionable notion of an innate death instinct. Existentialist literature provides a more satisfactory account of the persistence of feminine narcissism. Simone de Beauvoir makes use of the existentialist conception of "situation" in order to account for the persistence of narcissism in the feminine personality. A woman's situation, that is, those meanings derived from the total context in which she comes to maturity, disposes her to apprehend her body not as the instrument of her transcendence, but as "an object destined for another."[17]

Knowing that she is to be subjected to the cold appraisal of the male connoisseur and that her life prospects may depend on how she is seen, a woman learns to appraise herself first. The sexual objectification of women produces a duality in feminine consciousness. The gaze of the Other is internalized so that I myself become at once seer and seen, appraiser and the thing appraised. The adolescent girl, just beginning to grasp the role she is to assume

> becomes an object and sees herself as object; she discovers this new aspect of her being with surprise: it seems to her that she has been doubled; instead of coinciding exactly with herself, she now begins to exist outside.[18]

Narcissism, then, "consists in the setting up of the ego as a double, a stranger,"[19] while the identity of this "stranger" has yet to be established. Beauvoir's language seems hyperbolic: the stranger who inhabits my consciousness is not really a stranger at all, but *myself*.

For both psychoanalysis and existentialism, narcissism is at once a source of profound satisfaction and a temptation to be resisted. For Beauvoir, the narcissist seeks to escape the burdens of subjectivity by identifying her entire self with her bodily self. Such a person wants to retain sufficient awareness to enjoy her own finished and perfect thinghood: she wishes, at one and the same time, to become that which partakes of the nature of consciousness (the *pour-soi*) as well as that which does not (the *en-soi*), but this is impossible.[20] On this analysis, the pleasures of narcissism arise from self-deceived effort to escape the anguish of freedom.

For Freud, narcissistic satisfaction is not so metaphysical. "The first auto-erotic sexual gratifications," he tells us, "are experienced in connection with vital functions in the service of self-preservation."[21] But narcissism is an *infantile* libido-position. As the ego develops, it is supposed to "cathect" its libido away from itself, to other persons and groups of persons, to work, in short, to the world. This series of cathexes, in ordinary parlance, is called "maturation." So the woman tempted by sexual objectification to persist in her narcissism will undergo a kind of psychological infantilization, the perfect intrapsychic parallel to that pervasive infantilization to which we are subject in the larger society: our enforced dependency; manufactured incompetence; weakness and helplessness; our traditional exclusion from many areas of adult life; the requirement not only that we act like children, but that we look like children, too—smooth, soft, rounded, hairless, and, above all, young.[22]

At this point, it might be tempting to say of many women that they simply prefer the reverent and self-absorbed pleasures of the mirror to the challenges of freedom, that narcissistic satisfaction ties us tightly to "femininity" and hence to false consciousness. But let us look more closely. In narcissism, the self undergoes doubling: an Other, a "stranger" who is at the same time myself, is subject for whom my bodily being is object. This Other may take on a number of identities—that of a remembered or fantasized parental regard; a significant male Other; even a self struggling toward self-actualization and a wholesome affirmation of the body. But very often this Other is an interiorized representative of what I shall call the "fashion-beauty complex." Like the "military-industrial complex," the fashion-beauty complex is a major articulation of capitalist patriarchy. While an analysis of this complex structure lies beyond the scope of this essay, it is a vast system of corporations—some of which manufacture products, others services, and still others information, images, and ideologies— of emblematic public personages, and of sets of techniques and procedures. As family and church have declined in importance as the central producers and regulators of "femininity," the fashion-beauty complex has grown.

Overtly, the fashion-beauty complex seeks to glorify the female body and to provide opportunities for narcissistic indulgence. More important than this is its *covert* aim, which is to depreciate woman's body and deal a blow to her narcissism. We are presented everywhere with images of perfect female beauty— at the drugstore cosmetics display, the supermarket magazine counter, on television. These images remind us constantly that we fail to measure up. Whose nose is the right shape, after all, and whose hips are not too wide—or too narrow? The female body is revealed as a task, an object in need of transformation. "There are no ugly women," said Helena Rubinstein, "only lazy ones."[23] This project of transformation, as it is outlined in, for example, *Vogue*, is daunting. Every aspect of my bodily being requires either alteration or else heroic measures merely to conserve it. The taboo on aging demands that I try to trap my body and remove it from time; in the feminine ideal of *stasis*, we find once more a source of women's physical passivity.

I must cream my body with a thousand creams, each designed to act against a different deficiency, oil it, pumice it, powder it, shave it, pluck it, depilate it, deodorize it, ooze it into just the right foundation, reduce it overall through Spartan dieting or else pump it up with silicon. I must try to resculpture it on the ideal through dozens of punishing exercises. If home measures fail, I must take it to the figure salon, or inevitably, for those who can afford it, the plastic surgeon. There is no "dead time" in my day during which I do not stand under the imperative to improve myself: while waiting for the bus, I am to suck the muscles of my abdomen in and up to lend them "tone"; while talking on the telephone I am bidden to describe circles in the air with my feet to slim down my ankles. All these things must be done prior to the application of makeup, an art which aims once again to hide a myriad of deficiencies.

The fashion-beauty complex produces in woman an estrangement from her bodily being. One the one hand, I *am* it and am scarcely allowed to be anything else; on the other hand, I must exist perpetually at a distance from my physical self, fixed at this distance in a permanent posture of disapproval. Thus, insofar as the fashion-beauty complex shapes one of the introjected subjects for whom I exist as object, I sense myself as deficient, nor am I able to control in any way those images which give rise to the criteria by which these deficiencies appear. Breasts are bound in one decade, padded in another. One season eyebrows are thick and heavy, the next pencil-thin. Not long ago, the mannequins in Marshall Field's windows were dressed in what appeared to be Victorian christening gowns; more recently, the "harlot look" was all the rage. Perhaps the most pervasive image of all, the one which dominates the pages of *Vogue*, is not an image of woman at all, but of a beautiful adolescent boy.[24] All the projections of the fashion-beauty complex have this in common: they are images of *what I am not*. For me, attention to the ordinary standards of hygiene is not enough; I am unacceptable as I am. We can now grasp the nature of feminine narcissism with

more precision: it is *infatuation with an inferiorized body*. If this analysis is correct, narcissistic satisfaction is to some degree conditional upon a sense of successful adaptation to standards of feminine bodily presence generated by the enemies of women.

Earlier, I suggested the superiority of Beauvoir's account of feminine narcissism over standard Freudian explanations, not only because it stays clear of questionable theoretical constructions, for example, of a death instinct, but because it takes cognizance of woman's situation in a way Freudian theory does not. Essential to this situation, as we have seen, is the experience of sexual objectification, which leads many women to a virtually irresistible introjection of the subject for whom they are object. Now Beauvoir's account is certainly correct, but it is abstract and schematic. Narcissistic satisfaction is always *concrete*, that is, it is experienced under circumstances which are historically specific. Beauvoir does not make clear the relationship of certain experienced satisfactions to the material base of contemporary capitalist society, to the way in which such satisfactions are manipulated or the extent to which agents of a complex, sophisticated, and immensely profitable corporate structure have taken up residence within the feminine psyche.[25]

While in its objective structure the fashion-beauty complex recalls the military-industrial complex, in its subjective effects, it bears comparison to the Church. The Church cultivates in its adherents very profound anxieties about the body, most particularly about bodily appetites and sexual desires. It then presents itself as the only instrument able, through expiation, to take away the very guilt and shame it has itself produced. The fashion-beauty complex refines and deepens feminine anxieties which would accompany the status of sex object in any case; like the Church, it offers itself, its procedures and institutions, as uniquely able to diminish these anxieties. Magical physical transformations can be accomplished by the faithful like the spiritual transformations promised by the Church. There is evidence, for example, that the physical qualities of cosmetics—their texture, color, and gloss—are incorporated into the actual body images of the women who use them. Body care rituals are like sacraments. At best, they put a woman who would be lost and abandoned without them into what may feel to her like a state of grace; at worst, they exhibit the typical obsessive-compulsive features of much religious behavior. Feminists are widely regarded as the enemies of the family; we are also seen as enemies of the stiletto heel and the beauty parlor, in a word, as enemies of glamour. Hostility on the part of some women to feminism may have its origin here. The women's movement is seen not only to threaten profound sources of gratification and self-esteem but also to attack those rituals, procedures, and institutions upon which many women depend to lessen their sense of bodily deficiency.

The context within which we experience much narcissistic satisfaction bears the familiar marks of alienation. Earlier, I suggested that persons can be described as alienated or self-estranged if they suffer a splintering or fragmentation of such a nature as to prohibit the exercise of certain capacities the exercise of which is thought essential to a fully human existence. A truly "feminine" woman, then, has been seduced by a variety of cultural agents into being a body not only for another, but for herself as well. But when this happens, she may well experience what is in effect a taboo on the development of her other human capacities. In our society, for example, the cultivation of intellect has made a woman not more but less sexually alluring. The fragmentation which women undergo in the process of sexual objectification is evident too. What occurs is not just the splitting of a person into mind and body but the splitting of the self into a number of *personae*, some who witness and some who are witnessed; and, if I am correct, some internal witnesses are in fact introjected representatives of agencies hostile to the self. Women have lost control of the production of our own images, lost control to those whose production of these images is neither innocent nor benevolent, but obedient to imperatives which are both capitalistic and phallocentric. In sum, women experience a twofold alienation in the production of our own persons: the beings we are to be are mere bodily beings, nor can we control the shape and nature these bodies are to take.

At the end of Part 1, I posed this question: Is the claim that feminine narcissism involves self-estranged states of consciousness in any way compatible with the undeniable existence of narcissistic satisfaction? The shape of an answer has now emerged: the satisfactions of narcissism are real enough, but they are *repressive* satisfactions. "All liberation," says Marcuse, "depends on the consciousness of servitude and the emergence of this consciousness is always hampered by the predominance of needs and satisfactions which, to a great extent, have become the individual's own."[26] Repressive satisfaction fastens us to the established order of domination, for the same system which produces false needs also controls the conditions under which such needs can be satisfied. "False needs," it might be ventured, are needs which are produced through indoctrination, psychological manipulation, and the denial of autonomy; they are needs whose possession and satisfaction benefit not the subject who has them but a social order whose interest lies in domination. The price extracted for the satisfaction of repressive needs is high, for guilt, shame, and obsessional states of consciousness accompany the repressive satisfactions allowed us by the fashion-beauty complex. Repressive narcissistic satisfactions stand in the way of the emergence of an authentic delight in the body, too: the woman unable to leave home in the morning without "putting on her face" will never discover the beauty, character, and expressiveness her face already possesses.

III. Coda: Toward a Non-Repressive Narcissism

If feminine narcissism is a major ingredient in what is ordinarily regarded as "femininity," and if certain manifestations of "femininity" can be construed as modes of alienation, then it follows that the de-alienation of woman's existence will require a struggle against that excessive, damaged, and debilitating narcissism which now holds sway. But having concluded this, a host of new questions at once confronts us. How, in the face of those distortions in our relationship to the body produced by the established order of domination, can we arrive at a concept of nonrepressive narcissism anyhow? If the struggle against sexual objectification is successful, to what extent will the narcissistic needs of women be reduced? Might they disappear entirely? But if there are ineradicable narcissistic needs after all, how might such needs be satisfied in ways which do not damage the self?

Feminist strategy in regard to these issues has taken a number of forms. There has not been a concerted attack on feminine narcissism, but on sexual objectification, its root. The necessity and urgency of such a campaign is beyond question. But feminist practice as a whole has not been consistent in this regard. Some segments of the movement have protested sexual objectification with little understanding of its internalized psychological consequences and with no repudiation either in theory or in practice of conventional standards of dress and appearance. Other women, in rebellion against objectification, have adopted a practice in which both body display and the need to be admired are taboo. But if there are legitimate narcissistic needs, such asceticism ignores them. The women's movement has also put a very high priority on the development of the female body as instrument, on strength, agility, and physical competence. Training in self-defense and the campaign for equality in sports, in addition to their more immediate aims, open up to women new sources of self-esteem and satisfaction in embodiment. Struggles of this sort are indispensable, of course, but they do not exhaust what needs to be done, for we have consciousness not only of the body as instrument but as object for another as well; somatic awareness exists in both modes.

The interiorized witnesses to my bodily being do not form a harmonious unity: the contradictions which exist among them must be intensified. The *personae* who affirm the body must be strengthened. Those who are introjected representatives of agencies hostile to the self must be expelled from consciousness. The numerous exploitations of the fashion-beauty complex must be exposed at every opportunity and its idiotic image-mongering held up to a ridicule so relentless that incorporation into the self on which it depends will become increasingly untenable.[27] As part of our practice, we must create a new witness, a collective significant Other, integrated into the self but nourished and strengthened from without, from a revolutionary feminist community. This collective Other, while not requiring body display, will not taboo it either; it will allow and even encourage fantasy and play in self-ornamentation. Our ideas of the beautiful will have to be expanded and so altered that we will perceive ourselves and one another very differently than we do now. Much has been written about revolutionary aesthetics in connection with film, drama, and the visual arts, very little about a revolutionary aesthetic of the body. This is not surprising, since most revolutionary theory, in aesthetics as in other domains, has been the work of men, while the need for new ways of imagining the body is preeminently a need of women. The release of our capacity to apprehend the beautiful from the narrow limits within which it is now confined is part of what Marx meant or should have meant when he spoke in his most prophetic writing of an "emancipation of the senses."[28]

Notes

1. "How to Look Your Best All Your Life," *McCall's* (July 1979): 18.
2. In Lydia Sargent, ed., *Women and Revolution* (Boston: South End Press, 1981).
3. See the influential anthology *Capitalist Patriarchy and the Case for Socialist Feminism*, ed. Zillah R. Eisenstein (New York and London: Monthly Review Press, 1979).
4. Alison Jaggar, *Feminist Politics and Human Nature* (Totowa: Rowman and Allanheld, 1983).
5. See, e.g., Nancy Chodorow, *The Reproduction of Mothering* (Berkeley: University of California Press, 1978).
6. See, e.g., Eisenstein, *Capitalist Patriarchy*; Bridges and Hartmann, "The Unhappy Marriage of Marxism and Feminism"; Annette Kuhn and Ann Marie Wolpe, eds., *Feminism and Materialism* (London: Routledge and Kegan Paul, 1978); Christine Delphy, *The Main Enemy: A Materialist Analysis of Women's Oppression* (London: Women's Resource and Research Centre Publications, 1977); Jane Flax, "Do Feminists Need Marxism?" *Quest* 3(1976), and "A Materialist Theory of Women's Status," *Psychology of Women Quarterly* (Fall 1981); Gayle Rubin, "The Traffic in Women" in *Toward an Anthropology of Women*, ed. Rayna Reiter (New York: Monthly Review Press, 1975); Ann Ferguson, "Women as a Revolutionary Class in the U.S.," in *Between Labor and Capital*, ed. Pat Walker (Boston: South End Press, 1979); Sandra Harding, "What is the Real Material Base of Patriarchy and Capital?" in Sargent, *Women and Revolution*; Nancy Hartsock, "The Feminist Standpoint: Developing the Ground for a Specifically Feminist Historical Materialism," in *Discovering Reality: Feminist Perspectives on Epistemology, Metaphysics, Methodology and the Philosophy of Science*, ed. Sandra Harding and Merrill Hintikka (Dordrecht: Reidel, 1983); and Susan Rae Peterson, "Feminism, Marxism and Reproduction" (Paper read to the Society for Women in Philosophy, Eastern Division APA, December 1980).

    For two critiques of some lines of argument laid out in the above, see Iris Young, "Socialist-Feminism and the Limits of Dual Systems Theory," *Socialist Review* (March–June 1980); and Martha Gimenez, "The Oppression of Women: A Structuralist Marxist View," in *Structural Sociology: Theoretical Perspectives and Substantive Analysis*, ed. Ino Rossi (New York: Columbia University Press, 1982).
7. Karl Marx, "Estranged Labor," in *The Economic and Philosophic Manuscripts of 1844* (New York: International Publishers, 1964), 110.
8. For a fuller discussion, see Bertell Ollman, *Alienation: Marx's Conception of Man in Capitalist Society* (London: Cambridge University Press, 1971).
9. Iris Young, "Is There a Woman's World?—Some Reflections on the Struggle for our Bodies" (Lecture presented to The Second Sex—Thirty Years Later: A Commemorative Conference on Feminist Theory, sponsored by the New York Institute

for the Humanities, New York University, September 1979); see also her "Throwing Like a Girl: A Phenomenology of Feminine Body Comportment, Motility and Spatiality," *Human Studies* 13 (1980): 137–56.

10. For a fuller examination of both sexual objectification and cultural domination, see my paper "On Psychological Oppression," in *Feminity and Domination: Studies in the Phenomenology of Oppression* (New York: Routledge, 1990).

11. Sigmund Freud, "On Narcissism: An Introduction," in *General Selection from the Works of Sigmund Freud* (New York: Doubleday Anchor Books): 104.

12. My use of the term also conforms to Beauvoir's usage; I discuss her work below. The term "narcissism" has been used to refer to a normal stage of infantile development, a form of sexual perversion, a type of personality disorder seen with increasing frequency by contemporary clinicians (Kohut and Kernberg) and, most recently, the values and style of late capitalist culture (Lasch). For a trenchant critique of the latter, see Stephanie Engel, "Femininity as Tragedy, Reexamining the New Narcissism," *Socialist Review* 10(1980): 77–104.

13. Sigmund Freud from "Instincts and their Vicissitudes," *General Selection from the Works of Freud*, 81.

14. Freud, "The Psychology of Women," chap. 23, *New Introductory Lectures* (London: Hogarth Press, 1933). Penis envy is at the root of the "greater amount of narcissism attributed to women . . . their vanity is partly a further effect of penis-envy, for they are driven to rate their physical charms more highly as a belated compensation for their original sexual inferiority," 160.

15. Freud, "On Narcissism," from *General Selection from the Works of Sigmund Freud*, 112–13.

16. Helene Deutsch, *Psychology of Women*, vol. 1 (New York: Grune and Stratton, 1944), 105.

17. Simone de Beauvoir, *The Second Sex* (New York: Bantam Books, 1961), 300.

18. Ibid., 316.

19. Ibid., 375.

20. Ibid., 508.

21. Freud, *General Selection from the Works of Sigmund Freud*, 111.

22. See Susan Sontag's definitive treatment of the subject of women and aging, "The Double Standard of Aging," in *Psychology of Women: Selected Readings*, ed. Juanita Hill (New York: W. W. Norton and Co., 1979), 462–78.

23. Quoted in "Fashion, Beauty and the Feminist," *The Freewoman* (September–October 1978): 1.

24. Phyllis Chesler and Emily Jane Goodman, *Women, Money and Power* (New York: Morrow, 1976), 47–48. These images are not only unattainable but often incompatible as well. Thus in the same magazine, for example, women may be encouraged to look mysterious and seductive on one page, and apple-cheeked and virginal on the next.

25. While the fashion-beauty complex produces fears about the acceptability of the body, at the same time it feeds anxieties generated elsewhere. Two examples will suffice: first, the relatively recent entry of millions of women into a sex-segregated labor market where they must compete with other women on terms set by men; second, a growing divorce rate which in effect denies tenure in marriage and which tends to disadvantage women relative to men in the older age ranges.

26. Herbert Marcuse, *One-Dimensional Man* (Boston: Beacon Press, 1964), 7.

27. The original women's liberation demonstration of the feminist second wave, a burlesque of the Miss America Pageant in Atlantic City, was exemplary in this regard.

28. An earlier version of this paper was first presented at The Second Sex—Thirty Years Later: A Commemorative Conference on Feminist Theory, New York Institute of the Humanities, New York University, September 1979. Subsequent versions were presented at Claremont College, Augustana College, to Sapientia, the Dartmouth College Philosophy Colloquium, the Dartmouth Feminist Inquiry Seminar, the Boston Society for Women in Philosophy (SWIP), and at a session sponsored by SWIP at the Western Division meetings of the American Philosophical Association, 1981. Many people in discussions at those meetings contributed helpful criticisms and suggestions. I would like to thank the following persons in particular for helpful comments on earlier drafts of this paper: Ellin Ringler, Patricia Loose, Judith Gardiner, Ellen Rose, Iris Young, Alison Jaggar, Alan Soble, Jan Slagter, and Ann Garry.

e can confirm this notion of pregnancy as split subjectivity outside of the
hoanalytic framework that Kristeva uses. Reflection of the experience of
nancy reveals a body subjectivity that is de-centered, myself in the mode of
being myself.

s my pregnancy begins, I experience it as a change in my body, I become
rent from what I have been. My nipples become reddened and tender, my
y swells into a pear. I feel this elastic around my waist, itching, this round,
middle replacing the doughy belly with which I still identify. Then I feel a
tickle, a little gurgle in my belly, it is my feeling, my insides, and it feels
ewhat like a gas bubble, but it is not, it is different, in another place,
nging to another, another that is nevertheless my body.
he first movements of the fetus produce this sense of the splitting subject;
fetus' movements are wholly mine, completely within me, conditioning my
erience and space. Only I have access to these movements from their origin,
were. For months only I can witness this life within me, and it is only under
direction of where to put their hands that others can feel these movements. I
e a privileged relation to this other life, not unlike that I have to my dreams
thoughts, which I can tell someone, but which cannot be an object for both
us in the same way. Adrienne Rich reports this sense of the movements
hin me as mine, even though they are another's.

n early pregnancy, the stirring of the fetus felt like ghostly tremors of my own
ody, later like the movements of a being imprisoned within me; but both
ensations were *my* sensations, contributing to my own sense of physical and
osychic space (Rich 1976: 47).

Pregnancy challenges the integration of my body experience by rendering
d the boundary between what is within, myself, and what is outside, separate.
xperience my insides as the space of another, yet my own body.

Nor in pregnancy did I experience the embryo as decisively internal in Freud's
terms, but rather as something inside and of me, yet becoming hourly
and daily more separate, on its way to becoming separate from me and of
itself. . . .

    Far from existing in the mode of "inner space," women are powerfully and
vulnerably attuned both to "inner" and "outer" because for us the two are
continuous, not polar. (Rich 1976: 47–48)

The birthing process entails the most extreme suspension of the bodily
stinction between inner and outer. As the months and weeks progress, in-
easingly I feel my insides, strained and pressed, and increasingly feel the
ovement of a body inside me. Through pain and blood and water this inside
ing emerges between my legs, for a short while both inside and outside of me.
ter I look with wonder at my mushy middle and at my child, amazed that this
wling, flailing thing, so completely different from me, was there inside, a part
me.

Pregnant Embodiment:
Subjectivity and Alienation

IRIS MARION YOUNG

THE LIBRARY CARD CATALOG contains dozens of entries under the heading
"pregnancy": clinical treatises detailing signs of morbidity; volumes cataloging
studies of fetal development, with elaborate drawings; or popular manuals in
which physicians and others give advice on diet and exercise for the pregnant
woman. Pregnancy does not belong to the woman herself. It either is a state of
the developing fetus, for which the woman is a container; or it is an objective,
observable process coming under scientific scrutiny; or it becomes objectified by
the woman herself as a "condition" in which she must "take care of herself."
Except perhaps for one insignificant diary, no card appears listing a work which,
as Kristeva puts it, is "concerned with the subject, the mother as the site of her
proceedings" (1980: 237).

    We should not be surprised to learn that discourse on pregnancy omits
subjectivity, for the specific experience of women has been absent from most of
our culture's discourse about human experience and history. This essay considers
some of the experiences of pregnancy from the pregnant subject's viewpoint.
Through reference to diaries and literature, as well as phenomenological reflection on the pregnant experience, I seek to let women speak in their own voices.

    Section I describes some aspects of bodily existence unique to pregnancy. The
pregnant subject, I suggest, is de-centered, split, or doubled in several ways. She
experiences her body as herself and not herself. Its inner movements belong to
another being, yet they are not other, because her body boundaries shift and
because her bodily self-location is focused on her trunk in addition to her head.
This split subject appears in the eroticism of pregnancy, in which the woman
can experience an innocent narcissism fed by recollection of her repressed
experience of her own mother's body. Pregnant existence entails, finally, a

unique temporality of process and growth in which the woman can experience herself as split between past and future.

This description of the lived pregnant body both develops and partially criticizes the phenomenology of bodily existence found in the writings of Straus, Merleau-Ponty, and those of several other existential phenomenologists. It continues the radical undermining of Cartesianism that these thinkers inaugurated, but it also challenges their implicit assumptions of a unified subject and sharp distinction between transcendence and immanence. Pregnancy, I argue, reveals a paradigm of bodily experience in which the transparent unity of self dissolves and the body attends positively to itself at the same time that it enacts its projects.

Section II reflects on the encounter of the pregnant subject with the institutions and practices of medicine. I argue that with the present organization of these institutions and practices, women usually find such an encounter alienating in several respects. Medicine's self-definition as the curing profession encourages others as well as the woman to think of her pregnancy as a condition which deviates from normal health. The control over knowledge about the pregnancy and birth process that the physician has through instruments, moreover, devalues the privileged relation she has to the fetus and her pregnant body. The fact that in the contemporary context the obstetrician is usually a man reduces the likelihood of bodily empathy between physician and patient. Within a context of authority and dependence that currently structures the doctor-patient relation, moreover, coupled with the use of instruments and drugs in the birthing process, the pregnant and birthing woman often lacks autonomy within these experiences.

Before proceeding, it is important to note that this essay restricts the analysis to the specific experience of women in technologically sophisticated Western societies. The analysis presupposes, first, that pregnancy can be experienced for its own sake, noticed and savored. This entails that the pregnancy be chosen by the woman, either as an explicit decision to become pregnant, or at least choosing to be identified with and positively accepting of it. Most women in human history have not chosen their pregnancies in this sense. For the vast majority of women in the world today, moreover, and even for many women in this privileged and liberal society, pregnancy is not an experience they choose. So I speak in large measure for an experience that must be instituted, and for those pregnant women who have been able to take up their situation as their own.

I

The unique contribution of Straus, along with Merleau-Ponty and certain other existential phenomenologists, to the Western philosophical tradition has

consisted in locating consciousness and subjectivity in the body itself. T move to situate subjectivity in the lived-body jeopardizes dualistic metaphy altogether. There remains no basis for preserving the mutual exclusivit the categories subject and object, inner and outer, I and world. Straus pu this way:

> The meaning of 'mine' is determined in relation to, in contraposition to world, the Allon, to which I am nevertheless a party. The meaning of ' is not comprehensible in the unmediated antithesis of I and not-I, ow strange, subject and object, constituting I and constituted world. Ever points to the fact that separateness and union originate in the same g (Straus 1969: 29)

As Sarano (1966: 62–63) has pointed out, however, antidualist philos still tend to operate with a dualist language, this time distinguishing two f experiencing the body itself, as subject and as object, both transcending f and mere facticity. Reflection on the experience of pregnancy, I sha provides a radical challenge even to this dualism tacitly at work in losophers of the body.

To the extent that these existential phenomenologists preserve a di between subject and object, they do so at least partly because they as subject as a unity. In *The Phenomenology of Perception*, for example, Ponty locates the "intentional arc" that unifies experience in the b than in an abstract constituting consciousness. He does not, howeve the idea of a unified self as a condition of experience.

> There must be, then, corresponding to this open unity of the worl and indefinite unity of subjectivity. Like the world's unity, that invoked rather than experienced each time I perform an act tion, each time I reach a self-evident truth, and the universal I ground against which these effulgent forms stand out: it is t present thought that I achieve the unity of all my thoughts. (M 1962: 406).

Merleau-Ponty's later work, as well as more recent French however, suggests that this transcendental faith in a unified subje tion of experience may be little more than ideology (Coward an The work of Lacan, Derrida, and Kristeva suggests that the unit itself a project, a project sometimes successfully enacted by a mo contradictory subjectivity. I take Kristeva's remarks about pregna ing point:

> Pregnancy seems to be experienced as the radical ordeal of the subject: redoubling up of the body, separation and coexistenc an other, of nature and consciousness, of physiology and sp 1981: 31; cf. Kristeva 1980: 238).

The integrity of my body is undermined in pregnancy not only by this externality of the inside, but by the fact that the boundaries of my body are themselves in flux. In pregnancy I literally do not have a firm sense of where my body ends and the world begins. My automatic body habits become dislodged, the continuity between my customary body and my body at this moment is broken (Merleau-Ponty 1962: 82). In pregnancy my pre-pregnant body image does not entirely leave my movements and expectations, yet it is with the pregnant body that I must move. This is another instance of the doubling of the pregnant subject.

I move as if I could squeeze around chairs and through crowds as I could seven months before, only to find my way blocked by my own body sticking out in front of me, but yet not me, since I did not expect it to block my passage. As I lean over in my chair to tie my shoe, I am surprised by the graze of this hard belly on my thigh. I do not anticipate my body touching on itself, for my habits retain the old sense of my boundaries. In the ambiguity of bodily touch (Merleau-Ponty 1962: 93; Straus 1969: 46), I feel myself being touched and touching simultaneously, both on my knee and my belly. The belly is other, since I did not expect it there, but since I feel the touch upon it, it is me (cf. Straus 1963: 370).

Existential phenomenologists of the body usually assume a distinction between transcendence and immanence as two modes of bodily being. They assume that insofar as I adopt an active relation to the world, I am not aware of my body for its own sake. In the successful enactment of my aims and projects, my body is a transparent medium (Merleau-Ponty 1962: 138–39). For several of these thinkers, awareness of my body as weighted material, as physical, occurs only or primarily when his instrumental relation to the world breaks down, in fatigue or illness.

The transformation into the bodily as physical always means discomfort and malaise. The character of husk, which our live bodiness here increasingly assumes, shows itself in its onerousness, bringing heaviness, burden, weight (Plügge 1970: p. 298).

Being brought to awareness of my body for its own sake, these thinkers assume, entails estrangement, and objectification.

If, suddenly, I am no longer indifferent to my body, and if I suddenly give my attention to its functions and processes, then my body as a whole is objectified, becomes to me an other, a part of the outside world. And though I may also be able to feel its inner processes, I am myself excluded. . . . (Straus 1963: 245).

Thus the dichotomy of subject and object appears anew in the conceptualization of the body itself. These thinkers tend to assume that awareness of the body in its weight, massiveness, and balance is always an alienated objectification of my body, in which I am not my body and my body imprisons me. They also tend to assume that such awareness of my body must cut me off from the enactment of my projects; I cannot be attending to the physicality of my body and using it as the means to the accomplishment of my aims.

Certainly there are occasions when I experience my body only as a resistance, only as a painful otherness preventing me from accomplishing my goals. It is inappropriate, however, to tie such a negative meaning to all experience of being brought to awareness of the body in its weight and materiality. Sally Gadow (1980) has argued that in addition to experiencing the body as trans-parent mediator for our projects or an objectified and alienated resistance or pain, we also at times experience our bodily being in an aesthetic mode. That is, we can become aware of ourselves as body and take an interest in its sensations and limitations for their own sake, experiencing them as a fullness rather than a lack. While Gadow suggests that both illness and aging can be experiences of the body in such an aesthetic mode, pregnancy is most paradigmatic of such experience of being thrown onto awareness of one's body. Contrary to the mutually exclusive categorization between transcendence and immanence that underlies some theories, the awareness of my body in its bulk and weight does not impede the accomplishing of my aims.

This belly touching my knee, this extra part of me that gives me a joyful surprise when I move through a tight place, calls me back to the matter of my body even as I move about accomplishing my aims. Pregnant consciousness is animated by a double intentionality: my subjectivity splits between awareness of myself as body and awareness of my aims and projects. To be sure, even in pregnancy there are times when I am so absorbed in my activity that I do not feel myself as body, but when I move or feel the look of another I am likely to be recalled to the thickness of my body.

I walk through the library stacks searching for the *Critique of Dialectical Reason*, I feel the painless pull of false contractions in my back. I put my hand on my belly to notice its hardening, while my eyes continue their scanning. As I sit with friends listening to jazz in a darkened bar, I feel within me the kicking of the fetus, as if it follows the rhythm of the music. In attending to my pregnant body in such circumstances, I do not feel myself alienated from it, as in illness. I merely notice its borders and rumblings with interest, sometimes with pleasure, and this aesthetic interest does not divert me from my business.

This splitting focus both on my body and my projects has its counterpart in the dual location I give to myself on my body. Straus suggests that in everyday instrumental actions of getting about our business, comprehending, observing, willing, and acting, the "I" is located phenomenologically in our head. There are certain activities, however, of which dancing is paradigmatic, where the "I" shifts from the eyes to the region of the trunk. In this orientation that Straus calls "pathic" we experience ourselves in greater sensory continuity with the surroundings (Straus 1966a: 11–12).

The pregnant subject experiences herself as located in the eyes and trunk simultaneously, I suggest. She often experiences her ordinary walking, turning, sitting, as a kind of dance, movement that not only gets her where she is going, but in which she glides through space in an immediate openness. She is surprised sometimes that this weighted solidity which she feels herself becoming can still move with ease.

Pregnancy roots me to the earth, makes me conscious of the physicality of my body not as an object, but as the material weight that I am in movement. The notion of the body as a pure medium of my projects is the illusion of a philosophy which has not quite shed the Western philosophical legacy of humanity as spirit (Spelman 1982). Movement always entails awareness of effort and the feeling of resistance. In pregnancy this fact of existence never leaves me. I am an actor transcending through each moment to further projects, but the solid inertia and demands of my body call me to my limits, not as an obstacle to action, but only as a fleshly relation to the earth (Griffith 1970; cf. Spicker 1976). As the months proceed, the most ordinary efforts of human existence, like sitting, bending, and walking which I formerly took for granted, become apparent as the projects they themselves are. Getting up, for example, itself increasingly becomes a task which requires my attention (Straus 1966b; cf. Straus 1969: 35–37).

In the experience of the pregnant woman, this weight and materiality often produce a sense of power, solidity, and validity. Thus whereas our society often devalues and trivializes women, regards women as weak and dainty, the pregnant woman can gain a certain sense of self-respect.

> This bulk slows my walking and makes my gestures and my mind more stately. I suppose if I schooled myself to walk massively the rest of my life, I might always have massive thoughts (Lewis 1950: 83).

There was a time when the pregnant woman stood as a symbol of stately and sexual beauty (Rich 1976, chap. 4). While pregnancy remains an object of fascination, our own culture harshly separates pregnancy from sexuality. The dominant culture defines feminine beauty as slim and shapely. The pregnant woman is often not looked upon as sexually active or desirable, even though her own desires and sensitivity may have increased. Her male partner, if she has one, may decline to share in her sexuality, and her physician may advise her to restrict her "sexual activity." To the degree that a woman derives a sense of self-worth from looking "sexy" in the manner promoted by dominant cultural images, she may experience her pregnant body as ugly and alien.

Though the pregnant woman may find herself desexualized by others, at the same time she may find herself with a heightened sense of her own sexuality. Kristeva suggests that the pregnant and birthing woman renews connection to the repressed, pre-conscious, pre-symbolic aspect of existence. Instead of being a unified ego, the subject of the paternal symbolic order, the pregnant subject straddles the spheres of language and instinct. In this splitting of the subject, the pregnant woman recollects a primordial sexual continuity with the maternal body which Kristeva calls "juissance" (Kristeva 1980: 242; cf. Hirsch 1981).

The pregnant woman's relation to her body can be an innocent narcissism. As I undress in the morning and evening, I gaze in the mirror for long minutes, without stealth or vanity. I do not appraise myself, ask if I look good enough for others, but like a child take pleasure in discovering new things in my body. I turn to the side and stroke the taut flesh that protrudes under my breasts.

Perhaps the dominant culture's desexualization of the pregnant body helps make possible such self-love, when it happens. The culture's separation of pregnancy and sexuality can liberate her from the sexually objectifying gaze which alienates and instrumentalizes her when in her nonpregnant state. The leer of sexual objectification regards the woman in pieces, as the possible object of a man's desire and touch (Bartky 1982). In pregnancy the woman may experience some release from this alienating gaze. The look focusing on her belly is not one of desire, but of recognition. Some may be repelled by her, find her body ridiculous, but the look that follows her in pregnancy does not alienate her, does not instrumentalize her with respect to another's desire. Indeed in this society which still often narrows women's possibilities to motherhood, the pregnant woman often finds herself looked at with approval.

> As soon as I was visibly and clearly pregnant, I felt, for the first time in my adolescent and adult life, not-guilty. The atmosphere of approval in which I was bathed—even by strangers in the street, it seemed—was like an aura I carried with me, in which doubts, fears, misgivings, met with absolute denial. This is what women have always done (Rich 1976: 6).

In classical art this "aura" surrounding motherhood depicts repose (cf. Kristeva 1980). The dominant culture projects pregnancy as a time of quiet waiting. We refer to the woman as "expecting," as though this new life were flying in from another planet, and she sat in her rocking chair by the window, occasionally moving the curtain aside to see if the ship is coming. The image of uneventful waiting associated with pregnancy reveals clearly how much the discourse of pregnancy leaves out the subjectivity of the woman. From the point of view of others pregnancy is primarily a time of waiting and watching, when nothing happens.

For the pregnant subject, on the other hand, pregnancy has a temporality of movement, growth, and change. The pregnant subject is not simply a splitting in which the two halves lie open and still, but a dialectic. The pregnant woman experiences herself as a source and participant in a creative process. Though she does not plan and direct it, neither does it merely wash over her; rather she *is* this process, this change. Time stretches out, moments and days take on a depth because she experiences more changes in herself, her body. Each day, each week she looks at herself for signs of transformation.

Were I to lose consciousness for a month, I could still tell that an appreciable time had passed by the increased size of the fetus within me. There is a constant sense of growth, of progress, of time, which, while it may be wasted for you personally, is still being used, so that even if you were to do nothing at all during those nine months, something would nevertheless be accomplished and a climax reached (Lewis 1950: 78).

For others the birth of an infant may be only a beginning, but for the birthing woman it is a conclusion as well. It signals the close of a process she has been undergoing for nine months, the leaving of this unique body she has moved through, always surprising her a bit in its boundary changes and inner kicks. Especially if this is her first child she experiences the birth as a transition to a new self that she may both desire and fear. She fears a loss of identity, as though on the other side of the birth she herself became a transformed person, such that she would "never be the same again."

Finally her "time" comes, as is commonly said. During labor, however, there is no sense of growth and change, but the cessation of time. There is no intention, no activity, only a will to endure. I only know that I have been lying in this pain, concentrating on staying above it, for a long time because the hands of the clock say so, or the sun on the wall has moved to the other side of the room.

Time is absolutely still. I have been here forever. Time no longer exists. Always, Time holds steady for birth. There is only this rocketing, this labor (Chesler 1979: 116).

II

Feminist writers often use the concept of alienation to describe female existence in a male dominated society and culture (Foreman 1977; Young 1979; Bartky 1982; Greenspan 1983). In this section I argue that the pregnant subject's encounter with obstetrical medicine in the United States often alienates her from her pregnant and birthing experience. Alienation here means the objectification or appropriation by one subject of another subject's body, action, or product of action, such that she or he does not recognize the objectification as having its origins in her or his experience. A subject's experience or action is alienated when it is defined or controlled by a subject who does not share one's assumptions or goals. I will argue that a woman's experience in pregnancy and birthing is often alienated because her condition tends to be defined as a disorder, because medical instruments objectify internal process in such a way that they devalue a woman's experience of those processes, and because the social relations and instrumentation of the medical setting reduce her control over her experience from her.

Through most of the history of medicine its theoreticians and practitioners did not include the reproductive processes of women within its domain. Once women's reproductive processes came within the domain of medicine, they were defined as diseases. Indeed, by the mid-nineteenth century, at least in Victorian England and America, being female itself was symptomatic of disease. Medical writers considered women inherently weak and psychologically unstable, and the ovaries and uterus as the cause of a great number of diseases and disorders, both physical and psychological (Ehrenreich and English 1978, chaps. 2 and 3).

Contemporary obstetricians and gynecologists do usually take pains to assert that menstruation, pregnancy, childbirth, and menopause are normal body functions which occasionally have a disorder. The legacy which defined pregnancy and other reproductive functions as conditions requiring medical theory, however, has not been entirely abandoned.

Rothman (1979: 36) points out that even medical writers who explicitly deny that pregnancy is a disease view normal changes associated with pregnancy, such as lowered hemoglobin, water retention, and weight gain, as "symptoms" requiring "treatment" as part of the normal process of prenatal care. Though 75–88 percent of pregnant women experience some nausea in the early months, some obstetrical textbooks refer to this physiological process as a neurosis that "may indicate resentment, ambivalence and inadequacy in women ill-prepared for motherhood" (quoted in Corea 1977: 76). Obstetrical teaching films entitled "Normal Delivery" depict the use of various drugs and instruments, as well as use of paracervical block and the performance of episiotomy (Rothman 1979: 36).

A continued tendency on the part of medicine to treat pregnancy and childbirth as dysfunctional conditions derives, first, from the way medicine defines its purpose. Though medicine has extended its domain to include many bodily and psychological processes which ought not to be conceptualized as illness or disease, such as child development, sexuality, and aging, as well as women's reproductive functions, medicine continues to define itself as the practice which seeks cure for disease. Pellegrino and Thomasma (1981), for example, define the goal of medicine as "the relief of perceived lived body disruption," and "organic restoration to a former or better state of perceived health or well-being" (72).

> When a patient consults a physician, he or she does so with one specific purpose in mind: to be healed, to be restored and made whole, that is, to be relieved of some noxious element in physical or emotional life which the patient defines as disease—a distortion of the accustomed perception of what is a satisfactory life (Pellegrino and Thomasma 1981: 122).

These are often not the motives which prompt pregnant women to seek the offices of the obstetrician. Yet because medicine continues to define itself as the curing profession, it can tend implicitly to conceptualize women's reproductive processes as disease or infirmity.

A second conceptual ground for the tendency within gynecological and obstetrical practice to approach menstruation, pregnancy, and menopause as "conditions" with "symptoms" that require "treatment" lies in the implicit male bias in medicine's conception of health. The dominant model of health assumes that the normal, healthy body is unchanging. Health is associated with stability, equilibrium, a steady state. Only a minority of persons, however, namely adult men who are not yet old, experience their health as a state in which there is no regular or noticeable change in body condition. For them a noticeable change in their bodily state usually does signal a disruption or dysfunction. Regular, noticeable, sometimes extreme change in bodily condition, on the other hand, is an aspect of the normal bodily functioning of adult women. Change is also a central aspect of the bodily existence of healthy children and healthy old people, as well as some of the so-called disabled. Yet medical conceptualization implicitly uses this unchanging adult male body as the standard of all health.

This tendency of medical conceptualization to treat pregnancy as disease can produce alienation for the pregnant woman. She often has a sense of bodily well-being during her pregnancy and often has an increased immunity to common diseases like colds, flu, etc. As we saw in the previous section, moreover, she often has a bodily self-image of strength and solidity. Thus while her body may signal one set of impressions, her entrance into the definitions of medicine may lead her to the opposite understanding. Even though certain discomforts associated with pregnancy, such as nausea, flatulence, and shortness of breath, can happen in the healthiest of women, her internalization of various discussions of the fragility of pregnancy may lead her to define such experience as signs of weakness.

Numerous criticisms against the use of instruments, drugs, surgery, and other methods of intervention in obstetrical practice have been voiced in recent years (Arms 1975; Haire 1973; Laslie 1982). I do not wish to reiterate them here, nor do I wish to argue that the use of instruments and drugs in pregnancy and childbirth is usually inappropriate or dangerous. The instrumental and intervention orientation that predominates in contemporary obstetrics, however, can contribute to a woman's sense of alienation in at least two ways.

First, the normal procedures of the American hospital birthing setting render the woman considerably more passive than she need be. Most hospitals, for example, do not allow the woman to walk around even during early stages of labor, despite the fact that there is evidence that moving around can lessen pain and speed the birthing process. Routine breaking of the amniotic sac enforces this bed confinement. Women usually labor and deliver in a horizontal or near horizontal position, reducing the influence of gravity and reducing the woman's ability to push. The use of intravenous equipment, monitors, and pain-relieving drugs all inhibit a woman's capacity to move during labor.

Second, the use of instruments provides means of objectifying the pregnancy and birth which alienate a woman because it negates or devalues her own experience of those processes. As the previous section described, at a phenomenological level the pregnant woman has a unique knowledge of her body processes and the life of the fetus. She feels the movements of the fetus, the contractions of her uterus, with an immediacy and certainty that no one can share. Recently invented machines tend to devalue this knowledge. The fetal heart sensor projects the heartbeat of the six week old fetus into the room so that all can hear it in the same way. The sonogram is receiving increasing use to follow the course of fetal development. The fetal monitor attached during labor records the intensity and duration of each contraction on white paper; the woman's reports are no longer necessary for charting the progress of her labor. Such instruments transfer some control over the means of observing the pregnancy and birth process from the woman to the medical personnel. The woman's experience of these processes is reduced in value, replaced by more objective means of observation.

Alienation within the context of contemporary obstetrics can be further produced for the pregnant woman by the fact that the physician attending her is usually a man. Humanistic writers about medicine often suggest that a basic condition of good medical practice is that the physician and patient share the lived-body experience (Pellegrino and Thomasma 1981: 114). If the description of the lived-body experience of pregnancy in the previous section is valid, however, pregnancy and childbirth entail a unique body subjectivity which is difficult to empathize with unless one is or has been pregnant. Since the vast majority of obstetricians are men, then, this basic condition of therapeutic practice usually cannot be met in obstetrics. Physicians and pregnant women are thereby distanced in their relationship, perhaps more than others in the doctor-patient relation. The sexual asymmetry between physician and patient also produces a distance because it must be de-sexualized. Pre-natal check-ups follow the same procedure as gynecological examinations, requiring an aloof matter of factness in order to preclude attaching sexual meaning to them (Emerson 1970).

There is a final alienation the woman experiences in the medical setting, which derives from the relations of authority and subordination that usually structure the doctor-patient relation in contemporary medical practice. Many writers have noted that medicine has increasingly become an institution with broad social authority on a par with the legal system, or even organized religion (Freidson 1970; Zola 1972; Raymond 1982). The relationship between doctor and patient is usually structured as superior to subordinate. Physicians often project an air of fatherly infallibility and resist having their opinions challenged;

the authoritarianism of the doctor-patient relations increase as the social distance between them increases (Ehrenreich and Ehrenreich 1978: 59).

This authority that the physician has over any patient is amplified in gynecology and obstetrics by the dynamic of gender hierarchy. In a culture that still generally regards men as more important than women, and gives men authority and power over women in many institutions, the power the doctor has over the knowledge and objectification of her body processes, as well as his power to direct the performance of her office visits and her birthing, are often experienced by her as another form of male power over women (Kaiser and Kaiser 1974).

Philosophers of medicine have pointed out that the concept of health is much less a scientific concept than a normative concept referring to human well-being and the good life (Engelhardt 1976; Whitbeck 1981; Pellegrino and Thomasma 1981: 74–76). Above I have argued that there exists a male bias in medicine's concept of health insofar as the healthy body is understood as the body in a steady state. This argument suggests that medical culture requires a more self-consciously differentiated understanding of health and disease (Dallery 1983). Contemporary culture has gone to a certain extent in the direction of developing distinct norms of health and disease for the aged, the physically impaired, children, and hormonally active women. Such developments should be encouraged and medical theorists and practitioners should be vigilant about tendencies to judge physical difference as deviance.

Moreover, to overcome the potentialities for alienation which, I have argued, exist in obstetrical practices, as well as other medical practices, medicine must shed its self-definition as primarily concerned with curing. Given that nearly all aspects of human bodily life and change have come within the domain of medical institutions and practices, such a definition is no longer appropriate. There are numerous life states and physical conditions in which a person needs help or care, rather than medical or surgical efforts to alter, repress, or speed a body process. The birthing woman certainly needs help in her own actions, being held, talked to, coached, dabbed with water, and having someone manipulate the emergence of the infant. Children, old people, and the physically impaired often need help and care though they are not diseased. Within current medical and related institutions there exist professionals who perform these caring functions. They are usually women, usually poorly paid, and their activities are usually seen as complementing and subordinate to the direction of activities like diagnostic tests, drug and surgical therapies by the physicians, usually men. The alienation experienced by the pregnant and birthing woman would probably be lessened if caring were distinguished from curing, and took on a practical value that did not subordinate it to curing.

Finally, and perhaps most importantly, the alienation of the pregnant and birthing woman will be eliminated by her acquiring greater autonomy and control over those processes. As MacIntyre argues (1977), the physician's claim to authority, and hence medical institutions, should be transformed so that they allow for far greater autonomy to those in need of care. There are signs that the pressure of consumer groups, holistic health groups, and the women's health movement, as well as movements within the health professions, are already having some effect in promoting such a transformation. A humanistic orientation toward medicine should encourage such institutional changes and ensure that their benefits do not only extend to those with education and a comfortable income.

References

Arms, S. (1975). *Immaculate Deception: A New Look at Women and Childbirth in America.* Boston: Houghton Mifflin.

Bartky, S. L. (1979). "On Psychological Oppression." In *Philosophy and Women*, edited by Bishop and Weinzweig, 330–41. Belmont, Calif.: Wadsworth Publishing Co.

———. (1982). "Narcissism, Feminity, and Alienation." *Social Theory and Practice* 8: 127–143.

Chesler, P. (1979). *With Child: A Diary of Motherhood.* New York: Thomas Y. Crowell.

Corea, C. (1977). *The Hidden Malpractice: How American Medicine Treats Women as Patients and Professionals.* New York: William Morrow.

Coward, R., and Ellis, J. (1977). *Language and Materialism.* London: Routledge and Keegan Paul.

Dallery, J.; Lupton, J. J.; and Toth, E. (1983). *The Curse: A Cultural History of Menstruation.* New York: E. P. Dutton Co.

Ehrenreich, G., and Ehrenreich, J. (1978). "Medicine and Social Control." In *The Cultural Crisis of Modern Medicine*, edited by John Ehrenreich, 1–28. New York: Monthly Review Press.

Ehrenreich, B., and English D. (1978). *For Her Own Good.* Garden City, N.Y.: Doubleday.

Emerson, J. (1970). "Behavior in Private Places: Sustaining Definitions of Reality in Gynecological Examinations." In *Recent Sociology No. 2*, edited by H. Dreitzel, 74–97. London: Macmillan.

Engelhardt, H. T., Jr. (1976). "Human Well-Being and Medicine: Some Basic Value Judgements in the Biomedical Sciences." In *Science, Ethics, and Medicine*, edited by Engelhardt and Callahan, 120–39. Hastings-on-Hudson, N.Y.: Institute of Society, Ethics, and the Life Sciences.

Foreman, A. (1977). *Femininity as Alienation.* London: Pluto Press.

Freidson, E. (1970). *The Profession of Medicine.* New York: Dodd and Mead Co.

Gadow, S. (1980). "Body and Self: A Dialectic." *Journal of Medicine and Philosophy* 5: 172–85.

Greenspan, M. (1983). *A New Approach to Women and Therapy.* New York: McGraw-Hill.

Griffith, R. M. (1970). "Anthropodology: Man-a-foot." In *The Philosophy of the Body: Rejections of Cartesian Dualism*, edited by Spicker, 273–92. Chicago: Quadrangle Books.

Haire, D. (1973). "The Cultural Warping of Childbirth." *Environmental Child Health* 19: 171–91.

Hirsch, M. (1981). "Mothers and Daughters." *Signs* 7: 200–222.

Kaiser, B., and Kaiser, K. (1974). "The Challenge of the Women's Movement to American Gynecology." *American Journal of Obstetrics and Gynecology* 120: 652–61.

Kristeva, J. (1980). "Motherhood According to Giovanni Bellini." In *Desire in Language*, translated by Gora, Jardine, and Roudiez, 237–70. New York: Columbia University Press.

Kristeva, J. (1981). "Women's time." Translated by Jardine and Blake. *Signs* 7: 13–35.

Laslie, A. (1982). "Ethical Issues in Childbirth." *Journal of Medicine and Philosophy* 7: 179–96.

Lewis, A. (1950). *An Interesting Condition.* Garden City, N.Y.: Doubleday.

MacIntyre, A. (1977). "Patients as agents." In *Philosophical Medical Ethics: Its Nature and Significance*, edited by Spicker and Engelhardt, 197–212. Dordrecht, Holland: D. Reidel.

Merleau-Ponty, M. (1962). *The Phenomenology of Perception.* Translated by Colin Smith. Atlantic Highlands, N.J.: Humanities Press.

Pellegrino, E. D., and Thomasma, D. C. (1981). *A Philosophical Basis of Medical Practice.* New York: Oxford University Press.

Plügge, H. (1970). "Man and His Body." In *The Philosophy of the Body*, edited by Spicker, 293–311. Chicago: Quadrangle Books.

Raymond, J. (1982). "Medicine as Patriarchal Religion." *Journal of Medicine and Philosophy* 7: 197–216.

Rich, A. (1976). *Of Woman Born.* New York: W. W. Norton (Bantam Paperback Edition).

Rothman, B. K. (1979). "Women, Health, and Medicine." In *Women: A Feminist Perspective*, edited by Freeman, 27–40. Palo Alto, Calif.: Mayfield Publishing Co.

Sarano, J. (1966). *The Meaning of the Body.* Translated by James H. Farley. Philadelphia: Westminster Press.

Scully, D. (1979). *Men Who Control Women's Health.* Boston: Houghton-Mifflin.

Spelman, E. V. (1982). "Woman as Body: Ancient and Contemporary Views." *Feminist Studies* 8: 109–23.

Spicker, S. (1976). "Terra Firma and Infirma Species: From Medical Philosophical Anthropology to Philosophy of Medicine." *Journal of Medicine and Philosophy* 1: 105–35.

Straus, E. (1963). *The Primary World of the Senses.* London: The Free Press.

Straus, E. (1966a). "Forms of Spatiality." In *Phenomenological Psychology*, 3–37. New York: Basic Books.

Straus, E. (1966b). "The Upright Posture." In *Phenomenological Psychology*, 137–65. New York: Basic Books.

Straus, E. (1969). *Psychiatry and Philosophy*, New York: Springer-Verlag.

Whitbeck, E. (1981). "A Theory of Health." In *Concepts of Health and Disease: Interdisciplinary Perspectives*, edited by Caplan, Engelhardt, and McCartney, 611–26. Reading, Mass.: Addison-Wellesley.

Young, I. M. (1979). "Is There a Woman's World?—Some reflections on the struggle for our bodies." Proceedings of The Second Sex—Thirty Years Later, A Commemorative Conference on Feminist Theory, New York Humanities Institute (mimeograph).

Zola, I. K. (1972). "Medicine as an Institution of Social Control." *The Sociological Review* 2: 487–504.

PART III

Race

ALIENATION DUE TO RACIAL oppression has many of the features we have seen in the alienation of other groups. Alienation is imposed in some cases by stark coercion; in others by the apparently "helping hand" of a well-meaning member of a more powerful group. Alienation here too becomes self-imposed: Fanon depicts the self-hatred of the African in France.

He explains how the very language we use alienates because it is the language of those in power. English—as is the French language Fanon discussed—is a white man's language in which we, for instance, point to the "dark" side of things to refer to what is concealed because it is shameful. That is not a langue in which a person can easily express his or her pride in being black or brown. For some, there is the problem of Fanon: whether to retain their first language and thus cut themselves off from many possibilities that are attractive but require education in France and in French. For Spanish-speaking people in the United States there exists a similar problem. It is aggravated by the open hatred for the Spanish language that is widespread and manifested in recent campaigns to make English the official language in the United States and the only first language to be taught in our schools. But for others, the language problem is different: black people who have been English speakers for generations no longer have a separate language of their own. But their language is a vehicle of intense hostility to their appearance and their culture.

The selections, in this part, also bring to the fore new aspects of alienation. There is a tendency to think of two sorts of people in a society: those who impose alienation on others, and those who are the victims of alienation. But each person has many different social roles and positions and thus some may be alienated in one context, but may, in a different context, be counted among those visiting alienation on others. That was June Jordan's situation in the Bahamas. There her relative affluence put her in a position of power over the maids and waiters. They saw her as belonging to the oppressors— especially because the racial oppression Blacks experience in the West Indies is not as grinding as that experienced by Blacks in the United States.

These complexities that make us both alienated and contributors to the alienation of others also raise questions about the relations between alienated groups: to the extent that we live out lives prescribed for us by others, and live in worlds not of our own making, are there enemies and friends in those worlds who would not be enemies or friends if we lived in our own worlds or were genuinely ourselves? Oppressed groups often do to other groups what is done to them. This is perplexing because we expect that those who suffer oppression therefore must sympathize with those whose alienation is different, even if no less severe. But Jordan reminds us that the intricacies of our own alienation also affect our relationships to other groups: as long as we are alienated our worlds are defined for us and so are our friends and our enemies.

Implicit in Jordan's observation that we are both alienated and alienate others is the awareness that we live in multiple worlds: we are not all of one piece. Maria Lugones tries to develop that difficult metaphor by talking about "world"-travel. That concept is powerful because it allows us some understanding of how we can love someone without suffering her alienation and oppression. It also allows us to be clearer about the different roles we play in the world, as being both "arrogant perceivers" and the victims of "arrogant perception." Finally, Lugones begins to distinguish different ways in which we are complicit in our own alienation: there is a difference between "animating" an "arrogant perception"—living out someone's conception of me even if I reject it explicitly—and fully "inhabiting" that world when I see myself in the same derogatory stereotypes through which others see me.

Howard McGary raises questions similar to those raised in the Introduction, but provides different answers to them. Liberalism can understand alienation, he thinks, but will not be effective in acting against it. Of equal importance is his insistence that alienated groups have struggled, and are struggling, against alienation and often do so very successfully. African-Americans, he reminds us, have created powerful communities for themselves. They have and still do live in worlds of their own making within a larger world that is terribly hostile to them. As a consequence he is a great deal more sanguine than many other writers about the extent of alienation among African-Americans.

Playfulness, "World"-Travelling, and Loving Perception

MARIA LUGONES

THIS ESSAY WEAVES TWO aspects of life together. My coming to consciousness as a daughter and my coming to consciousness as a woman of color have made this weaving possible. This weaving reveals the possibility and complexity of a pluralistic feminism, a feminism that affirms the plurality in each of us and among us as richness and as central to feminist ontology and epistemology.

The essay describes the experience of "outsiders" to the mainstream of, for example, White/Anglo organization of life in the United States and stresses a particular feature of the outsider's existence: the outsider has necessarily acquired flexibility in shifting from the mainstream construction of life where she is constructed as an outsider to other constructions of life where she is more or less "at home." This flexibility is necessary for the outsider but it can also be willfully exercised by the outsider or by those who are at ease in the mainstream. I recommend this willful exercise which I call "world"-travelling and I also recommend that the willful exercise be animated by an attitude that I describe as playful.

As outsiders to the mainstream, women of color in the United States practice "world"-travelling, mostly out of necessity. I affirm this practice as a skillful, creative, rich, enriching, and, given certain circumstances, as a loving way of being and living. I recognize that much of our travelling is done unwillfully to hostile White/Anglo "worlds." The hostility of these "worlds" and the compulsory nature of the "travelling" have obscured for us the enormous value of this aspect of our living and its connection to loving. Racism has a vested interest in obscuring and devaluing the complex skills involved in it. I recommend that we affirm this travelling across "worlds" as partly constitutive of cross-cultural and cross-racial loving. Thus I recommend to women of color in the United States that we learn to love each other by learning to travel in each other's "worlds."

On the other hand, the essay makes a connection between what Marilyn Frye has named "arrogant perception" and the failure to identify with persons that one views arrogantly or has come to see as the products of arrogant perception. A further connection is made between this failure of identification and a failure of love, and thus between loving and identifying with another person. The sense of love is not the one Frye has identified as both consistent with arrogant perception and as promoting unconditional servitude. "We can be taken in by this equation of servitude with love," Frye (1983: 73) says, "because we make two mistakes at once: we think, of both servitude and love that they are selfless or unselfish." Rather, the identification of which I speak is constituted by what I come to characterize as playful "world"-travelling. To the extent that we learn to perceive others arrogantly or come to see them only as products of arrogant perception and continue to perceive them that way, we fail to identify with them—fail to love them—in this particularly deep way.

IDENTIFICATION AND LOVE

As a child, I was taught to perceive arrogantly. I have also been the object of arrogant perception. Though I am not a White/Anglo woman, it is clear to me that I can understand both my childhood training as an arrogant perceiver and my having been the object of arrogant perception without any reference to White/Anglo men, which is some indication that the concept of arrogant perception can be used cross-culturally and that White/Anglo men are not the only arrogant perceivers. I was brought up in Argentina watching men and women of moderate and of considerable means graft the substance[1] of their servants to themselves. I also learned to graft my mother's substance to my own. It was clear to me that both men and women were the victims of arrogant perception and that arrogant perception was systematically organized to break the spirit of all women and of most men. I valued my rural "gaucho" ancestry because its ethos has always been one of independence in poverty through enormous loneliness, courage, and self-reliance. I found inspiration in this ethos and committed myself never to be broken by arrogant perception. I can say all of this in this way only because I have learned from Frye's "In and Out of Harm's Way: Arrogance and Love." She has given me a way of understanding and articulating something important in my own life.

Frye is not particularly concerned with women as arrogant perceivers but as the objects of arrogant perception. Her concern is, in part, to enhance our understanding of women "untouched by phallocratic machinations" (Frye 1983: 53), by understanding the harm done to women through such machinations. In this case she proposes that we could understand women untouched by arrogant perception through an understanding of what arrogant perception does to women. She also proposes an understanding of what it is to love women that is inspired by a vision of women unharmed by arrogant perception. To love women is, at least in part, to perceive them with loving eyes. "The loving eye is a contrary of the arrogant eye" (Frye 1983: 75).

I am concerned with women as arrogant perceivers because I want to explore further what it is to love women. I want to explore two failures of love: My failure to love my mother and White/Anglo women's failure to love women across racial and cultural boundaries in the United States. As a consequence of exploring these failures I will offer a loving solution to them. My solution modifies Frye's account of loving perception by adding what I call playful "world"-travel.

It is clear to me that at least in the United States and Argentina women are taught to perceive many other women arrogantly. Being taught to perceive arrogantly is part of being taught to be a woman of a certain class in both the United States and Argentina, and it is part of being taught to be a White/Anglo woman in the United States, and it is part of being taught to be a woman in both places: to be both the agent and the object of arrogant perception. My love for my mother seemed to me thoroughly imperfect as I was growing up because I was unwilling to become what I had been taught to see my mother as being. I thought that to love her was consistent with my abusing her (using, taking for granted, and demanding her services in a far-reaching way that, since four other people engaged in the same grafting of her substance onto themselves, left her little of herself to herself) and was to be in part constituted by my identifying with her, my seeing myself in her: to love her was supposed to be of a piece with both my abusing her and with my being open to being abused. It is clear to me that I was not supposed to love servants: I could abuse them without identifying with them, without seeing myself in them. When I came to the United States I learned that part of racism is the internalization of the propriety of abuse without identification: I learned that I could be seen as a being to be used by White/Anglo men and women without the possibility of identification, that is, without their act of attempting to graft my substance onto theirs, rubbing off on them at all. They could remain untouched, without any sense of loss.

So, women who are perceived arrogantly can perceive other women arrogantly in their turn. To what extent those women are responsible for their arrogant perceptions of other women is centainly open to question, but I do not have any doubt that many women have been taught to abuse women in this particular way. I am not interested in assigning responsibility. I am interested in understanding the phenomenon so as to understand a loving way out of it.

There is something obviously wrong with the love that I was taught and something right with my failure to love my mother in this way. But I do not think that what is wrong is my profound desire to identify with her, to see myself in her; what is wrong is that I was taught to identify with a victim of enslavement.

What is wrong is that I was taught to practice enslavement of my mother and to learn to become a slave through this practice. There is something obviously wrong with my having been taught that love is consistent with abuse, consistent with arrogant perception. Notice that the love I was taught is the love that Frye (1983: 73) speaks of when she says, "We can be taken in by this equation of servitude with love." Even though I could both abuse and love my mother, I was not supposed to love servants. This is because in the case of servants one is and is supposed to be clear about their servitude and the "equation of servitude with love" is never to be thought clearly in those terms. So, I was not supposed to love and could not love servants. But I could love my mother because deception (in particular, self-deception) is part of this "loving." Servitude is called abnegation and abnegation is not analyzed any further. Abnegation is not instilled in us through an analysis of its nature but rather through a heralding of it as beautiful and noble. We are coaxed, seduced into abnegation not through analysis but through emotive persuasion. Frye makes the connection between deception and this sense of "loving" clear. When I say that there is something obviously wrong with the loving that I was taught, I do not mean to say that the connection between this loving and abuse is obvious. Rather I mean that once the connection between this loving and abuse has been unveiled, there is something obviously wrong with the loving given that it is obvious that it is wrong to abuse others.

I am glad that I did not learn my lessons well, but it is clear that part of the mechanism that permitted my not learning well involved a separation from my mother: I saw us as beings of quite a different sort. It involved an abandoning of my mother while I longed not to abandon her. I wanted to love my mother, though, given what I was taught, "love" could not be the right word for what I longed for.

I was disturbed by my not wanting to be what she was. I had a sense of not being quite integrated, my self was missing because I could not identify with her, I could not see myself in her, I could not welcome her world. I saw myself as separate from her, a different sort of being, not quite of the same species. This separation, this lack of love, I saw, and I think that I saw correctly as a lack in myself (not a fault, but a lack). I also see that if this was a lack of love, love cannot be what I was taught. Love has to be rethought, made anew.

There is something in common between the relation between myself and my mother as someone I did not use to be able to love and the relation between myself or other women of color in the United States and White/Anglo women: there is a failure of love. I want to suggest here that Frye has helped me understand one of the aspects of this failure, the directly abusive aspect. But I also think that there is a complex failure of love in the failure to identify with another woman, the failure to see oneself in other women who are quite different from oneself. I want to begin to analyze this complex failure.

Notice that Frye's emphasis on independence in her analysis of loving perception is not particularly helpful in explaining this failure. She says that in loving perception, "the object of the seeing is another being whose existence and character are logically independent of the seer and who may be practically or empirically independent in any particular respect at any particular time" (Frye 1983: 77). But this is not helpful in allowing me to understand how my failure of love toward my mother (when I ceased to be her parasite) left me not quite whole. It is not helpful since I saw her as logically independent from me. It also does not help me to understand why the racist or ethnocentric failure of love of White/Anglo women—in particular of those White/Anglo women who are not pained by their failure—should leave me not quite substantive among them. Here I am not particularly interested in cases of White women's parasitism onto women of color but more pointedly in cases where the failure of identification is the manifestation of the "relation." I am particularly interested here in those many cases in which White/Anglo women do one or more of the following to women of color: they ignore us, ostracize us, render us invisible, stereotype us, leave us completely alone, interpret us as crazy. All this *while we are in their midst.* The more independent I am, the more independent I am left to be. Their world and their integrity do not require me at all. There is no sense of self-loss in them for my own lack of solidity. But they rob me of my solidity through indifference, an indifference they can afford and which seems sometimes studied. (All of this points of course toward separatism in communities where our substance is seen and celebrated, where we become substantive through this celebration. But many of us have to work among White/Anglo folk and our best shot at recognition has seemed to be among White/Anglo women because many of them have expressed a *general* sense of being pained at their failure of love.)

Many times White/Anglo women want us out of their field of vision. Their lack of concern is a harmful failure of love that leaves me independent from them in a way similar to the way in which, once I ceased to be my mother's parasite, she became, though not independent from all others, certainly independent from me. But of course, because my mother and I wanted to love each other well, we were not whole in this independence. White/Anglo women are independent from me, I am independent from them, I am independent from my mother, she is independent from me, and none of us loves each other in this independence.

I am incomplete and unreal without other women. I am profoundly dependent on others without having to be their subordinate, their slave, their servant.

Frye (1983: 75) also says that the loving eye is "the eye of one who knows that to know the seen, one must consult something other than one's own will and interests and fears and imagination." This is much more helpful to me so long as I do not understand Frye to mean that I should not consult my own interests nor that I should exclude the possibility that my self and the self of the one I love may be importantly tied to each other in many complicated ways. Since I am emphasizing here that the failure of love lies in part in the failure to identify and since I agree with Frye that one "must consult something other than one's own will and interests and fears and imagination," I will proceed to try to explain what I think needs to be consulted. To love my mother was not possible for me while I retained a sense that it was fine for me and others to see her arrogantly. Loving my mother also required that I see with her eyes, that I go into my mother's world, that I see both of us as we are constructed in her world, that I witness her own sense of herself from within her world. Only through this travelling to her "world" could I identify with her, because only then could I cease to ignore her and to be excluded and separate from her. Only then could I see her as a subject even if one subjected and only then could I see at all how meaning could arise fully between us. We are fully dependent on each other for the possibility of being understood and without this understanding we are not intelligible; we do not make sense; we are not solid, visible, integrated; we are lacking. So travelling to each other's "worlds" would enable us to *be* through *loving* each other.

Hopefully, the sense of identification I have in mind is becoming clear. But if it is to become clearer, I need to explain what I mean by a "world" and by "travelling" to another "world."

In explaining what I mean by a "world" I will not appeal to travelling to other women's worlds. Rather I will lead you to see what I mean by a "world" the way I came to propose the concept to myself: through the kind of ontological confusion about myself that we, women of color, refer to half-jokingly as "schizophrenia" (we feel schizophrenic in our goings back and forth between different "communities") and through my effort to make some sense of this ontological confusion.

"Worlds" and "World" Travelling

Some time ago I came to be in a state of profound confusion as I experienced myself as both having and not having a particular attribute. I was sure I had the attribute in question and, on the other hand, I was sure that I did not have it. I remain convinced that I both have and do not have this attribute. The attribute is playfulness. I am sure that I am a playful person. On the other hand, I can say, painfully, that I am not a playful person. I am not a playful person in certain worlds. One of the things I did as I became confused was to call my friends, far away people who knew me well, to see whether or not I was playful. Maybe they could help me out of my confusion. They said to me, "Of course you are playful" and they said it with the same conviction that I had about it. Of course I am playful. Those people who were around me said to me, "No, you are not playful. You are a serious woman. You just take everything seriously." They were just as sure about what they said to me and could offer me every bit of evidence that one could need to conclude that they were right. So I said to myself: "Okay, maybe what's happening here is that there is an attribute that I do have but there are certain worlds in which I am not at ease and it is because I'm not at ease in those worlds that I don't have that attribute in those worlds. But what does that mean?" I was worried both about what I meant by "worlds" when I said "in some worlds I do not have the attribute" and what I meant by saying that lack of ease was what led me not to be playful in those worlds. Because you see, if it was just a matter of lack of ease, I could work on it.

I can explain some of what I mean by a "world." I do not want the fixity of a definition at this point, because I think the term is suggestive and I do not want to close the suggestiveness of it too soon. I can offer some characteristics that serve to distinguish between a "world," a utopia, a possible world in the philosophical sense, and a world-view. By a "world" I do not mean a utopia at all. A utopia does not count as a world in my sense. The "worlds" that I am talking about are possible. But a possible world is not what I mean by a "world" and I do not mean a world-view, though something like a world-view is involved here.

For something to be a "world" in my sense it has to be inhabited at present by some flesh and blood people. That is why it cannot be a utopia. It may also be inhabited by some imaginary people. It may be inhabited by people who are dead or people that the inhabitants of this "world" met in some other "world" and now have in this "world" in imagination.

A "world" in my sense may be an actual society given its dominant culture's description and construction of life, including a construction of the relationships of production, of gender, race, etc. But a "world" can also be such a society given a non-dominant construction, or it can be such a society or *a* society given an idiosyncratic construction. As we will see it is problematic to say that these are all constructions of the same society. But they are different "worlds."

A "world" need not be a construction of a whole society. It may be a construction of a tiny portion of a particular society. It may be inhabited by just a few people. Some "worlds" are bigger than others.

A "world" may be incomplete in that things in it may not be altogether constructed or some things may be constructed negatively (they are not what "they" are in some other "world"). Or the "world" may be incomplete because it may have references to things that do not quite exist in it, references to things like Brazil, where Brazil is not quite part of that "world." Given lesbian feminism, the construction of "lesbian" is purposefully and healthily still up in the air, in the process of becoming. What it is to be a Hispanic in this country is, in a dominant Anglo construction, purposefully incomplete. Thus one cannot really answer questions of the sort: "What is a Hispanic?" "Who counts as a Hispanic?" "Are Latinos, Chicanos, Hispanos, black dominicans, white cubans, korean-colombians, italian-argentinians hispanic?" What it is to be a "hispanic" in the varied so-called hispanic communities in the United States is also yet up in the air. We have not decided whether there is something like a "hispanic" in our varied "worlds." So, a "world" may be an incomplete visionary nonutopian construction of life or it may be a traditional construction of life. A traditional Hispano construction of Northern New Mexican life is a "world." Such a traditional construction, in the face of a racist, ethnocentrist, money-centered anglo construction of Northern New Mexican life is highly unstable because Anglos have the means for imperialist destruction of traditional Hispano "worlds."

In a "world" some of the inhabitants may not understand or hold the particular construction of them that constructs them in that "world." So, there may be "worlds" that construct me in ways that I do not even understand. Or it may be that I understand the construction, but do not hold it of myself. I may not accept it as an account of myself, a construction of myself. And yet, I may be *animating* such a construction.

One can "travel" between these "worlds" and one can inhabit more than one of these "worlds" at the very same time. I think that most of us who are outside the mainstream of, for example, the United States dominant construction or organization of life are "world-travellers" as a matter of necessity and of survival. It seems to me that inhabiting more than one "world" at the same time and "travelling" between "worlds" is part and parcel of our experience and our situation. One can be at the same time in a "world" that constructs one as stereotypically latin, for example, and in a "world" that constructs one as latin. Being stereotypically latin and being simply latin are different simultaneous constructions of persons that are part of different "worlds." One animates one or the other or both at the same time without necessarily confusing them, though simultaneous enactment can be confusing if one is not on one's guard.

In describing my sense of a "world," I mean to be offering a description of experience, something that is true to experience even if it is ontologically problematic. Though I would think that any account of identity that could not be true to this experience of outsiders to the mainstream would be faulty even if ontologically unproblematic. Its ease would constrain, erase, or deem aberrant experience that has within it significant insights into nonimperialistic under-standing between people.

Those of us who are "world"-travellers have the distinct experience of being different in different "worlds" and of having the capacity to remember other "worlds" and ourselves in them. We can say "That is me there, and I am happy in that 'world.'" So, the experience is of being a different person in different "worlds" and yet of having memory of oneself as different without quite having the sense of there being any underlying "I." So I can say "that is me there and I am so playful in that 'world.'" I say "That is *me* in that 'world'" not because I

recognize myself in that person, rather the first-person statement is noninferential. I may well recognize that that person has abilities that I do not have and yet the having or not having of the abilities is always an "I have . . ." and "I do not have . . .", that is, it is always experienced in the first person.

The shift from being one person to being a different person is what I call "travel." This shift may not be willful or even conscious, and one may be completely unaware of being different than one is in a different "world," and may not recognize that one is in a different "world." Even though the shift can be done willfully, it is not a matter of acting. One does not pose as someone else, one does not pretend to be, for example, someone of a different personality or character or someone who uses spaces or language differently than the other person. Rather one is someone who has that personality or character or uses space and language in that particular way. The "one" here does not refer to some underlying "I." One does not *experience* any underlying "I."

BEING AT EASE IN A "WORLD"

In investigating what I mean by "being at ease in a 'world,'" I will describe different ways of being at ease. One may be at ease in one or in all of these ways. There is a maximal way of being at ease, namely being at ease in all of these ways. I take this maximal way of being at ease to be somewhat dangerous because it tends to produce people who have no inclination to travel across "worlds" or have no experience of "world" travelling.

The first way of being at ease in a particular "world" is by being a fluent speaker in that "world." I know all the norms that there are to be followed, I know all the words that there are to be spoken. I know all the moves. I am confident.

Another way of being at ease is by being normatively happy. I agree with all the norms; I could not love any norms better. I am asked to do just what I want to do or think I should do. At ease.

Another way of being at ease in a "world" is by being humanly bonded. I am with those I love and they love me too. It should be noticed that I may be with those I love and be at ease because of them in a "world" that is otherwise as hostile to me as "worlds" get.

Finally one may be at ease because one has a history with others that is shared, especially daily history, the kind of shared history that one sees exemplified by the response to the "Do you remember poodle skirts?" question. There you are, with people you do not know at all. The question is posed and then they all begin talking about their poodle skirt stories. I have been in such situations without knowing what poodle skirts, for example, were and I felt so ill at ease because it was not *my* history. The other people did not particularly know each other. It is not that they were humanly bonded. Probably they did not have much politically in common either. But poodle skirts were in their shared history.

One may be at ease in one of these ways or in all of them. Notice that when one says meaningfully "This is *my* world," one may not be at ease in it. Or one may be at ease in it only in some of these respects and not in others. To say of some "world" that it is "*my* world" is to make an evaluation. One may privilege one or more "worlds" in this way for a variety of reasons: for example because one experiences oneself as an agent in a fuller sense than one experiences "oneself" in other "worlds." One may disown a "world" because one has first-person memories of a person who is so thoroughly dominated that she has no sense of exercising her own will or has a sense of having serious difficulties in performing actions that are willed by herself and no difficulty in performing actions willed by others. One may say of a "world" that it is "my world" because one is at ease in it, that is, being at ease in a "world" may be the basis for the evaluation.

Given the clarification of what I mean by a "world," "world"-travel, and being at ease in a "world," we are in a position to return to my problematic attribute, playfulness. It may be that in this "world" in which I am so unplayful, I am a different person than in the "world" in which I am playful. Or it may be that the "world" in which I am unplayful is constructed in such a way that I could be playful in it. I could practice, even though that "world" is constructed in such a way that my being playful in it is kind of hard. In describing what I take a "world" to be, I emphasized the first possibility as both the one that is truest to the experience of "outsiders" to the mainstream and as ontologically problema-tic because the "I" is identified in some sense as one and in some sense as a plurality. I identify myself as myself through memory and I retain myself as different in memory. When I travel from one "world" to another, I have this image, this memory of myself as playful in this other "world." I can then be in a particular "world" and have a double image of myself as, for example, playful and as not playful. But this is a very familiar and recognizable phenomenon to the outsider to the mainstream in some central cases: when in one "world" I animate, for example, that "world's" caricature of the person I am in the other "world." I can have both images of myself and to the extent that I can materialize or animate both images at the same time I become an ambiguous being. This is very much a part of trickery and foolery. It is worth remembering that the trickster and the fool are significant characters in many nondominant or outsider cultures. One then sees any particular "world" with these double edges and sees absurdity in them and so inhabits oneself differently. Given that latins are constructed in Anglo "worlds" as stereotypically intense—intense being a central characteristic of at least one of the anglo stereotypes of latins—and given that many latins, myself included, are genuinely intense, I can say to myself "I am intense" and take a hold of the double meaning. And furthermore, I can be stereotypically intense or be the real thing and, if you are Anglo, you do not know when I am which *because* I am Latin-American. As Latin-American I am an ambiguous being, a two-imaged self: I can see that gringos see me as

stereotypically intense because I am, as a Latin-American, constructed that way but I may or may not *intentionally* animate the stereotype or the real thing knowing that you may not see it in anything other than in the stereotypical construction. This ambiguity is funny and is not just funny, it is survival-rich. We can also make the picture of those who dominate us funny precisely because we can see the double edge; we can see them doubly constructed; we can see the plurality in them. So we know truths that only the fool can speak and only the trickster can play out without harm. We inhabit "worlds" and travel across them and keep all the memories.

Sometimes the "world"-traveller has a double image of herself and each self includes as important ingredients of itself one or more attributes that are *incompatible* with one or more of the attributes of the other self: for example being playful and being unplayful. To the extent that the attribute is an important ingredient of the self she is in that "world," that is, to the extent that there is a particularly good fit between that "world" and her having that attribute in it and to the extent that the attribute is personality or character central, that "world" would have to be changed if she is to be playful in it. It is not the case that if she could come to be at ease in it, she would be her own playful self. Because the attribute is personality or character central and there is such a good fit between that "world" and her being constructed with that attribute as central, *she* cannot become playful, she is unplayful. To become playful would be for her to become a contradictory being. So I am suggesting that the lack of ease solution cannot be a solution to my problematic case. My problem is not one of lack of ease. I am suggesting that I can understand my confusion about whether I am or am not playful by saying that I am both and that I am different persons in different "worlds" and can remember myself in both as I am in the other. I am a plurality of selves. This is to understand my confusion because *it is to come to see it as a piece* with much of the rest of my experience as an outsider in some of the "worlds" that I inhabit and of a piece with significant aspects of the experience of non-dominant people in the "worlds" of their dominators.

So, though I may not be at ease in the "worlds" in which I am not constructed playfully, it is not that I am not playful *because* I am not at ease. The two are compatible. But lack of playfulness is not caused by lack of ease. Lack of playfulness is not symptomatic of lack of ease but of lack of health. I am not a healthy being in the "worlds" that construct me unplayful.

PLAYFULNESS

I had a very personal stake in investigating this topic. Playfulness is not only the attribute that was the source of my confusion and the attitude that I recommend as the loving attitude in travelling across "worlds," I am also scared of ending up a serious human being, someone with no multidimensionality, with no fun in life, someone who is just someone who has had the fun constructed out of her. I am seriously scared of getting stuck in a "world" that constructs me that way. A world that I have no escape from and in which I cannot be playful.

I thought about what it is to be playful and what it is to play and I did this thinking in a "world" in which I only remember myself as playful and in which all of those who know me as playful are imaginary beings. A "world" in which I am scared of losing my memories of myself as playful or have them erased from me. Because I live in such a "world," after I formulated my own sense of what it is to be playful and to play I decided that I needed to "go to the literature." I read two classics on the subject: Johan Huizinga's *Homo Ludens* and Hans-Georg Gadamer's chapter on the concept of play in his *Truth and Method*. I discovered, to my amazement, that what I thought about play and playfulness, if they were right, was absolutely wrong. Though I will not provide the arguments for this interpretation of Gadamer and Huizinga here, I understood that both of them have an agonistic sense of "play." Play and playfulness have, ultimately, to do with contest, with winning, losing, battling. The sense of playfulness that I have in mind has nothing to do with those things. So, I tried to elucidate both senses of play and playfulness by contrasting them to each other. The contrast helped me see the attitude that I have in mind as the loving attitude in travelling across "worlds" more clearly.

An agonistic sense of playfulness is one in which *competence* is supreme. You better know the rules of the game. In agonistic play there is risk, there is *uncertainty*, but the uncertainty is about who is going to win and who is going to lose. There are rules that inspire hostility. The attitude of *playfulness is conceived as secondary to or derivative from play*. Since play is agon, then the only conceivable playful attitude is an agonistic one (the attitude does not turn an activity into play, but rather presupposes an activity that is play). One of the paradigmatic ways of playing for both Gadamer and Huizinga is role-playing. In role-playing, the person who is a participant in the game has a *fixed conception of him- or herself*. I also think that the players are imbued with *self-importance* in agonistic play since they are so keen on winning given their own merits, their very own competence.

When considering the value of "world"-travelling and whether playfulness is the loving attitude to have while travelling, I recognized the agonistic attitude as inimical to travelling across "worlds." The agonistic traveller is a conqueror, an imperialist. Huizinga, in his classic book on play, interprets Western civilization as play. That is an interesting thing for Third World people to think about. Western civilization has been interpreted by a white western man as play in the agonistic sense of play. Huizinga reviews western law, art, and many other aspects of western culture and sees agon in all of them. Agonistic playfulness leads those who attempt to travel to another "world" with this attitude to failure. Agonistic travellers fail consistently in their attempt to travel because what they do is to try to conquer the other "world." The attempt is not an attempt to try to erase the other "world." That is what assimilation is all about. Assimilation is the destruction of other people's "worlds." So, the agonistic attitude, the playful attitude given western man's construction of playfulness, is not a healthy, loving attitude to have in travelling across "worlds." Notice that given the agonistic attitude one *cannot* travel across "worlds," though one can kill other "worlds" with it. So for people who are interested in crossing racial and ethnic boundaries, an arrogant western man's construction of playfulness is deadly. One cannot cross the boundaries with it. One needs to give up such an attitude if one wants to travel.

So then, what is the loving playfulness that I have in mind? Let me begin with one example: We are by the riverbank. The river is very, very low. Almost dry. Bits of water here and there. Little pools with a few trout hiding under the rocks. But mostly it is wet stones, grey on the outside. We walk on the stones for awhile. You pick up a stone and crash it onto the others. As it breaks, it is quite wet inside and it is very colorful, very pretty. I pick up a stone and break it and run toward the pieces to see the colors. They are beautiful. I laugh and bring the pieces back to you and you are doing the same with your pieces. We keep on crashing stones for hours, anxious to see the beautiful new colors. We are playing. The playfulness of our activity does not presuppose that there is something like "crashing stones" that is a particular form of play with its own rules. Rather *the attitude that carries us through the activity, a playful attitude, turns the activity into play.* Our activity has no rules, though it is certainly intentional activity and we both understand what we are doing. The playfulness that gives meaning to our activity includes uncertainty, but in this case the uncertainty is an *openness to surprise.* This is a particular metaphysical attitude that does not expect the world to be neatly packaged, ruly. Rules fail to explain what we are doing. We are not self-important; we are not fixed in particular constructions of ourselves, which is part of saying that we are *open to self-construction.* We may not have rules, and when we do have rules, *there are no rules that are to us sacred.* We are not worried about competence. We are not wedded to a particular way of doing things. While playful we have not abandoned ourselves to, nor are we stuck in, any particular "world." We *are there creatively.* We are not passive.

Playfulness is, in part, an openness to being a fool, which is a combination of not worrying about competence, not being self-important, not taking norms as sacred, and finding ambiguity and double edges a source of wisdom and delight.

So, positively, the playful attitude involves openness to surprise, openness to being a fool, openness to self-construction or reconstruction and to construction or reconstruction of the "worlds" we inhabit playfully. Negatively, playfulness is characterized by uncertainty, lack of self-importance, absence of rules or a not taking rules as sacred, a not worrying about competence and a lack of abandonment to a particular construction of oneself, others, and one's relation to them. In attempting to take a hold of oneself and of one's relation to others in a particular "world," one may study, examine, and come to understand oneself. One may then see what the possibilities for play are for the being one is in that "world." One may even decide to inhabit that self fully in order to understand it better and find its creative possibilities. All of this is just self-reflection and it is quite different from resigning or abandoning oneself to the particular construction of oneself that one is attempting to take a hold of.

Conclusion

The are "worlds" we enter at our own risk, "worlds" that have agon, conquest, and arrogance as the main ingredients in their ethos. These are "worlds" that we enter out of necessity and which would be foolish to enter playfully in either the agonistic sense or in my sense. In such "worlds" we are not playful.

But there are "worlds" that we can travel to lovingly and travelling to them is part of loving at least some of their inhabitants. The reason why I think that travelling to someone's "world" is a way of identifying with them is because by travelling to their "world" we can understand *what it is to them and what it is to be ourselves in their eyes.* Only when we have travelled to each other's "worlds" are we fully subjects to each other (I agree with Hegel that self-recognition requires other subjects, but I disagree with his claim that it requires tension or hostility).

Knowing other women's "worlds" is part of knowing them and knowing them is part of loving them. Notice that the knowing can be done in greater or lesser depth, as can the loving. Also notice that travelling to another's "world" is not the same as becoming intimate with them. Intimacy is constituted in part by a very deep knowledge of the other self and "world" travelling is only part of having this knowledge. Also notice that some people, in particular those who are outsiders to the mainstream, can be known only to the extent that they are known in several "worlds" and as "world"-travellers.

Without knowing the other's "world," one does not know the other, and without knowing the other one is really alone in the other's presence because the other is only dimly present to one.

Through travelling to other people's "worlds" we discover that there are "worlds" in which those who are the victims of arrogant perception are really subjects, lively beings, resistors, constructors of vision even though in the mainstream construction they are animated only by the arrogant perceiver and are pliable, foldable, file-awayable, classifiable. I always imagine the Aristotelian slave as pliable and foldable at night or after he or she cannot work anymore (when he or she dies as a tool). Aristotle tells us nothing about the slave *apart from the master.* We know the slave only through the master. The slave is a tool of the master. After working hours he or she is folded and placed in a drawer till the next morning. My mother was apparent to me mostly as a victim of arrogant perception. I was loyal to the arrogant perceiver's construction of her and thus disloyal to her in assuming that she was exhausted by that construction. I was unwilling to be like her and thought that identifying with her, seeing myself in her, necessitated that I become like her. I was wrong both in assuming that she was exhausted by the arrogant perceiver's construction of her and in my understanding of identification, though I was not wrong in thinking that identification was part of loving and that it involved in part seeing myself in her. I came to realize through travelling to her "world" that she is not foldable and pliable, that she is not exhausted by the mainstream argentinian patriarchal construction of her. I came to realize that there are "worlds" in which she shines as a creative being. Seeing myself in her through travelling to her "world" has meant seeing how different from her I am in her "world."

So, in recommending "world"-travelling and identification through "world"-travelling as part of loving other women, I am suggesting disloyalty to arrogant perceivers, including the arrogant perceiver in ourselves, and to their constructions of women. In revealing agonistic playfulness as incompatible with "world"-travelling, I am revealing both its affinity with imperialism and arrogant perception and its incompatibility with loving and loving perception.

Note

1. Grafting the substance of another to oneself is partly constitutive of arrogant perception. See M. Frye (1983: 66).

References

Frye, Marilyn. (1983). *The Politics of Reality: Essays in Feminist Theory*. Trumansburg, New York: Crossing Press.
Gadamer, Hans-Georg. (1975). *Truth and Method*. New York: Seabury Press.
Huizinga, Johan. 1968. *Homo Ludens*. Buenos Aires, Argentina: Emece Editores.

The Negro and Language

FRANTZ FANON

I ASCRIBE A BASIC importance to the phenomenon of language. That is why I find it necessary to begin with this subject, which should provide us with one of the elements in the colored man's comprehension of the dimension of *the other*. For it is implicit that to speak is to exist absolutely for the other.

The black man has two dimensions. One with his fellows, the other with the white man. A Negro behaves differently with a white man and with another Negro. That this self-division is a direct result of colonialist subjugation is beyond question. . . . No one would dream of doubting that its major artery is fed from the heart of those various theories that have tried to prove that the Negro is a stage in the slow evolution of monkey into man. Here is objective evidence that expresses reality.

But when one has taken cognizance of this situation, when one has understood it, one considers the job completed. How can one then be deaf to that voice rolling down the stages of history: "What matters is not to know the world but to change it."

This matters appallingly in our lifetime.

To speak means to be in a position to use a certain syntax, to grasp the morphology of this or that language, but it means above all to assume a culture, to support the weight of a civilization. Since the situation is not one-way only, the statement of it should reflect the fact. Here the reader is asked to concede certain points that, however unacceptable they may seem in the beginning, will find the measure of their validity in the facts.

The problem that we confront in this chapter is this: The Negro of the Antilles will be proportionately whiter—that is, he will come closer to being a real human being—in direct ratio to his mastery of the French language. I am not unaware that this is one of man's attitudes face-to-face with Being. A man who has a language consequently possesses the world expressed and implied by that language. What we are getting at becomes plain: Mastery of language affords remarkable power. Paul Valéry knew this, for he called language "the god gone astray in the flesh."[1]

In a work now in preparation I propose to investigate this phenomenon.[2] For the moment I want to show why the Negro of the Antilles, whoever he is, has always to face the problem of language. Furthermore, I will broaden the field of this description and through the Negro of the Antilles include every colonized man.

Every colonized people—in other words, every people in whose soul an inferiority complex has been created by the death and burial of its local cultural originality—finds itself face-to-face with the language of the civilizing nation; that is, with the culture of the mother country. The colonized is elevated above his jungle status in proportion to his adoption of the mother country's cultural standards. He becomes whiter as he renounces his blackness, his jungle. In the French colonial army, and particularly in the Senegalese regiments, the black officers serve first of all as interpreters. They are used to convey the master's orders to their fellows, and they too enjoy a certain position of honor.

There is the city, there is the country. There is the capital, there is the province. Apparently the problem in the mother country is the same. Let us take a Lyonnais in Paris: He boasts of the quiet of his city, the intoxicating beauty of the quays of the Rhône, the splendor of the plane trees, and all those other things that fascinate people who have nothing else to do. If you meet him again when he has returned from Paris, and especially if you do not know the capital, he will never run out of its praises: Paris, city of light; the Seine; the little garden restaurants; know Paris and die. . . .

The process repeats itself with the man of Martinique. First of all on his island: Basse-Pointe, Marigot, Gros-Morne, and, opposite, the imposing Fort-de-France. Then, and this is the important point, beyond his island. The Negro who knows the mother country is a demigod. In this connection I offer a fact that must have struck my compatriots. Many of them, after stays of varying length in metropolitan France, go home to be deified. The most eloquent form of ambivalence is adopted toward them by the native, the-one-who-never-crawled-out-of-his-hole, the *bitaco*. The black man who has lived in France for a length of time returns radically changed. To express it in genetic terms, his phenotype undergoes a definitive, an absolute mutation.[3] Even before he had gone away, one could tell from the almost aerial manner of his carriage that new forces had been set in motion. When he met a friend or acquaintance, his greeting was no longer the wide sweep of the arm: with great reserve our "new man" bowed slightly. The habitually raucous voice hinted at a gentle inner stirring as of rustling breezes. For the Negro knows that over there in France there is a stereotype of him that will fasten on to him at the pier in Le Havre or Marseille: "Ah come from Mahtinique, it's the fuhst time Ah've eveh come to

France." He knows that what the poets call the *divine gurgling* (listen to Creole) is only a halfway house between pidgin-nigger and French. The middle class in the Antilles never speak Creole except to their servants. In school the children of Martinique are taught to scorn the dialect. One avoids *Creolisms*. Some families completely forbid the use of Creole, and mothers ridicule their children for speaking it.

> My mother wanting a son to keep in mind
> if you do not know your history lesson
> you will not go to mass on Sunday in
> your Sunday clothes
> that child will be a disgrace to the family
> that child will be our curse
> shut up I told you you must speak French
> the French of France
> the Frenchman's French
> French French.[4]

Yes, I must take great pains with my speech, because I shall be more or less judged by it. With great contempt they will say of me, "He doesn't even know how to speak French."

In any group of young men in the Antilles, the one who expresses himself well, who has mastered the language is inordinately feared; keep an eye on that one, he is almost white. In France one says, "He talks like a book." In Martinique, "He talks like a white man."

The Negro arriving in France will react against the myth of the *R*-eating man from Martinique. He will become aware of it, and he will really go to war against it. He will practice not only rolling his *R* but embroidering it. Furtively observing the slightest reactions of others, listening to his own speech, suspicious of his own tongue—a wretchedly lazy organ—he will lock himself into his room and read aloud for hours—desperately determined to learn *diction*.

Recently an acquaintance told me a story. A Martinique Negro landed at Le Havre and went into a bar. With the utmost self-confidence he called, "Waiterrr! Bing me a beeya." Here is a genuine intoxication. Resolved not to fit the myth of the nigger-who-eats-his-*R*'s, he had acquired a fine supply of them but allocated it badly.

There is a psychological phenomenon that consists in the belief that the world will open to the extent to which frontiers are broken down. Imprisoned on his island, lost in an atmosphere that offers not the slightest outlet, the Negro breathes in this appeal of Europe like pure air. For, it must be admitted, Aimé Césaire was generous—in his *Cahier d'un retour au pays natal*. This town of Fort-de-France is truly flat, stranded. Lying there naked to the sun, that "flat, sprawling city, stumbling over its own common sense, winded by its load of endlessly repeated crosses, pettish at its destiny, voiceless, thwarted in every direction, incapable of feeding on the juices of its soil, blocked, cut off, confined, divorced from fauna and flora."[5]

Césaire's description of it is anything but poetic. It is understandable, then, when at the news that he is getting into France (quite like someone who, in the colloquial phrase, is "getting a start in life") the black man is jubilant and makes up his mind to change. There is no thematic pattern, however; his structure changes independently of any reflective process. In the United States there is a center directed by Pearce and Williamson; it is called Peckham. These authors have shown that in married couples a biochemical alteration takes place in the partners, and, it seems, they have discovered the presence of certain hormones in the husband of a pregnant woman. It would be equally interesting—and there are plenty of subjects for the study—to investigate the modifications of body fluids that occur in Negroes when they arrive in France. Or simply to study through tests the psychic changes both before they leave home and after they have spent a month in France.

What are by common consent called the human sciences have their own drama. Should one postulate a type for human reality and describe its psychic modalities only through deviations from it, or should one not rather strive unremittingly for a concrete and ever new understanding of man?

When one reads that after the age of twenty-nine a man can no longer love and that he must wait until he is forty-nine before his capacity for affect revives, one feels the ground give way beneath one. The only possibility of regaining one's balance is to face the whole problem, for all these discoveries, all these inquiries lead only in one direction: to make man admit that he is nothing, absolutely nothing—and that he must put an end to the narcissism on which he relies in order to imagine that he is different from the other "animals."

This amounts to nothing more or less than *man's surrender*.

Having reflected on that, I grasp my narcissism with both hands and I turn my back on the degradation of those who would make man a mere mechanism. If there can be no discussion on a philosophical level—that is, the plane of the basic needs of human reality—I am willing to work on the psychoanalytic level—in other words, the level of the "failures," in the sense in which one speaks of engine failures.

The black man who arrives in France changes because to him the country represents the Tabernacle; he changes not only because it is from France that he received his knowledge of Montesquieu, Rousseau, and Voltaire, but also because France gave him his physicians, his department heads, his innumerable little functionaries—from the sergeant-major "fifteen years in the service" to the policeman who was born in Panissieres. There is a kind of magic vault of distance, and the man who is leaving next week for France creates round himself a magic circle in which the words *Paris, Marseille, Sorbonne, Pigalle* become the keys to the vault. He leaves for the pier, and the amputation of his being diminishes as the silhouette of his ship grows clearer. In the eyes of those who have come to see him off he can read the evidence of his own mutation, his power. "Good-by bandanna, good-by straw hat. . . ."

Now that we have got him to the dock, let him sail; we shall see him again. For the moment, let us go to welcome one of those who are coming home. The "newcomer" reveals himself at once; he answers only in French, and often he no longer understands Creole. There is a relevant illustration in folklore. After severel months of living in France, a country boy returns to his family. Noticing a farm implement, he asks his father, an old don't-pull-that-kind-of-thing-on-me peasant, "Tell me, what does one call that apparatus?" His father replies by dropping the tool on the boy's feet, and the amnesia vanishes. Remarkable therapy.

There is the newcomer, then. He no longer understands the dialect, he talks about the Opéra, which he may never have seen except from a distance, but above all he adopts a critical attitude toward his compatriots. Confronted with the most trivial occurrence, he becomes an oracle. He is the one who knows. He betrays himself in his speech. At the Savannah, where the young men of Fort-de-France spend their leisure, the spectacle is revealing: everyone immediately waits for the newcomer to speak. As soon as the school day ends, they all go to the Savannah. This Savannah seems to have its own poetry. Imagine a square about 600 feet long and 125 feet wide, its sides bounded by worm-eaten tamarind trees, one end marked by the huge war memorial (the nation's gratitude to its children), the other by the Central Hotel; a miserable tract of uneven cobbles, pebbles that roll away under one's feet; and, amid all this, three or four hundred young fellows walking up and down, greeting one another, grouping—no, they never form groups, they go on walking.

"How's it going?"

"O.K. How's it with you?"

"O.K."

And that goes on for fifty years. Yes, this city is deplorably played out. So is its life.

They meet and talk. And if the newcomer soon gets the floor, it is because they were *waiting for him*. First of all to observe his manner: the slightest departure is seized upon, picked apart, and in less than forty-eight hours it has been retailed all over Fort-de-France. There is no forgiveness when one who claims a superiority falls before the standard. Let him say, for instance, "It was not my good fortune, when in France, to observe mounted policemen," and he is done for. Only one choice remains to him: throw off his "Parisianism" or die of ridicule. For there is also no forgetting: when he marries, his wife will be aware that she is marrying a joke, and his children will have a legend to face and to live down.

What is the origin of this personality change? What is the source of this new way of being? Every dialect is a way of thinking, Damourette and Pichon said. And the fact that the newly returned Negro adopts a language different from that of the group into which he was born is evidence of a dislocation, a separation. Professor D. Westermann, in *The African Today* (p. 331), says that the Negroes' inferiority complex is particularly intensified among the most educated, who must struggle with it unceasingly. Their way of doing so, he adds, is frequently naive: "The wearing of European clothes, whether rags or the most up-to-date style; using European furniture and European forms of social intercourse; adorning the Native language with European expressions; using bombastic phrases in speaking or writing a European language; all these contribute to a feeling of equality with the European and his achievements."

On the basis of other studies and my own personal observations, I want to try to show why the Negro adopts such a position, peculiar to him, with respect to European languages. Let me point out once more that the conclusions I have reached pertain to the French Antilles; at the same time, I am not unaware that the same behavior patterns obtain in every race that has been subjected to colonization.

I have known—and unfortunately I still know—people born in Dahomey or the Congo who pretend to be natives of the Antilles; I have known, and I still know, Antilles Negroes who are annoyed when they are suspected of being Senegalese. This is because the Antilles Negro is more "civilized" than the African; that is, he is closer to the white man; and this difference prevails not only in the back streets and on boulevards but also in public service and the army. Any Antilles Negro who performed his military service in a Senegalese infantry regiment is familiar with this disturbing climate: on one side he has the Europeans, whether born in his own country or in France, and on the other he has the Senegalese. I remember a day when, in the midst of combat, we had to wipe out a machine gun nest. The Senegalese were ordered to attack three times, and each time they were forced back. Then one of them wanted to know why the *toubabs*[6] did not go into action. At such times, one no longer knows whether one is *toubab* or "native." And yet many Antilles Negroes see nothing to upset them in such European identification; on the contrary, they find it altogether normal. That would be all we need, to be taken for niggers! The Europeans despise the Senegalese, and the Antilles Negro rules the black roost as its unchallenged master. Admittedly as an extreme example, I offer a detail that is at least amusing. I was talking recently with someone from Martinique who told me with considerable resentment that some Guadeloupe Negroes were trying to "pass" as Martinicans. But, he added, the lie was rapidly discovered, because they are more savage than we are; which, again, means they are farther away from the white man. It is said that the Negro loves to jabber; in my own case, when I think of the word *jabber* I see a gay group of children calling and shouting for the sake of calling and shouting—children in the midst of play, to the degree to which play can be considered an initiation into life. The Negro loves to jabber, and from this theory it is not a long road that leads to a new proposition: the Negro is just a child. The psychoanalysts have a fine start here, and the term *orality* is soon heard.

But we have to go farther. The problem of language is too basic to allow us to hope to state it all here. Piaget's remarkable studies have taught us to distinguish the various stages in the mastery of language, and Gelb and Goldstein have shown us that the function of language is also broken into periods and steps. What interests us here is the black man confronted by the French language. We are trying to understand why the Antilles Negro is so fond of speaking French.

Jean-Paul Sartre, in *Orphée Noir*, which prefaces the *Anthology de la nouvelle poésie nègre et malgache*, tells us that the black poet will turn against the French language; but that does not apply in the Antilles. Here I share the opinion of Michel Leiris, who, discussing Creole, wrote not so long ago:

> Even now, despite the fact that it is a language that everyone knows more or less, though only the illiterate use it to the exclusion of French, Creole seems already predestined to become a relic eventually, once public education (however slow its progress, impeded by the insufficiency of school facilities everywhere, the paucity of reading matter available to the public, and the fact that the physical scale of living is often too low) has become common enough among the disinherited classes of the population.

And, the author adds:

> In the case of the poets that I am discussing here, there is no question of their deliberately becoming "Antilleans"—on the Provençal picturesque model— by employing a dead language which, furthermore, is utterly devoid of all external radiance regardless of its intrinsic qualities; it is rather a matter of their asserting, in opposition to white men filled with the worst racial prejudices, whose arrogance is more and more plainly demonstrated to be unfounded, the integrity of their personalities.[7]

If there is, for instance, a Gilbert Gratiant who writes in dialect, it must be admitted that he is a rarity. Let us point out, furthermore, that the poetic merit of such creation is quite dubious. There are, in contrast, real works of art translated from the Peul and Wolof dialects of Senegal, and I have found great interest in following the linguistic studies of Sheik Anta Diop.

Nothing of the sort in the Antilles. The language spoken is officially French; teachers keep a close watch over the children to make sure they do not use Creole. Let us not mention the ostensible reasons. It would seem, then, that the problem is this: In the Antilles, as in Brittany, there is a dialect and there is the French language. But this is false, for the Bretons do not consider themselves inferior to the French people. The Bretons have not been civilized by the white man.

By refusing to multiply our elements, we take the risk of not setting a limit to our field; for it is essential to convey to the black man that an attitude of rupture has never saved anyone. While it is true that I have to throw off an attacker who is strangling me, because I literally cannot breathe, the fact remains solely on the physiological foundation. To the mechanical problem of respiration it would be unsound to graft a psychological element, the impossibility of expansion.

What is there to say? Purely and simply this: When a bachelor of philosophy from the Antilles refuses to apply for certification as a teacher on the ground of his color, I say that philosophy has never saved anyone. When someone else strives and strains to prove to me that black men are as intelligent as white men, I say that intelligence has never saved anyone; and that is true, for, if philosophy and intelligence are invoked to proclaim the equality of men, they have also been employed to justify the extermination of men.

Before going any farther I find it necessary to say certain things. I am speaking here, on the one hand, of alienated (duped) blacks, and, on the other, of no less alienated (duping and duped) whites. If one hears a Sartre or a Cardinal Verdier declare that the outrage of the color problem has survived far too long, one can conclude only that their position is normal. Anyone can amass references and quotations to prove that "color prejudice" is indeed an imbecility and an iniquity that must be eliminated.

Sartre begins *Orphée Noir* thus: "What then did you expect when you un-bound the gag that had muted those black mouths? That they would chant your praises? Did you think that when those heads that our fathers had forcibly bowed down to the grounds were raised again, you would find adoration in their eyes?"[8] I do not know; but I say that he who looks into my eyes for anything but a perpetual question will have to lose his sight; neither recognition nor hate. And if I cry out, it will not be a black cry. No, from the point of view adopted here, there is no black problem. Or at any rate if there is one it concerns the whites only accidentally. It is a story that takes place in darkness, and the sun that is carried within me must shine into the smallest crannies.

Dr. H. L. Gordon, attending physician at the Mathari Mental Hospital in Nairobi, declared in an article in *The East African Medical Journal* (1943): "A highly technical skilled examination of a series of 100 brains of normal Natives has found naked eye and microscopic facts indicative of inherent new brain inferiority. . . . Quantitatively," he added, "the inferiority amounts to 14.8 percent."[9]

It has been said that the Negro is the link between the monkey and man— meaning, of course, white man. And only on page 108 of his book does Sir Alan Burns come to the conclusion that "we are unable to accept as scientifically proved the theory that the black man is inherently inferior to the white, or that he comes from a different stock. . . ." Let me add that it would be easy to prove the absurdity of statements such as this: "It is laid down in the Bible that the separation of the white and black races will be continued in heaven as on earth, and those blacks who are admitted into the Kingdom of Heaven will find themselves separately lodged in certain of those many mansions of Our Father that are mentioned in the New Testament." Or this: "We are the chosen people—look at the color of our skins. The others are black or yellow: That is because of their sins."

Ah, yes, as you can see, by calling on humanity, on the belief in dignity, on love, on charity, it would be easy to prove, or to win the admission, that the black is the equal of the white. But my purpose is quite different: what I want to do is help the black man to free himself of the arsenal of complexes that has been developed by the colonial environment. M. Achille, who teaches at the Lycée du Parc in Lyon, once during a lecture told of a personal experience. It is a universally known experience. It is a rare Negro living in France who cannot duplicate it. Being a Catholic, Achille took part in a student pilgrimage. A priest, observing the black face in his flock, said to him, "You go 'way big Savannah what for and come' long us?" Very politely Achille gave him a truthful answer, and it was not the young fugitive from the Savannah who came off the worse. Everyone laughed at the exchange and the pilgrimage proceeded. But if we stop right here, we shall see that the fact that the priest spoke pidgin-nigger leads to certain observations:

1. "Oh, I know the blacks. They must be spoken to kindly; talk to them about their country; it's all in knowing how to talk to them. For instance. . . ." I am not at all exaggerating: a white man addressing a Negro behaves exactly like an adult with a child and starts smirking, whispering, patronizing, cozening. It is not one white man I have watched, but hundreds; and I have not limited my investigation to any one class but, if I may claim an essentially objective position, I have made a point of observing such behavior in physicians, policemen, employers. I shall be told, by those who overlook my purpose, that I should have directed my attention elsewhere, that there are white men who do not fit my description.

To these objections I reply that the subject of our study is the dupes and those who dupe them, the alienated, and that if there are white men who behave naturally when they meet Negroes, they certainly do not fall within the scope of our examination. If my patient's liver is functioning as it should, I am not going to take it for granted that his kidneys are sound. Having found the liver normal, I leave it to its normality, which is normal, and turn my attention to the kidneys: as it happens, the kidneys are diseased. Which means simply that, side by side with normal people who behave naturally in accordance with a human psychology, there are others who behave pathologically in accordance with an inhuman psychology. And it happens that the existence of men of this sort has determined a certain number of realities to the elimination of which I should like to contribute here.

Talking to Negroes in this way gets down to their level, it puts them at ease, it is an effort to make them understand us, it reassures them. . . .

The physicians of the public health services know this very well. Twenty European patients, one after another, come in: "Please sit down. . . . Why do you wish to consult me? . . . What are your symptoms? . . ." then comes a Negro or an Arab: "Sit there boy. . . . What's bothering you? . . . Where does it hurt, huh? . . ." When, that is, they do not say: "You not feel good, no?"

2. To speak pidgin to a Negro makes him angry, because he himself is a pidgin-nigger-talker. But, I will be told, there is no wish, no intention to anger him. I grant this; but it is just this absence of wish, this lack of interest, this indifference, this automatic manner of classifying him, imprisoning him, primitivizing him, decivilizing him, that makes him angry. If a man who speaks pidgin to a man of color or an Arab does not see anything wrong or evil in such behavior, it is because he has never stopped to think. I myself have been aware, in talking to certain patients, of the exact instant at which I began to slip. . . .

Examining this seventy-three-year-old farm woman, whose mind was never strong and who is now far gone in dementia, I am suddenly aware of the collapse of the *antennae* with which I touch and through which I am touched. The fact that I adopt a language suitable to dementia, to feeble-mindedness; the fact that I "talk down" to this poor woman of seventy-three; the fact that I condescend to her in my quest for a diagnosis, are the stigmata of a dereliction in my relations with other people.

What an idealist, people will say. Not at all: it is just that the others are scum. I make it a point always to talk to the so-called *bicots*[10] in normal French, and I have always been understood. They answer me as well as their varying means permit; but I will not allow myself to resort to paternalistic "understanding."

"G'morning, pal. Where's it hurt? Huh? Lemme see—belly ache? Heart pain?"

With that indefinable tone that the hacks in the free clinics have mastered so well.

One feels perfectly justified when the patient answers in the same fashion. "You see? I wasn't kidding you. That's just the way they are."

When the opposite occurs, one must retract one's pseudopodia and behave like a man. The whole structure crumbles. A black man who says to you: "I am in no sense your boy, Monsieur. . . ." Something new under the sun.

But one must go lower. You are in a bar, in Rouen or Strasbourg, and you have the misfortune to be spotted by an old drunk. He sits down at your table right off. "You—Africa? Dakar, Rufisque, whorehouse, dames, café, mangoes, bananas. . . ." You stand up and leave, and your farewell is a torrent of abuse: "You didn't play big shot like that in your jungle, you dirty nigger!"

Mannoni has described what he calls the Prospero complex. We shall come back to these discoveries, which will make it possible for us to understand the psychology of colonialism. But we can already state that to talk pidgin-nigger is to express this thought: "You'd better keep your place."

I meet a Russian or German who speaks French badly. With gestures I try to give him the information that he requests, but at the same time I can hardly forget that he has a language of his own, a country, and that perhaps he is a lawyer or an engineer there. In any case, he is foreign to my group, and his standards must be different.

When it comes to the case of the Negro, nothing of the kind. He has no culture, no civilization, no "long historical past."

This may be the reason for the strivings of contemporary Negroes: to prove the existence of a black civilization to the white world at all costs.

Willy-nilly, the Negro has to wear the livery that the white man has sewed for him. Look at children's picture magazines: out of every Negro mouth comes the ritual "Yassuh, boss." It is even more remarkable in motion pictures. Most of the American films for which French dialogue is dubbed in offer the type-Negro: "Sho' good!"

In one of these recent films, *Requins d'acier*, one character was a Negro crewman in a submarine who talked the most classic dialect imaginable. What is more, he was all *nigger*, walking backward, shaking at the slightest sign of irritation on the part of a petty officer; ultimately he was killed in the course of the voyage. Yet I am convinced that the original dialogue did not resort to the same means of expression. And, even if it did, I can see no reason why, in a democratic France that includes sixty million citizens of color, dubbing must repeat every stupidity that crosses the ocean. It is because the Negro has to be shown in a certain way; and from the Negro in *Sans Pitié*—"Me work hard, me never lie, me never steal"—to the servant girl of *Duel in the Sun* one meets the same stereotype.

Yes, the black man is supposed to be a good nigger; once this has been laid down, the rest follows of itself. To make him talk pidgin is to fasten him to the effigy of him, to snare him, to imprison him, the eternal victim of an essence, of an *appearance* for which he is not responsible. And naturally, just as a Jew who spends money without thinking about it is suspect, a black man who quotes Montesquieu had better be watched. Please understand me: watched in the sense that he is starting something. Certainly I do not contend that the black student is suspect to his fellows or his teachers. But outside university circles there is an army of fools: what is important is not to educate them, but to teach the Negro not to be the slave of their archetypes.

That these imbeciles are the product of a psychological-economic system I will grant. But that does not get us much farther along.

When a Negro talks of Marx, the first reaction is always the same: "We have brought you up to our level and now you turn against your benefactors. Ingrates!

Obviously nothing can be expected of you." And then too there is that bludgeon argument of the plantation owner in Africa: our enemy is the teacher.

What I am asserting is that the European has a fixed concept of the Negro, and there is nothing more exasperating than to be asked: "How long have you been in France? You speak French so well."

It can be argued that people say this because many Negroes speak pidgin. But that would be too easy. You are on a train and you ask another passenger: "I beg your pardon, sir, would you mind telling me where the dining car is?"

"Sure, fella. You go out door, see, go corridor, you go straight, go one car, go two car, go three car, you there."

No, speaking pidgin-nigger closes off the black man; it perpetuates a state of conflict in which the white man injects the black with extremely dangerous foreign bodies. Nothing is more astonishing than to hear a black man expressing himself properly, for then in truth he is putting on the white world. I have had occasion to talk with students of foreign origin. They speak French badly: Little Crusoe, alias Prospero, is at ease then. He explains, informs, interprets, helps them with their studies. But with a Negro he is completely baffled; the Negro has made himself just as knowledgeable. With him this game cannot be played, he is a complete replica of the white man. So there is nothing to do but to give in.[11]

After all that has just been said, it will be understood that the first impulse of the black man is to say *no* to those who attempt to build a definition of him. It is understandable that the first action of the black man is a *reaction*, and, since the Negro is appraised in terms of the extent of his assimilation, it is also understandable why the newcomer expresses himself only in French. It is because he wants to emphasize the rupture that has now occurred. He is incarnating a new type of man that he imposes on his associates and his family. And so his old mother can no longer understand him when he talks to her about his *duds*, family's *crummy joint*, the *dump* . . . all of it, of course, decked out with the appropriate accent.

In every country of the world there are climbers, "the ones who forget who they are," and, in contrast to them, "the ones who remember where they came from." The Antilles Negro who goes home from France expresses himself in dialect if he wants to make it plain that nothing has changed. One can feel this at the dock where his family and his friends are waiting for him. Waiting for him not only because he is physically arriving, but in the sense of waiting for the chance to strike back. They need a minute or two in order to make their diagnosis. If the voyager tells his acquaintances, "I am so happy to be back with you. Good lord, it is hot in this country, I shall certainly not be able to endure it very long," they know: a European has got off the ship.

In a more limited group, when students from the Antilles meet in Paris, they have the choice of two possibilities:

—either to stand with the white world (that is to say, the real world), and, since they will speak French, to be able to confront certain problems and incline to a certain degree of universality in their conclusions;

—or to reject Europe, "Yo,"[12] and cling together in their dialect, making themselves quite comfortable in what we shall call the *Umwelt* of Martinique; by this I mean—and this applies particularly to my brothers of the Antilles—that when one of us tries, in Paris or any other university city, to study a problem seriously, he is accused of self-aggrandizement, and the surest way of cutting him down is to remind him of the Antilles by exploding into dialect. This must be recognized as one of the reasons why so many friendships collapse after a few months of life in Europe.

My theme being the disalienation of the black man, I want to make him feel that whenever there is a lack of understanding between him and his fellows in the presence of the white man there is a lack of judgment.

A Senegalese learns Creole in order to pass as an Antilles native: I call this alienation.

The Antilles Negroes who knows him never weary of making jokes about him: I call this a lack of judgment.

It becomes evident that we were not mistaken in believing that a study of the language of the Antilles Negro would be able to show us some characteristics of his world. As I said at the start, there is a retaining-wall relation between language and group.

To speak a language is to take on a world, a culture. The Antilles Negro who wants to be white will be the whiter as he gains greater mastery of the cultural tool that language is. Rather more than a year ago in Lyon, I remember, in a lecture I had drawn a parallel between Negro and European poetry, and a French acquaintance told me enthusiastically, "At bottom you are a white man." The fact that I had been able to investigate so interesting a problem through the white man's language gave me honorary citizenship.

Historically, it must be understood that the Negro wants to speak French because it is the key that can open doors which were still barred to him fifty years ago. In the Antilles Negro who comes within this study we find a quest for subtleties, for refinements of language—so many further means of proving to himself that he has measured up to the culture.[13] It has been said that the orators of the Antilles have a gift of eloquence that would leave any European breathless. I am reminded of a relevant story: In the election campaign of 1945, Aimé Césaire, who was seeking a deputy's seat, addressed a large audience in the boys' school in Fort-de-France. In the middle of his speech a woman fainted. The next day, an acquaintance told me about this, and commented: "*Français a té tellement chaud que la femme là tombé malcadi.*"[14] The power of language!

Some other facts are worth a certain amount of attention: for example,

Charles-Andre Julien introducing Aimé Césaire as "a Negro poet with a university degree," or again, quite simply, the expression, "a great black poet."

These ready-made phrases, which seem in a commonsense way to fill a need—for Aimé Césaire is really black and a poet—have a hidden subtlety, a permanent rub. I know nothing of Jean Paulhan except that he writes very interesting books; I have no idea how old Roger Caillois is, since the only evidences I have of his existence are the books of his that streak across my horizon. And let no one accuse me of affective allergies; what I am trying to say is that there is no reason why André Breton should say of Césaire, "Here is a black man who handles the French language as no white man today can."[15]

Notes

1. *Charmes* (Paris: Gallimard, 1952).
2. *Le Langage et L'agressivité.*
3. By that I mean that Negroes who return to their original environments convey the impression that they have completed a cycle, that they have added to themselves something that was lacking. They return literally full of themselves.
4. Léon-G. Damas, "Hoquet," in *Pigments*, ed. Leopold S.-Senghor, *Anthologie de la nouvelle poésie nègre et malgache* (Paris: Presses Universitaires de France, 1948), 15–17.
5. *Cahiers* (Paris: Présence Africaine, 1956), 30.
6. Literally, this dialect word means *European*; by extension it was applied to any officer (translator's note).
7. "Martinique-Guadeloupe-Haiti," *Les Temps Modernes* (February 1950): 1347.
8. Jean-Paul Sartre, *Orphée Noir*, in *Anthologie de la nouvelle poésie nègre et malgache* (Paris: Presses Universitaires de France, 1948), ix.
9. Quoted in Sir Alan Burns, *Colour Prejudice* (London: Allen and Unwin, 1948), 101.
10. Vulgar French for *Arab* (translator's note).
11. "I knew some Negroes in the School of Medicine . . . in a word, they were a disappointment; the color of their skin should have permitted them to give *us* the opportunity to be charitable, generous, or scientifically friendly. They were derelict in this duty, this claim on our good will. All our tearful tenderness, all our calculated solicitude were a drug on the market. We had no Negroes to condescend to, nor did we have anything to hate them for; they counted for virtually as much as we in the scale of the little jobs and petty chicaneries of daily life." Michel Salomon, "D'un juif à des nègres," *Présence Africaine*, no. 5, 776.
12. A generic term for *other people*, applied especially to Europeans.
13. Compare for example the almost incredible store of anecdotes to which the election of any candidate gives rise. A filthy newspaper called the *Canard Déchaîné* could not get its fill of overwhelming Monsieur B. with devastating Creolisms. This is indeed the bludgeon of the Antilles: *He can't express himself in French.*
14. "*Le français (l'elegance de la forme) etait tellement chaud que la femme est tombée en transes*" (His French [the refinement of his style] was so exciting that the woman swooned away).
15. Introduction to *Cahier d'un retour au pays natal*, p. 14.

Alienation and the African-American Experience

HOWARD McGARY

THE TERM "ALIENATION" INVOKES a variety of responses. For liberals, to be alienated signals a denial of certain basic rights, for example, the right to equality of opportunity or the right to autonomy.[1] Progressive thinkers, on the other hand, believe that alienation involves estrangement from one's work, self, or others because of capitalism.[2] However, recent discussions of alienation have cast doubt on whether either of these theories totally capture the phenomenon. Drawing on the experiences of people of color, these theorists maintain that to be alienated is to be estranged in ways that cannot be accounted for by liberal and Marxist theories of alienation.[3]

The concept of alienation is often associated with Marx's conception of human beings in capitalist societies. However, non-Marxists have also used the term alienation to explain the experiences of human beings in relationship to their society, each other, their work, and themselves. But liberal theories of alienation have been criticized by Marxists for two reasons: First they see liberal theories of alienation as a psychological condition that is said to result from a denial of basic individual rights rather than the result of systematic failure. Second, liberals have an account of human nature that is unhistorical; one that fails to consider the changes in human nature that result from changes in social conditions.

For the Marxist, alienation is not simply a theory of how people feel or think about themselves when their rights are violated, but a historical theory of how human beings act and how they are treated by others in capitalist society. The Marxist theory of alienation is an explanatory social theory that places human beings at the center of the critique of social-economic relations. Marx's human being is not a stagnant given, but a product of an explanatory social theory. For Marx alienation is something that all human beings experience in capitalist societies, it is not something that certain individuals undergo because they are neurotic or the victims of some unjust law or social practice.

It is clear that African-Americans have not always been recognized and treated as American citizens or as human beings by the dominant white society. Both of these forms of denial have had serious negative consequences and numerous scholars have discussed what these denials have meant to African-Americans and to the rest of society. However, it does not directly follow from the fact of these denials that African-Americans are alienated because of these things. In this essay, I shall attempt to understand this new challenge to the liberal and Marxist theories of "alienation" and its impact, if any, on the masses of African-Americans.

THE NEW ACCOUNT OF ALIENATION

According to the new account of alienation that is drawn from the experiences of people of color, alienation exists when the self is deeply divided because the hostility of the dominant groups in the society forces the self to see itself as loathsome, defective, or insignificant, and lacking the possibility of ever seeing itself in more positive terms. This type of alienation is not just estrangement from one's work or a possible plan of life, but an estrangement from ever becoming a self that is not defined in the hostile terms of the dominant group.

The root idea here is not just that certain groups are forced to survive in an atmosphere in which they are not respected because of their group membership, but rather because they are required to do so in a society that is openly hostile to their very being. The hostility, according to this new account of alienation, causes the victims to become hostile toward themselves. Those who are said to be alienated in this way are thought to be incapable of shaping our common conception of reality and thus they play little, if any, role in their self-construction. The self is imposed upon them by social forces, and what is even more disturbing, no individual self can change the social forces that impose upon members of certain groups their negative and hostile self-conceptions.

Is this new account of alienation just another way of saying that people of color have had their humanity called into question? We might begin to explore this question by examining the claim that having one's humanity recognized and respected means having a say about things that matter in one's life, and having such a say means that one is unalienated. To be more specific, having opinions about things and the ability and freedom to express one's opinions is the mark of the unalienated person. This response is helpful, but it does not fully capture what recent writers have meant by alienation. It assumes that the alienated self is secure, but constrained by external forces that prevent the person from becoming fully actualized: from having one's voice recognized and respected in the moral or political process.

The above account of what it means to recognize and respect a person's humanity fails to fully appreciate that human selves result, at least in part, from social construction. How we define who we are, our interests, and our relationship with others, involves a dynamic process of social interaction. To assume that what recent writers have meant by alienation is the failure by some to be able to express and have their opinions heard misses the mark. This view of things assumes that (1) people are clear about their interests, but have not been allowed to express them and (2) those who have power and privilege will be able to understand and fairly assess claims made by those who lack power and privilege if they were only allowed to express their opinions. Even if (1) and (2) are true, we still have not captured what recent writers have meant by alienation. This account focuses incorrectly on what the self is prevented from doing by forces external to it. However, the new account of alienation primarily concentrates on the fragility and insecurity of the self caused by the way people who are victims view and define themselves. According to this view, even if the external constraints were removed, the self would still be estranged because it has been constructed out of images that are hostile to it.

One might think that these new accounts of alienation are not saying anything new because Americans (including African-Americans) have always believed that people should be free to decide what kind of persons they want to be provided that in doing so they don't violate the rights of others. At least in principle, Americans have endorsed this idea. If this is so, what is new in these recent accounts of alienation? Perhaps we can gain some insight into this question by taking a closer look at the African-American experience.

African-Americans have had a paradoxical existence in the United States. On the one hand, they have rightfully responded negatively to the second-class status that they are forced to endure. While on the other hand, they believe that America should and has the potential to live up to the ideas so eloquently expressed in the Bill of Rights and in Martin Luther King, Jr.'s, "I Have a Dream" speech.[4] It is clear that there was a time when African-Americans were prevented from participating in the electoral process and from having a say in the shaping of basic institutions. Many would argue that there are still barriers that prevent African-Americans from participating in meaningful ways in these areas. If this is so, does this mean that most (many) African-Americans are alienated from themselves and the dominated society?

African-American leaders from the moderate to the militant have emphasized the importance of African-Americans making their own decisions about what is in their interests.[5] The right to self-determination has been seen as a crucial weapon in the battle against the evils of racial discrimination. These thinkers have also recognized that one must have an adequate understanding of one's predicament if one is to devise an effective strategy for overcoming the material and psychological consequences of racial injustice. Insight into the African-

American experience has come from a variety of sources. Some of these insights have been offered by social and political theorists, while others have been advanced by people in literature and the arts.

Ralph Ellison, in his brilliant novel, *The Invisible Man*, describes what he takes to be a consuming evil of racial discrimination.[6] According to Ellison, African-Americans are not visible to the white world. They are caricatures and stereotypes, but not real human beings with complex and varied lives. In very graphic terms, Ellison reveals what it is like to be black in a world where black skin signifies what is base and superficial. Ellison skillfully describes how blacks are perceived by white society, but he also tells us a great deal about how blacks perceive themselves. It is clear that African-Americans have struggled to construct an image of themselves different from the ones perpetrated by a racist society, but this is not an easy thing to do. W. E. B. DuBois spoke to the struggle and dilemma that confronts African-Americans when he identified what he calls "the problem of double consciousness." In *The Souls of Black Folk* he writes:

> It is a peculiar sensation, this double-consciousness, this sense of always looking at one's self through the eyes of others, of measuring one's soul by the tape of a world that looks on in amused contempt and pity. One ever feels his twoness—an American, a Negro; two warring ideals in one dark body, whose dogged strength alone keeps it from being torn asunder.[7]

DuBois is pointing to what he takes to be the mistaken belief held by many blacks and whites, namely that a person cannot be both black and an American. According to DuBois, for far too many people this was a contradiction in terms. DuBois strongly disagreed and spent a great deal of his energy arguing against this conclusion. But why this false view was held by so many people can be traced to an inadequate conception of what it means to be "black" and what it means to be "American." According to DuBois, race and class exploitation contributed greatly to these false conceptions. For DuBois, it was no surprise that African-Americans had such a difficult time identifying their true interests.

THE LIBERAL RESPONSE

Liberal political theorists rarely discuss alienation. This is in large part because alienation is seen as something that comes from within. For them alienation often is the result of injustice, but even so, it is something that can be overcome if only the individual would stand up for her rights. Liberals may realize that this might come at some serious personal cost to the individual, but they believe that the individual can and should bear these costs if they are to remain autonomous unalienated beings. For example, liberals often sympathize with white, highly educated, wealthy women who live alienated lives, but they believe that it is within the power of these women to end their estrangement or alienation even though it may be extremely difficult for them to do so. The critics of the liberal account of women's oppression have argued that liberals fail to see that capitalism and the negative stereotyping of women causes even educated and economically secure women to be at the mercy of sexist practices and traditions.

The critics of liberalism have also argued that liberalism places too much emphasis upon individuality and thus the theory fails to recognize how our conceptions of who we are and what we see as valuable are tied to our social relations. They insist that we are not alone in shaping who we are and in defining our possibilities. Society, according to these critics, plays a more extensive role than liberals are willing to admit.

Although liberals have recognized the alienation that people experience in modern society, their individual rights framework has not readily lent itself to an in-depth analysis of this phenomenon. However, I disagree with the critics of liberalism when they contend that the individual rights framework is inadequate to describe the nature of alienation. I shall attempt to show that liberals can describe the nature of alienation in capitalist society even though the theory is inadequate when it comes to addressing what the liberals must admit to be a violation of important rights.

Liberal theorists might characterize this new form of alienation in terms of a denial of the rights to such things as autonomy and self-determination and these denials rob persons of their freedom. Alienation on their accounts is just another way of saying that people are unfree and further that they don't appreciate that this is so. But if the liberal response is to be helpful, we need to know more precisely in what sense alienation is a denial of important rights, for example, the right to be free.

In what sense is the alienated person unfree? Can a person be alienated even if they have basic constitutional rights, material success, and a job that calls upon her abilities and talents in interesting ways? Some theorists think so. If alienation is a lack of freedom as the liberal theory suggests, in what sense are the people who have constitutional rights and material well-being unfree? The liberal theorist, Joel Feinberg, has discussed the lack of freedom in terms of constraints.[8] If we define alienation as constraint, then the alienated person is unfairly constrained in the ways that he or she can conceive of themselves in a culture that defines them in stereotypical terms. But what are these constraints? To borrow Feinberg's terminology, are these constraints external or internal? According to Feinberg, "external constraints are those that come from outside a person's body-cum-mind, and all other constituents, whether sore muscles, headaches, or refractory 'lower' desires, are internal to him."[9]

If we employ the language of constraints to understand alienation as a kind of unfreedom, should we view this unfreedom in terms of external or internal constraints or both? On a liberal reading of DuBois's and Ellison's characterizations of the African-American experience, this experience is characterized by a denial of opportunities because of a morally irrelevant characteristic, a person's race. It is plausible to interpret them in this way because this is clearly one of the consequences of a system of racial discrimination. However, I believe that they had much more in mind. The focus on the denial of opportunities is the standard liberal way of understanding the consequences of racial injustice. This is why you find liberal writers like Feinberg discussing freedom in terms of the absence of constraints and John Rawls concentrating on designing social institutions such that offices and positions are open to all under conditions of self-respect.[10] The focus by liberals has been primarily on what goes on outside of the body-cum-mind.

This is not to say that they completely ignore such psychological harms as self-doubt and a lack of self-respect that can result from injustice. In fact, Feinberg notes that things like sickness can create internal constraints which serve to limit a person's freedom.[11] Rawls, as well, appreciates the impact that injustice can have on a person's psyche. Thus he spends some time expounding on the connection between justice and a healthy self-concept.[12] He argues that in a just society social institutions should not be designed in ways that prevent people from having the social bases for self-respect. So both Feinberg and Rawls recognize that such things as freedom and justice go beyond removing inappropriate external constraints. But nonetheless, I don't think that Feinberg and Rawls can fully capture the insight offered by DuBois and Ellison because their emphasis on the external constraints causes them to underestimate the internal ways that people can be prevented from experiencing freedom.

Since Isaiah Berlin's distinction between positive and negative freedom, liberals have recognized that such things as ignorance and poverty can limit a person's freedom.[13] Recognition of the limitations caused by internal constraints has led some liberals to argue that a society can not be just if it does not address internal constraints on people's freedom. Such liberals would be open to the idea that an examination of the African-American experience would reveal the obvious and subtle ways that a lack of education and material well-being can lead to a sense of estrangement, a lack of self-respect. They would argue that this is true even when formal equality of opportunity can be said to exist. On their view, the real problem is not having laws that guarantee equality under the law, but finding ways to make real these guarantees. For them it is not so much how African-Americans are viewed by the rest of society, but rather that they should be treated in ways that make it possible for them to act and choose as free persons. According to this view, even if people are hated by the rest of the community provided that they are guaranteed equal protection under the law and steps are taken to ensure real equality of opportunity then things are just. These liberals insist that there is a large area of human affairs that should escape government scrutiny. In these areas, people should be able to pursue their own conceptions of the good provided that they don't cause direct harm to others. I should add that these liberals also believe that those who fail to provide such necessities as food and education to those who are in need of them cause direct harm by failing to do so.

However, some communitarian critics of liberalism have argued that this way of understanding the requirements of justice underestimates the importance of how we form a healthy self-concept in a community.[14] They emphasize the importance of being seen and treated as a full member of society as opposed to a person who must be tolerated. They question the wisdom and usefulness of attempting to find impartial norms that will guarantee each person the right to pursue his own unique conception of the good constrained by an account of the right defined by impartial reasoning. This concern has lead some communitarians to reject the search for impartial ideals of justice in favor of a method of forging a consensus about justice through a process of democratically working across differences through open dialogue. According to this view, we will not be able to put aside our partialities, but we can confront them through discourse.

Communitarians would contend that African-Americans or any minority group that has been despised and subjugated will feel estranged from the dominated society if they are merely tolerated and not accepted and valued for their contributions. They believe that the liberalism of Feinberg, Rawls, and Nozick can at best produce toleration, but not acceptance. But this view, of course, assumes that we can identify some common goods (ends) to serve as the foundation for our theory of justice. This is something that liberals who give priority to the right over the good deny.

The communitarians, whether they realize it or not, have pointed to a persistent problem for African-Americans. The problem of recognition. How do African-Americans become visible in a society that refuses to see them other than through stereotypical images? One need only turn to the history of black social and political thought to see that African-Americans have wrestled with the question of what the appropriate means are for obtaining recognition and respect for a people who were enslaved and then treated as second-class citizens. Some argued that emigration was the only answer, while others maintained that less radical forms of separation from white society would do. On the other side, others contend that blacks could obtain recognition only if they assimilated or fully integrated into white society.[15] Neither of these approaches so far have been fully tested, so it is hard to say whether either approach can adequately address the problem of the lack of recognition for blacks in a white racist society.

The new alienation theorists believe that liberals cannot adequately describe or eliminate the kind of estrangement experienced by African-Americans and other oppressed racial groups. Is this so? Yes and no. I shall argue that liberals can describe the experience of estrangement using the vocabulary of rights and opportunities, but I don't think that they can eliminate this experience and stay faithful to their liberal methodology.

Typically when we think of a person being denied rights or opportunities we think of rather specific individuals and specific actions which serve as the causes of these denials. For example, we might think of a specific employer refusing to hire a person because he or she is black. The black person in this case is denied job-related rights and opportunities by a specific person. But even if we changed our example to involve groups rather than individuals, the new alienation theorists would maintain the experience of estrangement that they describe goes beyond such a description. According to their account, African-Americans who have their rights respected and don't suffer from material scarcity still are estranged in a way that their white counterparts are not.

Are these theorists correct or do prosperous and highly regarded middle-class and wealthy African-Americans serve as counterexamples to the above claim? Don't such persons enjoy their rights and opportunities? If not, what rights and opportunities are they being denied? I believe that rights and opportunities are being denied, but it is more difficult to see what they are in such cases. I think that liberals can contend that middle-class and wealthy African-Americans are still alienated because they are denied their right to equal concern and respect in a white racist society. Even though they may be able to vote, to live in the neighborhood of their choice, and to send their children to good schools, they are still perceived as less worthy because of their race. The dominant attitude in their society is that they are less worthy than whites. The pervasive attitude is not benign. It acts as an affront to the self-concept of African-Americans and it causes them to expend energy that they could expend in more constructive ways. The philosopher, Laurence Thomas, graphically describes this experience in a letter to the *New York Times*.[16] For example, African-Americans are too aware of the harm caused by being perceived by the typical white as thieves no matter what their economic and social standing might be. African-Americans because of the dominant negative attitudes against them as a group are denied equal concern and respect.

It is difficult to see that this attitude of disrespect is a denial of rights because we most often associate political rights with actions and not with attitudes. In fact, it sounds awkward to say that I have a right that you not have a certain attitude towards me. This statement seems to strike against the very heart of liberalism. However in reality it does not. Liberals can and do say that human beings should be accorded such things as dignity and respect, and they believe that this entails taking a certain attitude or disposition towards others as well as acting or refraining from acting in particular ways. So, it is not that they cannot account for the particular estrangement that blacks experience because of the attitude of disrespect generated by the dominant society, but they don't seem to have the theoretical wherewithal to resolve the problem.

Since liberals assign great weight to individual liberty, they are reluctant to interfere with actions that cause indirect harm. So even though they recognize that living in a society that has an attitude of disrespect towards African-Americans can constitute a harm, and a harm caused by others, they are reluctant to interfere with people's private lives in order to eliminate these harms.

How can liberals change white attitudes in a way that is consistent with their theory? They could mount an educational program to combat false or racist beliefs. Liberals have tried this, but given their strong commitment to things like freedom of thought and expression, and the fact that power and privilege is attached to seeing nonwhites as less worthy, educational programs have only had modest success in changing white attitudes. Critics of such educational programs argue that these programs can never succeed until racism is seen as unprofitable.

Let us assume that the critics are correct. Can liberals make racism unprofitable and respect individual liberty, one of the cornerstones of their theory? There are two basic approaches available to liberals: they can place sanctions on all harmful racist attitudes or provide people with incentives to change their racist attitudes. But in a democracy, the will of the majority is to prevail. If the attitude of disrespect towards African-Americans is as pervasive as the new alienation theorists suggest, then it is doubtful there will be the general will to seriously take either of the approaches. I don't think that liberals can eliminate harmful racist attitudes without adopting means that would be judged by the white majority as unjustified coercion. However, they can adequately describe the alienation that African-Americans experience, even if they cannot eliminate it.

THE MARXIST ACCOUNT

The Marxist explanation of the African-American condition assumes that the problems experienced by this group can be traced to their class position. Capitalism is seen as the cause of such things as black alienation. For the Marxist, a class analysis of American society and its problems provides both a necessary and sufficient understanding of these things. According to the Marxist, alienation be it black or white is grounded in the labor process. Alienated labor, in all of its forms, is based in private property and the division of labor. On their account, if we eliminate a system of private property and the division of labor into classes, we will eliminate those things that make alienated relations possible.

The Marxist does recognize that political and ideological relations can and do formulate in capitalist societies, and that these relations do appear to have the autonomy and power to shape our thinking and cause certain behaviors. But, for the Marxist, these relations only appear to be fundamental when in reality they are not. They can always be reduced or explained by reference to a particular mode of production. Racism is ideological; an idea that dominates across class lines. However class divisions explain racial antagonisms, it is not the other way around.[17] But Marxists don't stop here. They also contend that in order to eliminate racism, we must eliminate class divisions, where class is defined in terms of one's relationship to the means of production.

Classical Marxists would oppose the new account of alienation advanced by recent theorists. The classical Marxists would insist that all forms of alienation no matter how debilitating or destructive can be explained in terms of the mode of production in which people are required to satisfy their needs. For them, it is not a matter of changing the way blacks and whites think about each other or the way blacks think of themselves, because ideas don't change our material reality, relationships with others, or our self-conceptions. Our material conditions (mode of production) shape our ideas and our behavior.

On this account, African-Americans are estranged from themselves because of their laboring activity or lack of it. They view themselves in hostile terms because they are defined by a mode of production that stultifies their truly human capacities and reduces them to human tools to be used by those who have power and influence. This all sounds good, but many black theorists (liberal and progressive) have been skeptical of this account of the causes and remedy for black alienation and oppression. They argue that the condition of black workers and white workers are different and that this difference is not merely a difference in terms of things like income and social and political status or class position. The difference cuts much deeper. In a white racist society, blacks (workers and capitalists) are caused to have a hostile attitude towards their very being that is not found in whites. The new alienation theorists contend that the classical Marxist explanation of African-American alienation is too limiting. It fails to recognize that alienation occurs in relationships apart from the labor process. W. E. B. DuBois, although a dedicated Marxist, claimed that the major problem of the twentieth century was race and not class. Some theorists have contended that Marxists are too quick in dismissing the significance of race consciousness.[18] I think the facts support their conclusion. In the next section, I will focus directly on this issue of African-American alienation.

AFRICAN-AMERICANS AND ALIENATION

I believe that the atmosphere of hostility created against African-Americans by our white racist society does amount to a serious assault on the material and psychological well-being of its African-American victims. I also believe that this assault can, and in some cases does, lead to the types of alienation discussed above. However, I disagree with those who conclude that most or all African-Americans suffer from a debilitating form of alienation that causes them to be estranged and divided in the ways described in the new account of alienation. I also reject the implication that most or all African-Americans are powerless, as individuals, to change their condition. The implication is that group action as opposed to individual effort is required to combat this form of alienation. There is also the implication that revolution and not reform is required in order to eliminate this form of alienation.

I don't wish to be misunderstood here. It is not my contention that capitalism is superior to socialism, but only that it is possible for African-Americans to combat or overcome this form of alienation described by recent writers without overthrowing capitalism.

Are African-Americans, as a group, alienated or estranged from themselves? I don't think so. Clearly there are some African-Americans who have experienced such alienation, but I don't think this characterizes the group as a whole. African-Americans do suffer because of a lack of recognition in American society, but a lack of recognition does not always lead to alienation. Even though African-Americans have experienced hostility, racial discrimination, and poverty, they still have been able to construct and draw upon institutions like the family, church, and black community to foster and maintain a healthy sense of self in spite of the obstacles that they have faced.

Although African-Americans have been the victims of a vicious assault on their humanity and respect, they have been able to form their own supportive communities in the midst of a hostile environment. During the long period of slavery in this country, African-Americans were clearly the victims of an extremely hostile environment. If there ever was a time a group could be said to be the victims of the assault caused by white racism, slavery was such a time. Slaves were denied the most basic rights because they were defined and treated as chattel. Some scholars, like Stanley Elkins, have argued that slavery did cause African-Americans as a group to become less than healthy human beings.[19] On the other hand, there are a group of scholars who argue that slaves and their descendants were able to maintain healthy self-concepts through acts of resistance and communal nourishment.[20] I tend to side with this latter group of scholars.

What is crucial for the truth of their position is the belief that supportive communities can form within a larger hostile environment that can serve to brunt the assault of a hostile racist social order. This, of course, is not to say that these communities provide their members with all that is necessary for them to flourish under conditions of justice, but only that they provide enough support to create the space necessary for them to avoid the deeply divided and estranged selves described in some recent work on alienation.

The history and literature of African-Americans is rich with examples of how communities have formed to provide the social and moral basis for African-Americans to have self-respect even though they were in the midst of a society that devalued their worth. Once again, I think it bears repeating. I don't deny that a hostile racist society creates the kind of assault that can lead to alienation, but only that this assault can be and has been softened by supportive African-American communities.

The sociologist, Orlando Patterson, disagrees. Patterson has argued that African-Americans are alienated because slavery cut them off from their African culture and heritage and denied them real participation in American culture and heritage. He characterizes this phenomenon as "natal alienation."[21] African-Americans, on Patterson's account, feel estranged because they don't believe that they belong. They are not Africans, but they also are not Americans. One might argue that the present move from "black American" to "African-American" is an attempt to address the phenomenon of natal alienation. According to Patterson, the past provides us with crucial insight into the present psyches of African-Americans. On his view, slavery is a powerful tool that helps to explain the present condition and behavior of African-Americans, including the present underclass phenomenon.[22]

I disagree with Patterson's conclusions. He falls prey to the same shortcoming that plagues the liberal and the Marxist accounts of the African-American experience. They all fail to appreciate the role of ethnic communities in the lives of individuals and groups. Although DuBois never played down the horrors and harms of racism, he refused to see the masses of black people as a people who were estranged or alienated from themselves. In fact, in his *Souls of Black Folk*, DuBois describes how black people have been able to draw strength from each other as members of a community with shared traditions, values, and impulses.[23] Being anchored in a community allows people to address and not just cope with things like oppression and racism.

The work of the historian John Blassingame can also be used to call into question Patterson's natal alienation thesis and it also provides some support for the importance of community in the lives of African-Americans. Blassingame argued that even during the period of antebellum slavery, there was still a slave community that served to allow for a sense of self-worth and social cohesiveness for slaves. In my own examination of slave narratives, first-hand accounts by slaves and former slaves of their slave experiences, I found that all slaves did not suffer from a form of moral and social death.[24] By moral and social death, I mean the inability to choose and act as autonomous moral and social agents. Of course this is not to deny that slavery was a brutal and dehumanizing institution, but rather that slaves developed supportive institutions and defense mechanisms that allowed them to remain moral and social agents.

But what about the presence of today's so-called black underclass? Does this group (which has been defined as a group that is not only poor, poorly educated, and victimized by crime, but also as a group with a breakdown of family and moral values) squarely raise the issue of black alienation or estrangement? Some people think so. They argue that Patterson's natal alienation thesis is extremely informative when comes to understanding this class. Others reject the natal alienation thesis, but remain sympathetic to the idea that where there once was a black community or institutions that served to prevent the erosion of black pride and values, these structures no longer exists to the degree necessary to ward off the harms of racism and oppression.

In *The Truly Disadvantaged*, William J. Wilson argues that large urban African-American communities are lacking in the material and human resources to deal with the problems brought on by structural changes and the flight of the middle class.[25] According to Wilson, these communities, unlike communities in the past, lack the wherewithal to overcome problems that are present to an extent in other poor communities. If Wilson is correct, there may not be the resources in present-day African-American communities to ward off the assault of a hostile racist society. I am not totally convinced by Wilson's argument, but I think his work and the work of the supporters of the new account of alienation make it clear that there needs to be further work which compares African-American communities before the development of the so-called "black underclass" with urban African-American communities today.

At this juncture, I wish to distinguish my claim that supportive African-American communities have helped to combat the effects of a racist society from the claims of neo-black conservatives like Shelby Steele. In *The Content of our Character*,[26] Steele argues that African-Americans must confront and prosper in spite of racism. Steele's recommendations have a strong individualist tone. He argues, like Booker T. Washington, that racism does exist but that African-Americans who are prudent must recognize that if they are to progress, they must prosper in spite of it. In fact, Steele even makes a stronger claim. He argues that African-Americans have become accustomed to a "victims status" and use racism as an excuse for failing to succeed even when opportunities do exist.

I reject Steele's conclusions. First, I don't think that individual blacks acting alone can overcome racism. Individual blacks who succeed in this country do so because of the struggles and sacrifices of others, and these others always extend beyond family members and friends. Next, I reject Steele's claim that the lack of progress by disadvantaged African-Americans is due in any significant way to their perception of themselves as helpless victims. Such a claim depends upon a failure to appreciate the serious obstacles that African-Americans encounter because of their race. Even if it is true that African-American advancement is contingent on African-Americans helping themselves, it does not follow that African-Americans should be criticized for failing to adopt dehumanizing means because they are necessary for their economic advancement.

African-Americans should not be viewed as inferior to other groups, but they should also not be seen as superior. Racial injustice negatively impacts the motivational levels of all people. African-Americans are not the exception. Steele makes it seem as if poor and uneducated African-Americans lack the appropriate values to succeed. He contends that the opportunities exist, but that too many African-Americans fail to take advantage of them because they cannot break out of the victim mentality. I reject this line of reasoning. As I have argued elsewhere,[27] this way of thinking erroroneously assumes that most disadvantages result from a lack of motivation. When in reality it would take exceptional motivational levels to overcome the injustices that African-Americans experience. Because some African-Americans can rise to these levels, it would be unreasonable to think that all could. Steele underestimates the work that must be done to provide real opportunities to members of the so-called black underclass who struggle with racism on a daily basis.

I would like to forestall any misunderstandings about my emphasis on the role that supportive communities play in the lives of oppressed groups. I am not maintaining that African-Americans don't experience alienation because they are able to draw strength from supportive communities. My point is that supportive communities can, in some cases, minimize the damaging effects caused by a racist society. Nor is it my contention to deny that African-Americans and other groups must constantly struggle to maintain a healthy sense of self in a hostile society that causes them to experience self-doubt and a range of other negative states.

Notes

1. Liberal thinkers tend to argue that alienation results when human beings can no longer see themselves as being in control or comfortable in their social environment, and they contend that this discomfort occurs when crucial rights are violated, e.g., the right to autonomy. In an interesting twist on the liberal position, Bruce A. Ackerman, *Social Justice and the Liberal State* (New Haven, Conn.: Yale University Press, 1980), esp. 346–47, argues that the right to mutual dialogue is necessary to protect the autonomy of individuals in a community.
2. See, e.g., Jon Elster, *Karl Marx: A Reader* (Cambridge: Cambridge University Press, 1986), chap. 2; Bertell Ollman, *Alienation* (Cambridge: Cambridge University Press, 1976), part 3; and Robert C. Tucker, ed., *The Marx-Engels Reader* (New York: W. W. Norton and Co., 1978), 73–75, 77–78, 252–56, 292–93.
3. See Frantz Fanon, *Black Skin / White Masks* (New York: Grove Press, 1967), chap. 1; June Jordan, "Report from the Bahamas," in *On Call* (Boston: South End Press, 1985), 39–50.
4. A famous speech delivered by Martin L. King, Jr., at the March on Washington, D.C., August 1963.
5. See Howard Brotz, ed. *Negro Social and Political Thought 1850–1920* (New York: Basic Books, 1966).
6. Ralph Ellison, *The Invisible Man* (New York: New American Library, 1953).
7. W. E. B. DuBois, *The Souls of Black Folk* (New York: New American Library, 1969), 45.
8. Joel Feinberg, *Social Philosophy* (Englewood Cliffs, N. J.: Prentice-Hall, Inc., 1973), chap. 1.

9. Feinberg, *Social Philosophy*, 13.
10. John Rawls, *A Theory of Justice* (Cambridge: Harvard University Press, 1971), section 67.
11. Feinberg, 1969, p. 13.
12. John Rawls, *A Theory of Justice*, 440–46.
13. Isaiah Berlin, *Two Concepts of Liberty* (Oxford: Clarendon Press, 1961).
14. See Alasdair MacIntyre, *After Virtue* (Notre Dame: Notre Dame University Press, 1981), chap. 17; and Michael Sandel, *Liberalism and the Limits of Justice* (Cambridge: Cambridge University Press, 1982), 59–65, 173–75.
15. Howard McGary, Jr., "Racial Integration and Racial Separatism: Conceptual Clarifications," in *Philosophy Born of Struggle*, ed. Leonard Harris (Dubuque, Iowa: Kendall/Hunt Publishing Co., 1983), 199–211.
16. Laurence Thomas, *New York Times*, op-ed, August 13, 1990.
17. See Bernard Boxill, "The Race-Class Question," in Harris, *Philosophy Born of Struggle*, 107–16.
18. See, e.g., Howard McGary, Jr., "The Nature of Race and Class Exploitation," in *Exploitation and Exclusion*, ed. A. Zegeye, L. Harris and J. Maxted (London: Hans Zell Publishers, 1991), 14–27; and Richard Schmitt, "A New Hypothesis about the Relations of Class, Race and Gender: Capitalism as a Dependent System," *Social Theory and Practice* 14, no. 3 (1988): 345–65.
19. Stanley Elkins, *Slavery: A Problem in American Institutional and Intellectual Life* (Chicago: University of Chicago Press, 1976).
20. John Blassingame, *The Slave Community: Plantation Life in the Antebellum South* (New York: Oxford University Press, 1972), esp. 200–216.
21. Orlando Patterson, *Slavery and Social Death* (Cambridge: Harvard University Press, 1982).
22. Orlando Patterson, "Towards a Future That Has No Past: Reflections on the Fate of Blacks in America," *The Public Interest* 27 (1972).
23. DuBois, *The Souls of Black Folk*.
24. See Howard McGary and Bill E. Lawson, *Between Slavery and Freedom: Philosophy and American Slavery* (Bloomington: Indiana University Press, 1992).
25. William J. Wilson, *The Truly Disadvantaged* (Chicago: University of Chicago Press, 1987).
26. Shelby Steele, *The Content of Our Characters: A New Vision of Race in America* (New York: St. Martin's Press, 1990), esp. chaps. 3 and 4.
27. Howard McGary, Jr., "The Black Underclass and the Question of Values," in *The Underclass Question*, ed. William Lawson (Philadelphia: Temple University Press, 1992), 57–70.

Report from the Bahamas

JUNE JORDAN

I AM STAYING IN a hotel that calls itself the Sheraton British Colonial. One of the photographs advertising the place displays a middle-aged Black man in a waiter's tuxedo, smiling. What intrigues me most about the picture is just this: While the Black man bears a tray full of "colorful" drinks above his left shoulder, both of this feet, shoes, and trouser legs, up to ten inches above his ankles, stand in the also "colorful" Caribbean saltwater. He is so delighted to serve you he will wade into the water to bring you Banana Daquiris while you float! More precisely, he will wade into the water, fully clothed, oblivious to the ruin of his shoes, his trousers, his health, and he will do it with a smile.

I am in the Bahamas. On the phone in my room, a spinning complement of plastic pages offers handy index clues such as CAR RENTAL and CASINOS. A message from the Ministry of Tourism appears among these travellers tips. Opening with a paragraph of "WELCOME," the message then proceeds to "A PAGE OF HISTORY," which reads as follows:

> New World History begins on the same day that modern Bahamian history begins—October 12, 1492. That's when Columbus stepped ashore—British influence came first with the Eleutherian Adventurers of 1647—After the Revolutions, American Loyalists fled from the newly independent states and settled in the Bahamas. Confederate blockade-runners used the island as a haven during the War between the States, and after the War, a number of Southerners moved to the Bahamas. . . .

There it is again. Something proclaims itself a legitimate history and all it does is track white Mr. Columbus to the British Eleutherians through the Confederate Southerners as they barge into New World surf, land on New World turf, and nobody saying one world about the Bahamian people, the Black peoples, to whom the only thing new in their island world was this weird succession of crude intruders and its colonial consequences.

This is my consciousness of race as I unpack my bathing suit in the Sheraton British Colonial. Neither this hotel, nor the British, nor the long ago Italians, nor the white Delta airline pilots belong here, of course. And every time I look at the photograph of that fool standing in the water with his shoes on I'm about to have a West Indian fit, even though I know he's no fool; he's a middle-aged Black man who needs a job and this is his job—pretending himself a servile ancillary to the pleasures of the rich. (Compared to his options in life, I am a rich woman. Compared to most of the Black Americans arriving for this Easter weekend on a three nights, four days' deal of bargain rates, the middle-aged waiter is a poor Black man.)

We will jostle along with the other (white) visitors and join them in the tee shirt shops or, laughing together, learn ruthless rules of negotiation as we, Black Americans as well as white, argue down the price of handwoven goods at the nearby straw market while the merchants, frequently toothless Black women seated on the concrete in their only presentable dress, humble themselves to our careless games:

"Yes? You like it? Eight dollar."

"Five."

"I give it to you. Seven."

And so it continues, this weird succession of crude intruders that, now, includes me and my brothers and my sisters from the North.

This is my consciousness of class as I try to decide how much money I can spend on Bahamian gifts for my family back in Brooklyn. No matter that these other Black women incessantly weave words and flowers into the straw hats and bags piled beside them on the burning dusty street. No matter that these other Black women must work their sense of beauty into these things that we will take away as cheaply as we dare, or they will do without food.

We are not white, after all. The budget is limited. And we are harmlessly killing time between the poolside rum punch and "The Native Show on the Patio" that will play tonight outside the hotel restaurant.

This is my consciousness of race and class and gender identity as I notice the fixed relations between these other Black women and myself. They sell and I buy or I don't. They risk not eating. I risk going broke on my first vacation afternoon.

We are not particularly women anymore; we are parties to a transaction designed to set us against each other.

"Olive" is the name of the Black woman who cleans my hotel room. On my way to the beach I am wondering what "Olive" would say if I told her why I chose the Sheraton British Colonial; if I told her I wanted to swim. I wanted to sleep. I did not want to be harassed by the middle-aged waiter, or his nephew. I did not want to be raped by anybody (white or Black) at all and I calculated that my safety as a Black woman alone would best be assured by a multinational hotel

corporation. In my experience, the big guys take customer complaints more seriously than the little ones. I would suppose that's one reason why they're big; they don't like to lose money anymore than I like to be bothered when I'm trying to read a goddamned book underneath a palm tree I paid $264 to get next to. A Black woman seeking refuge in a multinational corporation may seem like a contradiction to some, but there you are. In this case it's a coincidence of entirely different self-interests: Sheraton/cash = June Jordan's short-run safety.

Anyway, I'm pretty sure "Olive" would look at me as though I came from someplace as far away as Brooklyn. Then she'd probably allow herself one indignant query before righteously removing her vacuum cleaner from my room; "and why in the first place you come down you without your husband?"

I cannot imagine how I would begin to answer her.

My "rights" and my "freedom" and my "desire" and a slew of other New World values; what would they sound like to this Black woman described on the card atop my hotel bureau as "Olive the Maid"? "Olive" is older than I am and I may smoke a cigarette while she changes the sheets on my bed. Whose rights? Whose freedom? Whose desire?

And why should she give a shit about mine unless I do something, for real, about hers?

It happens that the book that I finished reading under a palm tree earlier today was the novel *The Bread Givers* by Anzia Yezierska. Definitely autobiographical, Yezierska lays out the difficulties of being both female and "a person" inside a traditional Jewish family at the start of the 20th century. That any Jewish woman became anything more than the abused servant of her father or her husband is really an improbable piece of news. Yet Yezierska managed such an unlikely outcome for her own life. In *The Bread Givers*, the heroine also manages an important, although partial, escape from traditional Jewish female destiny. And in the unpardonable, despotic father, the Talmudic scholar of that Jewish family, did I not see my own and hate him twice, again? When the heroine, the young Jewish child, wanders the streets with a filthy pail she borrows to sell herring in order to raise the ghetto rent and when she cries, "Nothing was before me but the hunger in our house, and no bread for the next meal if I didn't sell the herring. No longer like a fire engine, but like a houseful of hungry mouths my heart cried, 'herring—herring! Two cents apiece!'" who would doubt the ease, the sisterhood of conversation possible between that white girl and the Black women selling straw bags on the streets of paradise because they do not want to die? And is it not obvious that the wife of that Talmudic scholar and "Olive," who cleans my room here at the hotel, have more in common than I can claim with either one of them?

This is my consciousness of race and class and gender identity as I collect wet towels, sunglasses, wristwatch, and head towards a shower.

I am thinking about the boy who loaned this novel to me. He's white and he's

Jewish and he's pursuing an independent study project with me, at the State University where I teach whether or not I feel like it, where I teach without stint because, like the waiter, I am no fool. It's my job and either I work or I do without everything you need money to buy. The boy loaned me the novel because he thought I'd be interested to know how a Jewish-American writer used English so that the syntax, and therefore the cultural habits of mind expressed by the Yiddish language, could survive translation. He did this because he wanted to create another connection between us on the basis of language, between his knowledge/his love of Yiddish and my knowledge/my love of Black English.

He has been right about the forceful survival of the Yiddish. And I had become excited by this further evidence of the written voice of spoken language protected from the monodrone of "standard" English, and so we had grown closer on this account. But then our talk shifted to student affairs more generally, and I had learned that this student does not care one way or the other about currently jeopardized Federal Student Loan Programs because, as he explained it to me, they do not affect him. He does not need financial help outside his family. My own son, however, is Black. And I am the only family help available to him and that means, if Reagan succeeds in eliminating federal programs to aid minority students, he will have to forget about furthering his studies, or he or I or both of us will have to hit the numbers pretty big. For these reasons of difference, the student and I had moved away from each other, even while we continued to talk.

My consciousness turned to race, again, and class.

Sitting in the same chair as the boy, several weeks ago, a graduate student came to discuss her grade. I praised the excellence of her final paper; indeed it had seemed to me an extraordinary pulling together of recent left-brain/right-brain research with the themes of transcendental poetry.

She told me that, for her part, she'd completed her reading of my political essays. "You are so lucky!" she exclaimed.

"What do you mean by that?"

"You have a cause. You have a purpose to your life."

I looked carefully at this white woman; what was she really saying to me?

"What do you mean?" I repeated.

"Poverty. Police violence. Discrimination in general."

(Jesus Christ, I thought, is that her idea of lucky?)

"And how about you?" I asked.

"Me?"

"Yeah, you. Don't you have a cause?"

"Me? I'm just a middle-aged woman: a housewife and a mother. I'm nobody."

For a while, I made no response.

First of all, speaking of race and class and gender in one breath, what she said meant that those lucky preoccupations of mine, from police violence to nuclear wipeout, were not shared. They were mine and not hers. But here she sat, friendly as an old stuffed animal, beaming good will or more "luck" in my direction.

In the second place, what this white woman said to me meant that she did not believe she was "a person" precisely because she had fulfilled the traditional female functions revered by the father of that Jewish immigrant, Anzia Yezierska. And the woman in front of me was not a Jew. That was not the connection. The link was strictly female. Nevertheless, how should that woman and I, another female, connect beyond this bizarre exchange?

If she believed me lucky to have regular hurdles of discrimination then why shouldn't I insist that she's lucky to be a middle-class white Wasp female who lives in such well-sanctioned and normative comfort that she even has the luxury to deny the power of the privileges that paralyze her life?

If she deserts me and "my cause" where we differ, if, for example, she abandons me to "my" problems of race, then why should I support her in "her" problems of housewifely oblivion?

Recollection of this peculiar moment brings me to the shower in the bathroom cleaned by "Olive." She reminds me of the usual Women's Studies curriculum because it has nothing to do with her or her job: you won't find "Olive" listed anywhere on the reading list. You will likewise seldom hear of Anzia Yezierska. But yes, you will find, from Florence Nightingale to Adrienne Rich, a white procession of independently well-to-do women writers. (Gertrude Stein / Virginia Woolf / Hilda Doolittle are standard names among the "essential" women writers).

In other words, most of the women of the world—Black and First World and white who work because we must—most of the women of the world persist far from the heart of the usual Women's Studies syllabus.

Similarly, the typical Black History course will slide by the majority experience it pretends to represent. For example, Mary McLeod Bethune will scarcely receive as much attention as Nat Turner, even though Black women who bravely and efficiently provided for the education of Black people hugely outnumbered those few Black men who led successful or doomed rebellions against slavery. In fact, Mary McLeod Bethune may not receive even honorable mention because Black History too often apes those ridiculous white history courses which produce such dangerous gibberish as the Sheraton British Colonial "history" of the Bahamas. Both Black and white history courses exclude from their central consideration those people who neither killed nor conquered anyone as the means to new identity, those people who took care of every one of the people who wanted to become "a person," those people who still take care of the life at issue: the ones who wash and who feed and who teach and who diligently decorate straw hats and bags with all of their historically unrequired gentle love: the women.

> Oh the old rugged cross
> on a hill far away
> Well I cherish the old rugged cross.

It's Good Friday in the Bahamas. Seventy-eight degrees in the shade. Except for Sheraton territory, everything's closed.

It so happens that for truly secular reasons I've been fasting for three days. My hunger has now reached nearly violent proportions. In the hotel sandwich shop, the Black woman handling the counter complains about the tourists; why isn't the shop closed and why don't the tourists stop eating for once in their lives. I'm famished and I order chicken salad and cottage cheese and lettuce and tomato and a hard-boiled egg and a hot cross bun and apple juice.

She eyes me with disgust.

To be sure, the timing of my stomach offends her serious religious practices. Neither one of us apologizes to the other. She seasons the chicken salad to the peppery max while I listen to the loud radio gospel she plays to console herself. It's a country Black version of "The Old Rugged Cross."

As I heave much chicken into my mouth tears start. It's not the pepper. I am, after all, a West Indian daughter. It's the Good Friday music that dominates the humid atmosphere.

> Well I cherish the old rugged cross

And I am back, faster than a 747, in Brooklyn, in the home of my parents where we are wondering, as we do every year, if the sky will darken until Christ has been buried in the tomb. The sky should darken if God is in His heavens. And then, around 3 P.M., at the conclusion of our mournful church service at the neighborhood St. Phillips, and even while we dumbly stare at the black cloth covering the gold altar and the slender unlit candles, the sun should return through the high gothic windows and vindicate our waiting faith that the Lord will rise again, on Easter.

How I used to bow my head at the very name of Jesus: ecstatic to abase myself in deference to His majesty.

My mouth is full of salad. I can't seem to eat quickly enough. I can't think how I should lessen the offense of my appetite. The other Black woman on the premises, the one who disapprovingly prepared this very tasty break from my fast, makes no remark. She is no fool. This is a job that she needs. I suppose she notices that at least I included a hot cross bun among my edibles. That's something in my favor. I decide that's enough.

I am suddenly eager to walk off the food. Up a fairly steep hill I walk without hurrying. Through the pastel desolation of the little town, the road brings me to a confectionary pink and white plantation house. At the gates, an unnecessarily large statue of Christopher Columbus faces me down, or tries to. His hand is fisted to one hip. I look back at him, laugh without deference, and turn left.

It's time to pack it up. Catch my plane. I scan the hotel room for things not to forget. There's that white report card on the bureau.

"Dear Guests:" it says, under the name "Olive." "I am your maid for the day. Please rate me: Excellent. Good. Average. Poor. Thank you."

I tuck this momento from the Sheraton British Colonial into my notebook. How would "Olive" rate *me*? What would it mean for us to seem "good" to each other? What would that rating require?

But I am hastening to leave. Neither turtle soup nor kidney pie nor any conch shell delight shall delay my departure. I have rested, here, in the Bahamas, and I'm ready to return to my usual job, my usual work. But the skin on my body has changed and so has my mind. On the Delta flight home I realize I am burning up, indeed.

So far as I can see, the usual race and class concepts of connection, or gender assumptions of unity, do not apply very well. I doubt that they ever did. Otherwise why would Black folks forever bemoan our lack of solidarity when the deal turns real. And if unity on the basis of sexual oppression is something natural, then why do we women, the majority of people on the planet, still have a problem?

The plane's ready for takeoff. I fasten my seatbelt and let the tumult inside my head run free. Yes: race and class and gender remain as real as the weather. But what they must mean about the contact between two individuals is less obvious and, like the weather, not predictable.

And when these factors of race and class and gender absolutely collapse is whenever you try to use them as automatic concepts of connection. They may serve well as indicators of commonly felt conflict, but as elements of connection they seem about as reliable as precipitation probability for the day after the night before the day.

It occurs to me that much organizational grief could be avoided if people understood that partnership in misery does not necessarily provide for partnership for change: *When we get the monsters off our backs all of us may want to run in very different directions.*

And not only that: even though both "Olive" and "I" live inside a conflict neither one of us created, and even though both of us therefore hurt inside that conflict, I may be one of the monster she needs to eliminate from her universe and, in a sense, she may be one of the monsters in mine.

I am reaching for the words to describe the difference between a common identity that has been imposed and the individual identity any one of us will choose, once she gains that chance.

That difference is the one that keeps us stupid in the face of new, specific information about somebody else with whom we are supposed to have a connection because a third party, hostile to both of us, has worked it so that the two of us, like it or not, share a common enemy. *What happens beyond the idea of that enemy and beyond the consequences of that enemy?*

I am saying that the ultimate connection cannot be the enemy. The ultimate connection must be the need that we find between us. It is not only who you are, in other words, but what we can do for each other that will determine the connection.

I am flying back to my job. I have been teaching contemporary women's poetry this semester. One quandary I have set myself to explore with my students is the one of taking responsibility without power. We had been wrestling ideas to the floor for several sessions when a young Black woman, a South African, asked me for help, after class.

Sokutu told me she was "in a trance" and that she'd been unable to eat for two weeks.

"What's going on?" I asked her, even as my eyes startled at her trembling and emaciated appearance.

"My husband. He drinks all the time. He beats me up. I go to the hospital. I can't eat. I don't know what / anything."

In my office, she described her situation. I did not dare to let her sense my fear and horror. She was dragging about, hour by hour, in dread. Her husband, a young Black South African, was drinking himself into more and more deadly violence against her.

Sokutu told me how she could keep nothing down. She weighed ninety pounds at the outside, as she spoke to me. She'd already been hospitalized as a result of her husband's battering rage.

I knew both of them because I had organized a campus group to aid the liberation struggles of Southern Africa.

Nausea rose in my throat. What about this presumable connection: this husband and this wife fled from that homeland of hatred against them, and now what? He was destroying himself. If not stopped, he would certainly murder his wife.

She needed a doctor, right away. It was a medical emergency. She needed protection. It was a security crisis. She needed refuge for battered wives and personal therapy and legal counsel. She needed a friend.

I got on the phone and called every number in the campus directory that I could imagine might prove helpful. Nothing worked. There were no institutional resources designed to meet her enormous, multifaceted, and ordinary woman's need.

I called various students. I asked the chairperson of the English Department for advice. I asked everyone for help.

Finally, another one of my students, Cathy, a young Irish woman active in campus IRA activities, responded. She asked for further details. I gave them to her.

"Her husband," Cathy told me, "is an alcoholic. You have to understand about alcoholics. It's not the same as anything else. And it's a disease you can't treat any old way."

I listened, fearfully. Did this mean there was nothing we could do?

"That's not what I'm saying," she said. "But you have to keep the alcoholic part of the thing central in everybody's mind, otherwise her husband will kill her. Or he'll kill himself."

She spoke calmly; I felt there was nothing to do but to assume she knew what she was talking about.

"Will you come with me?" I asked her, after a silence. "Will you come with me and help us figure out what to do next?"

Cathy said she would but that she felt shy: Sokutu had come from South Africa. What would she think about Cathy?

"I don't know," I said. "But let's go."

We left to find a dormitory room for the young battered wife.

It was late, now, and dark outside.

On Cathy's VW that I followed behind with my own car was the sticker that reads BOBBY SANDS FREE AT LAST. My eyes blurred as I read and reread the words. This was another connection: Bobby Sands and Martin Luther King, Jr., and who would believe it? I would not have believed it; I grew up terrorized by Irish kids who introduced me to the word "nigga."

And here I was following an Irish woman to the room of a Black South African. We were going to that room to try to save a life together.

When we reached the little room, we found ourselves awkward and large. Sokutu attempted to treat us with utmost courtesy, as though we were honored guests. She seemed surprised by Cathy, but mostly Sokutu was flushed with relief and joy because we were there, with her.

I did not know how we should ever terminate her heartfelt courtesies and address, directly, the reason for our visit: her starvation and her extreme physical danger.

Finally, Cathy sat on the floor and reached out her hands to Sokutu.

"I'm here," she said quietly, "Because June has told me what has happened to you. And I know what it is. Your husband is an alcoholic. He has a disease. I know what it is. My father was an alcoholic. He killed himself. He almost killed my mother. I want to be your friend."

"Oh," was the only small sound that escaped from Sokutu's mouth. And then she embraced the other student. And then everything changed and I watched all of this happen so I know that this happened: this connection.

And after we called the police and exchanged phone numbers and plans were made for the night and for the next morning, the young South African woman walked down the dormitory hallway, saying goodbye and saying thank you to us.

I walked behind them, the young Irish woman and the young South African, and I saw them walking as sisters walk, hugging each other, and whispering and sure of each other and I felt how it was not who they were but what they both know and what they were both preparing to do about what they know that was going to make them both free at last.

And I look out the windows of the plane and I see clouds that will not kill me and I know that someday soon other clouds may erupt to kill us all.

And I tell the stewardess No thanks to the cocktails she offers me. But I look about the cabin at the hundred strangers drinking as they fly and I think even here and even now I must make the connection real between me and these strangers everywhere before those other clouds unify this ragged bunch of us, too late.

PART IV

Disability

MANY MEMBERS OF ALIENATED groups are prevented from participating fully in the society. Some have learned the lessons of the wider society too well and come to agree with the social estimation of their group, and thus to have a degree of self-hatred. Unique in this respect is the group to which we now turn. The self-hatred of people with physical disabilities may in some ways be the most severe and insidious of all. Irving Kenneth Zola, the author of the two pieces in this section, is a professor of sociology at Brandeis University and a well-known authority on medical sociology. He contracted polio when young and now walks with braces and canes.

Zola points out that for most alienated groups, the dominant culture has at least *officially* abandoned the mythologies of its superiority—white superiority, male superiority, European superiority—yet the myth of able-bodied superiority remains.

Disabilities bring special problems. The aged can argue that to be old is not worse than being young but merely different, and even in some ways superior. "Youth is wasted on the young" captures some of this sentiment. This affirmation of the inherent excellence of a previously despised group, and the consequent relegation of beliefs to the contrary to the realm of prejudice and bigotry is an important step in the liberation of oppressed groups. This first step is much more difficult for the handicapped. As Zola argues, one problem here is that one cannot deny the intrinsic desirability of sound health. It would be absurd for those who have handicaps to carry banners saying "Proud to Have Polio" or "Physical Disability: Get One."

Other features of alienation for the handicapped are shared with other alienated groups. Our culture tends to overlook the person and see only his or her disability. This is another example of the sort of "objectification" Sandra Bartky discussed in her essay. We say that a person has a cold, has the measles, has chicken pox, but we say that a person *is* an asthmatic, *is* a diabetic, *is* a polio victim, *is* a paraplegic, *is* a cripple. We speak of "the handicapped," or "asthmatics," or "the blind" as if this physical fact about them were their only salient characteristic, as if this physical feature were so important that one can confidently lump all those who have it into a single group, whose similarities will outweigh their differences. Yet obviously, a person's illness and disabilities, no matter how severe, do not define who that person is, do not even begin to exhaust a person's individuality. A handicapped person may be evil, kind, loving, have only one usable leg, be unable to see very well, be artistic, be stupid . . . all of these are only small parts of any whole human being. But for the disabled, this part, no matter how significant for the person herself, is seen by the rest of the world as characterizing the whole.

The handicapped, especially those for whom moving about in public is difficult, tend to be invisible. We never see handicapped people in advertisements or on television and their lesser mobility often keeps them indoors and out of sight. They are segregated in special institutions or lack access to areas that are supposedly public, but accessible only to those with full use of their bodies. Many, like Franklin D. Roosevelt, "pass": Roosevelt never allowed himself to be photographed with his crutches, in his wheelchair, or from the waist down. When even the president of the United States feels compelled to pretend that he is able-bodied, you can imagine the difficulties those less powerful have.

Along with many ethnic minorities, those with handicaps share a stigma of "overcoming" with its concomitant blaming of the victim and the sometimes paradoxical effect of limiting rather than increasing abilities. They are urged to try to do things as much as possible like those without handicaps do them, to "overcome" their handicap. Zola says that his obsession with doing as much with his legs as possible led him for many years to struggle to walk, whereas now he uses his wheelchair, greatly increasing his mobility and speed. Wheelchair marathoners could never finish a marathon using their legs, but finish a good hour ahead of the fastest runners when using their chairs.

One feature of handicapped experience they share with the old: they face those who are neither handicapped nor old with unwelcome truths, they are the messengers we kill for the unpalatable message. We may become physically disabled or contract chronic illnesses; we shun those who remind us of the frailty of all our bodies. As Zola points out, handicapped have recently begun referring to nonhandicapped as the TAB, the Temporarily Able-bodied.

One lesson of the women's movement that is applicable to the handicapped is that physical differences ought to be a signal for a culture to provide the means to live a full life, to fully participate, despite such differences, rather than being used as excuses to deny full participation. If women on the whole are not as good as men in lifting heavy objects, then jacks and forklifts can be invented. If one is unable to climb stairs, that's what ramps and elevators are for. Rather than use such departures from the "norm" as an excuse to exclude people (you can't be an executive, because you can't climb the stairs to the executive suite), we should be seeing them as occasions for the full exercise of our ingenuity to allow everyone to participate. Almost all of us are deficient in some respect. We might ask college professors to run the hundred yard dash in under fifteen seconds in order to be tenured. Slow, wheezing, out-of-shape college professors would be denied access to their profession. Since the ability to run even moderately fast is not a major factor in the jobs of most professors, we don't do this. Yet we do something very like it when we deny jobs to people who can't climb stairs because they're in wheelchairs, rather than providing them with ramps and elevators.

Communications Barriers between the Worlds of 'Able-Bodiedness' and 'Disability'

IRVING K. ZOLA

ON GETTING PEOPLE TO LISTEN

"WHY DOESN'T ANYONE UNDERSTAND what it's like?" is a lament of many who try to convey to others the nature of having a disability. It is a story rooted deep in Western culture. Slater (1970) put it well:

> Our ideas about institutionalizing the aged, psychotic, retarded and infirm are based on a pattern of thought that we might call The Toilet Assumption— the notion that unwanted matter, unwanted difficulties, unwanted complexities and obstacles will disappear if they are removed from our immediate field of vision. . . . Our approach to social problems is to decrease their visibility: out of sight, out of mind. . . . The result of our social efforts has been to remove the underlying problems of our society farther and farther from daily experience and daily consciousness, and hence to decrease in the mass of the population, the knowledge, skill, resources, and motivation necessary to deal with them.

It is, however, increasingly less acceptable to exile "problem" bearers in faraway colonies, asylums, and sanitaria. A recent compromise has been to locate them in places which, if not geographically distant, are socially distant places with unfree access, like ghettos, special housing projects, nursing homes, or hospitals. This too is imperfect. So a final strategy makes them socially indistinct. They are stereotyped. But I never fully appreciated the resultant distancing and isolation until it happened to me! I use two canes, wear a long leg brace on my right leg, a knee and ankle brace on my left, a back support, and walk stiff-legged with a pronounced limp. All in all, I think of myself as fairly unusual in appearance and thus easily recognizable. And yet for years I have had the experience of being "mistaken" for someone else. Usually I was in a new place and a stranger would greet me as Tom, Dick, or Harry. After I explained that I was not he, they would usually apologize saying, "You look just like him." Inevitably I would meet this Tom, Dick, or Harry and he would be several inches shorter or taller, forty pounds heavier or lighter, a person using crutches or a wheelchair. I was continually annoyed and even puzzled how anyone could mistake "him" for the "unique me." What eventually dawned on me was that to many I was "hand-icapped" first and foremost. So much so that in the eyes of the "able-bodied" I and all others like me "looked alike."

But more is going on here than the traditional stereotyping of a stigmatized ethnic group. The social invisibility of people with a disability has a more insidious development. Young children care little about skin color, or Semitic or Oriental features. Only as they grow older are they eventually taught to attend to these. Quite the opposite is true with regard to physical disability. When small children meet a person using a wheelchair or wearing a brace they are curious and pour forth questions like, "Why are you wearing this? What is it? Do you take it off at night? How high up does it go? Can I touch it?" If, however, there are any adults or parents within hearing they immediately become fidgety and admonish the child.

"It's not nice to ask such things" or "It's not nice to stare at people who are. . . ." The feature in question—the limp, the cane, the wheelchair, the brace, the stutter, the scarring—is quite visible and of great interest to children, but he or she is taught to ignore it. They are not, of course, taught that it is an inconsequential characteristic, but with effect, if not in words, that it is an uncomfortable and all-encompassing one. They are taught to respond globally and not particularistically: to recognize a person with a disability when they see one but to ignore the specific characteristics of the disability. Is it any wonder that a near-universal complaint is, "Why can't people see me as someone who *has* a disability rather than someone who *is* disabled?" Young children first perceive it that way but are quickly socialized out of it.

But why all this effort? Why this distancing of those with chronic illness or a disability? Why are we so threatening that we must be made socially invisible? The answer is found both in the nature of society and the nature of people.

In many countries in the Western world there is a premise that with great effort and the right technique there is no problem that cannot be solved, no force of nature unharnessed. It should thus be no great surprise that we simi-larly claim that there is no disease that cannot be cured. And so there is a continual series of wars; against heart disease, cancer, stroke, birth defects, mental illness. They are wars worthy enough in themselves but ones which promise nirvana over the next hill, a society without disease. It is, however, but a mirage (Dubos 1961).

I am not arguing for any cessation in these campaigns to prevent disease and disability. Rather, I am concerned with their side effects. People no longer die. Doctors simply lost the battle to save them. With society so raging against the anthropomorphic killer "diseases," should it be a surprise that some of the anger at the diseases spills on its bearers? In this context, people with disabilities become objects, the permanent reminders of a lost and losing struggle, the symbol of a past and continuing failure. To see how intolerant we are of failure think for a moment of how we in our respective countries have reacted to Vietnam veterans. Whether we were of the left or of the right, we both wanted to push the events of that era out of our minds and as a result treated the survivors of that war shabbily.

Finally, the discomforting confrontation of the "able-bodied" with the "disabled" is not just a symbolic one. For there is a hidden truth to the statement often heard when such a meeting occurs, the shudder and occasional sigh, "I'm glad it's not me." But the relief is often followed by guilt for ever thinking such a thought: a guilt one would just as soon also not deal with. Thus, the threat to be removed lies not merely in society's failure but in the inevitability of one's own. The discomfort that many feel in the presence of those who are aging, dying, or have a disability, *is* the reality that it *could* just as well be they and some day it will. For, like it or not, we will all one day get to grow old and to die.

And in this high-technology world this means dying *not* of natural causes and old age but of some chronic disease. But this is a reality we never tire of denying.

All this then is the baggage that we, with a disability, carry with us in our daily interactions.

ON THE DIFFICULTY IN TELLING

The story of having a disability or illness is difficult to tell as well as to hear. There is thus a complementary question to the one with which I opened this talk: "Why can't *I* make anyone understand what it's like to have a disability?" To me, the different emphasis implies that the spokesperson may be at a loss "to tell it like it is." Part of the problem may lie in the vantage point of the speakers. Erving Goffman (1963) once noted that "minority" group spokespersons may occupy those positions precisely because they are successful adapters and thus in many ways closer to the "normals." Yet to that extent, they are ironically less representative of the group they are supposed to represent. For instance, I and many other "successful mainstream adapters" have not numbered among our close friends and acquaintances *any* people with disabilities: an "alienation" from our disability which has escalated almost to the level of an unconscious principle. Moreover, almost every written "success" story as well as every "success" I have met (including myself) usually regards, as a key element, the self-conception: "I never think of myself as handicapped." Yet the degree to which this is true may have made it virtually impossible to tell anyone what it is like to have a disability in a world of "able-bodied." In a real sense, we don't know. Thus, what the public learns from our example is decidedly limited.

Franklin Delano Roosevelt is a case in point. To the world in general and to people with disabilities in particular he was the ultimate of successful adaptation. For after contracting polio and left "functionally paraplegic" he went on to become president of the United States. What better evidence of success? And yet the newer biographies reveal a man not so pleasant an individual, not so happy with his lot, and possessed of certain drives and needs that for another person less famous might have been labelled clinically pathologic. Moreover, whatever his political achievements, his social success was a more limited one. The public knew that he had polio, used a wheelchair regularly and crutches rarely, but he was careful never to "confront" the public. He never allowed himself to be photographed in a wheelchair or on crutches. He passed photogenically. But few of us can so control, manipulate, and overcome our environment. So too with the other folk heroes of disease. They are not little people, not the millions, but the few who are so successful that they also "passed"; the person with polio who later broke track records, the pianist who had limited vision, the singer who had a colostomy. They were all so good that no one knew or had to be aware of their "handicap" and therein lay part of their glory.

But it is the "success" stories which are more familiar to the public which are in some ways more destructive. A specific example sticks painfully in my mind. I am a sports fan and, as such, an avid watcher of major events. The 1976 Olympics found me glued to my TV set and I was pleasantly surprised by a documentary which related to me quite personally. I think it was called "Six Who Overcame" and told how six athletes had overcome some problem (five were directly physical) and gone on to win Olympic gold medals. One story really grabbed me. It was about Wilma Rudolph, a woman who had polio as a child. Through pictures and words, her struggle was recreated. Love, caring, exercise, and hard work repeated endlessly until she started to walk slowly with crutches and then, abandoning them, began to run. And there in the final frames she was sprinting down the track straining every muscle. With tears streaming down my face, I shouted: "Go on, Wilma! Do it! Do it!" And when she did I collapsed, exhausted and exhilarated. But scarcely ninety minutes later, I was furious. For a basic message of the film sank in. In each case the person overcame. But overcame what? Wilma's polio was not my polio! And all the love, caring, exercise, and hard work could *never* have allowed me to win a running race, let alone compete in one.

My point is that in almost all the success stories that get to the public, there is a dual message. The first one is very important: that just because we have polio, cancer, multiple sclerosis, mental illness, or have limited use of our eyes, ears, mouth, and limbs, our lives are *not* over. We can still learn, be happy, be lovers, spouses, parents, and even achieve great deeds. It is the second message which I have recently begun to abhor. It states that if a Franklin Delano Roosevelt or a Wilma Rudolph could *overcome* their disability, so could and should all. And if we fail, it's *our* problem, *our* personality, *our* weakness. And all this further masks what chronic illness and disability are all about. For our lives or even our adaptations do not center around one single activity or physical achievement but around many individual and complex ones. Our daily living is not filled with dramatic accomplishments but with mundane ones. And most of all, our physical difficulties are not temporary ones to be overcome once and for all but ones we must face again and again for the rest of our lives. That's what chronic means!

ON THE STORY TO BE TOLD

Now, this great achievement syndrome effects not only the general public but also the achievers. We are paid the greatest of compliments when someone tells us "You know, I never think of you as handicapped." And we gladly accept it. We are asked, "How did you make it against such great odds?" And we answer the question. And yet in both the accepting and the answering we further distance ourselves from the problems of having a disability. In a sense they become both emotionally and cognitively inaccessible. I am not using these words lightly. I do indeed mean emotionally and cognitively inaccessible.

Let me illustrate with a personal example. I do a great deal of long-distance travelling and, as such, often find my jet flight located on the furthest runway from the entrance. Adjusting to this, I ordinarily allow myself an extra twenty to thirty minutes to get there. I regard this for most of my life as a minor inconvenience. And if perchance you had asked me then if I experienced any undue tiredness or unavoidable soreness, I would have firmly and honestly answered, "No." But in 1977, a new "consciousness" altered all this (Zola 1982). Piqued at why I should continue to inconvenience myself I began to regularly use a wheelchair for all such excursions. I thought that the only surprise I would encounter would be the dubious glances of other passengers, when, after reaching my destination, I would rise unassisted and walk briskly away. In fact I was occasionally regarded as if I had in some way "cheated." Much more disconcerting, however, was that I now arrived significantly more energetic, more comfortable, freer from cramps and leg sores than in my previous decades of travelling. The conclusion I drew was inevitable. I had *always* been tired, uncomfortable, cramped, and sore after a long journey. But with no standard of comparison, these feelings were incorporated into the cognitive reality of what travelling was for me. I did not "experience" the tiredness and discomfort. They were cognitively inaccessible.

What I am contending is shockingly simple. The very process of successful adaptation not only involves divesting ourselves of any identification with having a disability, but also denying the uncomfortable features of that life. To not do so might have made our success impossible! But this process had a cost. One may accept and forget too much.

The experience of having a disability need not, however, be as isolating as it once was. There is a movement of people with disabilities to reclaim their rights (Scotch 1984). People with various disabilities now see that they have much in common both with each other (Harris 1986) and with other minority groups (Hahn 1985). We realize that we can take greater control and care over our lives and our health.

This talk has presented one set of experiences and concerns. I am sure the specific details and hardships of having a disability vary from person to person. But not the core problem. The story is inevitably difficult to both hear and tell. To the teller, it is especially hard to acknowledge. Indeed, to even think of the world in such a realistic, paranoid way might make it too depressing a reality to tolerate. As such, the only defense, the only way to live for far too long has been to deny it. But then it becomes socially invisible to *all*. We are sadly left as Slater (1970) has articulated: both those with physical disabilities and those without, *all* are deprived of the very knowledge, skill, resources, and motivation necessary to promote change.

References

Dubos, R. J. (1961). *Mirage of Health: Utopias, Progress and Biological Change*. New York: Doubleday (quote is from flyleaf).

Goffman, E. (1963). *Stigma: Notes on Management of Spoiled Identity*. Englewood Cliffs, N. J.: Prentice-Hall, 105–235.

Hahn, H. (1985). "Disability Policy and the Problem of Discrimination." *American Behavioural Scientist* 28: 293–318.

Harris, L., and Associates. (1986). *Disabled Americans Self-Perceptions: Bringing Disabled Americans into the Mainstream*. Study No. 854009. New York: International Centre for the Disabled.

Scotch, R. K. (1984). *From Good Will to Civil Rights: Transforming Federal Disability Policy*. Philadelphia: Temple University Press.

Slater, P. E. (1970). *Pursuit of Loneliness: American Culture at the Breaking Point*. Boston: Beacon Press, 15.

Zola, I. K. (1982). *Missing Pieces—A Chronicle of Living with a Disability*. Philadelphia: Temple University Press.

Four Steps on the Road to Invalidity: The Denial of Sexuality, Anger, Vulnerability, and Potentiality

IRVING K. ZOLA

BACKGROUND

A NUMBER OF YEARS ago I lived in a place in the Netherlands called Het Dorp (Zola 1982). This was a village specifically created for people with severe physical disabilities and chronic diseases. When I lived there almost every villager agreed that the six aims of the founders: to guarantee every inhabitant the right to privacy, work, recreation, religion, culture, and self-governance were, if not solved, at least being worked on seriously. Yet these "six building blocks of happiness" were just that, building blocks, a foundation which awaited an edifice. Ironically, the satisfaction of these basic needs did not so much make us thankful for what we had been given but provided us the time and opportunity to be aware of what we had lost; emotional needs that seemed to have been taken away, or never granted. As a result, those of us with a disability necessarily spend much of our time in a continuing effort to reclaim what we have lost: the right to act sexy, get angry, be vulnerable, and have possibilities. These basic needs do not seem like the kind of things that one person can give to another, but they are needs whose satisfaction the rest of society has helped impede and deny. It is the fact as well as the implication of this I wish to illuminate in this essay.

On Being Sexy

I probably need to say the least about sexuality. Sexuality is one of the first things "to go" when one becomes ill, and its return, often framed in standard jokes, supposedly indicates recovery. Much is made of sickness being a period of social withdrawal, when one feels less attractive and less interested in sex. And when one becomes permanently disabled, the attractiveness, the ability, and the interest to engage in sex are often regarded as similarly impaired.

More and more I realize that this is true only as long as sex is associated exclusively with youth and physical attractiveness. Our society does not like to picture people who are weak, sick, and even dying, having needs for sexual intimacy. It is regarded as unseemly. Such people are thought to have better things to do with their time than holding or being held. Yet my personal experience and professional observation has taught me to distrust this notion. The desire I believe is always there but it is shunted aside, suppressed by fear. We do not express or even show our wishes because we have learned that in our condition of disablement or disfigurement no one could (or should) find us sexually attractive.

I need to take a brief aside here about what "should" be. Several years ago I was consulting with a sexuality and disability counselling program, and the staff were discussing a project of sexual experimentation in Sweden. It involved able-bodied counsellors being sexually involved with people with severe disabilities. It was ultimately discontinued; *not* because of the experimentation, *nor* because of any lack of success *but* because it was found that many of the counsellors were enjoying themselves. They actually began to find these very physically disabled people attractive and *that* was regarded as shocking if not sick.

To return to my original point, those with a physical disability withdraw or deny the need for intimate contact not through lack of desire but fear of rejection. A self-fulfilling prophecy has thus been created.

Still another dilemma in dealing with sexuality amongst the disabled is a certain male and culture-boundedness in thinking. Thus it seems that the existence of sexuality is either denied entirely or if recognized is located entirely in the genitals: and the male genitals at that. What society in general and the rehabilitation literature in particular seem to have focused on is sex as capacity and technique. Thus if the researchers are not counting the marriage and divorce rates, or the number of children, they are measuring the number, frequency, and type of orgasm. And where those with a chronic disability are concerned the research and clinical efforts are on compensatory techniques, ways to stimulate or simulate ejaculations and erections, ways to reclaim some lost or weakened ability. And while I agree that sex involves many skills, it seems to be foolish and limited to focus on *one* organ, *one* ability, *one* sensation to the neglect and exclusion of all others. Sex and loving can surely involve the genitals and what is euphemistically called penetration. But we can also touch, show, and experience love in our fingers, hands, feet, tongues, lips, eyes, ears, and words.

The loss of bodily sensation and function associated with many disorders, and its replacement with a physical as well as psychological numbness, has made sexuality a natural place to begin the process of reclaiming some of one's selfhood. But as the self is located in no single place, neither is sexuality.

ON GETTING ANGRY

The dilemma of anger for those with a disability was summed up best by a friend of mine. For months, she had what she called "weak spells" and then she learned that the condition would be permanent, that she had indeed a debilitating progressive disorder. While there were many things about this that bothered her, one in particular stuck in her throat: "Now that I've got this problem I just can't afford to be angry with anyone. I need them too much." And so began with her, and with many others, a lengthy process of learning to be nice in the face of one after another upsetting event.

Now while this may have roots in certain Judeo-Christian values, it has certainly been made an essential personality ingredient of many people with chronic disabilities. For most of the contemporary history, to be a complainer in the hospital (or doctor's office) was a road that led nowhere. In a sense we were taught that we had no right to complain; everything that could be done was being done. Everyone was busy and overworked and besides: "Weren't we grateful?" This gratitude has been our curse. In the first place, being sick made us by definition so dependent that any expressions of dissatisfaction became a threat to the continued care which we could not easily get elsewhere. And in the second place, our anger was regarded as inappropriate because it indicated we were not sufficiently "grateful" for all that *was* being done for us.

The idea of suppressing one's anger has still another social function as seen in the cliched consolation: "Be grateful for what you've got. Look at all those who are worse off than you." The words are as frequent as the lack of solace they provide. My observation is that such "consolations" most typically occurred when someone was feeling "down" about their condition and expressed this rather depressingly to someone who did not have any obvious physical "difficulty." The inevitable reply was intended to have a reassuring effect, but it was, in fact, far more effective as a "silencer." Passed off as an attempt to prevent us from "wallowing in self pity," its real function may have been to protect the listener. Making us look at those "worse-off" than us rather than those "better-off" prevented us from being envious and even resentful of our able-bodied friends. For they were the ones we wanted to shout at for having what we didn't have and being so smug about it, for not knowing what it's like and not letting us explain.

Whatever else this process produces, it cannot help but be detrimental. On the one hand, it deprives us of an almost universal need—the need if not the right—to be angry. Some of the more common expressions of sublimated anger are not open to us. Often we do not have the physical strength to hit a pillow or kick a chair. And when we use what we have at our disposal, we are either condemned or run unusual risks. When a friend became so frustrated at his wife's behavior that he rammed his wheelchair into a wall, the hospital staff labelled him self-destructive. Someone with the complications of diabetic retinopathy cannot swing their arms for fear of hemorrhaging. To these can be added the countless other people who because of their disorder have been warned by their physician *not* to exert themselves, *not* to worry too much, or *not* to get too excited. In short, they are instructed not to feel anything too intensely, especially anger.

Thus, with virtually no acceptable avenues for expression, those with a chronic disability are forced either to turn their anger in on themselves or to blunt it. To the degree that we succeed in the latter we become increasingly unfeeling, and often so distanced from ourselves that virtually nothing can touch us. In this way we provide the basis for the stereotype in the professional literature which describes us as "difficult to reach." If, on the other hand, we turn the anger inward, it is likely to take the form of depression. Is it thus any wonder that study after study document the high degree of depression among those with a chronic disability? This depressed state is not merely a primary reaction to our losses, our dependency, our sickness, and thus something for us "to realistically come to grips with," it is every bit as much a socially induced defense, the result of our enforced inability to express anger. Society's gain by this process is straightforward. Since depression is considered the result of one's inadequate adaptation and resources, it can be more easily ignored as the individual's problem. Anger, on the other hand, whatever its cause, has an outward expression and direction. As such it at very least demands involvement if not response.

For those with a disability, the issue of anger goes, however, beyond the ability to express it. While it may be more blessed to give than to receive, where anger is concerned the two go hand in hand. If we are to be encouraged to be angry at things that bother us, then we must also be prepared to receive anger if *we* bother someone else. Though such a statement seems perfectly obvious, its daily application is not. And through the years I have grown aware that people are very wary about being openly angry or critical of someone with a disability. And yet one of the greatest putdowns one can inflict on another (as the feminist movement has pointed out) is contained in the phrase: "I'm afraid that you won't be able to take it." Since all of us have done things to upset others, to be denied their resentment is to be taken unseriously and to be deemed unworthy of response, to make the provoking action almost unreal.

It is thus that a full circle of anger-denial is completed. On the one hand, those of us with a disability are unable to express our anger and on the other we are protected from seeing why anyone might be angry at us. What was originally fostered by our physical and medical dependency has ultimately been translated and reinforced as a *modus vivendi* for our social dependency.

ON FEELING VULNERABLE

Of all the emotional qualities I have dealt with, vulnerability is, perhaps, the hardest in which to find some path between denial and "narcissistic self-indulgence" or what is more commonly called "self-pity." There is an almost instinctual drive towards narcissism in all of us which is, in many ways, curtailed by society. For those who have a disability, this drive is difficult to resist. In the physiological state of having an illness, our body cries out for attention. In the social position of having an illness we are deprived of all our usual sources of action, distraction, and entertainment. Both situations force us even more into ourselves. The usual sterile environment of long-term "care" institutions further exacerbate this tendency. All of these features might seem to demand strictures against the focusing on one's weaknesses. And yet I suspect that these tendencies become problems precisely because society allows for little, if any, admission of vulnerability. The strictures against crying, particularly for males is a prime example. The fear is that once started, it, like self-pity, will never stop. My own observation is that those people with an oversupply of tears are the ones who have been unable to mourn their losses fully, especially when they first occurred. As a result, they "leak" and mourn a little bit all of the time.

Most of us are shut off from our losses prematurely. We are pushed to get on with the future and forget what is past or left behind. To mark the generally recognized losses and transition, there are, however, at least ceremonial rituals; from divorce proceedings to retirement parties, from funerals to wakes. Moreover, specific "mourning" periods are set aside; from specified times during which one cannot remarry after a divorce or death to the daily ritual kaddish said for a year by the orthodox Jewish male. Though many of these ceremonies have become attenuated, at least the forms exist. A chronic disease or disability, whatever else it may mean, also constitutes a loss—of time, of capacity, of function, of appearance—and as such it has to be acknowledged and mourned before it, too, can be put aside. In a logical way the mourning may also not be a once and forever thing, for unlike the departure of a person whose loss we may only occasionally be reminded of, the physical loss of a function or bodily part is with us all the time. Our braces, limps, drugs, weaknesses are a constant reminder. From this perspective it may be remarkable that we are not "crying" all the time.

In short, if those of us with disabilities are not made "sick" by the loss, we surely are by the ways we are forced to deal with it. The current approaches make us lose perspective. With little opportunity to confront our realities, we find ourselves thought of as distant because we refuse to acknowledge our big problems, or crybabies because we dwell so much on the small ones. Yet this is the very trap we are forced into by a society which neither acknowledges our losses nor our need to express them. And without this, all are losers: we for not being able to fully clarify our needs and the society for not being able to hear them.

ON HAVING POSSIBILITIES

The issue of potentiality epitomizes the "damned if you do, damned if you don't" dilemmas often facing those with a chronic condition. In trying to plan our lives, we are either pushed to regard our physical difficulty as the all-encompassing touchstone *or* to claim that we are just like everyone else, needing and wanting no special consideration. These alternatives are paralleled by two social defense mechanisms, what Miller and Gynne (1972) have called the "warehousing" and "horticultural" modes. In a sense, society uses both approaches at the same time. The "warehousing" perspective, where the individual is seen permanently "in need" of help, is the prevalent mode in most institutional and interpersonal arrangements facing the disabled. The "horticultural" model of "unlimited" possibilities is the standard by which people are measured *before* society gives up and "warehouses" them. Though one may appear conservative and one liberal, both have a history and result detrimental to those with a disability.

The "warehousing" perspective develops out of the view that the lives of people with a disability are entirely determined by their physical conditions. Much of this view is rooted in a certain reality. Our early lives as "chronically disabled" are essentially spent under medical supervision if not medical dominion. For the most part our conditions are known and our physical dependence, be it on medicine, prostheses, or people, obvious. This is a reality so overpowering, so visible, so continually confronting that it is difficult to resist. Still weakened by our physical condition we find ourselves the recipients of rehabilitation programs where further assumptions are perpetuated about our abilities and our best interests. This trend is exacerbated by the fact that most programs operate within a medical perspective: a perspective in which the giver of help and the recipient are most distant from one another and where the latter must place oneself completely in the hands of the former with few if any questions permitted. Finally, medicine is a very pragmatic applied science focusing very heavily on practicalities. As a result, there is a push to focus more on the practical possibilities of our limitations than the unknown potentialities of our strengths.

Freeing oneself from a "warehousing" or physicalist perspective is not easy. Like the Women's Movement, we, too, find ourselves railing against the

assumption that "Anatomy is Destiny" and the consequent perspective which traps us into some roles and excludes us from others. On the other hand, the seductiveness of the "everything is possible horticultural" mode can be equally entrapping. Any message that implies that with sufficient effort there is no physical problem that could not be overcome is not, however, "the curse" I seek when I ask for "possibilities." To be always held up to some arbitrary overoptimum standard can only be more depressing when one can't make it, or when once achieved, one can never give it up. Just because an individual *can* do something physical does not mean that he or she *should*. While for some people it might be very important, if not essential to their self-image, to spend two hours dressing by themselves or several more writing a single-page letter, many would just as soon spend their time and energy elsewhere. By spending so much time and energy on basic tasks, we eliminate the possibility of even realizing other possibilities. Most tritely, we find ourselves too tired to think and, thus, in a sense to live more fully. What is often misunderstood is that this is by no means an individual decision, but one again where many of us feel we are living up to someone else's ideals. No matter that for many an external monitor is absent, the socialization process has taken, the message has been internalized.

Thus, to emphasize the individual personal qualities as the reasons for success in overcoming difficulties (and the reason for failure if the barriers prove insurmountable) is self-serving for the individual and the society. For individuals who have lost so much it rewards us at a cost of making us ignore not only what we owe to those who helped us, but what we share with those who did not make it. To the society this emphasis merely allows the further disavowal of any responsibility, and more important, any accountability for the process which makes a chronically disabled person's entry or reentry into life so difficult. Were my family poorer and less pushy, my friends fewer and less caring, my champions less willing to fight the system, then all my personal qualities and strengths would have been for naught. On the other hand, if we lived in a less healthist, capitalist, and hierarchical society which spent less time finding ways to exclude and disenfranchise people and more ways to include and enhance the potentialities of everyone, then there wouldn't have been so much for me to overcome (Zola 1977).

In Conclusion

Two words summarize what faces an individual with a disability. Infantilization is the process. Invalidation is the result. Having an illness calls forth ill feelings, behavior, and even treatment, a state of dependency most characteristic of children. When the temporary acute state becomes permanent, then too, unfortunately, do the childlike qualities inherent in the role. But even more the necessities of being "dependent" do this. In a society which frowns not only on being dependent but also upon being nurturant to one's peers, the able-bodied has only one sanctioned model for making both her / himself, and the person needing help, psychologically comfortable: the model of the "well parent" and the "sick child." It is, thus, a two-sided bind. Only children can continually demand help, and only parents can be continually expected to give it. Thus, in recognizing our needs for dependence and nurturance we take the only roles open to us.

The process of infantilization is, however, not only in the roles but in the content. Parents usually set limits on both their children's physical activity and their emotional expression. In particular, parents deny children their sexuality, anger, and vulnerability (i.e., we tell them not to be a crybaby, etc.) and put limits on their potentiality (i.e., the parents and the society determine when they are ready to engage in certain activities). But for children there is, theoretically, a time limit. When society engages in the same process with adults, the infantilization inevitably leads to invalidation.

References

Miller, E. S., and Gynne, G. V. (1972). *A Life Apart—A Study of Residential Institutions for the Physically Handicapped and the Young Chronic Sick*. London: Tavisstock Publications.

Zola, I. K. (1977). "Healthism and Disabling Medicalization." In I. Illich, I. K. Zola, J. McKnight, H. Shaiken, *Disabling Professions*, 41–67. London: Marion Boyars.

Zola, I. K. (1982). *Missing Pieces: A Chronicle of Living with a Disability*. Philadelphia Temple University Press.

PART V

Old Age

ON A LONG TRAIN ride from New Orleans to the West Coast a few years ago, I had a chance to talk to a remarkable woman: lively, intelligent, candid, curious, funny. In other words, a remarkable person altogether. But I must confess that to some extent I saw her not as simply a remarkable human being, but as a remarkable old person like the fabled talking dog, where you marvel not at how well the dog talks but that it can talk at all. I marveled that she failed to live up to my stereotypes about age, for she was at least sixty, yet "youthful" in appearance and attitude. She wore jeans and a sweatshirt, and her white hair was ponytailed behind her smooth face. She had just retired from the merchant marine and was taking trains around the country looking for a good place to live. She was vibrant, optimistic, flexible, all things that I deemed "youthful."

In other words, I reacted toward her in a way very similar to the way bigoted whites react to blacks who are more like whites in speech and demeanor than like the stereotype of blacks. I was delighted that she was not what I thought she ought to be because of her age.

Such an experience illustrates that age is generally regarded as a catastrophe, as simply a loss of the supreme good of youth. Age is treated like a disease or a disability: as a deviation from a presumed desirable normality. Euphemisms like "senior citizen" reveal our distaste for the old. The function of euphemism, after all, is to sugarcoat something seen as shameful or bad. We need no euphemisms for the young. They are not "junior citizens," they are unapologetically "young." But when people are old, we think it impolite to refer so nakedly to their age, as we think it impolite to refer to someone's recent bankruptcy. It cannot, we think, be polite or kind to remind someone so plainly that he is no longer young but rapidly approaching death.

To be old can be a source of capacity, as it was in the many cultures where the old were regarded as the wise, to be looked to for advice and counsel. There have been times and cultures where there was no shame involved in being old, where to be old was to have a central and respected place. But the dominant culture in the United States is not like that, though traces of such attitudes linger in some minority cultures, such as that of some American Indians. But the dominant culture no longer builds its society around the elders. There is confusion about who the old are, and a tendency to think of them as having no purpose or value, now that they no longer have the purposes and values they had when younger. The old change from being productive and active citizens, workers, lovers, child rearers, teachers, and carpenters, to being simply old, without any socially recognized useful functions, marginalized, trivialized, disrespected-alienated.

Many of the old of course have been marginalized all their lives. These old—old Black people, old gays, old Indians, old women, old workers—have always been alienated. They find that age, rather than being a welcome time of rest from the struggle, simply adds one more layer of disrespect to those they have experienced all their lives.

Sexism, for example, persists and even intensifies as women become old. To a much greater degree than men, women are trapped by the cultural demand to be young. A middle-aged man can be distinguished and attractive and can often have the company, social and sexual, of younger women. It is rare for a middle-aged woman to date a much younger man, and when she does, there is a certain absurdity and desperation to it that leads many to pity her. Women, more than men, are defined by the physical attributes of youth. She must be pretty and lithe and firm. As a woman's skin wrinkles, as her waist thickens and her breasts sag, she loses much of what gave her value in men's eyes to begin with. Women begin to lose their value to men with the first onset of the loss of the twenty-year-old body and skin. As Shevy Healey points out, this view of old age leads to old people trying to pass themselves off as young, and, like all forms of passing, it betrays the self-hatred of the passing person. A black who tries to pass as white not only reveals the existence of racism in her society, but reveals that she hates herself for being black. So too with the old who desperately try to remain young, with face-lifts, and wigs, and cosmetics, and liposuction—what Healey calls a "personal attempt to cling to the mainstream of life and avoid the fate of the outcast."

Very likely this depth of marginalization, this insistence on pushing the old out of sight and out of mind, this almost obsessional insistence on staying young, stems from our fear of losing our youth, and its accompaniment, our inevitable death. The old, like the very ill or the handicapped, remind us too forcefully of our own eventual fate, for death following on old age awaits all of us who do not die young.

For most then, old age is a time of intensified alienation. For those lucky enough to not suffer alienation in their youth and middle age, old age introduces them to alienation. For the majority who have all their lives experienced one or more forms of alienation, old age adds yet another layer. And as people increasingly live longer, old age becomes a greater proportion of life as a whole. Whites in the industrialized West now routinely live a quarter to a third of their lives as "old"—if we define that as over sixty. By alienating our elderly we see to it that for many of us, old age is a time of disability and marginalization and loneliness, when it need not be so. Rather than treating the inevitability of death as a reason for making all of life as joyful as possible, we allow it to poison the last portion of life.

Growing to be an Old Woman:
Age and Ageism

SHEVY HEALEY

IN MY LATE FIFTIES, and then my sixties, I heard, "I can't believe you're that old. You don't look that old." At first that felt like a compliment. Then I became a bit uneasy. It reminded me of early prefeminist days when I was complimented by some men for being "smarter," "more independent" than those "other" women. What was I now—a token "young"?

Slowly other experiences began to accumulate, reminding me of a real change in my life status.

First, I moved. And while I found easy acceptance among older people in the community, when younger people talked to me they invariably would say something like, "You remind me of my grandmother." Grandmother?! I felt labelled and diminished somehow.

Recently, I have, in fact, become a grandmother. I found most young friends expected me—automatically—to "be" a certain way. Many of those expecta-tions were in accord with what I felt. Some were not. I did not instantly fall in love with my grandson. I was much more drawn to my daughter and what she was experiencing. I must admit that I am now a doting grandmother, but being put in a particular slot about that was a bit disquieting, as though all of my reactions could be gauged in advance and belonged to the generic group "grandmother" rather than to me.

I attended a Women's Action for Nuclear Disarmament (WAND) meeting at which a young M.D. spoke about his research with children all over the world and their responses to the atom bomb. His talk was stimulating, and after the meeting I went up to him to comment on his research. I had the most peculiar feeling of being looked through, as though, what could I, this gray-haired woman in very casual dress, know about research design. I felt patronized, a feeling I wasn't used to.

I lost some money recently through bad judgment and suddenly had the realization that I would never be able to replace it. I do not have enough time left to be able to earn that money again.

I looked in the mirror and saw lots of wrinkles. I had a hard time fitting that outward me with the me inside. I felt like the same person, but outside I looked different. I checked into a face-lift, with much trepidation. What a seduction took place in that doctor's office! He told me he would make me less strange to myself. I would look more like I felt! I became frightened by the whole process. Who was I then? This face? What I felt like inside? How come the two images were not connected? My own ageism told me that how I looked outside was ugly. But I felt the same inside, not ugly at all.

Finally, death entered my life as a direct reality. My oldest friend died of cancer three years ago. My father died two years ago after what turned out to be needless surgery. Another close friend died last month after a year of struggling with cancer. My mother is dying slowly and painfully after suffering a massive stroke. The realization hit me that I can expect this kind of personal contact with death to occur with greater and greater frequency.

Not just my chronological age, but life itself was telling me that I was becoming an older/old woman.

Just at this time I found Barbara Macdonald and Cynthia Rich through their book *Look Me in the Eye—Old Women, Aging and Ageism*. I join with May Sarton who said, "*Look Me in the Eye* is a tremendously stirring recognition of what we are doing to ourselves as we grow older and a rousing attack on what is being done to us. . . . To me personally as I enter my 72nd year, the book has come as a revelation, hitting me hard with the shock of recognition."

But why am I, a woman in her sixties, who has explored the stereotyping of sexism, racism, of the physically disabled, just now looking at ageism? Even to pose the question goes a way towards answering it. Because, in our society, to be old is so awful, one best not think of it. "Old" is equated with "awful" in every respect, with regard to function, thought, action, appearance. I mentioned the Old Woman's League (OWL) to a friend and her instant response was, "What an awful name!"

Think of all the adjectives that are most disrespectful in our society. They are all part of the ageist stereotyping of old women: pathetic, powerless, querulous, complaining, sick, weak, conservative, rigid, helpless, unproductive, wrinkled, asexual, ugly, unattractive, and on, ad nauseam. There is, by the way, an exception to this, and that is the stereotype of the wise old woman. She, of course, never complains, is never sick, and although no one really would want to *be* with her, occasionally it might be fine to sit at her feet!

How did this happen, this totally denigrating picture of old women? To understand this phenomenon we must look at sexism, for ageism is inextricably tied to sexism and is the logical extension of its insistence that women are only valuable when they are attractive and useful to men.

Under the guise of making themselves beautiful, women have endured torture and self-mutilation, cramped their bodies physically, maimed themselves mentally, all in order to please and serve men better, as men defined the serving, because only in that service could women survive.

Foot-binding, for example, reminds us how false and relatively ephemeral those external standards of beauty and sexuality are. We can feel horror at what centuries of Chinese women had to endure. Do we feel the same horror at the process which determines that gray hair, wrinkled skin, fleshier bodies are not beautiful, and therefore ought to be disguised, pounded, starved to meet an equally unrealistic (and bizarre) standard set by the patriarchy? Women spend their lives accepting the premise that to be beautiful one must be young, and only beauty saves one from being discarded. The desperation with which women work to remove signs of aging attests only to the value they place upon themselves as desirable and worthwhile, in being primarily an object pleasing to men. Women's survival, both physical and psychological, has been linked to their ability to please men, and the standards set are reinforced over and over by all the power that the patriarchy commands. The final irony is that all of us, feminists included, have incorporated into our psyches the self-loathing that comes from not meeting that arbitrary standard.

As we alter and modify our bodies in the hopes of feeling good, we frequently achieve instead an awful estrangement from our own bodies. In the attempt to meet that arbitrary external standard, we lose touch with our own internal body messages, thus alienating ourselves further from our own sources of strength and power.

What does this have to do with aging and ageism? Having spent our lives estranged from our own bodies in the effort to meet that outer patriarchal standard of beauty, it is small wonder that the prospect of growing old is frightening to women of all ages. We have all been trained to be ageist. By denying our aging we hope to escape the penalties placed upon growing old. But in so doing we disarm ourselves in the struggle to overcome the oppression of ageism.

To deal with our own feelings about aging we must scrupulously examine how we have been brainwashed to believe that three-inch feet are beautiful, or whatever equivalent myth is currently being purveyed. The old have done what all oppressed people do: they have internalized the self-hatred embodied in the ageist stereotyping. First they try to pass, at least in their own minds if not in the minds of others. They separate themselves from those "others," the old people. They are youthful. I know a woman who at eighty described how she visited the "old folks' home." She was not "one of them." That's not cute on her part. It is simply an expression of how she has incorporated that "old" is "awful," and she wants no part of that powerlessness and marginality. She has found a way to affirm herself, but it's at the expense of others. For all people who try to pass the price is high. In passing you are saying that who you are at sixty, seventy, eighty is *not* OK. You are OK only to the degree that you are like someone else, someone younger, who has more value in the eyes of others.

It is difficult to hold on to one's own sense of self, to one's own dignity when all around you there is no affirmation of you. At best there may be a patronizing acknowledgment; at worst, you simply do not exist.

The oppressed old woman is required to be cheerful. But if you're smiling all the time, you acquiesce to being invisible and docile, participating in your own "erasure." If you're not cheerful then you are accused of being bitter, mean, crabby, complaining! A real catch-22.

Old people are shunted off to their own ghettoes. Frequently they will say they like it better. But who would not when, to be with younger people is so often to be invisible, to be treated as irrelevant and peripheral, and sometimes even as disgusting.

What then is the reality of being old? With all due respect to the problems of younger sisters, to lump older women from forty to ninety is more than inaccurate. It perpetuates the ageist assumption that there are no special conditions, problems, dilemmas for old women worthy of being addressed. When discussion of aging begins and remains primarily about women in their forties and fifties, it reinforces the invisibility of the old woman, and diminishes the importance of the last twenty-five years of life.

We need to begin the systematic examination from a feminist perspective of the issues involved in women's aging, the condition of old women and our society's ageism. As the pervasiveness of ageist thinking becomes apparent, both in our culture and in the feminist movement itself, we will need to carefully scrutinize many of our basic assumptions, attitudes, and values.

We have systematically denigrated old women, kept them out of the mainstream of productive life, judged them primarily in terms of failing capacities and functions, and then found them pitiful. We have put old women in nursing "homes" with absolutely no intellectual stimulation, isolated from human warmth and nurturing contact, and then condemned them for their senility. We have impoverished, disrespected, and disregarded old women, and then dismissed them as inconsequential and uninteresting. We have made old women invisible so that we do not have to confront our patriarchal myths about what makes life valuable or death painful.

Having done that, we then attribute to the process of aging *per se* all the evils we see and fear about growing old. It is not aging that is awful, nor whatever physical problems may accompany aging. What is awful is how society treats old women and their problems. To the degree that we accept and allow such treatment we buy the ageist assumptions that permit this treatment.

What then does it really mean to grow old? For me, first of all, to be old is to be *myself*. No matter how patriarchy may classify and categorize me as invisible and powerless, I exist. I am an ongoing person, a sexual being, a person who struggles, for whom there are important issues to explore, new things to learn, challenges to meet, beginnings to make, risks to take, endings to ponder. Even though some of my options are diminished, there are new paths ahead.

Secondly, I subscribe to Macdonald's view that "age in our society gives us a second opportunity (or places the demand on us, if that is how it feels) to finally deal with our difference, if we have not done so before; to move out of that safe harbor of acceptability." Here the difference we have to deal with is our own aging. Neither to run from being old nor to succumb to being more acceptable as a "young" old. We have the opportunity to deal with what is different, special, unique about being older and old, to find a belonging with other women as they examine the issue of aging, no matter what their age.

Finally, for me the largest issue of all is to deal with the appropriate task of my own age, to learn to live with loss and death, to prepare for my own death. Do I frighten some of you? I have just spoken the unspeakable. In our culture, death is to be avoided at all costs, to be struggled against, and when it comes, to be hidden—in a funeral parlor—away from sight. We so fear death that we have permitted our medical establishment, which neglects old people in life, to keep them from death beyond all reason and dignity. To face the challenge of dying with grace—that is power.

As an old woman I am approaching what in some respects is the greatest power of my life. I am truly freed from the role of wife, mother, daughter, career woman. I can in truth seek to take charge of my life. A bit scary for one whose whole life has been lived subject to external disciplines, now to explore what is important to me, not simply to respond to others. I perceive for myself a twofold task: to attend to the current business of living with vigor and involvement, while at the same time attending to the unfinished business of my life, putting old rancors in perspective, letting go of pettiness, acknowledging love.

To the degree that I deny my aging I cripple my ability to deal with my living and my dying. To deal with both means most particularly to find and accept my own place in the world, in the universe.

Ageism and the
Politics of Beauty

CYNTHIA RICH

IF YOU ARE A younger woman, try to imagine what everything in society tells you not to imagine: that you are a woman in your seventies, eighties, nineties, or older, and yet you are still you. Even your body is yours. It is not, however, in the language of the embalmers, "well-preserved," and though the male world gives you troubles for it, you like it that way. Apart from those troubles you find sometimes a mysterious integrity, a deep connection to life, that comes to you from having belonged to a body that has been large and small, thin and fat, with breasts and hips of many different sizes and shapes and skin of different textures.

In your fifties and sixties when your eyebrows and pubic hair and the hair on your head began to thin, it bothered you at first. But then you remembered times when you tweezed your eyebrows, shaved your pubic hair and legs and underarms, or took thinning shears to your head. "Too much" hair, "too little" hair—now you know that both are male messages.

One day you pick up a book that you find rich and nourishing—for example, *Getting Home Alive* by Aurelia and Rosario Morales, published by a feminist press. It's a political book and a sensuous book, and you like the way its politics and its sensuality seem merged. Rosario is a younger woman in her fifties, with a warmth of connection to other people, especially women. It is when you come to a chapter about aging that abruptly the connection—with you—is broken. You find Rosario writing with dread and loathing at the thought that one day she must live inside the body of a woman who looks like you.

Stop! / I don't want my scalp / shining through a few thin hairs. / Don't want my neck skin to hang—/ neglected cobweb—in the corner of my chin. / Stop! at ruckling ruches of skin / at soft sags, / bags of tongue tickling breast and belly, / at my carved face.

Neglected cobweb. Bags of tongue. It shouldn't take this guided tour for any

180

of us to recognize that an old woman must find it insulting, painful, personally humiliating to be told in print that other women in her community find her body disgusting. What you—the old woman—find especially painful is that Morales, *Sojourner* (where this excerpt was first printed), and Firebrand (who published the book) would surely protest if Jewish features, black features, or the features of any other marginalized group, were described—whether in the form of the outsider's contempt or the insider's self-hatred—with this kind of revulsion. They would not think of their protest as censorship of literary expression. They would know that such attitudes do deep damage to a work artistically, as well as humanly and politically.

Yet clearly there are not the same standards about speaking with disgust about the bodies of old women. So the message has a double sting. The "ugliness" of your physical being is not a cruel opinion but an accepted fact; you have not even the right to be insulted. How is it that you, the old woman, find yourself in this place?

I believe the revulsion towards old bodies is only in part, as Morales suggests— she ends the poem, "*No quiero morir*"—a fear of death. (Of course, there is no reason why women over sixty should have to hear such insults whether they remind us of death or not.) Or else, everybody would find soldiers going to battle repugnant, young women with leukemia disgusting, the tubercular Violetta in *Traviata* loathsome. This is a death-obsessed and death-fearing society, that's true enough. But the dying *young* woman has always been a turn-on.

No, there is another more deeply antiwoman source for this disgust. Once again, it is men who have defined our consciousness and, as Susan Sontag noted ten years ago, in aging as in so much else, a double standard reigns. Even old men—who if powerless are sometimes viewed by younger men *as if* they were old women—seek out much younger women for erotic companions and usually find them. In white Western society, the old woman is distasteful to men because she is such a long way from their ideal of flattering virginal inexperience. But also she outlives them, persists in living when she no longer serves them as wife and mother, and if they cannot make her into Grandma, she is—like the lesbian—that monstrous woman who has her own private reasons for living apart from pleasing men. On the one hand, she is a throwaway, on the other a threat.

White men have provided the world with little literature, sculpture, or painting in which the old woman's body is seen through the eyes of desire, admiration, love, wonder, playfulness, tenderness. Instead they have filled our minds with an extensive literature and imagery of disgust, which includes a kind of voyeuristic fascination with what they see as the obscenity of female aging. Men's disgust for old women's bodies, with its language of contempt (shrivelled, sagging, drooping, wizened, ravaged, liver spots, crow's feet, old bag, etc.) is so familiar to us that it feels like home.

Still, if this were all, how is it that twenty years of ground-breaking feminism have not led us to rise up to challenge such a transparent, gross form of woman-hating? An honest answer to that question is painful but essential, and in *Look Me in the Eye*, Barbara Macdonald named the key to our resistance. Younger women can no longer afford to ignore the fact that we learned early on to pride ourselves on our distance from, and our superiority to, old women.

While I was thinking about this article, the picture of an old woman caught my eye from the comic pages. The three frames of "The Wizard of Id" (November 24, 1987) show an old woman, with thin hair pulled to a tiny topknot on her head, her breasts and hips a single balloon. The Wizard, her jaunty old husband (hand debonairly on hip, leg crossed with a flair), has bragged: "The king and I are judging a beauty contest tonight." She wags her finger. "That's degrading!" she exclaims through her downturned, toothless mouth. "My lady friends and I will picket!" The Wizard gets in the last word, which of course leaves her speechless: "That'll make a nice contrast."

This slice of mainstream media is jammed with political messages. Old women are ugly. Their view of things can be dismissed as just a way of venting their envy of young women. The old men, who have status and power, and therefore are the judges who matter, prize the young women's beauty and judge old women's bodies to be contemptible. The old woman has no defense since she too knows old women are ugly. And: the young woman's body in fact gains in value when set beside that of an old woman.

So younger women have not only unthinkingly adopted an ageist stance and woman-hating language from men, but the old woman's low currency temporarily drives up our own. As the "plain" white woman is at least not black, the "plainest" young woman is at least not old. The system gives us a vested interest in maintaining the politics of beauty and in joining in the oppression of old women.

The principal source of the distaste for old women's bodies should be perfectly familiar. It is very similar to the distaste anti-Semites feel toward Jews, homophobes feel toward lesbians and gays, racists toward blacks—the drawing back of the oppressor from the physical being of the oppressed. This physical revulsion travels deep; it is like fear. It feels entirely "natural" to the oppressor: he / she believes that everybody who claims to feel differently is simply hiding it out of politeness or cowardice.

When I was twelve, I had an argument with my grandmother. (Because of ageism, I feel a need to point out that she was no more racist than most white Baltimoreans of all ages in the 1940s.) It was probably my first political argument, and I felt both shaky and strong. Buttressed by a book on what in the forties was called "tolerance," I didn't see why little black girls couldn't go to my school. I can still remember her voice as she bypassed the intelligent argument, "But just think—would you want one to come to your house and spend the night?" *Yes, but would you want to marry one?* Physical revulsion is an ideal tool for maintaining oppressive systems, an instant check whenever reason or simple fairness starts to lead us on to more liberal paths.

To treat old women's minds as inconsequential or unstable is in one sense more serious, more dangerous than disgust for their bodies. But most women find that the more our bodies are perceived as old, the more our minds are dismissed as irrelevant. And if we are more than our bodies (whatever that means), we also are our bodies. If you find my body disgusting, no promises that you admire or love my mind can assure me that I can trust you.

No, the issue of "beauty" and "ugliness" is not frivolous. I think of two white women who are in their sixties. One, a lesbian psychologist from a working-class radical home, has written about the compelling urge she felt to have a face-lift—until she became aware that what she was dealing with was not her own ugliness, but the ugly projections of others, and became instead an activist against ageism. The other, a former airplane pilot and now a powerful photographer, has made a series of self-portraits that document, mercilessly, the bruises and scars of her own face-lift. These are not conforming Nancy Reagans. These are creative, independent, gutsy women, and they heard the message of society quite accurately: the pain of an operation for passing is less than the pain of enduring other people's withdrawal.

One example of the increased danger when an old woman's body is seen as less valuable than a young woman's is that she is unlikely to receive equal treatment by the medical profession, male or female. Old women attest to this fact. Recent research agrees. A UCLA study confirms that old women with breast cancer are treated less thoroughly than younger women, so that their lives are "needlessly shortened."

In her pamphlet, *Ageism in the Lesbian Community* (Crossing Press), Baba Copper points to the daily erosions of "ugly." She observes that the withdrawal of eroticism between women "which takes place after middle age (or at the point when a woman no longer passes for young) *includes withdrawal of the emotional work which women do to keep the flow of social interactions going*: teasing, touching, remembering details, checking back, supporting" (emphasis mine).

I hear a voice: "All of this may be true. But aren't you trying to place the heavy boot of political correctness on the mysteries of attraction?" No. But obviously the fewer women we can be drawn to because they are "too" Jewish or fat or Asian or old, the more impoverished our lives. And also: if we can never feel that mysterious attraction bubbling up towards an old woman, a disabled woman, a Hispanic woman, we can pretty well suspect that we are oppressive to such women in other ways.

Sometimes I sense a presumption that the fact that each of us is growing older gives us all license to speak of old women's bodies in insulting and degrading ways—or even makes this particular form of woman-hating somehow admirable and honest. Yet the fact that one of us may well in the next twenty years become disabled or fat doesn't make feminist editors eager to hear the details of any "honest" loathing we may feel for the bodies of disabled or fat women.

It does not surprise me that ageism is still with us, since eradicating oppressive attitudes is hard, ongoing, embarrassing, painful, gut work. But as a movement we have developed many sensitivities that are at least well beyond those of the mainstream. And we are quite familiar by now with the basic dynamics that almost all oppressions have in common (most of which we learned from the insights of the civil rights movement and other liberation movements). Erasure. Stereotyping. Internalized self-hatred, including passing when possible. The attempt to prove the oppression is "natural." Impugning of the mental and emotional capacities. Blame-the-victim. Patronizing. Tokenizing, Segregation. Contempt mingled with fear. And physical revulsion. So it seems almost incredible that we have not learned to identify these most flagrant signals of ageism.

How can we begin to change? We can—especially those of us in our forties and fifties—stop the trend of examining in public how disgusted we are at the thought of the bodily changes of growing old. This does not display our moral courage. It reveals our insensitivity to old women who have to hear once more that we think their bodies are the pits. We can recognize the ideas of beauty are socialized into us and that yes, Virginia, we *can* begin to move in the direction of resocializing ourselves. We can work (for ourselves and for any revolution we might imagine) to develop a deeper and more resonant—dare I say more *mature*—concept of beauty?

I am looking at two photographs. One is of Septima Clark, on the back of the book she wrote in her late eighties about her early and ongoing work in the civil rights movement. The other is a postcard of Georgia O'Keeffe from a photo twenty years before her death. The hairs on their scalps are no longer a mass, but stand out singly. O'Keeffe's nose is "too" strong, Clark's is "too" broad. O'Keeffe's skin is "wizened," Clark's is "too" dark. Our task is to learn, not to look insultingly beyond these features to a soul we can celebrate, but instead to take in these bodies as part of these souls—exciting, individual, beautiful.

PART VI

Nature

SO FAR, ALIENATION HAS always referred to the position of a particular social group in relation to a larger and, more importantly, more powerful group. Groups, and the persons belonging to them, are alienated to the extent that their lives are shaped for them by others, and their identities are, therefore, not fully their own. For, living in a world that one would not have chosen, one comes to be a person one does not recognize. The struggle against alienation is, therefore, the struggle for fuller self-determination.

But in thinking about alienation from nature, we appear to confront a very different sort of problem. Here it is all of humanity, whether powerful or not, that is thought to be estranged from its natural environment, the rain forests of the Andes, the ozone layer, the earth's atmosphere. This is what Bill McKibben believes.

With that he joins a venerable Western tradition. Our culture is fond of certain tales and myths about the aboriginal, the savage, the native, all those peoples thought to have lived in a Golden Age where they were one with nature. The stories told of peoples in harmony with the earth and its creatures, who took from the earth only what they needed and returned what they could, who did not pollute or exploit, and who were respectful of nature. We find this story in many places: the biblical account of the Garden of Eden, Rousseau's "noble savages," romanticized versions of the lives of American Indians, tales of the South Seas. The corollary morality tale sees the rise of civilization, culture, and technology as displacing these chthonic beings in favor of creatures alienated from nature. Adam and Eve leave the Garden of Eden with a mandate to subdue nature and to use the animals for their own purposes. Rousseau's "noble savages" degenerate in society. Native Americans are violently displaced by the wasteful and polluting industrial European cultures. And the heirs of those Europeans view nature as material to be exploited, polluted, and overpopulated as necessary to suit their purposes. What is left of nature is no longer our home, it is a rural Disneyland that we visit for spectacle, for recreation, for amusement, for escape. And if Bill McKibben is right, ultimately we have destroyed nature. There is no more wilderness, there is nothing that we have not brushed with our acid touch. We have finally overcome our alienation from nature not by returning to it but by destroying it.

Steven Vogel, on the other hand, argues that this view of nature as something separate from humans is itself an expression of our alienated state. Vogel argues that for Marx the "natural" environment is a human environment, a product of human labor, and thus to see it as an independent force, a "natural" entity, as Gaia for example, is to express our alienation from it. Nature is no such thing and our alienation consists in part in not recognizing that the natural world is a humanly built, or at least humanly shaped, world. Thus Vogel agrees with McKibben that there is no refuge from the social world, that there is no "natural" nature, but suggests that far from lamenting this fact, we recognize that at least since the rise of capitalism, it has always been thus. To recognize this is to begin to overcome our alienation. As Vogel says "To overcome the alienation would mean to reassert the sociality of the environment." Here alienation consists, once again, of finding ourselves in a world in which we do not recognize ourselves, because we did not make it. Our relation to natural resources has developed piecemeal as a consequence of decisions made by many different persons. Until very recently, no one gave much thought to the damage we do to forests, and to lakes, and to the atmosphere, and few realized that natural resources are limited.

In one way, this seems like alienation as we found it before: lack of control over our lives, because someone else has arranged them for us without asking us. But now there seems to be also a difference: there does not seem to be an identifiable other group that we can hold responsible for our alienation. Women can blame men; whites are to blame for the alienation of people of color. But who is to blame for the alienation of the disabled, or the old? In those cases of alienation it is not quite as easy to identify the culprit. We have seen other examples where those who are alienated are also implicated in the alienation of others. We have also seen cases where the alienated are complicit in their own alienation. Assigning blame for alienation is much easier in some cases than in others. An important aspect of many kinds of alienation is that it comes over us, and we do not quite understand its origins.

Assigning blame for alienation is often important, precisely because the alienated tend to blame themselves for their sense that they do not know where or who they are. They mistakenly take upon themselves the responsibility for being different and being made to suffer for that difference. But, in the end, alienation is cured only if the alienated can get a stronger hand in shaping their world.

That is true also of alienation from nature. In practice, both McKibben and Vogel agree on that. The remedies are for us to seriously rethink our uses of natural resources and to change our habits and our social organization in order to preserve the resources we have for future generations.

The End of Nature

BILL McKIBBEN

NATURE, WE BELIEVE, TAKES forever. It moves with infinite slowness through the many periods of its history, whose names we can dimly recall from high school biology—the Cambrian, the Devonian, the Triassic, the Cretaceous, the Pleistocene. At least since Darwin, nature writers have taken pains to stress the incomprehensible length of this path. "So slowly, oh, so slowly, have the great changes been brought about," John Burroughs wrote in 1912. "The Orientals try to get a hint of eternity by saying that when the Himalayas have been ground to powder by allowing a gauze veil to float against them once in a thousand years, eternity will only have just begun. Our mountains have been pulverized by a process almost as slow." We have been told that man's tenure is as a minute to the earth's day, but it is that vast day that has lodged in our minds. The age of the trilobites began six hundred million years ago. The dinosaurs lived for a hundred and fifty million years. Since even a million years is utterly unfathomable, the message is: Nothing happens quickly. Change takes unimaginable—"geological"—time.

This idea about time is essentially misleading, for the world as we know it, the world with human beings formed into some sort of civilization, is of quite comprehensible duration. People began to collect in a rudimentary society in the north of Mesopotamia some twelve thousand years ago. Using twenty-five years as a generation, that is four hundred and eighty generations ago—I have photographs of four. That is, I can think back one ninety-sixth of the way to the start of civilization. A skilled genealogist could easily get me one-fiftieth of the distance back. And I can conceive of how most of those forebears lived. From the work of archaeologists and from accounts like those in the Bible I have some sense of daily life at least as far back as the time of the Pharaohs, which is almost half way. Three hundred and twenty generations ago, Jericho was a walled city of three thousand souls. Three hundred and twenty is a large number, but not in the way that six hundred million is a large number, not inscrutably large. And within those twelve thousand years of civilization time is not uniform. The world as we really know it dates back to the Renaissance. The world as we *really* know it dates back to the Industrial Revolution. The world as we feel comfortable in it dates back to perhaps 1945.

In our words, our sense of an unlimited future, which is drawn from that apparently bottomless well of the past, is a delusion. True, evolution, grinding on ever so slowly, has taken billions of years to create us from slime, but that does not mean that time always moves so ponderously. Over a lifetime or a decade or a year, big and impersonal and dramatic changes can take place. We have accepted the idea that continents can drift in the course of aeons, or that continents can die in a nuclear second. But normal time seems to us immune from such huge changes. It isn't, though. In the last three decades, for example, the amount of carbon dioxide in the atmosphere has increased more than 10 percent, from about three hundred and fifteen parts per million to about three hundred fifty parts per million. In the last decade, an immense "hole" in the ozone layer has opened up above the South Pole each fall, and, according to the Worldwatch Institute, the percentage of West German forests damaged by acid rain has risen from less than 10 percent to more than 50 percent. Last year, for perhaps the first time since that starved Pilgrim winter at Plymouth, America consumed more grain than it grew. Burroughs again: "One summer day, while I was walking along the country road on the farm where I was born, a section of the stone wall opposite me, and not more than three or four yards distant, suddenly fell down. Amid the general stillness and immobility about me, the effect was quite startling. . . . It was the sudden summing-up of half a century or more of atomic changes in the material of the wall. A grain or two of sand yielded to the pressure of long years, and gravity did the rest."

In much the same comforting way that we think of time as imponderably long, we consider the earth to be inconceivably large. Although with the advent of space flight it became fashionable to picture the planet as a small orb of life and light in a dark, cold void, that image never really took hold. To any one of us, the earth is enormous, "infinite to our senses." Or, at least, it is if we think about it in the usual horizontal dimensions. There is a huge distance between my house, in the Adirondack Mountains, and Manhattan—it's a five-hour drive through one state in one country of one continent. But from my house to Allen Hill, near town, is a trip of five and a half miles. By bicycle it takes about twenty minutes, by car seven or eight. I've walked it in an hour and a half. If you turned that trip on its end, the twenty-minute pedal past Bateman's sandpit and the graveyard and the waterfall would take me to the height of Mt. Everest—almost precisely to the point where the air is too thin to breathe without artificial assistance. Into that tight space, and the layer of ozone above it, are crammed all that is life and all that maintains life.

This, I realize, is a far from novel observation. I repeat it only to make the case I made with regard to time. The world is not as large as we intuitively believe—space can be as short as time. For instance, the average American car driven the average American distance—ten thousand miles—in an average American year releases its own weight in carbon into the atmosphere. Imagine every car on a busy freeway pumping a ton of carbon into the atmosphere, and the sky seems less infinitely blue.

Along with our optimistic perceptions of time and space, other relatively minor misunderstandings distort our sense of the world. Consider the American failure to convert to the metric system. Like all schoolchildren of my vintage, I spent many days listening to teachers explain liters and meters and hectares and all the other logical units of measurement, and then promptly forgot about it. All of us did, except the scientists, who always use such units. As a result, if I read that there will be a rise of 0.8 degree Celsius in temperature between the year 2000, it sounds less ominous than a rise of a degree and a half Fahrenheit. Similarly, a ninety-centimeter rise in sea level sounds less ominous than a one-yard rise—and neither of them sounds all that ominous until one stops to think that over a beach with a normal slope such rise would bring the ocean ninety meters (that's two hundred and ninety-five feet) above its current tide line. In somewhat the same way, the logarithmic scale we use to determine the acidity or alkalinity of our soils and our waters—pH—distorts reality for anyone who doesn't use it on a daily basis. Normal rainwater has a pH of 5.6. But the acidified rain that falls on Buck Hill, behind my house, has a pH of 4.6 to 4.2, which is from ten to fourteen times as acid as normal.

Of all such quirks, though, probably the most significant is an accident of the calendar: we live too close to the year 2000. Forever we have read about the year 2000. It has become a symbol of the bright and distant future, when we will ride in air cars and talk on video phones. The year 2010 still sounds far off, almost unreachably far off, as if it were on the other side of a great body of water. But 2010 is as close as 1970—as close as the breakup of the Beatles—and the turn of the century is no farther in front of us than Ronald Reagan's election to the presidency is behind. We live in the shadow of a number, and that makes it hard to see the future.

Our comforting sense, then, of the permanence of our natural world—our confidence that it will change gradually and imperceptibly, if at all—is the result of a subtly warped perspective. Changes in our world which can affect us can happen in our lifetime—not just changes like wars but bigger and more sweeping events. Without recognizing it, we have already stepped over the threshold of such a change. I believe that we are at the end of nature.

By this I do not mean the end of the world. The rain will still fall, and the sun will still shine. When I say "nature," I mean a certain set of human ideas about the world and our place in it. But the death of these ideas begins with concrete changes in the reality around us, changes that scientists can measure. More and more frequently, these changes will clash with our perceptions, until our sense of nature as eternal and separate is finally washed away and we see all to clearly what we have done.

For the moment, though, forget about the higher temperatures and the dead trees and the other effects. The physical consequences of increasing the level of carbon dioxide will be staggering, but no more staggering than the simple fact of what we have already done. Carbon dioxide levels have gone up significantly, and globally. Elevated levels can be measured far from industry and miles above the ground. And the changes are irrevocable. They are not possibilities. They cannot be wished away, and they cannot be legislated away. To prevent them, we would have had to clean up our collective act many decades ago. We have done this ourselves—by driving our cars, running our factories, clearing our forests, growing our rice, turning on our air conditioners. In the years since the Civil War, and especially in the years since the Second World War, we have changed the atmosphere—changed it enough so that the climate will change dramatically. Most of the major events of human history gradually lose their meaning: wars that seemed at the time all-important are now a series of dates that schoolchildren don't even try to remember; great feats of engineering crumble in the desert. But now the way of life in one part of the world in one half century is altering every inch and every hour of the planet.

Most mornings, I hike up the hill outside my back door. Within a hundred yards, the woods swallow me up, and there is nothing to remind me of human society—no trash, no stumps, no fences, not even a real path. Looking out from the high places, you can't see road or house; it is a world apart from man. But once in a while someone will be cutting wood farther down the valley, and the snarl of a chain saw will fill the woods. It is harder these days to get caught up in the timelessness of the forests, for man is nearby. The sound of the chain saw doesn't blot out all the noises of the forest, or drive the animals away, but it does drive away the feeling that you are in another, separate, wild sphere.

Now that we have changed the most basic forces around us, the noises of that chain saw will always be in the woods. We have changed the atmosphere, and that is changing the weather. The temperature and the rainfall are no longer entirely the work of some uncivilizable force but instead are in part a product of our habits, our economies, our way of life. Even in the most remote wilderness, where the strictest laws forbid the falling of a single tree, the sound of that saw will be clear, and a walk in the woods will be changed by its whine. The world outdoors will mean the same thing as the world indoors, the hill the same thing as the house. An idea can become extinct, just like an animal or a plant. The idea in this case is "nature"— the wild province, the world apart from man, under whose rules he was born and died. We have not ended rainfall or sunlight. The wind still blows—but not from some other sphere, some inhuman place. It is too early to tell exactly how much harder the wind will blow, how much hotter the sun will shine. That is for the future. But their *meaning* has already changed.

The argument that nature is ended is complex; profound objections to it are possible, and I will try to answer them. But to understand what is ending requires some attention to the past. Not the ancient past, not the big bang or the primal soup—the European exploration of the New World is far enough back, since it is man's *idea* of nature that is important to this discussion, and it was in response to that wild country that much of our modern notion of nature developed. North America was not unaltered by man when the Europeans arrived, but its previous occupants had treated it fairly well. Most of it was still wilderness on the eve of the Revolution, when William Bartram, one of America's first professional naturalists, set out from his native Philadelphia to tour the South. Though some of the land through which he travelled had been settled (he spent a number of nights on plantations), the settlement was sparse, and the fields of indigo and rice gave way quickly to wilderness—not the dark and forbidding wilderness of European fairy tales but a blooming, humming, fertile paradise. Every page of his diary of the journey through "North & South Carolina, Georgia, East & West Florida, the Cherokee Country, the Extensive Territories of the Musogulges, or Creek Confederacy, and the Country of the Chactaws" shouts of the fecundity, the profligacy, of that fresh land: "I con-tinued several miles [over] verdant swelling knolls, profusely productive of flowers and fragrant strawberries, their rich juice dyeing my horse's feet and ankles." When he stops for dinner, he picks a wild orange, and stews a fresh-caught trout in its juices over his fire.

Whatever direction he struck off in, Bartram found vigorous beauty. His diary brims over with the grand Latin binomials of a thousand plants and animals (*Kalmia latifolia*, "snowy mantled" *Philadelphus inodorus*, *Rheum rheponticum*, *Magnolia grandiflore*) and also with the warm common names—the bank martin, the water wagtail, the mountain cock, the chattering plover, the bumblebee. But the roll call of his adjectives is even more indicative of his mood. In the account of a single evening, he musters fruitful, fragrant, sylvan (twice), mod-erately warm, exceeding pleasant, charming, fine, joyful, most beautiful, pale gold, golden, russet, silver (twice), ultramarine, velvet-black, orange, prodi-gious, gilded, delicious, harmonious, soothing, tuneful, sprightly, elevated, cheerful (twice), high and airy, brisk and cool, clear, sweet, and healthy. And where he can't see, he imagines marvels: the fish disappearing into subterranean streams, "where, probably, they are separated from each other, by innumerable paths, or secret rocky avenues; and after encountering various obstacles, and beholding new and unthought-of scenes of pleasure and disgust, after many days absence from the surface of the world emerge again from the dreary vaults, and appear exulting in gladness, and sporting the transparent waters of some far distant lake." But he is no Disney—this is no "Fantasia." He is a scientist recording his observations, and words like "cheerful" and "sweet" seem to be technical descriptions of the untouched world in which he wandered.

This sort of joy in the natural world was not a literary convention, a given. Much of literature regarded wilderness as ugly and crude until the Romantic movement of the late eighteenth century; Andrew Marvell, for one, referred to mountains as "ill-designed excrescences." This silliness changed into a new silliness with the Romantics. Chateaubriand's immensely popular *Atala* describes the American wilderness as full of bears "drunk with grapes, and reeling on the branches of elm trees." But the rapturous fever took on a healthier aspect in this country. Most of the pioneers, to be sure, saw a buffalo as something to hunt, a forest as something to cut down, a flock of passenger pigeons as a call for heavy artillery (farmers would bring their hogs to feed on the carcasses raining down in the slaughter), but there were always a good many—even, or especially, among the hunters and loggers—who recognized and described the beauty and order of this early time.

Over time, though, we've reconciled ourselves to the idea that we'll not be the first up any hill. The wonder of nature does not depend on its freshness. The Grand Canyon is so grand that we don't mind not being the first people to see it. But still we feel the need for pristine places. We have legislated wilderness, set aside big tracts of land where, in the words of the federal statute, "the earth and its community of life are untrammeled by man." Even if we don't visit them, they matter to us. The Arctic National Wildlife Refuge, on Alaska's northern shore, is reached by just a few hundred people a year, but it has a vivid life in the minds of many more, who are upset that oil companies want to drill there. They are upset not only because it might harm the caribou but because here is a vast space free of roads and buildings and antennas—a blank spot.

When Rachel Carson wrote *Silent Spring*, she was able to find some parts of the Arctic still untouched—no DDT in the fish, the beaver, the beluga, the caribou, the moose, the polar bear, the walrus. The cranberries, the salmonberries, and the wild rhubarb all tested clean, though two snowy owls, probably as a result of their migrations, carried small amounts of the pesticide, as did fat samples from several Eskimos who had been away to a hospital in Anchorage. In other words, as pervasive a problem as DDT was and is, one could always imagine that somewhere a place existed free of its taint. (And, largely as a result of Carson's book, there are more and more such places.) As pervasive and growing as the problem of acid rain surely is, at the moment places still exist with a rainfall of an acceptable pH. And if we wished to stop acid rain we could: experimenters have raised tents over groves of trees to demonstrate that if the acid bath ceases a forest will return to normal. Even the radiation from an event as nearly universal as the explosion at the Chernobyl nuclear power plant has begun to fade, and Scandinavians can once more eat some of the vegetables they grow. The idea of wilderness, then, can survive most of man's destruction of nature. If the ground is dusty and trodden, we look at the sky; if the sky is smoggy, we travel to some place where it's clear; if we can't travel to some place where it's clear, we imagine ourselves in Alaska or Australia or some other place where it is, and that works nearly as well. Nature is durable in our imaginations. The idea of wildness has outlasted the exploration of the entire globe. Standing in the middle of a grimy English mill town, George Orwell reflected, "In spite of hard trying, man has not yet succeeded in doing his dirt everywhere. The earth is so vast and still so empty that even in the filthy heart of civilization you find fields where the grass is green instead of gray; perhaps if you looked for them you might even find streams with live fish in them instead of salmon tins."

But now the basis of that faith is lost. The idea of nature will not survive the new, global pollution—the carbon dioxide and the methane and the like. This new rupture with nature is different both in scope and in kind from salmon tins in an English stream. We have deprived nature of its independence, and that is fatal to its meaning. Nature's independence *is* its meaning.

If you travel by plane and dog team and snowshoe to the farthest corner of the Arctic and it is a mild summer day, you will not know whether the temperature is what it is "supposed" to be or whether you are standing in the equivalent of a heated room. If the wind is howling and the temperature is twenty below, might it otherwise be forty below? Since most of us get to the North Pole only in our minds, our situation is more like this: if, in July, there's a heat wave in London, it won't be a natural phenomenon. It will be a man-made phenomenon—an amplification of what nature intended, or a total invention. Or it *might* be a man-made phenomenon, which amounts to the same thing. The storm that could have snapped the hot spell may never form, or may veer off in some other direction—not by the laws of nature but by the laws of nature as rewritten by man. If the sun feels sweet on the back of your neck, well, that's fine, but it isn't nature. What has happened is the extinction of summer and its replacement with something else that will be called "summer." This new summer will retain some of the season's relative characteristics—it will be hotter than the rest of the year, for instance, and it will be the time of year when crops grow—but it will not be summer, just as even the best prosthesis is not a leg. Those "record highs" and "record lows" that the weathermen are always talking about are meaningless now. They imply a connection between the past and the present which doesn't exist. And, of course, climate determines an enormous amount of the rest of nature—where the forests stop and the tundra or the prairies begin, where the rain falls and where the arid deserts squat, where the wind blows strong and steady, where the glaciers form, how fast the lakes evaporate, and how high the seas rise.

About half a mile from my house, right at the head of a small lake, the town has installed a streetlight. It is the only one for miles, and it is a good thing that it is there; without it, a car or two each summer would miss the turn and end up in the drink. Still, it intrudes on the dark. Most of the year, once the summer people have left, there is another light to be seen. On a starry night, the Milky Way stands out like a marquee; on a cloudy night, you can walk in pitch-black darkness, unable to see even the dog trotting at your side. But then, around a bend, there is the streetlamp, breaking up the feeling of the night. And now it is as if we had put a huge lamp in the sky and cast that same prosaic light everywhere.

We will have a hard time accepting this new state of affairs. Even the most far-seeing naturalists of an earlier day failed to comprehend that the atmosphere, the climate, could be dramatically altered. Thoreau, complaining about the logging that eventually destroyed every stand of virgin timber between the Atlantic and the Mississippi, said that soon the East "would be so bald that every man would have to grow whiskers to hide its nakedness, but, thank God, the sky was safe." And John Muir, the Scottish-born explorer of Yosemite, wrote one day in his diary, about following a herd of grazing sheep through the valley, "Thousands of feet trampling leaves and flowers, but in this mighty wilderness they seem but a feeble band, and a thousand gardens will escape their blighting touch. They cannot hurt the trees, though some of the seedlings suffer, and should the woolly locusts be greatly multiplied, as on account of dollar value they are likely to be, then the forests, too, may in time be destroyed. Only the sky will then be safe." George Perkins Marsh, the first modern environmentalist, who knew over a century ago that cutting down forests was a disastrous idea, wrote, "The revolutions of the seasons, with their alternations of temperature, and of length of day and night, the climate of different zones, and the general condition and movements of the atmosphere and the seas, depend upon causes for the most part cosmical, and, of course, wholly beyond our control."

Even as it dawns on us what we have done, there will be plenty of opportunity to forget—at least, for a while—that anything has changed. It isn't natural beauty that is ended; in the same way that smog breeds spectacular sunsets, there may be new, unimagined beauties. What will change is the meaning that beauty carries, for when we look at a sunset we see, or think we see, many things beyond a particular arrangement of orange and purple and rose.

It is also true that this is not the first huge rupture in the globe's history. Some thirty times since the earth formed, "planetesimals" at least ten miles in diameter and travelling at sixty times the speed of sound have crashed into the earth, releasing perhaps a thousand times as much energy as would be liberated by the explosion of all present stocks of nuclear weapons; such events, some scientists say, may have destroyed up to 90 percent of all living organisms. Ice ages have come and gone. On a larger scale, the sun has steadily increased its brightness, growing nearly 30 percent more luminous since life on earth began, forcing that life to keep forever scrambling to stay ahead (a race it will eventually lose, though not for some billions of years). Or consider an example more closely resembling the sharp divide we have now crossed. About two billion years ago, the spread of a particular kind of cyanobacteria caused, in short order, an increase in atmospheric oxygen from one part in a million to one part in five—that is, from one ten-thousandth of a percent to twenty-one percent. Compared with that, the increase in carbon dioxide from two hundred and eighty to five hundred and sixty parts per million is as the hill behind my house to Annapurna. "This was by far the greatest pollution crisis the earth has ever endured," the microbiologist Lynn Margulis writes in "Microcosmos." Oxygen poisoned most microbial life, which, Margulis points out, "had no defense against this cataclysm except the standard way of DNA replication and duplication, gene transfer, and mutation." And, indeed, these adaptations produced the successful oxygen-utilizing life forms that now dominate the earth.

But each of these examples is different from what we now experience, for they were "natural," as opposed to man-made. A pint-size planet cracks into the earth; the ice advances and retreats; the sun, by the immutable laws of stars, burns brighter until its inevitable explosion; genetic mutation sets certain bacteria to spew out oxygen until they dominate the planet—a strictly natural pollution.

One could argue that the current crisis, too, is "natural," since man is part of nature. This echoes the views of the early Greek philosophers who made no distinction between matter and consciousness: nature included everything. The British scientist James Lovelock wrote some years ago that "our species with its technology is simply an inevitable part of the natural scene"; that is, we are little more than mechanically advanced beavers. According to this view, to say that human beings have "ended" nature, or even damaged nature, makes no sense. But it is a debater's point, a semantic argument. When I say that we have ended nature, I mean not that natural processes have ceased but that we have ended the thing that has—at least, in modern times—defined nature for us: its separation from human society.

That separation has been real. I sit writing here in my office. On the wall facing me is a shelf of reference books, and underneath them a typewriter and a computer. Visible through the window is a steep mountain, with nearly a mile of bare ridge and a pond almost at the peak. The mountain and the office are separate parts of my life; I do not think of them as connected. At night, it's dark out there; save for the streetlamp by the lake, there's not a light for twenty miles to the west and thirty to the south. But in here the light shines. Its beams stretch a few yards into the night and then falter, turn to shadow and black. In the winter, it's cold out there, but in here the fire burns until near dawn, and when it dwindles the oil burner kicks in. What happens in here I control; what happens out there has always been the work of some independent force. It is this separate nature I am talking about when I use the word—"nature," if you like.

Scientists may argue that natural processes still rule, that the chemicals even now trapping the earth's reflected heat or eating away the ozone or acidifying this rain are proof that nature is still in charge—still our master. Some have talked about God as present in the interstices of the atom, or in the mysteries of quantum theory, or in the double helix of DNA and other bits of "information." To all but the few who really understand the math, however, this is a minor and secondhanded comfort—an occult, esoteric knowledge. We draw our lesson from what we can see and feel and hear around us. The nature that matters is not the whirling fuzziness of electrons and quarks and neutrinos, which will continue unchanged; it is not the vast fields and fluxes that scientists can find with their telescopes. The nature that matters is the temperature, and the rain, and the leaves turning color on the maples, and the raccoons around the garbage can.

The invention of nuclear weapons may have marked the beginning of the end of nature; we possessed, finally, the ability to overmaster it, to leave an indelible imprint everywhere, all at once. "The nuclear peril is usually seen in isolation from the threats to other forms of life and their ecosystems, but in fact it should be seen as the very center of the ecological crisis—as the cloud-covered Everest of which the more immediate, visible kinds of harm to the environment are the mere foothills," Jonathan Schell wrote in *The Fate of the Earth*. And, indeed, at the time he was writing—less than a decade ago—it was hard to conceive of a threat of the same magnitude. Global warming was one obscure theory among many; nuclear weapons were unique—and remain so, if only for the speed with which they work. But the nuclear dilemma is at least open to human reason. We can decide not to use the weapons—even to reduce and perhaps eliminate them. And the horrible power of these weapons, which has been amply demonstrated in Japan and on Bikini and under Nevada and many times in our imaginations, had led us fitfully in that hopeful direction.

By contrast, the various processes that lead to the end of nature have been essentially beyond human thought. Only a few people, for instance, knew that carbon dioxide would warm up the world, and for a long time they were unsuccessful in their efforts to alert the rest of us. Now it is too late—not too late (as I shall discuss) to ameliorate some of the changes, and so perhaps avoid the worst of their consequences. But a shift in weather is inevitable.

The passing of nature as we have known it, like the passing of any large idea, will have its recognizable effects both immediately and over time. In 1893, when Frederick Jackson Turner announced to the American Historical Association that the frontier was closed, no one was aware that the frontier had been the defining force in American life. But in its absence this was understood. One reason we pay so little close attention to the separate natural world around us is that it has always been there and we have presumed that it always would be. As it disappears, its primary importance will become clearer, in the same way that some people think they have put their parents out of their lives, until the day comes to bury them.

Above all, the world displays a lovely order, an order comforting in its intricacy. And the most appealing part of this harmony, perhaps, is its permanence—the sense that we are part of something with roots stretching back nearly forever and branches reaching forward just as far. Purely human life provides only a partial fulfillment of this desire for a kind of immortality. But the earth and all its processes—the sun growing plants; flesh feeding on these plants; flesh decaying to nourish more plants, to name just one cycle—give us some sense of an enduring role. John Muir expressed this sense of immortality beautifully. Born to a stern Calvinist father, who used a belt to help him memorize the Bible, Muir eventually escaped to the woods, travelling to the Yosemite Valley of California's Sierra Nevadas. The journal of his first summer there is filled with a breathless joy at the grandeur around him. Again and again in that Sierra June—"the greatest of all the months of my life"—he uses the word "immortality," and he uses it in a specific way, designed to contrast with his father's grim and selfish religion. Time ceases to have its normal meaning in those hills: "Another glorious Sierra day in which one seems to be dissolved and absorbed and sent pulsing onward we know not where. Life seems neither long nor short, and we take no more heed to save time or make haste than do the trees and stars. This is true freedom, a good practical sort of immortality." To someone in a mood like this, space is no more of a limitation than time: "We are now in the mountains and they are in us . . . making every nerve quiver, filling every pore and cell of us. Our flesh-and-bone tabernacle seems transparent as glass to the beauty about us, as if truly an inseparable part of it, thrilling with the air and trees, streams and rocks, in the waves of the sun—a part of all nature, neither old nor young, sick nor well, but immortal."

Some dim recognition that God and nature are intertwined has led us to pay at least lip service to the idea of "stewardship" of the land. If there is a God, He probably does want us to take good care of the planet, but He may want something even more radical. The Old Testament contains in the book of Job one of the most far-reaching defenses ever written of wilderness—of nature free from the hand of man. The argument gets at the heart of what the loss of nature will mean to us. Job is, of course, a just and prosperous man brought low. He refuses to curse God, but he does demand a meeting with Him and an explanation of his misfortune. Job refuses to accept the reasoning of his orthodox friends—that he has unknowingly sinned and is therefore being punished. Their view—that the earth revolves around man, and every consequence is explained by man's actions—doesn't satisfy Job, because he knows he is innocent.

Finally, God arrives, a voice from the whirlwind. But instead of engaging in deep metaphysical discussion He talks at some length about nature, about creation. "Where were you when I laid the earth's foundation?" He asks. In an exquisite poem He lists His accomplishments, His pride in His creation always evident. Was Job there when He "put the sea behind closed doors?" Job was not; therefore, Job cannot hope to understand many mysteries, including why rain falls "on land where no one lives, to meet the needs of the lonely wastes and make grass sprout upon the ground."

"Behold now Behemoth," God roars. "He eateth grass as an ox. Lo now, his strength is in his loins. And his force is in the muscles of his belly. He moveth his tail like a cedar. . . . His bones are as tubes of brass. His limbs are like bars of iron. . . . Behold, if a river overflow he trembleth not. He is confident, though Jordan swell even to his mouth. Shall any take him when he is on the watch, or pierce through his nose with a snare?" The answer, clearly, is not: not all nature is ours to subdue.

Nature has provided a way for us to recognize God, and to talk about who He is—even, as in Job, a way for God to talk about who He is. So what will the end of nature as we have known it mean to our understanding of God and of man? For those of us who have tended to locate God in nature—who looked upon spring, say, as a sign of His existence and a clue to His meaning—what does it mean that we have destroyed the old spring and replaced it with a new one, of our own devising? We as a race turn out to be stronger than we suspected— much stronger. In a sense, we turn out to be God's equal, or, at least, His rival—able to destroy creation. This idea has been building for a while. "We became less and less capable of seeing ourselves as small within creation, partly because we thought we could comprehend it statistically, but also because we were becoming creators, ourselves, of a mechanical creation by which we felt ourselves greatly magnified," the essayist Wendell Berry writes. "Why, after all, should one get excited about a mountain when one can see almost as far from the top of a building, much farther from an airplane, farther still from a space capsule?" And our nuclear weapons obviously created the possibility that we could exercise godlike powers. But the possibility is different from the fact. Though we seem to have recognized the implications of nuclear weapons and begun to back away from them, we have shown no such timidity in our wholesale alteration of nature. We are in charge now, like it or not. When God asks, as He does in Job, "Who shut in the sea with doors . . . and prescribed bounds for it?" and "Who can tilt the waterskins of the heavens?" we must now answer that it is us.

With this new power comes a deep sadness. I took a day's hike last fall, following the creek that runs by my door to the place where it crosses the main county road. It's a distance of maybe nine miles as the car flies, but rivers are far less efficient, and endlessly follow time-wasting, uneconomical meanders. The creek cuts some fancy figures, and so I was able to feel a bit exploratory—a budget Bob Marshall. In a strict sense, it wasn't much of an adventure. I stopped at the store for a liverwurst sandwich at lunchtime, the path was generally downhill, the temperature stuck at an equable fifty-five degrees, and since it was the week before the hunting season opened I didn't have to sing as I walked. It isn't Yosemite, this small valley, but its beauties are absorbing, and one can say, with Muir on his mountaintop, "Up here all the world's prizes seem as nothing."

And so what if it isn't nature primeval? One of my neighbors has left several kitchen chairs along his stretch of the bank, spaced at fifty-yard intervals, for comfort in fishing. At one old homestead, a stone chimney stands at each end of a foundation now filled by a graceful birch. Near the one real waterfall, a lot of rusty pipe and collapsed concrete testifies to the mill that once stood there. But these aren't disturbing sights; they're almost comforting—reminders of the way that nature has endured and outlived and with dignity reclaimed so many schemes and disruptions of man. (A mile or so off the creek, there's a mine where a hundred and fifty years ago a visionary tried to extract pigment for paint and pack it out by mule and sledge. He rebuilt after a fire; finally, an avalanche convinced him. The path in is faint now, but his chimney, too, still stands, a small Angkor Wat of free enterprise.) Large sections of the area were once farmed; but the growing season is not much more than a hundred days in a good year, and the limits established by that higher authority were stronger than the (powerful) attempts of individual men to circumvent them, and so the farms returned to forests, with only a dump of ancient bottles or a section of stone wall as a memorial. These ruins are humbling sights, reminders of the negotiations with nature which have established the world as we know it.

Changing socks in front of the waterfall, I thought back to the spring of 1987, when a record snowfall melted in only a dozen or so warm April days. A little to the south, a swollen stream washed out a highway bridge, closing the New York Thruway for months. The creek became a river, and the waterfall, normally one of those diaphanous-veil affairs, turned into a cataract. It filled me with awe to stand there then, on the shaking ground, and think, this is what nature is capable of. But as I sat there this time, and thought about the dry summer we'd just come through, there was nothing awe-inspiring or instructive, or even lulling, in the fall of the water. It suddenly seemed less like a waterfall than like a spillway to accommodate the overflow of a reservoir. That didn't decrease its beauty, but it changed its meaning. It has begun, or will soon begin, to rain and snow when the chemicals we've injected into the atmosphere add up to rain or snow—when they make it hot enough over some tropical sea to form a cloud and send it this way. In one sense, I will have no more control over this process than I ever did. But the waterfall seemed different, and lonelier. Instead of a world where rain had an independent and mysterious existence, I was living in a world where rain was becoming a subset of human activity: a phenomenon like smog or commerce or the noise from the skidder towing logs on the nearby road—all the things over which I had no control, either. The rain bore a brand: it was a steer, not a deer. And that was where the loneliness came from. There's nothing here except us.

At the same time that I felt lonely, though, I also felt crowded—without privacy. We go to the woods in part to escape. But now there is nothing except us, and so there is no escaping other people. As I walked in the autumn woods, I saw a lot of sick trees. With the conifers, I suspected acid rain. (At least I have the luxury of only suspecting; in too many places, they know.) And so who walked with me in the woods? Well, there were the presidents of the Midwestern utilities, who kept explaining why they had to burn coal to make electricity (cheaper, fiduciary responsibility, no *proof* it kills trees), and then there were the congressmen, who couldn't bring themselves to do anything about it (personally favor, but politics the art of compromise, very busy with the war on drugs), and before long the whole human race had arrived to explain its aspirations. We like to drive, it said, air-conditioning is a necessity nowadays, let's go to the mall. Of course, the person I was fleeing most fearfully was myself, for I drive, and I'm burning a collapsed barn behind the house next week because it is much the cheapest way to deal with it, and I live on about four hundred times the money that Thoreau conclusively proved was enough, so I've done my share to take this independent, eternal world and turn it into a science fair project.

Our local shopping mall has a club of people who go "mall-walking" every day. They circle the shopping center en masse—Caldor to Sears to J. C. Penney, circuit after circuit, with an occasional break to shop. This seems less absurd to me now than it did at first. I like to walk in the outdoors not solely because the air is cleaner but also because outdoors we venture into a sphere larger than we are. Mall-walking involves too many other people, and too many purely human sights, ever to be more than good-natured exercise. But now, out in the wild, the sunshine on one's shoulders is a reminder that man has cracked the ozone, that, thanks to us, the atmosphere absorbs where it once released. The greenhouse effect is a more apt name than those who coined it can have imagined. The carbon dioxide and the other trace gases act like the panes of glass of a greenhouse—the analogy is accurate. But it's more than that. We have built a greenhouse—a human creation—where once there bloomed a sweet and wild garden.

Or, just possibly, we could change our habits.

One very small example of an idea so large as to be unwieldy: To cope with the greenhouse world, people in the developed countries will probably begin to install much more energy-efficient washing machines. That would reduce somewhat the amount of carbon dioxide each of us puffs into the atmosphere. But what if, instead, people got together with their neighbors and agreed to buy a single washing machine for the entire block (not such a novel concept to people in big-city apartment houses)? And what if they also decided that instead of continually buying fashionable clothes they would reduce their wardrobes to a comfortable, or even uncomfortable, minimum? What if, in other words, we began to reject a pervasive individual consumerism, and began to alter a basic way we look at ourselves? Mightn't such a path, broadened to include other facets of daily life, offer the best way not only to avoid overheating the planet but also to keep from transforming it in the other sad ways I have discussed?

As long as the desire for endless material advancement drives us, there is no way to set limits. We are unlikely to develop genetic engineering to eradicate diseases and then not use it to manufacture perfectly efficient chickens; there is nothing in the logic of our beliefs that would lead us to draw that line. If there is one item that virtually all successful politicians on earth—socialist and fascist and capitalist—agree on, it is that "economic growth" is good, necessary, the proper end of organized human activity.

Our present environmental troubles, though, just might give us the chance to change the way we think. Spurred by the realization of what we have done, we might begin to think and then behave more humbly. As the effects of man's domination have become clearer in recent years, a new idea has begun to spread, both in America and abroad. Some environmentalists have begun to talk of two approaches to the world: the traditional anthropocentric view, and the biocentric vision of mankind as just another part of the world. This concept is foreign to most of us. My first sense of what it might mean came a couple of summers ago in Idaho, when I was camped next to a man who hikes almost every year from Mexico to Canada. A dozen times, he told me, he had met grizzly bears, the grandest mammals left on the continent: "The last one, he stood on his hind legs, clicked his jaws, woofed three times. I was too close to him, and he was just letting me know. Another one, he circled me about forty feet away and wouldn't look me in the eye. When you get that close, you realize you're part of the food chain."

The idea that man doesn't necessarily belong at the top—that the hierarchy we've spent many thousands of years establishing is dangerous to other species and also to ourselves—is a strange and powerful idea. The few philosophers and environmentalists interested in such a Copernican shift have taken to calling this alternative path "deep ecology"—as opposed to the "shallow ecology" of conventional environmentalism, which seeks merely to turn mankind into better stewards. Deep ecology suggests that instead of just giving better orders we learn to give fewer and fewer orders—to sink back into the natural world. Deep ecologists question the industrial basis of our civilization, the need to forever grow in wealth and numbers, the entire way we live. We should, they say, work toward a smaller world population—half the current one, maybe, or even less. And we should lay aside our desire for material advancement in favor of "doing with enough."

Such ideas are not blueprints; they aren't even outlines. But they are at least a starting point for those who seek to save a world fast vanishing. They are radical ideas, but we live at a radical moment. We live at the end of nature, the instant when the essential character of the world is changing. If our way of life is ending nature, it is not radical to talk about transforming our way of life. When I climb the hill out back, I often pause on a ledge from which I can see my house—the car in the driveway, the chimney above the stove. I love the life that that house represents, love it very much. But I love the hemlocks around me on the hill, too, and the coyotes, and the deer. And it seems that either that life down there must change or the life up here around me will change—the trees will wilt in the sun or else sprout in perfect, heat-tolerant, genetically improved rows.

Exactly what a humbler world would look like I cannot say. We are used to planning utopias, worlds engineered for human happiness. But this would be something different—an "atopia," perhaps, where the integrity of the planet, and not our desires, would be the engine. If our thinking changed, the details would follow of their own accord. Perhaps we might all begin to use the "appropriate technology" of "sustainable development" which we urge on Third World peasants—solar cookstoves, or bicycle-powered pumps. Probably many more of us would be growing our own food. Such solutions are not beyond our imagination. When we decided that accumulation and growth were our economic ideals, we invented wills and lending at interest and puritanism and supersonic aircraft. Why would we come up with ideas less powerful in an all-out race to do with less?

The difficulty in accomplishing this transformation is almost certainly more psychological than intellectual—less that we can't figure out major alterations in our way of life than that we don't want to. The people whose lives may point the way—Thoreau, say, or Gandhi—we dismiss as exceptional, a polite way of saying that there is no reason we should be expected to go where they pointed. The challenge they presented with the example of their lives is much more subversive than anything they wrote or said, for if they could live simply it's no use saying we couldn't. And maybe now we should—not just for moral or aesthetic reasons but for reasons of chemistry and physics.

Such a change would obviously be colossally difficult. For one thing, while we as individuals would have to change our habits, it would mean very little—save as a good gesture—for any one of us to, say, drive less. Most people have to be persuaded to drive less, and persuaded quickly; this is the first environmental crisis one can't escape by heading for the woods. It's also difficult for us to turn our backs on the idea of economic growth, because it has been sold as the answer to the poverty that afflicts most of the planet. For example, S. Fred Singer, the greenhouse skeptic, writes, "Drastically limiting the emission of carbon dioxide means cutting deeply into global energy use. But limiting economic growth condemns the poor, especially in the Third World, to continued poverty, if not outright starvation." I am sometimes dubious about the actual depth of feeling for the Third World such arguments imply; they mesh too conveniently with our desires. An overheated, ozone-depleted world would probably be crueller to the poor than to the rich, and if our desire is to alleviate poverty, limiting our standard of living and sharing our surplus would likely work as well. But I have no doubt about the power of arguments like Singer's to stall effective action of any sort if we are reluctant to take such action in the first place.

Still, problems like the inertia of affluence, the push of poverty, and the soaring population are traditional problems. We can think about them, deal with them, perhaps overcome them. In my lifetime, in this country, we have gone from Jim Crow to affirmative action, and there is no saying we can't do something similar with regard to the planet.

I fear that we won't, though, and for an entirely different set of reasons— reasons intimately linked to the unique and depressing moment in which we find ourselves. As we have seen, nature is already ending. And not only does its passing prevent us from returning to the world we previously knew but also, for a couple of powerful reasons, it makes any of the fundamental changes I've discussed even more unlikely than they might be in easier times.

In the first place, the end of nature is a plunge into the unknown, fearful as much *because* it is unknown as because the world may become hot or dry or whipped by hurricanes. But the type of shift in attitudes I've been describing— the deep ecology alternative, for instance—would make life even more un- predictable. One would have to begin to forgo the traditional methods of securing one's future—children, possessions, and so on. As the familiar world around us starts to change, every threatened instinct will have us scrambling to preserve at least our familiar style of life. We can—we may well—make the adjustments necessary for our survival. For instance, some of the early work in agricultural biotechnology has focused on inventing plants able to survive heat and drought. It seems the sensible thing to do—the way to keep life as "normal" as possible in the face of change. It leads, though, as I have said, to the second end of nature: the imposition of our artificial world in place of the broken natural one.

I got a glimpse of this particular future a few years ago, when I spent some time along the La Grande River in sub-Arctic Quebec. It is a barren land but beautiful—a taiga of tiny ponds and hummocks stretching to the horizon, carpeted in light-green caribou moss. There are trees—almost all black spruce, and all spindly, sparse. No one lived there save a small number of Indians and Eskimos—about the number the area could support. A decade or so ago, Hydro-Quebec, the provincial utility, decided to exploit the power of the La Grande by building three huge dams along a three-hundred-and-fifty-mile stretch of the river. The largest is the size of fifty-four thousand two-story houses, a Hydro-Quebec spokesman told me. Its spillway could carry the combined flow of all the rivers of Europe. Erecting it was a Bunyanesque task: eighteen thousand men carved the roads north through the taiga and poured the concrete. (Photographs show the cooks stirring spaghetti sauce with canoe paddles.) This is the perfect example of "environmentally sound" energy generation; the dams produce a tremendous amount of power without giving off any greenhouse gas. They are the sort of structure we will be clamoring to build as the warming progresses.

But environmentally sound is not the same as natural. The dams have altered an area larger than Switzerland. The flow of the Caniapiscau River has been partly reversed to provide more water for the turbines. In September of 1984, at least ten thousand caribou drowned trying to cross the river during their annual migration. They were crossing at their usual spot, but the river was not its usual size; it was so swollen that many of the animals were swept forty-five miles downstream. Every good argument—the argument that fossil fuels cause the greenhouse effect, the argument that in a drier, hotter world we will need more water, the argument that as our margin of security dwindles we must act to restore it—will lead us to more La Grande projects, more dams on the Colorado, more "management." Every argument that the warmer weather and increased ultraviolet are killing plants and causing cancer will have us looking to genetic engineering for salvation. And with each such step we will move farther from nature.

And as that happens the counterargument—the argument for nature—will grow ever fainter. Wendell Berry once argued that in the absence of a "fascination" with the wonder of the natural world "the energy needed for its preservation will never be developed"—that "there must be a mystique of the rain if we are ever to restore the purity of the rainfall." This makes sense when the problem is transitory—sulfur dioxide emissions drifting over the Adirondacks. But how can there be a mystique of the rain, now that every drop—even the drops that fall as snow on the Arctic, even the drops that fall deep in the remaining forest primeval—bears the permanent stamp of man? Having lost its separateness, nature loses its special power. Instead of being a category like God—something beyond our control—it is now a category like the defense budget or the minimum wage, a problem we must work out. This alone changes its meaning completely, and changes our reaction to it. The end of nature probably also makes us reluctant to attach ourselves to its remnants, for the same reason that we usually don't choose new friends from among the terminally ill. I love the mountain outside my back door—the stream that runs down a quarter-mile mossy chute, and the place where the slope flattens into an open plain of birch and oak. But I know that in some way I resist getting to know it better—for fear, weak-kneed as it sounds, of getting hurt. I fear that if I knew as well as a forester what sick trees look like I would see them everywhere. I find now that I like the woods best in winter, when it is harder to tell what might be dying, but I try not to love even winter too much, because of the January perhaps not so distant when the snow will fall as warm rain. There is no future in loving nature.

And there may not even be much past. Though Thoreau's writings grew in value and importance the closer we drew to the end of nature, the time fast approaches when he will be inexplicable, his notions less comprehensible to future men than cave paintings are to us. Thoreau writes of the land around Katahdin that it "was vast, Titanic, and such as man never inhabits. Some part of the beholder, even some vital part, seems to escape through the loose grating of his ribs. . . . Nature has got him at a disadvantage, caught him alone, and pilfers him of some of his divine faculty. She does not smile on him as in the plains. She seems to say sternly, Why came ye before your time. This ground is not prepared for you." That sentiment describes perfectly the last stage of the relationship of man to nature; though we had subdued her in the low places, the peaks, the poles, the jungles still rang with her pure message. But what will this passage mean in the years to come, when Katahdin, the "cloud factory," is ringed by clouds that are the work of man? When the great pines around its base have been genetically improved for straightness of trunk and "proper branch drop," or, more likely, have sprung from the cones of genetically improved trees that began a few miles and a few generations distant on some timber plantation? When the moose that ambles by is part of a herd whose rancher is committed to the enlightened notion that "conservation and profit can go hand in hand"? Soon Thoreau will make no sense. And when that happens the end of nature, which began with our alteration of the atmosphere and continued with the responses of the planetary managers and the genetic engineers, will be final. The loss of memory will be the eternal loss of meaning.

I understand perfectly well that defiance may bring prosperity, and a sort of security—that more hydropower will mean less carbon dioxide, and that genetic engineering will help the sick, and that much progress can still be made against human misery. And I have no plans to live in a cave, or even in an unheated cabin. If it took twelve thousand years to get where we are, it will take a few more generations to climb back down. But this could be the epoch in which people decide at least to go no farther along the path we have been following—when we make not only the necessary technological adjustments to preserve the world from overheating but also the necessary mental adjustments to insure that we will never again put our good ahead of everything else's. This is the path I choose, for it offers at least a shred of hope for a living, eternal, meaningful world.

As birds have flight, our special gift is reason. Part of that reason drives the intelligence that allows us to master DNA or build big power plants. But our reason could also keep us from following blindly the biological imperatives toward endless growth in numbers and territory. Our reason allows us to conceive of our species as a species, and to recognize the danger that our growth poses to it, and to feel something for the other species we threaten. Should we so choose, we could exercise our reason to do what no other animal can do: we could limit ourselves voluntarily, choose to remain God's creatures instead of making ourselves gods. What a towering achievement that would be, so much more impressive than the largest dam—beavers can build dams—because so much harder. Such restraint, not genetic engineering or planetary management, is the real challenge. If we now, today, began to limit our numbers and our desires and our ambitions, perhaps nature could someday resume its independent working. Perhaps the temperature could someday adjust itself down to its own setting, and the rain fall of its own accord.

Marx and Alienation
from Nature

STEVEN VOGEL

IT IS INCREASINGLY COMMON in contemporary discussions of science, technology, and society, especially those influenced by environmentalism, to find the claim that humans today are "alienated from nature." Typically proponents of this claim argue that the scientific-technological project itself expresses such an alienation, by treating nature as an inert and passive matter to be "dominated" by human will, and by failing to see that the complexity of the ecosystem places severe constraints on what can be done "to" nature without producing ecologically dangerous consequences. Humans, this view asserts, feel themselves to be independent of nature, and masters of it, and believe science makes it possible to bend nature to their will; in fact, however, they are *part* of nature, themselves subject to its laws, and any act to change it potentially rebounds back to humanity's (and nature's) own peril.

The clearest expression of our alienation, it is also claimed, lies in the way we treat the natural environment. Rather than learning from nature, from its complexity, its organismic and holistic character, we treat it as "mere matter" to be manipulated for purely human purposes, destroying forests and wetlands in the name of "development," killing lakes and streams with the acid pollution from modern industry, genetically engineering new species while callously allowing the extinction of thousands of old ones, etc. This form of environmentalism thus tends to be characterized by deep misgivings about human interventions into nature and natural processes, particularly large-scale technological ones; instead of attempting to master nature, it suggests, we ought to learn to live in harmony with nature, recognizing our bond to it and treating it with the respect and dignity its role as source of all life deserves.[1]

In this essay I wish to examine the notion of "alienation from nature," by

considering one of its intellectual roots: the account of nature in the work of
Marx. My claim is that this account provides a useful framework for thinking
about the relation between humans and nature, and about what an "alienated"
relation to nature might consist in, but at the same time that it leads to
conclusions very different from the ones drawn by the environmentalist position
I have just outlined. In particular, I think a consideration of Marx's account
suggests that although contemporary society is marked by alienation from something like nature, that alienation is not the result of our hubristic attempt to
dominate nature through technology, nor is it to be overcome by the decision
to refrain from large-scale interventions in natural processes, or by the resolution
to live in "harmony" with nature. Indeed, I will argue, the position just outlined
in a sense appears much more like a symptom of our alienation than a correct
account of it.

Much of my discussion of Marx's theory of alienation will be familiar, but its
relation specifically to questions about nature and the environment has rarely
been brought out.[2] Marx's account bears reconsideration precisely because its
implications are indeed so different from conclusions about the environment
that are today often taken for granted, particularly in a "leftist" or "progressive"
context. To be sure, Marx is sometimes criticized by environmentalists for holding a
purely utilitarian and "dominative" view of the relation between humans and
nature. But this criticism seems to me at best partial and misleading, and to beg
central questions; rather than judge Marx by the standard of contemporary
environmentalism, I would prefer to show the coherence and interest of his
position itself—and to suggest on the contrary the ways in which it helps to
clarify and to resolve some deep difficulties that environmentalism faces.

                                        I

Marx defines alienation in the famous section on "Estranged Labor" in the 1844
Manuscripts, explicitly associating it with an economic system based on private
property. Alienation, he writes, arises when

> the object which labor produces—labor's product—confronts it as *something
> alien*, as a *power independent* of the producer. . . . The worker puts his life into
> the object; but now his life no longer belongs to him but to the object. . . .
> The *alienation* of the worker in his product means not only that his labor
> becomes an object, an *external* existence, but that it exists *outside him*,
> independently, as something alien to him, and that it becomes a power on its
> own confronting him. It means that the life which he has conferred on the
> subject confronts him as something hostile and alien.[3]

For Marx, alienation thus has fundamentally to do with the relation of humans
to objects that they have produced—to objects of labor. Under alienation these

objects turn into alien and independent powers over and against humans, achieving a kind of sham self-sufficiency and externality in which the objects seem to be master over those who produced them. And the paradigm case of such alienation, Marx argues, occurs under the current economic system when the object produced by the worker is counted as adding to the wealth of the capitalist.[4] The "objectification" of the worker's labor—the process by which that labor (and, by extension, the worker's subjectivity or "life") is transmuted into an object, and so made "objective"—appears, Marx writes, instead as "loss of the object and bondage to it," as estrangement, alienation.[5]

The account of alienation in Marx thus directs us to the realm of "produced objects." By making labor into the central category of both his epistemology and his social theory, Marx draws our attention to the fact that most of what we call the "objective world," the world of objects, is in fact a world of *human* objects, objects produced by humans through labor. We are alienated from this world when we fail to recognize its humanity, when we are unable to see it as *our* world, our product, and when it accordingly begins to appear as an alien power over against us. In the *1844 Manuscripts* Marx speaks of this alienation of the human being from what he called (following Feuerbach) the human "species-being":

> In the practical creation of an objective world, in his *work upon* inorganic nature, man proves himself a conscious species-being. . . . Through this production, nature appears as *his* work and his reality. The object of labor is, therefore, the *objectification of man's species-life*: for he duplicates himself not only, as in consciousness, intellectually, but also actively, in reality, and therefore sees himself in a world that he has created. In tearing away from the man the object of his production, therefore, estranged labor tears from him his *species-life*, his real objectivity as a member of the species, and transforms his advantage over animals into the disadvantage that his inorganic body, nature, is taken away from him.[6]

It is precisely in this failure of humans to "see themselves in the world they have created" that the alienation consists.

In this framework "alienation from nature" seems a misnomer; it would be more correct to speak of "alienation from the environment," or from the "built environment." In the *Theses on Feuerbach* and *The German Ideology* Marx criticizes previous materialism (including Feuerbach's) for failing to see the material environment as the product of concrete human activity, and hence for falling into a simplistic naturalism in which humans appear as merely the passive products of external circumstances. Feuerbach, Marx writes in *The German Ideology*,

> does not see that the sensuous world around him is not a thing given direct from all eternity, remaining ever the same, but the product of industry and of the state of society; and, indeed, . . . it is an historical product, the result of the activity of a whole succession of generations, each standing on the

shoulders of the preceding one. . . . Even the objects of the simplest "sensuous certainty" are only given him through social development, industry and commercial intercourse. The cherry-tree, like almost all fruit-tree, was, as is well-known, only a few centuries ago transplanted by *commerce* into our zone, and therefore only *by* this action of a definite society in a definite age has it become "sensuous certainty" for Feuerbach.[7]

Against this, Marx's materialism, by emphasizing labor, asks us to look not at nature but at the transformation of nature by humans as the clue to understanding society. "Nature is man's inorganic body," Marx writes;[8] what humans do—"by nature"—is to transform nature, to remake it, through their labor. This is not to deny, he writes, "the priority of external nature"; clearly nature existed before humans. But today a nature entirely independent of human action is scarcely any longer to be found ("except perhaps on a few Australian coral islands of recent origin"[9]). Rather, it is "the nature which develops in human history" that is "man's *real* nature," he writes. "*Industry* is the *actual*, historical relationship of nature . . . to man. If, therefore, industry is conceived as the *exoteric* revelation of man's *essential powers*, we also gain an understanding of the *human* essence of nature or the *natural* essence of man." Thus "history itself is a *real* part of *natural* history," Marx writes, "of nature developing into man [*des Werdens der Natur zum Menschen*]."[10] History then is a *natural* process, the process of nature becoming humanized; and this applies above all to the history of "industry"—that is, of technology.

Marx is writing, of course, in a specifically economic context. It is the worker who is alienated, through the process of capitalist production. The worker quite literally through his or her labor produces the modern world of industry, and yet this world, argues Marx, comes to appear to him or her as an alien and hostile power, appears as the source of his or her oppression; indeed "the worker becomes all the poorer the more wealth he produces, the more his production increases in power and size . . . . The *devaluation* of the world of men is in direct proportion to the *increasing value* of the world of things."[11] In *The German Ideology* he writes that "man's own deed [*die eigne Tat des Menschen*] becomes an alien power opposed to him, which enslaves him instead of being controlled [*beherrscht*] by him."[12]

In the latter work alienation is explicitly associated with the division of labor, or more precisely with the particular form it takes under contemporary economic conditions.[13] Instead of seeing his or her product as something that directly satisfies the human needs of others, the worker views it merely as a means to an end—a troublesome necessity requisite to obtain the money for the satisfaction of his or her own needs. Thus whereas from an external standpoint we can see the production of the object as part of an overall system of mutual and interdependent production, in which the labor of all functions to satisfy the needs of all, this implicitly social and cooperative element to the act of production is hidden from the worker, who produces the object only because he or she has to in order to be paid.

Marx describes this as a contradiction between the worker's "particular" interest and the "common" interest of the society of which he or she forms a part, a contradiction which takes the form of alienation. Since the interdependence and mutuality implicit in capitalist production are never explicitly recognized as such by the producers themselves, the "common" interest appears as an alien interest, as a power external to and separate from the individual producers. It appears, in fact, in the form of "the market," the "laws of supply and demand," the "invisible hand," etc., which seem to rule over human productive activity although in fact they are rather its result. Marx calls this a "fixation [*Sichfestsetzen*] of social activity," a "consolidation of what we ourselves produce into a material power above us, growing out of our control," and goes on to say:

> The social power, i.e., the multiplied productive force that arises through the co-operation of different individuals caused by the division of labor, appears to those individuals, since their co-operation is not voluntary but has come about naturally [*naturwüchsig*], not as their own united power, but as an alien force existing outside them, of the origin and goal of which they are ignorant, which they thus are no longer able to control [*beherrschen*].[14]

Until the implicit sociality of production is recognized and made explicit, that is, production (our "own deed") will continue to appear in the form of an opaque and independent social system that humans are unable to master, and as a set of "economic laws" operating behind their backs. Abolishing alienation is thus not a matter of abolishing the sociality of production by abolishing the division of labor, but rather of explicitly recognizing this sociality by asserting conscious social control over production (through, for example, the democratic planning Marx associates with communism).[15] As long as the cooperative character of production remains implicit, it appears *naturwüchsig*—as something that has grown up "by nature," without any human intervention or planning, and hence comes to seem an independent and nonhuman power.[16]

In *Capital* and the notes that form the *Grundrisse*, the account of alienation appears in a more sophisticated form. Marx's earlier emphasis on labor as the central philosophical category reappears in his mature economic work as the assertion of a labor theory of value. It is central to Marx's argument that since labor is the only source of value, it follows that capital, labor's antithesis, *is* simply labor: "dead labor," as he calls it, or "congealed labor," the labor of past workers "embodied" concretely not only in the capitalist's wealth but in the machinery and the factories that serve as the environment for the oppression of current workers.[17] The analysis of capital thus has the same logical structure as the earlier analysis of alienation: the workers' labor is objectified, and its object, in the form of capital, turns into an independent and alien force over and against them. Further, Marx extends this to the social system as a whole. The mysteries he discovers at the heart of phenomena such as interest, profit, money, prices, etc., reveal them to be not primary phenomena at all but rather the reified form in which human productive activity appears under conditions of alienation—when, as he writes, "a definite social relation between men . . . assumes, in their eyes, the fantastic form of a relation between things."[18]

The center of Marx's analysis is of course the commodity, that "very queer thing, abounding in metaphysical subtleties and theological niceties."[19] A commodity is first of all the product of human labor, and this labor is the source of its value. But under conditions of capitalist production, Marx points out, it does not appear as such: rather, the value of the commodity appears as a natural fact about it, an "objective" fact independent of human action. Marx writes that

> a commodity is . . . a mysterious thing simply because in it the social charac-
> ter of men's own labor appears to them as an objective character of the
> products of that labor, as socially natural characteristics [gesellschaftliche
> Natureigenschaften] of those things and thus also because the social relation of
> the producers to their collective labor appears to them instead as a social
> relation, existing independently and outside them, between objects.[20]

The commodity, Marx writes, is a "social hieroglyphic"[21] in which the truth about contemporary social relations is written, but in an initially unreadable form. As in The German Ideology, Marx claims that it is above all the sociality of production that is hidden from us. Again, a relation between humans—that is, the implicit mutuality and cooperation of our labor—here appears only in the distorted and alienated form of a relation between things—that is, between the prices of external objects whose source in human labor, and thus whose connection to us, has been lost.[22] In the "free market" where these prices are expressed, Marx writes, our "own social action [Bewegung]" thus "takes the form of the action of objects [Sachen], which rule the producers instead of being ruled by them."[23]

In this analysis of the "fetishism of commodities" all the strands of the earlier discussions of alienation are brought together. The commodity is part of the "built environment," not a naturally occurring object but a product of human labor. The labor that produces it is implicitly social—that is, cooperative—labor: it is produced for the purpose of satisfying the needs of others. But this sociality remains only implicit, concealed as it is by the economic structures of private property and private exchange. Thus it can only reach expression in an alienated form, in which the human world of objects produced by labor comes to seem an independent, external, and "natural" world, and a power over and against the producers. The overcoming of alienation, then, would consist in the recognition and the explicit assertion of the sociality of labor by the associated human community. This is why it is central to Marx's vision of the future

Communist "realm of freedom" that the anarchy and *Naturwüchsigkeit* of the market be replaced by a system of conscious and democratically controlled social planning of production. Only in this way can humans regain control over their own objects, reassert their power over that which had come to seem alien and independent.

II

We can summarize, then, by saying that for Marx alienation arises from *the failure to recognize the human origin of objects that have been produced by human activity*, and that the overcoming of alienation is for him associated with *the achievement of this recognition*. The "human origin" of the objects, further, means in particular their *social* origin, as products of cooperative, social labor. Thus as I have argued above Marx's account points us toward a recognition of the sociality of the environment, of its character as "built," consisting almost entirely of products of human labor designed to fulfill human needs.

This seems to me a crucially important, and underappreciated, insight—above all in a discussion of "alienation from nature." The "environment" we inhabit, the world of objects we find around us, is an environment of objects built by humans—not "nature," if by this is meant a world of things untouched by human activity, but nature transformed, reworked, reshaped, humanized: plants into clothing, trees into furniture, iron and clay into houses, petroleum into plastics, sand into glass and microchips. As I look about me there is not a single object in my environment (nor, I would guess, in that of many readers) that is not in this sense literally a human object, the objectification of human, and indeed of social, labor. To choose a single object in the immediate environment, this wooden paperweight, for instance, and to think of all the humans involved in producing it—those who felled the tree, who cut the timber, who transported the logs from the forest, who formed it into its present shape, carved the decorations on it, polished it—but not only these, for each of them used tools in the process, and so there must be added to the list those who built the saws, the trucks, the lathes, the polishing machines, and then those who built the tools that made these in turn possible, and so on, stretching off into the past in a geometrically increasing manner—is to begin to recognize, in the image of human solidarity this potential infinity of labor suddenly reveals, the depth of the sociality hidden in each of the objects we find surrounding us.[24]

These objects indeed are, as Marx says, hieroglyphics for our interdependence, for the sociality of our activity, for the way we cooperatively and compulsively remake the world in our own image. But we fail to read the message they carry. We see the objects surrounding us as "mere things," as simply part of the external scenery we "naturally" find around us; indeed in general we barely see them at all.[25] We value them—if indeed we do—for their beauty, or their usefulness, or especially their price, but not as symbols of our connection, or of our power.

Marx's analysis, I am suggesting, implies that the "environment" from which we are alienated is a social environment, and that our alienation derives from our failure to recognize its sociality. To say that our environment is social is not merely to say that social forces and institutions—the market, the political system, gender roles, etc.—are as "real" to us as the physical objects that surround us; it is to point out that even those physical objects themselves are always already the result of social labor. Just as we are alienated from the social institutions around us when they come to appear not as the product of human action but rather like forces of nature—that is, independently given and unalterable facts entirely outside of our control—so too we are alienated from the objects around us when they appear to us not as the result of social labor but rather as mere "commodities", entering into mysterious relations with each other on the basis of a seemingly natural price. In the last analysis these aspects of the "social environment" cannot be separated: social institutions are not distinct from physical objects but are rather embodied in them (in bankbooks, voting booths, price tags, wedding rings, etc.), just as the physical objects with which we daily interact have the meanings they do only within the context of specific social institutions. "Alienation from the environment" is thus a single phenomenon, in which the products of our action—social institutions as well as physical objects—appear as external and independent forces whose connectedness to us has been lost. To overcome the alienation would mean to reassert the sociality of the environment: to see it consciously as our own, and explicitly and consciously to exert the kind of control over it that we already implicitly possess—to raise it, that is, from the *naturwüchsig* to the truly social.

But this sense of "alienation from the environment," and this notion of its overcoming, are certainly not those of much contemporary environmentalism. For Marx, I am arguing, recognizing our connectedness to the environment means recognizing its *sociality*; for the environmentalist position I began by outlining, on the other hand, our connectedness to the environment means rather our *rootedness in nature*, and the increasing sociality of the physical environment (the result of technological development) appears rather as a symptom of our denial of this connectedness, and hence of our increasing alienation. Thus for this view we overcome our alienation not by explicitly asserting the humanness of the environment, but by acknowledging and emphasizing the naturalness of humans—by learning to live in harmony with nature and to respect its laws instead of trying to dominate it, and above all by limiting the extent to which we act to transform it.

Such a position uses the word "alienation" in a sense radically different from that of Marx. What was essential to Marx's concept of alienation, I argued above, was the notion of an object produced by humans that comes to appear as an external and independent force above them; here that notion has disappeared, replaced by what seems like the opposite one—that of an object ("Nature") that really is an external and independent force, but which has mistakenly (and arrogantly) been viewed by us as human. By the same token, whereas for Marx the overcoming of alienation involves recognizing and reasserting the sociality of the object and hence abolishing the sham externality it presents to us, for this view we overcome alienation only by admitting the externality of the object, acquiescing in its power over us, and agreeing to live in accordance with its dictates. Let me suggest some reasons why I think this latter view is mistaken.

At first glance the whole dispute seems to turn on an ambiguity in the word "environment." The environment of which environmentalism speaks is not the world of directly human objects, of the commodities with which we surround ourselves, that I have described above, but rather the world of *nature*, the pre- and extrahuman natural environment that surrounds the human world. It is indeed precisely the increasing encroachment of the "human" world upon the "natural" one that contemporary environmentalism wishes to warn us against. But by seeing human activity in the world of nature as somehow an encroachment on it, or a violation of its "naturalness," such a view seems to be curiously guilty of just the sort of dualism it ascribes to the project of "dominating nature": somehow the activity of humans in transforming their environment, alone of all other species, is "unnatural."[26] Further, such a view fails to grasp Marx's point against Feuerbach that the cherry trees we admire as part of "nature" are in truth the result of earlier labor (see above, pp. 209–10). An enormous amount of what we naively see as "pure" nature has in fact already been the object of human action. True "wilderness"—in the sense of land never affected by human activity—is extremely rare in this country; even as "preserved" in national parks and the like (a preservation that itself is only the result of a social decision and a social act) it presents us not with "pure" nature but rather with something highly artificial: a piece of nature that has been withdrawn from the natural order in which human transformative activity plays such a crucial part.

The point is not that those who admire the cherry tree are laboring under an illusion and should only admire indigenous species, or that we ought to redouble our efforts to save whatever "pure" nature is left. The point is that the concepts "natural" and "human" are not mutually exclusive, as I have already argued: history, as Marx put it, is part of natural history.[27] Thus the cherry trees are part of nature, as are synthetic fibers, skyscrapers, and Tang—because we are. Hence ultimately the word "environment" is not ambiguous: we live in a single environment, not two, and it is a natural one—and so is increasingly becoming a human one as well.

Thus there is no point to preferring the "natural" to the "human" (nor, for that matter, for the opposite preference either); the distinction cannot be coherently be made, or at least cannot be made to do the work this version of environmentalism wants it to. If we wish to reserve the word "nature" for that part of the world that has not yet been transformed by humans, we may certainly do so—but only at the cost of making the claim that our technology is "unnatural" analytic. The real question isn't whether what we do "accords with nature"—of course it does, and trivially so. The question is whether we like what we have wrought. And if we find ourselves living in an environment of ugly shopping malls and endless superhighways, of dangerous nuclear power plants and toxic waste dumps, of rotting slums and polluted rivers, it is not because we have violated nature but because our own acts remain powers over and against us: because we have not yet exerted conscious social control over our activity, and so that activity remains under the sway of *Naturwüchsigkeit*, of alienation.

From this point of view the emphasis in the environmentalist position I am criticizing on nature's power over us, on its delicate harmony and complexity, and so on the dangers of attempting to change it, I want to suggest, represents not so much an analysis as a symptom of our alienation. In the call for reverence before nature's mystery, in the warning about the "limits to growth" and the need for us to curb our technology for fear of nature's "revenge," the world of objects surrounding us is once again asserted to be an alien and independent power over and against us; the world of humans is once again devalued in favor of the world of things. To use words like "domination" or "subjugation" of nature, to talk of it taking "revenge" on us, etc., is to employ categories appropriate to relations between persons as if they applied to relations with things. "Nature" is not a person, and to treat it like one, I want to argue, is precisely to reproduce the fetishism Marx criticized as characteristic of an alienated social order—an order in which facts about humans and human relations are falsely projected onto the world of objects.[28]

The environmentalism I am discussing talks of a reverence and love for nature, for its "holistic" character, its complexity, its unfathomable harmony—but its talk of nature's revenge, of the inevitability of catastrophe in the human attempt to "use" nature for our own ends, betrays a deeper fear of nature. The reverence it counsels is that of an impotent and terrified mortal before a jealous and angry God. Concepts such as that of the "ecosphere" as an indivisible whole, of the earth as a single organism ("Gaia"), etc., work to reinforce the notion of nature as a mammoth, complex, and frighteningly inhuman force that we cannot successfully change but to which we must rather adjust ourselves. In our attempt to "live in harmony" with nature, it seems that we make all the compromises; nature remains aloof, silent, stubborn—our master. I want to suggest that this view of nature, increasingly common over the last quarter century, represents *the projection onto nature (onto things) of a set of facts about society (about humans)*.

For it is society, it seems to me, that appears today as a complex unity that seems to transcend both our ability to understand it and any possibility of our changing it. In the face of mysterious and crushing abstract forces like the "market," the "arms race," the "global economy," etc., individual humans feel small and powerless; unable to affect such forces, we have to learn to "live in harmony" with them, to acquiesce, that is, in their power over us. It is that experience, I am saying, that is falsely projected onto nature in the environmentalist views under discussion.

Individuals in this society know all too well the feeling of being under the power of massive external forces they cannot control. This is just the fact of alienation described by Marx, and is I think an almost constant feature of the phenomenology of contemporary social life. But it is crucial, as a step towards overcoming this alienation, to see that these forces are the result of our own action, and thus that they can be controlled, that their *Naturwüchsigkeit* can be eliminated. Instead, the position I am criticizing goes in the opposite direction, mystifying the real situation further by ascribing these forces to an entirely nonhuman nature, and seeing any attempt to assert control over them as anthropocentric hubris. I have argued above that part of the solution to alienation is to recognize the sociality of the environment and so to dissolve its apparent independence and externality. In contrast, this view denies its sociality, wishes instead to reassert its independence and externality—and thus, I would argue, it partakes in, rather than working against, dominant illusions. It hypostasizes the ruling (and oppressive) social powers into a divine and unchangeable Nature ("Gaia"), and then dolefully warns against attempting to fight it—thus reinforcing, on a deep level, the very structures of oppression to which it believes itself opposed. Overcoming alienation requires increasing humans' faith in their own ability to change their own conditions, not criticizing it as hubris.

I have no wish to defend contemporary technology, nor to deny the threat it represents. On the contrary, I think environmentalism is quite correct to point to the real dangers posed to us by the technologies we employ today, and by the thoughtless, shortsighted, and unplanned—*naturwüchsig!*—ways in which they are introduced. The dangers of pollution, acid rain, soil erosion, ozone depletion, radioactive waste, etc.—and above all those of thermonuclear war—are ominous and profound; unchecked, the development of contemporary technology seems to be leading us towards an ecological catastrophe that might well mean the end of human life, or even of life itself, on earth.

But it is precisely contemporary technology that requires such a critique, and not technology as such. Contemporary technology takes place under the sign of alienation (in Marx's sense): it is a social product but appears like an autonomous force, responding to the imperatives of the market, or the balance of power, in ways we feel incapable of affecting. It is not the social character of our interventions in nature that deserves criticism but rather their very *Naturwüchsigkeit*—the fact that they have not been sufficiently socialized, that there exists no means of exerting over them democratic social control. Only when we find a way to assert that control, and so end our own alienation, will it be possible to begin to work for a technology that truly solves social problems instead of being an alien and autonomous force threatening to destroy us.

We are active participants in nature, which is to say we make our environment human by remaking nature. We change it through our labor in accordance with our needs and desires, and at the level of skill our knowledge and experience permits. Whether we do so well or poorly depends on the one hand on the current state of our understanding of nature and our skill in transforming it. But on the other hand (and much more importantly today, when our technological expertise has far surpassed the rationality of our social arrangements) it depends on our ability to articulate and to justify to ourselves socially what our needs and desires really are, and to determine rationally and democratically what we wish to do (and are willing to do, and to risk) to satisfy them. To the extent that we have not done this, and remain subject to a social system we do not know how to control, our technology will inevitably fail us. The solution thus is not to abolish technology, or the attempt to remake nature, but to establish democratic mechanisms of social decision making based on rational discourse about norms.[29]

III

Two concepts have been central in the preceding discussion, "humanization" and "recognition." I have argued that a certain strain in environmentalism arrives at a mistaken view of alienation from nature by failing to see that it is part of what it is to be human to produce a world of human (social) objects—to humanize nature. Alienation occurs not when we humanize nature but when we fail to recognize that that is what we are doing: when our act becomes an alien power over and against us. Humanization is thus constant, implicit in the use of tools from the species' beginning: but without recognition, the conscious assertion by society of its control over its own production, the humanization process occurs in a *naturwüchsig* manner, and becomes an external and independent force (becomes like nature), and so only appears in an alienated form.

The end of alienation means making explicitly true (true "for us") what is now only true "in itself"—producing a world of objects whose sociality is transparent, the result of conscious social decisions and cooperative social acts. In the *1844 Manuscripts* Marx writes that "man does not lose himself in his object"—that is, avoids alienation—

> only when the object becomes for him a *human* object or an objective human [*menschlicher Gegenstand oder gegenständlicher Mensch*]. This is possible only by the object becoming for him a *social* object [*gesellschaftlicher Gegenstand*] and

he himself becoming a social being, just as society becomes a being for him in this object. . . . It is only by objective reality becoming everywhere for humans in society the reality of essential human powers, human reality . . . that all *objects* become for him the *objectification* of himself, become objects which confirm and realize his individuality, become *his* objects.[30]

"Recognition" here does not denote merely a passive acknowledgment, as if alienation could be overcome simply by a change in attitude. To say we recognize the humanness of our products is at the same time to say we begin to produce different products, and in the process become different ourselves. A nonalienated relation to the world would require a change in our activity in the world: a change in technology that cannot be separated from changes in the way that technology is organized, or in the social order within which it is embedded. But it also means a change in us: a truly social world, a world of objects in which we see ourselves and our projects directly reflected, both requires and in turn helps to produce truly social humans. Thus the remaking of the world is at the same time a remaking of humanity.

Marx writes that "the *senses* of the social man *differ* from that of the non-social man," and adds that it is only through the objective development of humanity's essential powers—that is, through their expression in objects—that such truly social or human senses come into being. Indeed, he continues, this applies not merely to the ordinary senses but more broadly, to the "practical senses (will, love, etc.)," to all human relations to the world. "In a word, *human* sense, the humanity of the senses, comes to be by virtue of *its* object—*humanized nature.* . . . The objectification of the human essence, both in its theoretical and practical aspects, is required to make humanity's *sense human* [*die* Sinne *des Menschen* menschlich *zu machen*]."[31]

There is thus a complex dialectic at work here, in which our acts to "humanize" nature, once they are recognized for what they are, lose their alienated and *naturwüchsige* form, and so produce a new relation to nature, a new kind of humanization. This complexity is not sufficiently captured by the simplistic assimilation of all acts of humanization to alienated attempts at the "domination of nature." Such an assimilation seems to make a subtle version of the mistake for which Marx criticized Hegel—confusing objectification with alienation, that is to say, seeing the process of actively expressing one's humanity in the objective world as inevitably involving a loss of self and a separation from the object. The (justified) rejection of the wasteful and dangerous ways we misuse the environment today leads such a position to counsel a kind of passive "letting nature be," because it is unable to imagine any active human relation to the environment that is not one of "exploitation" and destructive misuse. Thus the current relation to the external world (one which takes place under alienation) appears as the only possible one, and all "humanization" of the environment appears as "domination" of it.

For Marx, on the other hand, the end of alienation means a new kind of humanization, a new relation to the world of objects:

> The eye has become a *human* eye, just as its *object* has become a social, *human* object, made by humans for humans. The senses . . . relate themselves to the *thing* [*Sache*] for the sake of the thing, but the thing itself is an *objective human* relation to itself and to humans. . . . Need or enjoyment have thus lost their *egotistical* nature, and nature has lost its mere *utility* [*Nützlichkeit*] by use becoming *human* use [*menschlichen Nutzen*].[32]

To see "use" only as exploitative, egotistical use, and to talk of all humanization as dominative is to fail to see that it might be possible to "relate to the thing for the sake of the thing" while still recognizing the thing as a human object, as an expression of a human relation. To see the environment as both already human and as potentially further humanizable is not necessarily to see it as unimportant, as "mere matter" to be manipulated, but rather perhaps to cherish it as an objective expression of our connection, of our own objectivity. It is thus hard to understand why such a view is criticized as an anthropocentric hubris that will lead to the environment's destruction. It would seem much more likely to lead to an increased respect for the environment—not the awe-filled respect of a helpless mortal before an omnipotent divinity, to be sure, but the self-respect of an autonomous and rational community, conscious both of its own achievement and its own responsibility.

Our problem today is not with nature so much as it is with a set of social arrangements that prevent humans from recognizing technology as their project, and so from changing it to satisfy *their* needs. Ruled by *Naturwüchsigkeit*, our technology has become a power outside our control, threatening in the near future to destroy us. But the solution to this—to our alienation from our environment, our failure to see it as ours—is then not to abdicate the human project of shaping nature for our own needs, but rather to bring it under democratic social control; it is not to set up "Nature" or "Gaia," as too much contemporary talk about nature and technology goes, as yet another nonhuman power independent of us we dare not change, but rather to recall humans to their own power, their own ability to change the world and to decide how they want to live. The point, that is, is not to dominate nature but to abolish *Naturwüchsigkeit*, the power uncomprehended social acts have over humans.

Notes

1. This account is particularly associated with what has come to be called the "deep ecology" movement, but can be found elsewhere as well, especially in more popular discussions of environmental issues. It has also been a common theme in certain feminist discussions of science and technology. For some examples, see William Devall and George Sessions, eds., *Deep Ecology* (Salt Lake City: Peregrine Smith Books, 1984); Arne Naess, "The Shallow and the Deep, Long-Range Ecology

Movement," *Inquiry* 16 (1973): 95–100; Theodore Roszak, *Where the Wasteland Ends* (London: Faber, 1973); Murray Bookchin, *The Ecology of Freedom* (Palo Alto: Cheshire Books, 1982); Fritjof Capra, *The Turning Point* (New York: Simon and Schuster, 1982); Jeremy Rifkin, *Algeny* (New York: Penguin, 1983); Susan Griffin, *Woman and Nature* (New York: Harper and Row, 1978); Carolyn Merchant, *The Death of Nature* (New York: Harper and Row, 1980). Note that I am certainly not claiming that *all* contemporary environmentalism argues in this manner.

2. Among the works that do touch this subject, see Alfred Schmidt, *The Concept of Nature in Marx* (London: NLB, 1973); George Lukács, *History and Class Consciousness* (Cambridge, MIT Press, 1972); Jürgen Habermas, *Knowledge and Human Interests* (Boston: Beacon Press, 1969); Louis Dupre, *The Philosophical Foundations of Marxism* (New York: Harcourt, Brace, 1966); and Andrew Feenberg, *Lukács, Marx, and the Sources of Critical Theory* (Totowa, N.J.: Rowman and Littlefield, 1981).

3. Karl Marx and Frederick Engels, *Collected Works*, vol. 3 (New York: International Publishers, 1975), 272. I will refer to the *Collected Works* in what follows as MECW.

4. MECW 3, 278.

5. MECW 3, 272.

6. MECW 3, 276–77 (translation somewhat altered). The German version of the *Manuscripts* is contained in Karl Marx and Friedrich Engels, *Werke*, Ergänzungsband (Berlin: Dietz Verlag, 1977), which I will refer to henceforth as *Manuskripte*; the reference here is on pp. 516–17.

7. MECW 5, 39. See also p. 40: "So much is this activity, this unceasing sensuous labor and creation, this production, the foundation of the whole sensuous world as it now exists that, were it interrupted for only a year, Feuerbach would not only find an enormous change in the natural world, but would very soon find that the whole world of man and his own perceptive faculty, nay his own existence, were missing."

8. MECW 3, 276.

9. MECW 5, 40.

10. MECW 3, 303–4 (*Manuskripte*, 543–44).

11. MECW 3, 271–72.

12. MECW 5, 47. See Karl Marx and Friedrich Engels, *Die Deutsche Ideologie* (Berlin: Dietz Verlag, 1953), 29.

13. See MECW 5, 46–54.

14. MECW 5, 47–48 (translation slightly altered). See Marx and Engels, *Die Deutsche Ideologie*, 31.

15. See, for instance, MECW 5, 81: "Communism differs from all previous movements in that it . . . for the first time consciously treats all naturally evolved [*naturwüchsigen*] premises as the creations of hitherto existing humans, strips them of their natural character [*Naturwuchsigkeit*], and subjects them to the power of the united individuals. . . . The conditions which capitalism creates are precisely the true basis for rendering it impossible that any conditions should exist independently of individuals, insofar as these conditions are . . . only a product of the preceding intercourse of individuals" (translation altered; see Marx and Engels, *Die Deutsche Ideologie*, 71.)

16. The concept of *Naturwuchsigkeit* is of central importance to Marx's analysis of alienation from the environment. It is unfortunate that there is no good English equivalent for it; the word "*naturwüchsig*" is typically translated as "natural," which fails to capture the difference between it and "*natürlich*." See Jeremy J. Shapiro, "The Slime of History" in *On Critical Theory*, ed. John O'Neill (New York: Seabury Press, 1976), 145–63.

17. See Karl Marx, *Grundrisse* (New York: Vintage Books, 1973), 453–54.

18. Karl Marx, *Capital*, vol. 1 (New York: Modern Library, n.d.), 83.
19. Marx, *Capital*, 81.
20. Marx, *Capital*, 83, translation altered. See Karl Marx, *Das Kapital*, Bd. 1 (Frankfurt: Verlag Marxistische Blatter, 1976), 86.
21. Marx, *Capital*, 85.
22. See *Grundrisse*, 156–57.
23. Marx, *Capital*, 86 (*Das Kapital*, 89.) See also p. 84 (*Das Kapital*, 87), where Marx talks oxymoronically of "material [*sachliche*] relations between persons and social relations between things [*Sachen*]."
24. John Locke, in the course of presenting his own version of the labor theory of value in the *Second Treatise of Civil Government*, writes (paragraph 43): "it is not barely the plough-man's pains, the reaper's and thresher's toil, and the baker's sweat, is to be counted into the bread we eat; the labor of those who broken the oxen, who digged and wrought the iron and stones, who felled and framed the timber employed about the plough, mill oven, or any other utensils, which are a vast number, requisite to this corn, from its being feed to be sown to its being made bread, must all be charged on the account of labor, and receive as an effect of that. . . . It would be a strange catalogue of things, that industry provided and made use of, about every loaf of bread, before it came to use, if we could trace them; iron, wood, leather, bark, timber, stone, bricks, coals, lime, cloth, dying drugs, pitch, tar, masts, ropes, and all the materials made use of in the ship, that brought any of the commodities made use of by any of the workmen, to any part of the work; all which it would be almost impossible, at least too long, to reckon up."
25. It is interesting to notice, for instance, that the tables philosophy professors point to in introductory courses as part of discussions of Cartesian doubt, or the chairs we kick as refutations of Berkeleian idealism (examples, supposedly, of those independent and external objects whose existence we need to assure ourselves of) are always built objects, human objects, social objects—and so, I would argue, in truth are objects whose epistemological status is a lot more complicated, and a lot closer to that of "language" or "morality" or other social institutions whose analysis is reserved for upper-level seminars, than we generally admit.
26. See on this point Richard Watson, "A Critique of Anti-Anthropocentric Biocentrism," *Environmental Ethics* 5 (1983), 245–56.
27. See p. 210 above.
28. Indeed, "Nature" is not even a thing—it is an abstraction; to treat individual entities and their relations as though they were merely expressions of "Nature" conceived of as an individual is already to fetishize it in the manner of idealist metaphysics. Marx makes this point in the highly interesting "*Sozialistische Bausteine*" section of vol. 2 of *The German Ideology*. See MECW 5, 470–83, esp. 473–74.
29. This point, of course, is central to Habermas's argument against Marcuse on the "ideological" nature of technology. See Habermas's *Toward a Rational Society* (Boston: Beacon Press, 1970), chaps. 4–6.
30. MECW 3, 301 (translation altered). See *Manuskripte*, 541.
31. MECW 3, 301–2 (translation altered). See *Manuskripte*, 541–42.
32. MECW 3, 300 (translation altered). See *Manuskripte*, 540. This is the same kind of point Marx makes at MECW 3, 299, where he writes that the *Aufhebung* "of private property—i.e., the *sensual* appropriation for and by humans of the human essence and of human life, of objective humanity, of human *works—should not be conceived in the sense of immediate*, one-sided enjoyment [*Genuß*], merely in the sense of *possessing*, of *having*" (translation altered; see *Manuskripte*, 539).

PART VII

What Is to Be Done?

IT HAS OFTEN BEEN asserted that alienation is an inescapable human condition that we cannot do anything about. This claim has some plausibility as long as we talk about alienation very abstractly. Once we take up alienation in all its concrete forms as the preceding readings have done we can see that there are remedies for alienation. Alienation is the result of very complex, but also very specific, historical conditions. These conditions came into being at a particular time. They can also be brought to an end. The remaining selections argue this more explicitly.

Roger Gottlieb's summary of alienation stresses one major source of it: the disenfranchisement of most of us in determining who we are. Disenfranchisement, moreover, is not limited to the realm of what is usually called "politics"—the electoral process and the workings of various governments—but includes mass-culture. Others decide for us who we are not only by means of familiar political decision making, but much more devastatingly by creating cultural definitions for us.

The road toward overcoming alienation lies clearly in the direction of reducing this disenfranchisement. We do not know a great deal about how to go about doing that. We saw in the first introductory essay that dominant political theory has studiously avoided looking at alienation. Few theorists have given sustained thought to questions of how to overcome it. In general, we know what that answer must be: more and better democracy will reduce alienation. Gottlieb's analysis makes clear that this is not just democracy in relation to electing public officials, but democracy in a much broader sense, that takes away the power of defining our identities from the media and other cultural institutions and, instead, allows all of us a hand in saying who we are.

Harry Boyte also talks about extending democracy, and, while his discussion appears to have to do with politics in a traditional sense, he insists again and again that building community organizations to reach specific goals always must have an underlying, long-term agenda, of empowering the membership. In Gottlieb's terms, the community organizations Boyte talks about fight alienation by fighting particular forms of disenfranchisement.

Minnie Bruce Pratt recounts, from her own experience, the complexities of overcoming alienation. Most of us are both victims and perpetrators of alienation. One's own alienation is intimately associated with the alienations one imposes on others. Liberating oneself is all of a piece with making possible the liberation of others.

Her autobiographical reflections show very clearly that the distinction often drawn and argued between first changing oneself and then changing society makes little sense. In working to change society, you need to reconsider your previous stances and practices, otherwise your "outreach" will only perpetuate past oppressions and, at best, be useless. If you change, you will also act and alter what you do—otherwise your change is merely verbal.

Changing the world and changing yourself takes work. An important part of that work is to find out about others. You need to read, to explore history. But you also need to find out more about your own family and background. You need to learn what your kind of people did to make the world better, and not only how they victimized others. But you also need to discover the history of people very different from you.

These selections have raised many questions about alienation, its different forms, and its origins. A new and very powerful question is now added to all of those. We have found that more democracy is a cure for alienation; but surely not what we usually mean by that term "democracy": political campaigns managed by professional "handlers" and "spin doctors" for candidates who may, or may not, turn out to do what they promised on the campaign trail.

The issue of alienation demands a fundamental rethinking of the concept and the practices of democracy. The essays by Boyte and Pratt make some suggestions about ways of doing that.

The Dominated Self

Roger Gottlieb

Two concepts from Hegel (1967) will help convey what I wish to say about how the self is dominated in contemporary society. In Hegel's description of the "Master-Slave" relation, the "Master" gets his sense of self and social position by coercing the obedience of the "Slave"—who sees *his* labor appropriated by another and his own identity lost in the relation. For Hegel, however, the Slave comes to realize that his "slavishness" makes possible the Master's sense of self. The Slave's obedience and labor—that is, his action—are, in Hegel's phrase, the "truth" of the Master's seeming (but false) self-sufficiency. It is just such a transformation of the "slaves" that has been arrested under advanced capitalism. We do not find the direct and personal relations of Master and Slave; rather, there are the impersonal, bureaucratized relations of mass society—or atomized individuals facing mass-produced images. More important, the oppressed in contemporary capitalist society seem almost permanently blocked from experiencing their lives as forms of action, and thus from seeing the manner in which their action constitutes the "hidden truth" that supports social authority. This blockage produces another self-consciousness that can be understood with the help of another Hegelian concept: the "unhappy consciousness." An unhappy consciousness alternates between its awareness that a yearned-for goal is unrealizable and a fantasized realization of that goal that is haunted by suppressed knowledge of actual failure. Hegel used the concept to refer to certain forms of spirituality; I believe that it has relevance also to contemporary mass society. Specifically, I believe that obedience to social authority—remaining in the "slave" relation—is supported by a society-wide unhappy consciousness.

In the contemporary encounter between rulers and ruled, says Richard Sennett (1981: 154, 26), "Personal authority is not based simply on abstract principles of right . . . the legitimacy of personal authority arises from a perception of differences in strength. The authority conveys, the subject perceives, that there is therefore something unattainable in the character of authority." Even when authorities are subject to criticism, "these powers also translate into images of human strength: of authorities who are assured, judge as superiors, exert moral discipline and inspire fear." In this era of frequently exposed governmental and corporate corruption and incompetence, Sennett is making a crucial point. Though we feel authority to be illegitimate, we still tie ourselves to it. We act in a rebelliousness originating in the desire to displease authority, rather than out of our own freely generated motivations. Or we complain continually about authority but require its existence as the scapegoat for all that is wrong in our lives. Or we use the authority as a kind of negative model: if only we had authorities who were the opposite of what we in fact have, all problems would vanish.

Sennett explains these tendencies as products of our desire to affix personal responsibility for pains caused by an impersonal capitalist market.[1] While there may be some truth in this reasoning, he ignores the possibility that we might take control of these impersonal forces and use them in our own interests. Capitalism created not only the market but also ideologies of individuality and political freedom. How then is freedom made to coexist with powerlessness? Why do we tolerate delegitimized authorities when we might constitute legitimate ones ourselves?

Part of the answer lies in the creation of the dominated self. The dominated self is an unhappy consciousness which, in its unhappiness, requires the "support" of social authority, even when that authority inspires a strong sense of illegitimacy. The dominated self of advanced capitalism is not defined by particular beliefs or values; indeed, contemporary capitalist hegemony is maintained despite significant shifts in the conscious beliefs of the general population concerning crucial political and economic issues. Rather, the dominated self is constructed around a fundamental lack, a sense of inadequacy and unreality.[2] A self that is felt as unreal, absent, or lacking is incapable of rational and powerful action, and so such a self sustains social authority even when that authority seems undemocratic and inexpert. Thus a critique of the powers that be is all too frequently joined with political passivity rather than with militant mass movements. Or, when the bonds of social authority are weakened, the action of the oppressed takes the form of a desperate search for a selfhood felt to be unachievable.

Let us take, for example, the media. In advanced capitalism, we consume a never-ending stream of images of human beings. These images purport to represent us but are unrecognizable. We are everywhere and always confronted by images of ourselves that represent not us but some other selves that are not us. The result is a permanent sense of unreality in our own lives: a permanent discrepancy between what we know ourselves to be and what we are represented to be, a discrepancy in which we persistently fail to be what we "are." What we are, again, *is not*—for we know that we are not those figures on the television or movie screen. What we are not, *is*: the interesting, beautiful, seductive images of mass culture have a reality that preempts our own shabby, boring, tired existence. In this complex sense, the media, like the state and the doctor, serve as authority figures. Their authority derives from the compelling power of the images they produce—just as the authority of the medieval church derived from the size of its cathedrals.

The media tell us who we are and who we should be. Our persistent inability to follow that direction results in an often unconscious sense of our own unreality and failure. As men, for instance, we are not those handsome, athletic, fun-loving, warm-hearted guys playing their hearts out for a Michelob Light. We do not have such good friends, after all, nor are we so athletic or good-looking. By contrast to them we are failures—in our relationships, our bodies, our lives. All we can do, at the next touch football game, is *pretend* that we are they—and suppress to the level of unconsciousness the nagging sense of unreality that inevitably accompanies the attempt. As women, we know that we are not those beautiful, well-dressed, perfectly put-together persons meeting handsome, successful men at expensive restaurants; or shifting with ease from career woman (by day) to a seductress (by night); or possessing, along with two children, the figure of a seventeen-year-old model. All of us sense that our family holidays never move with the satisfaction and perfect love of the ones in Hallmark ads. And each time a Christmas or a Thanksgiving family event occurs, there is, again, that persistent sense that it is not what it should be.

The general effect is a demand, by media-as-authority, that we be something we are not. And this includes that most insidious of demands: that we feel something we do not feel.[3] The images of mass culture do not only represent externalities—looks, money, accomplishments; the attention of beautiful women, handsome men, and doting families. They also represent certain interiorities—happiness, fulfillment, love, good humor, calm, sexual satisfaction. We face representations of ourselves that direct us to emotional states we are incapable of feeling. Betty Friedan (1968) described this situation—in regard to the frustration and depression of middle-class women of the 1950s—as "the problem that has no name." Certain women supposedly possessed everything that was guaranteed to make them fulfilled. Instead of fulfillment, they felt a profound sense of emptiness.

These reflections suggest that culture does not only tell people what to do or what authorities to obey; it also represents us to ourselves. A mass culture that persistently tells us we are something we are not induces a sort of cultural schizophrenia. Our persistent attempt to be what we are not—or to believe we are what we know we are not—can only create a numbing sense of personal unreality. Such an unhappy consciousness is incompatible with coherent, organized, and effective political action because it is incompatible with the taking of authority. Thus support for authority, even when that authority is considered illegitimate, becomes more comprehensible. An unreal self cannot provide direction for itself. Without authority, it is lost.

Another source of the dominated self involves the relation between the media and the state. The ideology of democracy requires that government seem to combine delegated authority and expertise, and that there be a free press, academic freedom, and the like. These institutions allow much of public life to become a series of crises requiring public attention and redress by authority: a Three Mile Island accident, a public building that falls apart a few years after it is built, a delay in natural gas shipments during the winter, a catastrophic rise in gasoline prices. At such times the media generates an enormous hue and cry. News conferences are held; television "specials" give analysis and opinion; radio talk shows hold discussions through the night; popular movies may be made on the topic. The fear and anger of the general population are represented for that population through images of public concern. Media-as-authority promise action to redress wrongs, solve problems, and restore public safety. Experts-as-authority provide analyses and devise programs.

The social function of these processes is to lead the general population to believe that the authorities are willing and able to handle the particular problem. Often, however, no really significant action need ever be taken. By the time the blue-ribbon commissions and governmental inquiries are concluded, the attention of the general population is focused on another "crisis" with *its* press conferences, television specials, and government statements. National attention was glued to the Three Mile Island plant during the incident and immediately afterward, but how many people noticed the issuing of the presidential commission's report a year later? How many people know what was in the report, or whether its recommendations were implemented?

In these cases, the general population is led to feel that the authorities, functioning on the basis of a popular mandate and scientific expertise, are dealing with a crucial social problem. Yet the speed and intensity with which public attention is focused on and then shifted away from social problems leads to an inability to keep track of the concrete relation between "public" outcry and public reality. All that is known is that nuclear power plants continue to have accidents; public contracting in Massachusetts continues to produce shoddy buildings at exorbitant costs; and energy continues to be controlled by oligopolies for private profit. The painful discrepancy between promise and fulfillment, the supposed capacity and interest of government and experts, and the actual inability and lack of desire to do anything, creates a widespread and numbing sense of *political* unreality. The manipulation of political issues furthers the increased political passivity of a general population in the face of a social order that seems, legally and ideologically, to support political activity. The belief that authority is subject to public scrutiny and responsive to crises coexists with the sense that nothing is really changing and that we are still getting screwed. Price-gouging corporations are widely criticized, crooked politicians removed from office, demonstrations mounted, a rash of muckraking books published. Yet little changes.

There is a relation between the unreality of our image of the public world of politics and the private world of consumption and feeling. Our exclusion from active participation and collective control of the public realm is "justified" by the (illusory) rewards of the private. Depoliticization is rationalized by material wealth and personal freedom to consume, to choose a "life-style," to express heterodox opinions, and to form and dissolve personal relationships. Because a democratic ideology is combined with mass powerlessness in the worlds of work and politics, too much is loaded onto the family, fashion, hobbies, the latest VCR, mobile home, lace underwear, or therapy group. Because consumerism and personal relationships cannot replace a fulfilling involvement in social and productive life, mass culture must offer highly distorted possibilities of what consumption and personal relationships can do for us. Commodities and "life-styles" must be represented as offering fulfillment in such a compelling and convincing way that their failure to do so will be internalized as our own. And it is not foolishness or stupidity that leads us to take these images so seriously. It is the fact that real needs are manipulated into false hopes.[4] Our needs for sexuality, love, community, and interesting life, family respect, and self-respect are transformed by the ubiquitous images of an unattainable reality into the sense that our sexuality, family, and personal lives are unreal. And it is this mechanism that sustains social authorities no longer believed to be legitimate.

The same mechanism contributes to the disunity of the oppressed, a psychic disunity that correlates to the fragmenting effects of labor segmentation and racial or gender antagonisms. In this psychic disunity we live out our lives isolated by the distorted images of our own inadequacy, or we are joined in a false unity that only reproduces our isolation.

We may utilize here Sartre's notion of a "series." Sartre (1976: 25) takes as an example of a series a group of people waiting for a bus. The unity of this group is their common relation to something outside of themselves: the absent bus and the hope that it will get them to work on time. No internal connections are forged within this group; indeed, each member is a threat to the others—a threat that the line is too long and that there will not be enough seats. The unity of millions of people desiring the same (unattainable) sex symbol on a television program or cheering the same athletic team possesses a similar falsity. The sexuality of the film star and the triumph of the victorious team are "for us," yet will never be ours. Our physical desire is awakened at the same time that we know it cannot be fulfilled—except in fantasy. Likewise, our rejoicing over "our" team's victory celebrates an action that is not taken by us and which will leave our lives exactly as they were before. The isolation of a fantasized desire shared by millions corresponds to the false solidarity of a meaningless triumph. In both cases real action is excluded. Surrogate action is all that remains: sex in which the Other is experienced as a fantasy; emotional responses to triumphs and failures of another.[5]

The size and complexity of modern mass culture means that the foregoing analysis needs to be extended. We require an account, for example, of the mass consumption of simulated tragedy in the world of soap operas, or the use of intergenerational relations as substitutes for political ones. We also need to understand the compatibility and tension between modern mass culture and the traditional cultures of religion and community. Most important, it is necessary to see how the totality of culture, despite its reproduction of social relations through the dominated self, may at times come into conflict with the social order.

Here, however, the major point is the manner in which the dominated self can coexist with a variety of ideologies and cultural norms. It makes little difference what people believe, think to be "right," or value if they are incapable of decisive, collective action. This point is crucial, for—just like pop music and women's fashions—much of the cognitive content of ideology is subject to rapid transformation. Whatever the images of success and adequacy, they must be inaccessible. As Greenspan (1983) has argued, for instance, the transition from the feminine mystique of the 1950s to the superwoman (career, motherhood, and sexuality combined) of the late 1970s leaves women feeling inadequate when they cannot live up to this new unrealizable ideal. Similarly, a "Father Knows Best" 1950s suburban family (white, middle-class, comfortable, "funny," and loving) no more matches the reality of most families than does the two-career, high-consumption, childless yuppie couple of the 1980s. Finally, the dominated self is compatible with certain fundamental changes in the locus of sexual repression and cultural images of fatherhood, family, and work. It was out of a particular configuration of these that Reich and the Frankfurt School developed their explanations of authoritarianism. Yet social authority remains, even while the cultural changes of the past fifty years have rendered much of their analysis somewhat obsolete. Puritan-style repression no longer links sexuality and social authority.

The dominated self, whatever particular thoughts or beliefs it possesses, maintains its general sense of unreality. And as an unreal self, it necessarily turns to the greater reality of social authorities as sources of strength, control, and direction—even when it possesses independent doubts or criticisms of those authorities. It will not rely on itself—or on others like it. Unity and action become impossible.

CRITICISMS AND RESPONSES

Some criticisms might be made of this analysis. If I am attempting to describe the "psychology of oppression," why have I chosen to describe the effects of structures or situations that seem so nearly universal? An upper-class, suburban white woman, after all, may be as distant from images of seductive, beautiful femininity as a black welfare mother. A corporate executive may enjoy less male camaraderie than the workers he exploits. Persecuted minorities may often have as much or more family warmth than members of the ruling class. Yet in each of these pairs, the former possess privileges and, in some cases, power at the latter's expense.

In fact, it might be argued, the structures of oppression are not based in a widespread, nearly universal "dominated self," an atomized relation to a generalized condition. Rather, they are rooted in the specific institutional and personal inequalities. To understand the psychology of oppression, then, would be to understand how taking a subordinate position affects the oppressed. For every "have not" felt by the oppressed, there is a corresponding "have" of the possessor group. Women's fear of male violence corresponds to a sense of power held by men. Working-class poverty corresponds to capitalist wealth. The high unemployment rate of blacks makes possible a lower one among whites.

Finally, someone could suggest, while some of the "Master-Slave" relations of contemporary society are impersonal, many are not. As I have already argued in chapter 9 [of *History and Subjectivity*], a significant part of male-female oppression is defined by personal relations. The psychology of oppression is operative in encounters between workers and managers, secretaries and their bosses, ordinary citizens and politicians, nurses or patients and doctors, students and teachers. The solution is, therefore, that the oppressed come to a personal and political realization of the true nature of their relation to their oppressors.

These criticisms, I believe, deepen rather than contradict my analysis. First, consider the sense of personal unreality conveyed by mass culture's images. Different types of oppression can be defined partly by reference to the degree to which people cannot find their lives represented by the culture in which they live. Just as different groups may have unequal access to material wealth, so they have unequal access to the "cultural wealth" of seeing a reflection of their lives in the surrounding public space. Despite the underlying unreality of most of the images of popular culture, it is clear that certain groups are closer to those images than others. White, upper-class, Gentile, nonhandicapped heterosexuals see themselves in these images in ways that black, Jewish, homosexual, or handicapped people cannot. Media-as-authority direct us to live a certain life, engage in certain activities, look a certain way. The closer one is to those images, the less one feels that devastating sense of unreality described above.

Similarly, media-as-authority enjoin us to have certain kinds of feelings. For instance, motherhood is represented as a blissful state in which perfect children play in clean (or soon to be clean) clothes, well protected by a totally devoted woman. Despite the unreality of this image, certain women can clearly find aspects of it easier in their lives than can others. A professional woman married to a husband somewhat touched by feminist ideals, with adequate income for quality day care and the best medical attention, will—all other things being equal—find motherhood less frustrating than will a welfare mother.

We may generalize this point by saying that an essential aspect of the oppression of various groups in our society is the disenfranchisement from the mass culture that surrounds them. Social authority is protected and reproduced by excluding certain groups from cultural and psychic representation and thus crippling their capacity to feel themselves as real.

If my analysis is correct, we would expect to see struggles against oppression include attempts by the oppressed to represent their own reality. And, in fact, we do. From the Harlem Renaissance and Black Nationalist movements of the 1920s to the "Black is Beautiful" slogan of the 1960s, politicized blacks have struggled for cultural self-representation. Contemporary feminists have transformed cultural representations of women and developed "woman-oriented" scholarship, music, and spiritual practices. Examples from sources as disparate as the pre–World War I German Social Democratic Party and Allende's Chile could also be offered.

Similarly, if my analysis is correct, we should see mass culture responding to upsurges among the oppressed by a process of co-optation. In this process the demands and concerns of the oppressed are "deflected": situation comedies about blacks or charming Hispanic-American junkmen, male homosexuals on soap operas, black women newscasters. In each case the demand of the oppressed—that, for instance, the reality of living as a black in a racist society be recognized—is both "accepted" and shown to be compatible with the existing order. If those blacks on television can adapt, why can't I? If Laverne and Shirley, two working-class "girls" who live together, have such camaraderie and good humor, why can't the rest of us? If this or that individual black or woman or Hispanic has "made it" as anchorperson or executive, my failure must be due to personal limitations (cf. Sennett and Cobb 1973). In each case, cultural self-representation is thwarted and the reality of the experiences of oppression obscured.

Moving to my second example of a source of the dominated self, we may note that just as all groups are not equally alienated from mass culture, so they are not all equally alienated from political processes. Not all see their fears and hopes manipulated and frustrated. To take an extreme instance, we might compare the political response to an urban fiscal crisis of a corporate executive and an unemployed autoworker. The unemployed autoworker is by and large a spectator, a consumer of the news bulletins and statements by government officials, bank presidents,and bureaucratic union leaders. Meanwhile, his services will suffer the most. He may lack the education to understand either the deeper roots of the fiscal crisis or the terminology of the various alternative proposals for curing it. At any rate, he knows that the effort needed to understand is not well spent. Since he has no input into these decisions, he will be better off looking for a job, fixing his house, or watching a baseball game at a bar. The corporate executive, by contrast, is financially cushioned against a rise in gas prices or layoffs of public school teachers. By training and temperament, he is capable of at least a superficial understanding of a fiscal crisis, alternative proposals to meet it, and the complicated institutions called on to act. He may know some of the bankers, politicians, or experts involved; in any event, he moves in the same social circles.

It is obvious that unemployed autoworkers and corporate executives possess unequal social authority, and that the political process in advanced capitalist society includes one and excludes the other. It is less obvious, however, that these differences are not limited to income or social position. What the corporate executive has and the unemployed worker has not is a general sense of the reality of this own being, a sense that his actions will have significant effects in the world. The familiar self-description—"I want to be somebody" and "I'm just a nobody"—sum up this phenomenon. To be oppressed is not simply to lack material goods, leisure, or opportunity. It is to be robbed of one's self.

Finally, my stress on the generalized cultural forms that create the dominated self do not exclude person-to-person interactions. Meetings between oppressor and oppressed may be between individuals, but these encounters express the collective realities of oppressor and oppressed. One does not leave behind the sense of unreality produced by impersonal forces when one confronts the oppressor in person. Nor does the oppressor leave behind the psychological advantage of having had some sense of power, some reflection in the generalized culture. A reality confronts an unreality. A slave faces a master. In this confrontation the power of the ruler is sustained by the material structure of the ruled's inability to feel him or herself as a reality.[6] Institutional power and wealth are joined with the psychological "wealth" of self-confidence and public recognition; institutional powerlessness and material poverty are joined to a lack of mastery of the techniques by which one represents oneself as knowledgeable, expert, and worthy of respect (Sennett 1981: 97–104; Ellman 1968).

In conclusion, then, we see that socialization processes begun in infancy and continued through adult life create adult personalities tied to present forms of domination or incapable of resisting them. The failures of the economy provide, at best, a spur to cracking through the resistant shell of internalized social control or the crippling effects of the dominated self. At such times, however, the oppressed face two formidable obstacles. The unity of the ruling class is expressed mainly (but not exclusively) in the state. Simultaneously, social differentiation keeps different segments of the working class from uniting politically. Consequently, our study of the transformation of Marxist theory now leads to an examination of the social primacy of politics.

Notes

1. A similar argument is developed at length in Schmitt's *Alienation and Class* (1983). Schmitt claims that alienation emerged when capitalism combined individual freedom and personal powerlessness.
2. I am opposing Marcuse's account in *One-Dimensional Man* (1964) in which he claimed that repressive desublimation, which made for what might be called a "happy consciousness" among the ruled, was responsible for the absence of radical political activity.
3. The alienation of experience was a basic theme of the "anti-psychiatry" movement of the 1960s (Laing 1960, 1967).
4. This type of analysis was performed on changing sexual mores by Marcuse's concept of "repressive desublimation." Marcuse (1964) argued that the seeming end of sexual puritanism masked a continued repression. The impersonal sex of the sexual revolution, he maintained, did not liberate our sexuality but simply changed the form of sexual repression.
5. This may be one way to make sense of Althusser's often-quoted but highly obscure claim (1971: 162) that "ideology is a 'representation' of the imaginary relationships of individuals to their real conditions of existence."
6. In Foucault's (1975) account of the "gaze" in medicine and the penal system, subject groups (patients or prisoners) are rendered passive before a seemingly objective source of knowledge and power.

References

Althusser, Louis. (1971). *Lenin and Philosophy and Other Essays*. New York: Monthly Review Press.

Ellman, Mary. (1968). *Thinking about Women*. New York: Harcourt, Brace, and World.

Foucault, Michel. (1975). *The Birth of the Clinic: An Archeology of Medical Perception*. New York: Vintage.

Friedan, Betty. (1968). *The Feminine Mystique*. New York: Dell.

Greenspan, Miriam. (1983). *A New Approach to Women and Therapy*. New York: McGraw-Hill.

Hegel, G. W. F. (1967). *The Phenomenology of Mind*. New York: Harper and Row.

Laing, Ronald D. (1960). *The Divided Self*. New York: Penguin.

Laing, Ronald D. (1967). *The Politics of Experience*. New York: Ballantine.

Sartre, Jean-Paul. (1976). *Critique of Dialectical Reason*. London: NLR.

Schmitt, Richard. (1983). *Alienation and Class*. Cambridge: Schenkman.

Sennett, Richard. (1981). *Authority*. New York: Random House.

Sennett, Richard, and Cobb, Jonathan. (1973). *The Hidden Injuries of Class*. New York: Random House.

Public Freedom

HARRY C. BOYTE

THE EXHILARATION OF THE sixties grew from a particular experience of *public freedom*,[1] based on a recognition by ordinary citizens that they can gain the power to affect the decisions which shape their worlds through participation in public life. Today, when the country faces a complex web of dangers, challenges, and the burdens of the Gulf War, we also have far more extensive foundations on which to build a renewed politics of freedom. A look at lessons from subsequent organizing efforts highlights the possibilities.

A cottage industry of films, documentaries, songs, and other cultural expressions has recently looked back wistfully upon the 1960s. In this reading, the cultural and political vibrancy of that decade presents a stunning contrast to the discouraged, privatized, and shallow period that followed. Moreover, political demoralization gives every sign of continuing in the 1990s, the era *Newsweek* dubbed the "Decade of Anxiety."

It is as if the Baby Boom had been refashioned as a championship gymnast whose youthful glory makes the tired denouements of middle age all the more painful. From this perspective, alienation, understood as estrangement from our best possibilities, our promises, and our capacity, threatens to become the chronic condition of our time, not only the experience of the poorest and the most visibly "marginal."

Yet a different rendering of history is possible. A sea of democratic experiment spread through the nation over the past two decades, ranging from neighborhood organizations to battered women's shelters, environmental efforts to large citizen action groups. For instance, something like 8,000 community organizations now exist in America, often in poor and working-class urban settings, working on issues that range from housing to drugs, school reforms to urban gardening. From the vantage of such experience, the movements of the sixties simply *reintroduced* democratic themes that had once seemed extinguished. Two decades of organizing have produced significant advances in both the craft and the theory of democratic action.

Such experiences have yet to be integrated into a larger vision of political transformation. But here, the sixties activism provides important resources. "Freedom" was the structuring theme of the civil rights movement of the late 1950s and early 1960s in ways that have been little explored. In civil rights, freedom conveyed the conventional meaning of freedom *from* repressive conditions or restraint. Specifically it offered release from the degradation of segregation. Freedom today continues to have strong resonance in American culture but its current meaning is constricted to an individualized, privatized, and largely negative sense: freedom means usually simply the ability to do what one likes, without undue coercion.

In civil rights, freedom's most powerful meanings came from *public* dimensions, however. It suggested the positive freedom *to* participate as full, independent, and powerful citizens in public affairs on an ongoing basis, that experience that creates what Hannah Arendt called "public happiness." Precisely this public participation—in the movement's rallies, sit-ins, demonstrations, voter registration drives, Freedom Schools, and other activities—generated the movement spirit, despite opposition and situations of great danger.[2] Subsequent grassroots organizing have elaborated three aspects of public freedom present in the movement. In the first instance, freedom meant the end of contingency, or definition of one's being by "the other," and the alternative acts of individual and collective self-discovery and self-definition. In the second instance, freedom involved new experiences of power—what has come to be understood as the process of "organizing for power," or empowerment, in community action. Finally, freedom meant the ability to act with sophistication and effectiveness with others to shape the larger public world, beyond one's private and communal relationships. This experience of world creation was both critical to civil rights and also transitory and short-lived. The movement lacked the language and repertoire of skills essential to sustain a larger process of public reconstruction. Yet this process is essential to public freedom, understood not only as self-definition and empowerment but also as coauthorship of history.

SELF-NAMING

"Old woman, what is this freedom you love so well?" asks Ralph Ellison's protagonist in *Invisible Man*. "I guess now it ain't nothing but knowing how to say what I got up in my head," she replies. "But it's a hard job, son. Too much is done happen to me in too short a time. Hit's like I have a fever. Ever' time I starts to walk my head gits to swirling and I falls down."

The civil rights movement generated the capacity to speak—the ability to define oneself, to think, to talk, and to take initiative. Indeed, as its first act, the movement challenged the very *definition* of being "Negro" in southern society, the profound alienation that stemmed from being defined and dismissed by the other, by white society. "People were talking about becoming free, free of mind, and free in spirit," remembered Annie Devine, a leader in the movement in Canton, Mississippi. John Hulett of the Lowndes County Freedom Party argued that through the movement "people began to take on a new life and they see themselves as being men and women."

This process required collective action to overcome the pervasive fear that had worked to prevent opposition to the racial status quo. In turn, collective action depended upon free spaces, the activation of communal places that had an important measure of autonomy from external and dominant centers of power. Barber shops and beauty parlors, for instance, proved a central distribution center for literature in the movement's early days, because such institutions had no dependency on white society. "We ran special workshops for black beauticians. We used the shops all over the south as a center for literature and discussions because the beauticians didn't care what white people thought about them," recounted Myles Horton, director of Highlander Folk School. The movement also built on the legacy of the African-American church as a setting where blacks could define who they were and what they wanted, free of coercion.

Free spaces are settings rooted in people's everyday life experience. A central lesson out of successful organizing in recent history has been the importance of grounding democratic action in the concrete ties of daily life—what organizers often call "self-interests," not understood as narrow concerns but rather as those things that strongly move people into action.

Central to effective community organizing is a *listening* process that leads to understanding the community and its interests and everyday life patterns. "The starting of a People's Organization is not a matter of personal choice. You start with the people, their traditions, their prejudices, their habits, their attitudes, and all of those other circumstances that make up their lives," wrote Saul Alinsky, dean of this craft. Organization must be "rooted in the experience of the people themselves." Change should never be shortcut through ignorance or carelessness. "To know a people is to know their religions. It is to know the values, objectives, customs, sanctions and the taboos of these groups. It is to know them not only in terms of their relationships and attitudes toward one another but also in terms of what relationship all of them have toward the outside."

Moreover, free spaces are environments where people develop the capacity to define their own agenda in a world surfeited by professional language. Alinsky saw organizing in Chicago's Southside ghettoes as a "revolt against welfare colonialism," challenging the labelling processes which render poor and minority communities radically dependent upon professional help.

This reclaiming of authority from experts and professionals has subsequently proven critical. Thus, leaders of successful community efforts regularly describe the first step of action as a process of defining a reality for themselves. "When we started out, they said we couldn't do nothing cause we were poor folks, black and not experts," said Bertha Gilkey, a tenant leader who led a dramatic process of community regeneration in the once decimated St. Louis public housing project, Cochran Gardens. "I thought about that, and then decided that experts got us in trouble in the first place." When East Brooklyn Churches (EBC), a community organization that built thousands of low-cost single family homes in rubble-strewn blocks on the Brooklyn Borough, named their undertaking the "Nehemiah Plan," recalling the Old Testament prophet sent back to Jerusalem by the king of Persia in 420 to lead in the rebuilding of the city after the Babylonian captivity, the act of naming itself changed the undertaking. "The story connected our work to something real, not something bogus," explained Mike Gecan, organizer. "It got it out of the 'housing' field and the idea that you have to have a bureaucracy with 35 consultants to do anything. It made it a 'nonprogram,' something more than housing." Or as one EBC leader, Celina Jamieson, emphasized, "We are more than a Nehemiah Plan. We are about the central development of dignity and self-respect."

The freedom to define oneself and one's issues in one's own terms, in turn, is essential for any process of empowerment.

Empowerment

In the civil rights movement, freedom also meant empowerment, or the ability to act in the world. As SNCC Chair John Lewis put it, "being involved tended to free you . . . you saw yourself also as a free man, as the free agent, able to act." Fannie Lou Hamer described how the process of voter registration provided new experiences of self-direction and capacity. "Headin' your flock out of the chains and fetters of Egypt—taken' them yourself to register . . . taught us a lot about what we should do ourselves."

"Power" means the ability to act with effect. One never "empowers" others; empowerment is a process that people forge themselves as they come to develop their own capacity for action. This insight has become codified in community-organizing networks as a phrase that challenges the approach of service providers: "never do things for people that they can do for themselves."

Saul Alinsky argued for "the politics of stop-signs," focusing on concrete, immediate, and achievable goals as the first step in grass-roots empowerment. The point was that people needed success experience which they themselves "owned." Throughout *Reveille for Radicals*, his first book, he emphasized self-help, confidence-building collective success, and dramatic encounter as keys to organizing for power. "It is impossible to overemphasize the enormous importance of people's doing things themselves," Alinsky wrote in his chapter, "Psychological Observations on Mass Organization." "The objective is never an end in itself," Alinsky continued. "The efforts that are exerted in the actual earning of the objective are part of the achievement. . . . What you get by your own effort is really yours."

A recognition of the importance of self-help and successful group action is at the heart of organizing approaches taught in a variety of training centers, including Alinsky's Industrial Areas Foundation (IAF), and also the Midwest Academy, Grassroots Leadership, Advocacy Institute, Organize Training Center, National Training and Information Center, Gamiliel Foundation, and Pacific Institute for Community Organization, among others. Those who have felt marginal need an experience of collective efficacy. "We had a short term strategy and a long term strategy," was the way Gilkey put it. "The long term strategy was to rebuild Cochran Gardens as a good place to live. But we couldn't tell many people because they would think we were crazy. So our short term strategy was recognition that we could *do* something by ourselves and for ourselves." Gilkey and Cochran Garden tenants started by raising money through bake sales and other means to buy paint to paint their hall walls.

A focus on sustained empowerment changes the terms of politics from essentially moralized crusades into a pragmatic process. Community leaders and organizers were often active in sixties efforts, but they distinguish their work today from the sixties. Thus, it does little good to complain or moralize about "the establishment," like local business leadership. Power relations *exist*. The most effective way of dealing with the fact is to develop a practical attention to the ways of gaining power and changing the chemistry of power interactions from largely one-way encounters to a more interactive and relational process.

Doug Miles, a young civil rights activist in Baltimore in the 1960s who became a key figure in the Baltimore BUILD group said that by the late 1970s it was increasingly clear that exhortation and protest weren't successful. "Winning was just being able to say you were on the right side; it was a moral victory." When he became involved in BUILD, Miles learned a pragmatic rather than a moralized approach to power, aimed at mobilizing "organized people" both to counter and also to develop relationships with what they call the "organized money." "We learned that power isn't a dirty word," Miles recounted. "We learned the need for accountability. The difference between the world as it is and as it should be."

Free spaces, or settings over which people have a strong degree of control, are essential for such empowerment. The need for financial independence is often a critical element here. "The development of dues in the Citizens Action Program (CAP) in Chicago in the 1970s turned out to be a real key to our whole approach," argued Larry McNeil, recalling the experience that became a model for much subsequent organizing. "The organization wasn't dependent on government funds, or foundation money, or corporations. Members raised funds themselves." Self-sufficiency created the ability to determine organizational objectives and actions. In the mid-seventies, Joan Flanagan's *Grass Roots Fund-raising*, detailing ways for local groups to become self-supporting and indepen-dent of large institutional funders, has proven a vital resource for thousands of local efforts.

Winning real victories that people define for themselves and that matter in their lives is the lifeblood of grass-roots organizing. But such organizing can also become self-limiting, leading to a parochial "Not in My Backyard" (NIMBY) or single-issue stance. To move from a position of "protestor" to the experience of being a significant actor requires additional elements of skill and political language: a way of describing the heterogeneous public world beyond one's immediate circle of friends and community life in noninstrumental terms, and the skills and public arts that allow one to act in public affairs on a continuing basis with effectiveness.

PUBLIC CREATION

In the civil rights movement, freedom suggested more than an experience of self-definition, a legal status, or even the more intangible but potent qualities of empowerment and self-respect. It also entailed a new and strengthened sense of "citizenship," through which people came to experience themselves as par-ticipants in the governance of American society.

Such a vision of freedom as public participation and citizenship had old roots in the African-American tradition. Charles Gomillion had described earlier efforts to bring about political equality in Tuskegee, for instance, as "civic democracy . . . a way of life in which all citizens have the opportunity to participate in societal affairs."

This theme of public participation became a central motif in the movement. Indeed it formed the heart of efforts like the Citizenship Schools of the Southern Christian Leadership Conference and the Freedom Schools of the Student Nonviolent Coordinating Committee, adapted from Highlander.

Organized by Ella Baker, Septima Clark, Miles Horton, Dorothy Cotton, Andy Young, and others, the Citizenship and Freedom schools, while register-ing voters, also taught thousands of local leaders new approaches to citizen problem solving. "Teachers" and "students" were peers. Methods drew directly on the stories and experiences of participants. The formal political process was concretely connected to problems in people's daily lives. This experience could create a transformative sense of public life. Unita Blackwell, involved with the Mississippi Freedom Democratic Party, who later was elected mayor of Mayers-ville, Mississippi, described her experience: "We found ourselves involved in working in political work, and we still ain't figured all of it out yet, but it's been just wonderful." "What I remember," said one participant in the Selma movement, "was the happiness of the people. . . . We could . . . let everyone know that we were Americans, too."

Since the 1960s, citizen efforts have added to this tradition through developing an explicit language that stresses the need to move from resistance to transformation of the larger environment. Thus, the Midwest Academy training center, a resource for a large range of labor, community, women's, environmental, and other citizen groups over the past two decades, has recently begun to stress public responsibility for problem solving as well as organizing for power. As Kimberly A. Bobo, Jacquelyn Kendall, and Steve Max put it in their new book, *Organizing for Power*, "while much of our language remains the language of protest, citizen organizing now goes beyond that. Many organizations strive to enlarge the participation of ordinary people in public life with a problem-solving politics that has citizens at the core . . . citizens are taking on themselves civic responsibilities previously left to government."

Moreover, successful organizing has often framed such problem solving with the concept of *public life*, a diverse, challenging arena that is not simply instrumental but important in its own right. In public life, citizens reclaim responsibility and develop the power and skills and organizational means to address seriously public issues.

At the heart of such a politics is a political education. Ed Chambers, director of IAF since Alinsky died in 1972, describes the shift toward education as the major development in the network's fifty-year history. "We began to see every action as an opportunity for education and training," said Maribeth Larkin, an organizer with the Los Angeles United Neighborhood Organization.

Citizens thus become "co-creators of history" in the phrasing of Gerald Taylor, on IAF's national staff. Taylor sees this as the shift from protest to participation in governance. "When you've been out of power so long, there's a tendency not to want to be responsible or to be held accountable. But to participate—to develop a sense that you are creating history—one must move into power." "Moving into power" for Taylor means to "negotiate, compromise, understand that others have power and ways of viewing the world different than your own."

A conceptual framework that shows both the distinctions and the connections between public and private life proves a valuable resource for citizenship initiatives. In these terms, public life is a realm of difference, public work, accountability, respect and recognition, negotiation and bargaining; private life is an area of intimacy, spontaneity, similarity, and loyalty. There is nothing completely "either-or" about such distinctions—private life always has public dimensions; public life has personal elements. Moreover, such a political mapping builds on the sixties insight that "the personal is political." People's self-interests and passions, forged mainly from personal experience, are what lead people normally to public action.

While people usually enter public life through private concerns, they can act with far greater effectiveness if they recognize the different dynamics at work in public and private domains. In ways analogous to the legal distinction between substantive and procedural matters, this kind of mapping leads to a redefinition of the citizenry as not simply protestors or deliberators but as actors in the ongoing public problem solving.

"We would never have been able to challenge the priest to stop acting like our 'father' without this sort of training," said Beatrice Cortez, a president of San Antonio Communities Organized for Public Service (COPS) in the early 1980s. "You learn what's appropriate and inappropriate for politicians. They shouldn't try to get us to love them, for instance." Cortez frequently tells the story of her daughter, to illustrate how children can quickly pick up the point. Cortez had a COPS phone in her house, during her tenure as president of the organization. One day the mayor, Henry Cisneros—whom she had known for years—called up on the line. "My daughter answered and at first didn't know who it was. 'Who should I say is calling?' she asked." Cisneros said, "'Tell her it's a special friend.' Then she recognized his voice," Ms. Cortez continued. "She said, 'on this line, you're not a friend. I know who you are. You're the mayor!' I told her, 'you got that right, honey!'" Cortez subsequently found that in training Mexican communities in other parts of Texas in effective "public life," the distinction proved invaluable. "In these towns, politics has come to be equated with family ties. People get mixed up through marriage, godparents and don't want to challenge close ties."

Evocation of a "public realm" where dynamics of personal loyalty were not dominant did not undermine extended family patterns, nor consign "family concerns" to the private realm. But it positioned them in a way that allowed common work with people *beyond* traditional family ties.

These groups reverse the traditional attributes of public and private realms. "Private," in the IAF terms, is the more self-sacrificial and idealistic realm, while public is the world of "quid pro quo" and "self-interest." Moreover, public life in this view has value in its own right, but it also should serve the personal interests of families and private relations.

In contrast, the republican tradition across the centuries has privileged public life, sustaining in various forms Aristotle's metaphor of public life as like the body (politic), while private life is like limbs, that can be cut away if necessary. A more apt metaphor for community organizing's construction of public and private is the symbol of a tree. Roots serve as the "private" foundations of public life, while trunk and branch, symbols of the visible public world, are expressions of "maturity"—but continue to draw sustenance and support from their roots. Such a set of reversals has its counterparts in the communal and family issues that are taken up by groups like COPS. And they have led to a radical recasting of the nature of leadership and politics that encourages women, for instance, to take new roles. After COPS first election, every president of the organization was female.

These lessons of community activism are important but insufficient in themselves to generate a new politics of freedom. Community organizations, like everything in human affairs, are marked by their cultures and histories. Saul Alinsky came from an Orthodox Jewish background. The Eastern European Catholic values of his classic groups, like Back of the Yard in Chicago, still find echoes today in the vocabulary and values of organizations among poor, minority, and ethnic communities dedicated to ethnic heritage, religious traditionalism, family, community, hard work, and patriotism.

Community organizations' vocabularies are different than the world of the middle class, on the one hand. On the other, community organizing, classically creating a power base out of local institutions, is far more difficult in those urban areas today where churches or synagogues, small businesses, ethnic groups, political organizations, and labor unions have dramatically weakened. Organizing strategies, based on flamboyant direct acting and confrontation with local business interests and power brokers, are not directly transferable to the environments of the service world, where forms of power based on professionalized and expertise are dominant, but often hidden and invisible. A more multidimensional political pedagogy and strategy, in other words, is essential in order to develop a democratic politics that engage the vast range of constituencies in American society.

Project Public Life at the University of Minnesota's Humphrey Institute of Public Affairs has experimented successfully over the last two years with teaching concepts and skills of public life to reengage teens, young adults, and others in the political world in settings as diverse as high schools, nursing homes, and low income areas. Public Achievement, for instance, undertaken by Project Public Life with St. Paul mayor Jim Scheibel and Minnesota 4-H, has found that teens today have enormous interest in a "problem-solving politics" in which they design and manage their own projects. Public Achievement regularly brings together different teams of teenagers in public environments where they learn how to work practically across racial and income lines. Participants clearly distinguish this experience from community service and other conventional educational activities. "In school, the point is to do what we are asked to do," explained one leader in an effort to give students more voice in high school governance. "Regular education simply isn't designed to develop our political capacities or our feeling of power."

Project Public Life adapts the community organizing version of "public and private" to highlight an intermediate realm of communal life that cannot be taken for granted for many today. Community overlaps with public and private but is distinctive. Such a schema can be represented graphically:

PRIVATE	COMMUNITY	PUBLIC
family/friends	clubs/religious/community groups, professional groups, etc.	large institutions, public projects,
loyalty	covenant relations	accountability
similarity	familiarity	difference
intimacy/love	friendship	recognition/respect
spontaneity	task orientation/socializing	strategic action
personal power	community power	public power

In a problem-solving public world that grows from this sort of mapping, there are few saints or sinners but rather an interplay among a variety of interests, values, and ways of looking at experience. Knowledge is not simply divided between categories like "objective" and analytic or "subjective" and emotional. Different ways of knowing and perspectives are valued because they are helpful, in just the sense suggested by the Jainist fables of the six blind men surrounding an elephant who only know "the truth" of the elephant by pooling their knowledge. In a public sphere of actors, no one is simply a victim or an innocent. Power is not one-directional. The development of ethical standards and ground rules for public life is essential. But everyone bears a measure of responsibility for this process.

Such an approach gives new foundations to the intimations of public freedom that have emerged in recent history in Eastern Europe, Africa, China, and Latin America. It challenges the modern managerialism of technocratic capitalism. And it differs sharply from the "ideological" mode of communism or other revolutionary and totalizing ideologies that, in Czech leader Vaclav Havel's terms, "offers human beings the illusion of an identity and of morality while making it easier for them to part with them." The concept of a public realm of action, creation, and deliberation is something different:

> In a society which is really alive, there is always something happening . . . a constant succession of unique situations which provoke further and fresh movement. The mysterious, vital polarity of the continuous and the changing, the regular and the random, the foreseen and the unexpected, has its effect. . . .

Recent democratic movements like Havel's have suggested again a public life with worth because it is the arena for public creation: the place where one actively makes one's mark not through simply "doing one's thing" but through *adding value* to the world. Public freedom suggests the process through which people become creators of the world, no longer objects.

We have memories of this history creation by ordinary people a generation ago. We also have multiple lessons in the intervening time from which to draw.

There is yet to emerge a large-scale politics of freedom which expresses and sustains such insights. But a freedom movement is not as distant as imagined.

Notes

1. Thanks to Sara Evans and Peg Michels for their comments. An earlier version of this paper appeared in *Tikkun*.
2. This argument benefits from the vivid treatment of the theme of freedom in Richard H. King, in "Citizenship and Self-Respect: The Experience of Politics in the Civil Rights Movement," *Journal of American Studies* 22 (1988): 7–24. King argues that despite the extensive historiography of the civil rights movement, there has been strikingly little attention to the power and meanings of its "freedom language."

Identity: Skin, Blood, Heart

MINNIE BRUCE PRATT

WHERE DOES THE NEED come from, the inner push to walk into change, if by skin color, ethnicity, birth culture, we are women who are in a position of material advantage, where we gain at the expense of others, of other women? A place where *we* can have a degree of safety, comfort, familiarity, just by staying put. Where is our *need* to change what we were born into? What do we have to gain?

When I try to think of this, I think of my father: of how, when I was about eight years old, he took me up the front marble steps of the courthouse in my town. He took me inside, up the worn wooden steps, stooped under the feet of folks who had gone up and down to be judged, or to gawk at others being judged, up past the courtroom where my grandfather had leaned back in his chair and judged for over forty years, up to the attic, to some narrow steps that went to the roof, to the clock tower with a walled ledge.

What I would have seen at the top: on the streets around the courthouse square, the Methodist church, the limestone building with the county Health Department, Board of Education, Welfare Department (my mother worked there), the yellow brick Baptist church, the Gulf station, the pool hall (no women allowed), Cleveland's grocery, Ward's shoestore; then all in a line, connected, the bank, the post office, Dr. Nicholson's office, one door for whites, one for Blacks; then separate, the Presbyterian church, the newspaper office, the yellow brick jail, same brick as the Baptist church, and as the courthouse.

What I could not have seen from the top: the sawmill, or Four Points where the white mill folks lived, or the houses of Blacks in Veneer Mill quarters.

This is what I would and would not have seen, or so I think, for I never got to the top. When he told me to go up the steps in front of him, I tried to, crawling on hands and knees, but I was terribly afraid. I couldn't, or wouldn't, do it. He let me crawl down; he was disgusted with me, I thought. I think now that he wanted to show me a place he had climbed to as a boy, a view that had been his father's and his, and would be mine. But I was *not* him; I had not learned to take that height, that being set apart as my own—a white girl, not a boy.

Yet I was shaped by my relation to those buildings and to the people in the buildings, by ideas of who should be working in the Board of Education, of who should be in the bank handling money, of who should have the guns and the keys to the jail, of who should be *in* the jail; and I was shaped by what I didn't see, or didn't notice, on those streets.

Not the way your town was laid out, you say? True, perhaps, but each of us carries around those growing-up places, the institutions, a sort of backdrop, a stage set. So often we act out the present against a backdrop of the past, within a frame of perception that is so familiar, so safe that it is terrifying to risk changing it even when we know our perceptions are distorted, limited, constricted by that old view.

So this is one gain for me as I change: I learn a way of looking at the world that is more accurate, complex, multilayered, multidimensioned, more truthful—to see the world of overlapping circles, like movement on the mill-pond after a fish has jumped, instead of the courthouse square with me at the middle, even if I *am* on the ground. I feel the *need* to look differently because I've learned that what is presented to me as an accurate view of the world is frequently a lie; so that to look through an anthology of women's studies that has little or no work by women of color is to be up on that ledge about the town and be thinking that I see the town, without realizing how many lives have been pushed out of sight, beside unpaved roads. I'm learning that what I think that I *know* is an accurate view of the world is frequently a lie, as when I was in a discussion about the Women's Pentagon Action with several women, four of us Christian-raised, one Jewish. In describing the march through Arlington Cemetery, one of the four mentioned the rows of crosses. I had marched for a long time through that cemetery; I nodded to myself, visualized rows of crosses. No, said the Jewish woman, they were headstones with crosses or stars of David engraved above the names. We four objected; we all had seen crosses. The Jewish woman had some photographs of the march through the cemetery, laid them on the table. We saw rows and rows and rows of rectangular gravestones, and in the foreground, clearly visible, one inscribed with a name and a star of David.

So I gain truth when I expand my constricted eye, an eye that has only let in what I have been taught to see. But there have been other constrictions: the clutch of fear around my heart when I must deal with the *fact* of folks who exist, with their own lives, in other places besides the narrow circle I was raised in. I have learned that my fear is kin to a terror that has been in my birth culture for years, for centuries: the terror of a people who have set themselves apart and *above*, who have wronged others, and feel they are about to be found out and punished. It is the terror that in my culture has been expressed in lies about dirty Jews who kill for blood, sly Arab hordes who murder, brutal Indians who massacre, animal Blacks who rise in rebellion in the middle of the night and slaughter. It is the terror that has *caused* the slaughter of all those peoples. It is the terror that was my father, with his stack of John Birch newspapers, his belief in a Communist-Jewish-Black conspiracy. It is the desperate terror, the knowledge that something is *wrong*, and tries to end fear by attack.

When I am trying to understand myself in relation to folks different from me, when there are discussions, conflicts about anti-Semitism and racism among women, criticisms, criticisms of me, and I get afraid: when, for instance, in a group discussion about race and class, I say I feel we have too much about race, not enough about class, and a woman of color asks me in anger and pain if I don't think her skin has something to do with class, and I get afraid; when, for instance, I say carelessly to my Jewish lover that there were no Jews where I grew up, and she begins to ask me: how do I know? do I hear what I am saying? and I get afraid; when I feel my racing heart, breath, the tightening of my skin around me, literally defenses to protect my narrow circle, I try to say to myself:

Yes, that fear is there, but I will try to be at the edge between my fear and outside, on the edge at my skin, listening, asking what new thing will I hear, will I see, will I let myself feel, beyond the fear. I try to say to myself: To acknowledge the complexity of another's existence is not to deny my own. I try to say: When I acknowledge what my people, what those who are like me, have done to people with less power and less safety in the world, I can make a place for things to be different, a place where I can feel grief, sorrow, not to be sorry *for* the others, but to mourn, to expand my circle of self, follow my need to loosen the constrictions of fear, be a break in the cycle of fear and attack. When I can do this, that is a second gain.

To be caught within the narrow circle of the self is not just a fearful thing, it is a *lonely* thing. When I could not climb the steps that day with my father, it marked the last time I can remember us doing something together, just the two of us; thereafter, I knew on some level that my place was with women, not with him, not with men; later I knew more clearly that I did not want his view of the world. I have felt this more and more strongly since my coming out as a lesbian. Yet so much has separated me from other women, ways in which my culture set me apart by race, by ethnicity, by class. I understood abruptly one day how lonely this made me when a friend, a Black woman, spoke to me casually in our shared office, and I heard how she said my name, the drawn-out accent, so much like how my name is said at home.

Yet I know enough of her history and mine to know how much separated us: the chasm of murders, rapes, lynchings, the years of daily humiliations done by my people to hers. I went and stood in the hallway and cried, thinking of how she said my name like home, and how divided our lives were. It is a pain I come to over and over again, the more I understand the ways in which I have been kept from other women, and how I keep myself from them. The pain, when, for instance, I realize how *habitually* I think of my culture, my ethics, my morality, as the culmination of history, as the logical extension of what has gone before; the kind of thinking represented by my use, in the past, of the word *Judeo-Christian*, as if Jewish history and lives have existed only to culminate in Christian culture, the kind of thinking that the U.S. government is using now to promote Armageddon in the Middle East; the kind of thinking that I did until recently about Indian lives and culture in my region, as if Indian peoples have existed only in museums since white folks came to this continent in the 1500s; the kind of thinking that separates me from women in cultures different from mine, makes their experience less central, less important than mine. It is painful to keep understanding this separation within myself and in the world. Sometimes this pain feels only like despair; yet I have felt it also to be another kind of pain, where the need to be with other women can be the breaking through the shell around me, painful, but a coming through into a new place, where with understanding and change, the loneliness won't be necessary. And when this happens, then I feel a third gain.

How do we begin to change, and then keep going, and act on this in the world? How do we *want* to be different from what we have been? Sometimes folks ask how I got started, and I must admit that I did not begin by reasoning out the gains; this came later and helped me keep going.

But I began when I jumped from my edge and outside myself, into radical change, for love, simply love, for myself and for other women. I acted on that love by becoming a lesbian, falling in love with and becoming sexual with a particular woman; and this love led me directly, but by a complicated way, to work against racism and anti-Semitism.

It is another kind of breaking through to even write this, to put these words before you. I anticipate the critical voices that say, "Your sexuality is irrelevant to the serious issue of racism and anti-Semitism"; that say, "You are being psychologizing, individualistic"; the voices that say, "You should want to work on these issues because they are right, for justice, for general principles." I anticipate the other, perhaps subvocal, words: "Disgusting." "Perverted." "Unnatural." "Not fit to live."

I think these voices may be sounding now because I have heard them before: from folks on the street, from political co-workers, from women at my job, from the man I was married to, from my mother. They are the judging, condemning voices that despise me, that see me as dangerous, that put me in danger, because of *how I love*: because of my intimate, necessary, hopeful love, for which I have been punished and been made to suffer bitterly, *when I have disclosed it*.

I could conceal it from you. I could hide this part of myself as other light-skinned, European-looking folks in this country have hidden parts of themselves that kept them from fitting in, assimilating, being safe in white Christian culture: hidden their religion, or the poverty or working class of their people; or their ethnicity, any connection to "undesirable" people, to Jews, or Mediterranean or Middle Eastern peoples, or Native Indians, or Asian peoples, or to any people of color.

I could pass in this way, by hiding part of myself. I fit neatly into the narrow limits of what is "normal" in this country. Like most lesbians, I don't fit the stereotype of what a lesbian looks like; unless my hair is cut quite short and unless I wear the comfortable, sturdy clothes and shoes that are called "masculine," I look quite stereotypically "American," like the girl in the toothpaste ad.

But in this writing, I can not hide myself, because it is how I love that has brought me to change. I have learned what it is to lose a position of safety, to be despised for *who I am*. For being a lesbian, I have lost those I loved almost as myself, my children, and I have had my pride, as Barbara Deming says, "assaulted in its depth . . . since one's sexuality is so at the heart . . . at the heart of one."[1] It was my joy at loving another woman, the risks I took by doing so, the changes that brought me to it, and the losses, that broke through the bubble of skin and class privilege around me. Barbara Deming has called "liberation by analogy"[2] the fighting of someone else's fight because you can't for whatever reason acknowledge and fight your own oppression. So I speak here of how I came to my own fight, and to an understanding of how I am connected to the struggle of other women and other people different from myself.

In the fall of 1974, I moved with my husband and children to an eastern North Carolina town whose center was not a courthouse, but a market house, with a first story of four arched brick walls, a closed brick second story, a circle of streets around it. I heard the story of the market house at a dinner that welcomed my husband to his new job. In a private club overlooking the central circle, the well-to-do folks at the table, all white, chatted about history, the things sold in the past at the market house, the fruits and vegetables, the auctioned tobacco. "But not slaves," they said.

The Black man who was serving set down the dish, and broke through the anonymity of his red jacket. No, he said, there *were* slaves there: men, women, children sold away from their mothers. Going to the window, he looked down on the streets and gave two minutes of facts and dates; then he finished serving and left. The white folks smiled indulgently, and changed the subject. I recognized their look, from home. I was shocked that he had dared speak to them, yet somehow felt he had done so many times before, and knew, without letting myself know, that as he spoke, there stood behind him the house slaves who had risked whipping or worse when they whittled with their words at the white folks' killing ignorance.

What he told me was plain enough: This town was a place where some people had been used as livestock, chattel, slaves, cattle, capital, by other people; and this use had been justified by the physical fact of a different skin color and by the cultural fact of different ways of living. The white men and their families who had considered Black people to be animals with no right to their own children or to a home of their own still did not admit that they had done any wrong, nor that there had *been* any wrong, in *their* town. What he told me was plain enough: Be warned—they have not changed.

By the end of dinner, I had forgotten his words. They were about the past, seemed to have nothing to do with me returning, after almost ten years in university towns, to the landscape of my childhood, to a military town that was enlarged, urban, with buying and selling at its heart, the country club its social center rather than the church (but Blacks and Jews still not welcome), a town with a more conspicuous police presence, the U.S. Army's second largest home base, with combat veterans who had trained to the chant, "Here is my prick, here is my gun, one is for killing, the other for fun."

Every day I drove around the market house, carrying my two boys between home and grammar school and day care. To me it was an impediment to the flow of traffic, awkward, anachronistic. Sometimes in early spring light it seemed quaint. I had no knowledge and no feeling of the sweat and blood of people's lives that had been mortared into its bricks, nor of their independent joy apart from that place. What I was feeling was that I would spend the rest of my life going round and round in a pattern that I knew by heart: being a wife, a mother of two boys, a teacher of the writings of white men, dead men. I drove around the market house four times a day, travelling on the surface of my own life: circular, repetitive, like one of the games at the county fair, the ones with yellow plastic ducks clacking one after the other on a track, until they fall abruptly off the edge, into inevitable meaningless disappearance, unless, with a smack, one or two or three vanish from the middle, shot down by a smiling man with a gun.

For the first time in my life, I was living in a place where I was afraid because I was a *woman*. No one knew me by my family: there were no kindnesses because someone knew my mama or my pa, and no one was going to be nice to me because of my grandfather. I was only another woman, someone's wife, unless I was alone; then, walking down Hay Street to the library, I could be propositioned as a prostitute, or, driving at night on the Boulevard, threatened as a cunt. At home when I complained about the smiling innuendo of a gas station attendant, my husband said I should be complimented; this is a town where "R & R" stood for "Rape and Recreation."

Not such a surprising realization: to understand that women are used as sexual pets, or are violently misused, are considered prey. But, there it was—for the first time I felt myself to be, not theoretically, but physically and permanently, in the class of people labeled *women*, and felt that group to be relatively powerless and at the mercy of another class, *men*.

In the market town I began to try, steadily, to make a place like the memory, yet that would last longer than a morning or an evening: it was to be a place where I could live without the painful and deadly violence, without the domination; a place where I could live free, *liberated*, with other women. I began to do some political work, organized another consciousness-raising group. Then I fell in love with another woman, after she told a secret to the group. I thought I had come again to the place of intense curiosity, powerful creativity. It was March, it was April, wisteria, dogwood, pink tulip magnolia. I began to dream my husband was trying to kill me, that I was running away with my children on Greyhound buses through Mississippi. I began to dream that I was crossing a river with my children; women on the other side, but no welcome for me with my boys.

The place I wanted to reach was not a childish place, but my understanding of it was childish. I had not admitted that the safety of much of my childhood was because Laura Cates, Black and a servant, was responsible for me; that I had the walks with my father because the woods were "ours" by systematic economic exploitation, instigated, at that time, by his White Citizens' Council; that I was allowed one evening a month with woman friends because I was a wife who would come home at night. Raised to believe that I could be where I wanted and have what I wanted, as a grown woman I thought I could simply claim what I wanted, even the making of a new place to live with other women. I had no understanding of the limits that I lived within, nor of how much my memory and my experience of a safe space to be was based on places secured by omission, exclusion, or violence, and on my submitting to the limits of that place.

I should have remembered, from my childhood, Viola Liuzzo, who was trying to reach the place by another way, shot down in Lowndes County, Alabama, while driving demonstrators during the Selma-to-Montgomery march. Her death was justified by Klan leader Robert Shelton on the grounds that she "had five children by four different husbands"; "her husband hadn't seen her in two, three months"; "she was living with two nigger men in Selma"; "she was a *fat* slob with crud . . . all over her body"; "she was bra-less."[3] Liuzzo, Italian, white-but-not-white, gone over to the other side, damned, dead.

I didn't die, trying to make a new life for myself out of an old life, trying to be a lover of myself and other women in a place where we were despised. I didn't die, but by spring of the next year, by May, watching the redbud tree drop flowers like blood on the ground, I felt like I had died. I had learned that children were still taken from their mothers in that town, even from someone like me, if by my wildness, by sexual wildness, I placed myself in the wilderness with those feared by white Southern men: with "every wolf, panther, catamount and bear in the mountains of America, every crocodile in the swamps of Florida, every negro in the South, every devil in Hell."[4] I had learned that I could be either a lesbian or a mother of my children, either in the wilderness or on holy ground, but not both.

I should not have been surprised at the horror of my sophisticated liberal husband; he was also an admirer of the apologists for the Old South, like the poet who named woman and the land as the same: beautiful, white, pure, "the Proud Lady, of the heart of fire, / The look of snow. . . . The sons of the fathers shall keep her, worthy of / What these have done in love." But I was no longer pure; I had declined to be kept. I no longer qualified as sacred, eligible for the protection promised by a KKK founder, protection for "the [white] women of the South, who were the loveliest, most noble and best women in the world. . . ."[5] (I asked my father, in his extreme age, to tell me about his mother, the woman I'm named for; he could only say, "She was the best woman in the world.")

Why was I surprised when my husband threatened and did violence, threatened ugly court proceedings, my mother as character witness for him, restricted my time and presence with the children, took them finally and moved hundreds of miles away? I was no longer "the best of women"; what did I expect? But I *had* expected to have that protected circle marked off for me by the men of my kind as my "home"; I had expected to have that place with my children. I expected it as my *right*. I did not understand I had been exchanging the use of my body for that place.

I learned, finally; I stepped outside the circle of protection. I said, "My body, my womb, and the children of my womb are not yours to use." And I was judged with finality. Without my climbing the steps to the stale rectangular courtrooms of Cumberland County, I was given a judgment: without facing the judge, since my lawyer feared that "calling the attention of the court" to my lesbian identity would mean that I would never see my children again. I was dirty, polluted, unholy. I was not to have a home with my children again. I did not die, but the agony was as bitter as death: we were physically separated; they were seven and six, hundreds of miles away; I had held them before they were born and almost every day of their lives, and now I could not touch them. During this time I discovered that expressions I had thought to be exaggerations were true: if you are helpless with grief, you do, unthinkingly, wring your hands; you can have a need to touch someone that is like hunger, like thirst. The inner surface of my arms, my breasts, the muscles of my stomach were raw with my need to touch my children.

I could have stolen them and run away to a place where no one knew them, no one knew me, hidden them, and tried to find work, under some other name than my own. I could not justify taking them from all their kin, or their father, in this way. Instead, from this marriage I carried away my clothes, my books, some kitchen utensils, two cats. I also carried away the conviction that I had been thrust out into a place of terrible loss by laws laid down by men. In my grief, and in my ignorance of the past of others, I felt that no one had sustained such a loss before. And I did not yet understand that to come to a place of greater liberation, I had to risk old safeties. Instead I felt that I had no place, that, as I moved through my days, I was falling through space.

I became obsessed with justice: the shell of my privilege was broken, the shell that had given me a shape in the world, held me apart from the world, protected me from the world. I was astonished at the pain; the extent of my surprise revealed to me the degree of my protection.

I became determined to break the powers of the world: they *would* change, the powers that would keep me from touching my children because I touched another woman in love. Beyond five or six books on women's liberation, and the process of consciousness-raising, I had few skills and little knowledge of how to act for justice and liberation. I had no knowledge of any woman like me who had resisted and attempted to transform our home in preceding generations; I had no knowledge of other instances of struggle, whose example might have strengthened and inspired me in mine.

For instance, I knew nothing of the nearby Lumbee Indians, descendants of the folk who came into first contact with Raleigh's English in the 1500s, who four hundred years later had been part of a three-way segregated school system— white, Black, Indian—who succeeded in the 1950s in breaking up Klan rallies and cross burnings that had warned them to "keep their place."[6]

Even though I was teaching at a historically Black college, I had no understanding of the long tradition of Black culture and resistance in the town, which reached back before the Civil War, and had produced Charles W. Chesnutt, president in the 1870s of the school where I was then teaching, author of novels that described the town of the market house, political organizing by Blacks, their massacre by whites during the 1898 Wilmington elections, even the story of a white man returning to his hometown who dreamed of, and worked toward, a racially just society.[7]

I knew nothing of the nourishing of Jewish culture in that hostile Bible-Belt town, nor of Jewish traditions of resistance. I learned only much later that one of the few townspeople who I knew to be politically progressive, Monroe Evans, was Jewish; that his family had emigrated from Lithuania to escape the 1881 May Laws against Jews, the confiscation of property, limitations on travel and on the right to have homes, the conscription of Jewish children into the tsar's army, the violent pogroms; that they had struggled to make a place in the town, one of two or three Jewish families, trying to maintain their identity among folk who alternately asked them how big was Noah's ark or called them Christ-killer; how they learned Yiddish in the home, took weekend trips to Holt's Lake to gather with other Jews from small North Carolina towns, to break their isolation.[8]

Nor did I know of the huge rallies against the Vietnam War in the 1970s, masses of people around the market house, chanting in the streets, traffic stopped; nor that Carson McCullers, a woman very like me, living there in the thirties, had written of the maddening, rigid effects of military life and thinking, and of the small resistances of an Army wife.[9]

I knew nothing, then, of the lesbians stationed at Fort Bragg or Pope Air Force Base, who might spend all day scrubbing out jet fuel tanks, light-headed, isolated, inside a metal cavern, and come out at night to the Other Side, to dance with lovers, play pool no matter that the CID cruised by on Russell Street writing down license plate numbers, no matter the risk of being thrown out; and later I discovered Bertha Harris's novel of being a lesbian lover, with extravagant stories that might have been told in that bar—being a passing woman in the Wilmington shipyards, being lovers with a movie star, with "hair like gold electricity," hair like my lover's hair—a book that was published the year that I moved to the town that outrageous Bertha had long since grown up in and left.[10]

I knew nothing of these or other histories of struggle for equality and justice and one's own identity in the town I was living in—not a particularly big town, not liberal at all, not famous for anything, an almost rural eastern North Carolina town, in a region that you, perhaps, are used to thinking of as backward. Yet it was a place with so many resistances, so much creative challenge to the powers of the world, which is true of every county, town, or city in this country, each with its own buried history of struggle, of how people try to maintain their dignity within the restrictions placed around them, and how they struggle to break those restrictions.

But as yet I knew nothing of this. I entered the struggle, adding my bit to it, as if I were the first to struggle, joining with five or six other women like me, in the local NOW chapter. For the next few years, I worked on education programs (women working in the home, out of the home, women and health, power, education, the media, the military, women and rape, women in religion, minority women, women and North Carolina law); I worked on self-defense classes for women, on establishing a rape crisis line and a shelter for women who were being beaten, on editing a local newsletter, on producing women's cultural events, on nights and nights of phone calls for the ERA, on a fight with the local clerk of court to make him admit women's independent name changes, on day care, on Black women's studies courses and a daily women's news program at the college where I taught, on a county advisory group for women's issues where we struggled with the local Democratic machine to try to get a Black woman appointed as our coordinator, where we pressed for implementation of our recommendations with county money, and were perceived as so radical that the courthouse rumor was "Lesbians have taken over."

We wanted to change the world; we thought we knew how it needed changing. We knew we were outnumbered: in a town where the Berean Baptist Church owned its own fleet of buses and shuttled hundreds of its members to every legislative meeting to oppose the ERA, the handful of us in NOW were the only folks using the word "women's liberation." We tried everything we could think of to "reach more women."

We were doing "outreach," that disastrous method of organizing; *we* had gone forward to a new place, women together, and now were throwing back safety lines to other women, to pull them in as if they were drowning, to save them. I understood then how important it was for me to have this new place; it was going to be my home, to replace the one I had lost. I needed desperately to have a place that was mine with other women, where I felt hopeful. But because of my need, I did not push myself to look at what might separate me from other women. I relied on the hopefulness of all women together; what I felt, deep down, was hope that they would join me in my place, which would be the way I wanted it. I didn't want to have to *limit* myself.

I didn't understand what a limited, narrow space, and how short lasting, it would be, if only *my* imagination and knowledge and abilities were to go into the making and extending of it. I didn't understand how much I was still inside the restrictions of my culture, in my vision of how the world could be. I, and the other women I worked with, limited the effectiveness of our struggle for that place by our own racism and anti-Semitism.

With a minimal understanding of history, we knew that, because of civil rights work, Black women in town were probably organized, might be potential allies: so our first community forum had one panel out of six designated with the topic "minority women," and five of the twenty speakers for the day were Black women. This was in a day's activities which were planned, the speakers chosen, the location selected, and the publicity arranged, by three middle-class white women, me included, who had not *personally* contacted a single Black women's organization, much less considered trying to coplan or cosponsor with such a group; and who had no notion of the doubts or risks that Black women in that town might have about our endeavor. Neither did we consult our common sense to discover that "minority women" in Fayetteville included substantial numbers of Thai, Vietnamese, Cambodian, Laotian, Korean, and Japanese women, as well as Lumbee women and Latinas. Attendance at the forum was overwhelmingly white; we questioned our publicity instead of our perspective on power.

Similarly, our thinking about allies out of the civil rights movement of the sixties did not include the possibility that there might be Jewish women in town who had worked in that struggle, who might be interested in our work. Well-schooled by my past in how Jews (and Communists) were the source of "outsider trouble," the old theory that if Jews are present and visible, they must be in control, I did not turn this teaching around to question if the significant participation of Jews in civil rights work might not have had something to do with their own history of oppression. In fact, I didn't think of Jews as being *in* the town, even though I drove past a large and modern synagogue on Morganton Road every time I went to grocery shop. Blacks were definitely Southern, and American even though they'd come from Africa (the continent a blur to me), even though I'd heard men at home mouthing off about "Send them back." But a Black woman had raised me; Black women and men came in and out of my kinfolks' houses, cooking, cleaning; Black people worked *for* white people; I knew (I thought) what their place was. I had no place for Jews in the map of my thoughts, except that they had lived before Christ in an almost mythical Israel, and afterwards in Germany until they were killed, and that those in this country were foreign, even if they were here; they were always foreign, their place always somewhere else.

So I drove past the synagogue, and when we scheduled a discussion on religion, the two women who spoke were a professor of religion and a Methodist minister; no representation was requested from the women of the local Jewish congregation, since "religion" meant denominations of Christianity. We held the session on a Saturday because, after all, Sunday was when folks went to church, or just took it easy; we had no grasp that there might be some Jewish women who would want to come, but not be able, since their Sabbath was sundown Friday to sundown Saturday night.

My sense of the history of the town was distorted as my perspective on its demographics, or its geography, or its theology. When we were organizing a day's program on rape, I was concerned that Black women know and come, so I drove up and down Murchison Road to post flyers, ignoring my uneasiness, the training of years of warnings about which parts of a town were "safe" for me and which were not. I could have paused to trace that uneasiness to a fear of Black men: but I did not, nor did I wonder about the history of white women in relation to Black men, or white men to Black women, or *then* question what the feelings, not to mention the experience, of Black women in relation to rape might be, compared to mine. I stapled posters to telephone poles, I politely asked permission to place them in the windows of Black-owned businesses, without ever thinking the word "lynching," or wondering about how sexual violence was used racially by white men to keep Blacks and white women from joining force.

Nor when we were struggling so hard with ERA ratification, during miserable nights in a borrowed doctor's office, calling strangers' names listed on file cards, during the crisis when one of our key local representatives had a religious renewal and became a born-again Christian just before the vote, during none of the three votes, over six years, did I examine the long complicated relation between the struggle for women's suffrage and Black suffrage through constitutional amendments. I did not learn that white women's suffrage leaders, in-cluding Elizabeth Cady Stanton, had failed to take the long view required of coalition work in their disappointment over the Fifteenth Amendment being passed for manhood, rather than universal, suffrage. They had refused to make the reciprocal actions that would have pushed for post–Civil War voting rights enforcement for Black men in the South, so necessary for the success of revolutionary Reconstruction governments, and therefore, ultimately, for the establishment of legislatures favorable to Black and white women's suffrage.[11] I did not learn of the deliberate segregationist tactics, used by Susan B. Anthony, of refusing to organize Black women in the South for fear of alienating Southern white women from the suffrage movement.[12] Nor did I speculate over what could have happened had there been more support by Southern white women of voting rights for Blacks in the sixties and seventies: would Black legislators have been elected, more favorable to the ratification of the ERA? I puzzled over why Black women were not more active in the ERA campaign without figuring out how "women's rights" had been a code for "white women's rights."

When we worked to establish a battered women's shelter, even a temporary place where a woman could come be safe from male violence, I didn't wonder if it would be experienced as a "white woman's home" or if a Thai woman with perhaps her own language needs, a Jewish woman with perhaps her own food needs, a Black woman with perhaps a need not to experience white ignorance of her life, if any of these women or others might feel so dubious of their "safety" that they would choose not to come.

And even as we worked in all these ways to try to change the world, to make it safer (we thought) for all women, I did not reflect on how hesitant I was to mention my lesbian identity except to a trusted few women. I did not feel safe with many of my political co-workers; I had lost my children; I could still lose my job; and I could lose my place in this fragile new world-space for women I thought we were making. After all, our answer to attacks on the ERA "because it would legalize homosexual marriages" was to say that this just wouldn't happen. *I* didn't realize that there was nothing wrong with lesbians or gay men wanting public recognition of our relationships.

I was, in fact, not seeking liberation as my particular, complex self. I was working desperately to make the new place where I could live safely with other women, while denying publicly a basic part of myself, while not seeing the subtle and overt pressures on other women to also deny their different aspects, in order to exist in the outside world, and in order to come to our place. In newspaper interviews I spoke obliquely of conscious choices, alternatives, possibilities, but I did not yet understand with my heart Lillian Smith's statement that "our right to be different is, in a deep sense, the most precious right we human beings have."[13]

By 1979 I was watching the second wave of the women's movement, which had swept through this Southern town about ten years later than the rest of the country, be increasingly directed into electoral politics and social services, and less and less into grass-roots women's work. I knew that I felt painfully isolated as a lesbian, but I did not analyze this in the context of our tiny movement's failure to deal with issues of difference, nor did it occur to me, as Bettina Aptheker has said of women in the first wave of feminism, that ". . . in the context of American politics, the neglect of or acquiescence in racism would inevitably force . . . women into a more and more conservative and politically ineffectual mold."[14]

Instead I withdrew from our struggling projects, in the evenings didn't go to meetings but wrote poetry or read, stayed at home; it was so peaceful in my three-room apartment; at night I would burn candles on the mantlepiece, no sounds but the blapping of my typewriter, or maybe the rain on the porch roof outside, fresh smells coming through the screen front door. I did not have my children, but I had these rooms, a job, a lover, work I was making. I thought I had the beginnings of a place for myself.

But that year in November my idea of what kind of work it would take to keep my bit of safe space, my very idea of that space, my narrow conception, was shattered. In writing of the change in her own culture-bound perceptions, Joanna Russ speaks of "that soundless blow, which changes forever one's map of the world."[15] For me the blow was literal, the sound was rifle fire. In broad daylight, in Greensboro, North Carolina, about fifty miles from where I lived, Klansmen and Nazis drove into an anti-Klan demonstration, shouting "Nigger! Kike! Commie bastard!" They opened fire, killed five people: four white men, two of them Jews, one Black woman; labor union organizers, affiliated with the Communist Workers Party. The next day I saw in the newspaper an interview with Nancy Matthews, wife of one of the Klansmen. She said, "I knew he was a Klan member, but I don't know what he did when he left home. I was surprised and shocked. . . ."[16] But the Klansmen defended their getting out of their cars at the rally, rifles in hand, by saying they saw the car holding some Klansmen being attacked and were "rushing to their rescue."[17]

And I thought: I identify with the demonstrators; I am on *their* side; I've felt that danger. Yet in what way am I any different from this woman? Am I not surprised and shocked that this could happen? Yet it did, and there must be a history behind it. Do I have any notion, *any*, of what white men have been doing outside home, outside the circle of my limited white experience? I have my theory of how I lost my home because I was a woman, a lesbian, and that I am at risk because of who I am: then how do I explain the killing of Jews, Communists, a Black woman, the killing justified in the name of "protecting white women"?

I set out to find out what had been or was being done in my name. I took Nancy Matthews's words seriously, and began by asking what had happened outside my home, outside the circle of what I knew of me and my people where I grew up. I asked my mother. She recounted Klan activity in my Alabama hometown in the 1920s—marches, crossburnings, a white woman beaten for "immorality"—but she didn't know what they did to Blacks; our family was not implicated, but the contrary, she was proud to say: my grandfather the judge stood up to them, political death in that era, by refusing to prosecute Black men who had acted in self-defense.

I read Black history: Ida B. Wells's records show that Black men were lynched in my home county, and one in my hometown, for allegedly raping white women, in 1893, shortly after my grandfather opened his law practice there.[18] I wondered what he did then: anything? And my grandmother, for whom I was named: what did she do? what did she think? I gathered family letters and documents. They told me explicitly what had never been said by my kin: that on both the maternal and paternal sides of my family, we had owned slaves, twelve to fifteen, on small "family-sized" farms; that what place and money my family had got by the mid-nineteenth century, we had stolen from the work and lives of others; and that the very ground the crops grew in was stolen. I saw the government form that bountied 160 acres to my Great-Grandfather Williams for fighting the Seminoles in the Creek Wars, driving them from their homes in South Georgia, bounty, a bonus for "good work." I read transcripts of legal proceedings from after the Civil War, from testimony about the counties my folks had lived in, and where I had grown up: the voices of Black men and women came to me out of the grave, to tell of homes broken into or burned, the beatings, rapes, murders, during their attempts to secure Black suffrage and a redistribution of land, telling of the attacks by men determined to keep control in the name of white, Christian civilization.

These voices came to me, and I thought of my children and the grief and anger, the shame and failure, I felt because I had not been able to fight for them and have a home for me and them, against the man my husband, and other legal men, and the history of this town, with its market house point of interest where within some people's memory families *had* been sold apart from one another. The voices came, and I thought of my small but comfortable apartment, my modestly well-paying job at a Black college, gotten with my segregated-university education, gotten with the confidence and financial help of men and women who had occupied and held the security of a certain place, despite the upheaval of Reconstruction, for three and four generations.

During the time that I was first feeling all this information, again I lived in a kind of vertigo: a sensation of my body having no fixed place to be, the earth having opened, I was falling through space. I had had my home and children taken away from me. I had set out to make a new home with other women, only to find that the very ground I was building on was the grave of the people my kin had killed, and that my foundation, my birth culture, was mortared with blood.

Until this time, I had felt my expanding consciousness of oppression as painful but ultimately positive: I was breaking through to an understanding of my life as a woman, as a way to my *own* liberation; the cracking and heaving and buckling in my life was the process of freeing myself. I had felt keenly the pain of being punished for who I was, and had felt passionately the need for justice, for things to be set right. When, after Greensboro, I groped toward an understanding of injustice done to others, injustice done outside my narrow circle of being, and to folks *not* like me, I began to grasp, through my own experience, something of what that injustice might be, began to feel the extent of pain, anger, desire for change.

But I did not feel that my new understanding simply moved me into a place where I joined others to struggle *with* them against common injustices. Because *I* was implicated in the doing of some of these injustices, and I held myself, and my people, responsible, what my expanded understanding meant was that I felt in a struggle with myself, *against* myself. This breaking through did not feel like liberation but like destruction.

As in a story from my childhood, one of Poe's stories that I read late at night, I was scared but fascinated by the catastrophic ending: when the walls of a house split, zigzag, along a once barely noticeable crack, and the house of Usher crumbled with "a long tumultuous shouting sound like the voice of a thousand waters." A woman is the reason for the fall of that house, a place of "feudal antiquity"; she is the owner's twin sister who dies and is confined in a chamber deep under the house. The brother, who suffers from a continual and inexplicable terror, "the grim phantasm FEAR," becomes more terrified; his friend reads a romance to soothe him, a crude tale of a knight who conquers by slaying a dragon; the sounds in the story of ripping wood, grating clanging brass, piercing shrieks, begin to be heard in the very room where the two men are seated. In horror the brother reveals that he knew he had buried the sister alive, but he *had dared not speak*; the sounds are "the rending of her coffin and the grating of the iron hinges of her prison. . . ." At that moment, the doors rush open; the lady stands before them, bloody in white robes, and then falls upon her brother in violent death agonies, bearing him to the ground a corpse, shattering the house over them.

Read by me a hundred years after it was written in the 1840s, a time of intensifying Southern justification of slavery, Poe's description of the dread, nervousness, fear of the brother, pacing through the house from "whence for many years, he had not ventured forth" could have been a description of my father, trapped inside his beliefs in white supremacy, the purity of (white) women, the conspiracy of Jews and Blacks to take over the world. And the entombment of the lady was my "protection": the physical, spiritual, sexual containment which men of my culture have used to keep "their women" pure, our wombs to be kept sacred ground, not polluted by the dirty sex of another race; our minds, spirits, and actions to be Christian, not "common," but gentlewomanly, genteel, Gentile; thereby ensuring that children born of us are theirs, are "well-born," of "good" blood, skin, family; and that children raised by us will be "well-raised," not veering into wild actions, wayward behavior.

It was this protection that I felt one evening during the height of the civil rights demonstrations in Alabama, as the walls that had contained so many were cracking, when my father called me to his chair in the living room. He showed me a newspaper clipping, from some right-wing paper, about Martin Luther King, Jr., and told me that the article was about how King had sexually abused, used, young Black teenaged girls. I believe he asked me what I thought of this; I can only guess that he wanted me to feel that my danger, my physical, sexual danger, would be the result of the release of others from containment. I felt frightened and profoundly endangered, by King, by my father; I could not answer him. It was the first, the only time, he spoke of sex, in any way, to me.

This was the "protection" that I had romanticized in the hot thunderstormy summers of my adolescence as I read Tennyson's poetry, kings and queens, knights and ladies; and the "protection" that during the actual Crusades of 1095 to 1270 C.E. * meant metal chastity belts locked around the genitals of their wives by Christian European knights, who travelled to Jerusalem to free the holy places from "the pollution and filth of the unclean," the Islamic Persians, who, when Jerusalem was taken in 1099, were beheaded, tortured, burned in flames, while the Jews of the city were herded into a synagogue and burned alive.[19]

It was the safety offered by the Knights of the Ku Klux Klan in 1867 "as an institution of Chivalry" for the purpose of "protecting the homes and women of the South";[20] and in 1923 as "swift avenger of Innocence despoiled" and preservers of the sanctity of the home";[21] and in 1964 as working with "sincere Christian devotion" to stop "mongrelization of the white race by Blacks and Jews";[22] and in 1980 as defenders of the family and white civilization who, in Klan rituals "advance to the next step of knightly honor," are baptized, and vow that they are white American citizens, not Jews.[23] Within this "protection," the role of women, as described by California Klan Corps member Dorraine Metzger is to have "lots of babies to help the white race along . . . at least two or three babies because the minorities are just going crazy . . . babies, babies everywhere."[24] What this "chivalric" behavior has meant historically is the systematic rape of Black women;[25] the torture, mutilation, and killing of Black men (over 1,000 lynched between 1900 and 1915, many on the pretext of having raped a white woman);[26] the death of Leo Frank, a Jew (accused of being the "perverted" murderer of a young white girl, falsely convicted) lynched by the Knights of Mary Phagan, who became the core of a modern national Klan fifteen

---

*C.E. or common era, is an alternative to A.D., or *anno Domini*, "in the year of the Lord."

million strong at its height in the 1920s.[27] This "knightly honor" also meant the harassment and attempted intimidation of any of "their women" who rejected the "protection": the women who came South to teach Blacks during Reconstruction;[28] women who asserted their sexual autonomy during the twenties;[29] women who spoke out against segregation, racism, anti-Semitism from the forties to the sixties;[30] women who asserted economic autonomy by fighting to work in the mines in the seventies;[31] women who were openly lesbian at the International Women's Year Conference;[32] and women who are now doing anti-Klan organizing as open lesbians.[33]

It is this threatening "protection" that white Christian men in the U.S. are now offering. In his 1984 State of the Union Address President Reagan linked his election to a "crusade for renewal," "a spiritual revival" in America, denounced the "tragedy of abortion," stated that "families stand at the center of our society," and announced that this country has "brought peace where there was only bloodshed."[34] All this was in language that paralleled the words of Jerry Falwell's 1984 State of the Union Address in which the Moral Majority leader preached a "moral awakening" for the country and condemned the "decadence" of abortion and gay rights.[35] All this in a year when abortion clinics are being bombed by a group called the Army of God;[36] when the Klansmen and Nazis indicted in the Greensboro massacre have been acquitted by an all-white jury because U.S. Justice Department prosecution allowed them to plead that they were "patriotic citizens just like the Germans," who were also fighting against Communists;[37] when each U.S. citizen under the Reagan budget will pay $555 more to the military and $88 less to poor children and their mothers;[38] when a group of white farm wives visiting D.C. from the Midwest had U.S. policy in the Caribbean and Central America (including the invasion of Grenada) officially explained to them as a way to prevent "a Brown Horde," "a massive wave of immigration," if "communist takeovers" occur in the region.[39]

If I have come to the point of consciousness where I have begun to understand that I am entrapped *as* a woman, not just by the sexual fear of the men of my group, but also by their racial and religious terrors; if I have begun to understand that when they condemn me as a lesbian and a free woman for being "dirty," "unholy," "perverted," "immoral," it is a judgment that has been called down on people of color and Jews throughout history by the men of my culture, as they have shifted their justification for hatred according to their desires of the moment; if I have begun to understand something of the deep connection between my oppression and that of other folks, what is it that keeps me from acting, sometimes even from speaking out, against anti-Semitism and racism? What is it that keeps me from declaring against and rejecting this "protection" at every level?

The image from my childhood, from Poe's story, returns to me—the woman who escapes with superhuman effort, from a coffin whose lid is fastened down by screws, from a vault with iron doors of immense weight; she may free herself, but then she dies violently, carrying with her the home and her kin—catastrophe. Melodramatic, yet twenty years after I first read the story, when I began to admit to myself how I had been buried by my culture, coffined heart and body, and how this was connected to my sex, my race, my class, my religion, my "morality"; when I began to push through all this, I felt like my life was cracking around me.

I think this is what happens, to a more or less extreme degree, every time we expand our limited being: it is upheaval, not catastrophe, more like a snake shedding its skin than like death; the old constriction is sloughed off with difficulty, but there is an expansion, not a change in basic shape or color, but an expansion, some growth, and some reward for struggle and curiosity. Yet, if we are women who have gained privilege by our white skin *or* our Christian culture, but who are trying to free ourselves *as* women in a more complex way, we can experience this change as loss. Because it is—the old lies and ways of living, habitual, familiar, comfortable, fitting us like our skin, were *ours*.

Our fear of the losses can keep us from changing. What is it, exactly, that we are afraid to lose?

As I try to strip away the layers of deceit that I have been taught, it is hard not to be afraid that these are like wrappings of a shroud and that what I will ultimately come to in myself is a disintegrating, rotting *nothing*—that the values that I have at my core, from my culture, will only be those of negativity, exclusion, fear, death. And my feeling *is* based in the reality that the group identity of my culture has been defined, often, not by positive qualities, but by negative characteristics: by the *absence of* "no dogs, Negroes, or Jews." We have gotten our jobs, bought our houses, borne and educated our children by the negatives—no niggers, no kikes, no wops, no dagos, no spics, no A-rabs, no gooks, no queers.

We have learned this early, and so well. Every spring, almost, when I was in grammar school, our field trip would be an expedition to Moundville State Park, where part of our education was to file into a building erected over a "prehistoric" Indian burial ground, and stand overlooking the excavated clay, dug out so that small canyons ran between each body, the bundles of people's bones, separating each from each, as if water had eroded, except it was the hands of a probably white, probably Christian archaeologist from the university, meticulously breaking into the sacred ground. Floodlights exposed people curled or stretched in the final vulnerability of death, while we stood in the safe darkness of the balconies, looking down.

It has taken a long time for me to understand that this place was sacred not because it had been set aside for death, but because it was a place where spiritual and physical life returned to life, bones and bodies as seeds in the fertile darkness of the earth. It took me so long because so much in my culture is based on the principle that we are *not* all connected to each other, that folk who seem different should be excluded, or killed, and their living culture treated as dead objects.

No wonder, then, that if we have been raised up this way, when we begin to struggle with the reality of our anti-Semitism and racism, we may simply want to leave our culture behind, disassociate ourselves from it. In order to feel positively about ourselves, we may end up wanting not to *be* ourselves, and may start pretending to be someone else. Especially this may happen when we start learning about the strong traditions of resistance and affirmation sustained for centuries by the very folks *our* folks were trying to kill.

Without a knowledge of this struggle for social justice in our own culture, we may end up clothing our naked, negative selves with something from the positive traditions of identity which have served in part to help folks survive our people. We may justify this "cultural impersonation"[40] by our admiration and our need for heroines, as did one woman at an evening of shared spirituality which I attended: a Euro-American woman, very fair-haired and fair-complexioned, renamed herself in a ritual during which she took three women's names, each from a different tribe of native American people; she explicitly stated that the names represented powers and gifts she desired—those of healing, leadership, love—qualities she felt she was lacking in. We may justify taking the identity of another as our own by stating a shared victimization, as I have heard from some Christian-raised women when they have mentioned that they have "always felt like a Jew" because of how they have felt exclusion and pain in their lives; sometimes they have then used this feeling to assert that they were Jews and to justify a conversion to Judaism.

Sometimes the impersonation comes because we are afraid we'll be divided from someone we love if we are ourselves. This can take very subtle forms, as when I wrote a poem for my lover, whom I'd been dealing with about issues of Jewish-Gentile differences; anxious, without admitting it to myself, about the separation that opened at times between us, I blurred our difference in the poem by using images and phrases from a Jewish women's spiritual tradition as if they were from my *own*, using them to imply that she and I were in the same affirming tradition.

Sometimes we don't pretend to *be* the other, but we take something made by the other and use it for our own, as I did for years when I listened to Black folk singing church songs, hymns, gospels, and spirituals, the songs of suffering, enduring, and triumph. Always I would cry, baffled as to why I was so moved. I understood myself only after I read a passage in Mary Boykin Chesnutt's diary in which she described weeping bitterly at a slave prayer meeting where the Black driver shouted "like a trumpet"; she said, "I would very much have liked to shout too."[41] Then I understood that I was using Black people to weep for me, to express *my* sorrow at my responsibility, and that of my people, for their oppression; and I was mourning because I felt they had something I didn't, a closeness, a hope, that I and my folks had lost because we had tried to shut other people out of our hearts and lives.

Finally I understood that I could feel sorrow during their music, and yet not confuse their sorrow with mine, or use their resistance for mine. *I needed to do my own work*, express my sorrow and my responsibility myself, in my own words, by my own actions. I could hear their songs like a trumpet to me: a startling, an awakening, a reminder, a challenge, as were the struggles and resistance of other folk, but not take them as replacement for my own work.

In groups of white women I sometimes hear a statement like this: "We have to work on our own racism; after all, white people are responsible, so we shouldn't expect women of color to help us, or to show us where we are going wrong, or tell us what to do." And I believe a similar generalization may be beginning to be made about anti-Semitism: "Christian-raised women should take responsibility, and not expect Jewish women to explain our mistakes." I agree with both of these statements, but I think we will act on them only when we know and *feel* them as part of a positive process of recreating ourselves, of making a self that is not the negative, the oppressor.

I believe that we don't want to be like the U.S. government stealing Native American land for national parks and bomb test sites, nor like Boy Scouts who group by ancient tribal place-names to practice dimly understood dances to perform at shopping malls. If we don't want to perpetuate the Euro-American tradition of theft, of *taking* from others, in large and small ways, I believe we must remember our relation to other women in the context of a national history in which we can tour the U.S. Capitol, with its elaborate murals about freedom and its statues to liberty, but if we ask about the builders, we will *not* be told: "The building was the work of hired-out slaves."[42] We must think about our relation to other women and their work if we can attend a celebration of International Women's Day, as I did this year, hear accounts of the brave women organizing in New York's garment district, how their work was the foundation for our work, but we are *not* told: "Sixty-five percent of the women in the striking shirtwaist makers, of the 'Uprising of the 20,000,' were Jewish women, and six of the women on the board of Local 25 who led them were Jews."[43]

When we begin to understand that we have benefitted, for no good reason, from the lives and work of others, when we begin to understand how false much of our sense of self-importance has been, we do experience a loss—our self-respect. To regain it, we need to find new ways to be *in* the world, those very actions a way of creating a positive self.

Part of this process, for me, has been to acknowledge to myself that there are things I *do not know*—an admission hard on my pride, and harder to do than it sounds—and to try to fill up the emptiness of my ignorance about the lives of

Jewish women and women of color. It has also been important for me to acknowledge to myself that most of my learning has been based on the work of these women: that I would never have grasped the limits on my understanding and action if I had not read the work of North American Indian women—Leslie Silko, Joy Harjo, the anthology *A Gathering of Spirit*, edited by Beth Brant; the work of Black women—Toni Morrison, Alice Walker, Audre Lorde, *Home Girls: A Black Feminist Anthology*, edited by Barbara Smith; the work of Jewish women—Muriel Rukeyser, Ruth Seid, Anzia Yezierska, the lesbian anthology *Nice Jewish Girls*, edited by Evelyn Torton Beck; and the work of Asian-American women, Latinas, and other women of color in such collections as *The Third Woman*, edited by Dexter Fisher, *Cuentos: Stories by Latinas*, edited by Alma Gomez, Cherrie Moraga, and Mariana Romo-Carmona, and *This Bridge Called My Back: Writings by Radical Women of Color*, edited by Gloria Anzaldúa and Cherrie Moraga.[44]

And part of my regaining my self-respect has been to struggle to reject a false self-importance by acknowledging the foundation of liberation effort in this country *in* the work of women, and men, who my folks have tried to hold down. For me this has meant not just reading the poetry, fiction, essays, but learning about the long history of political organizing in the U.S. by men and women trying to break the economic and cultural grip a Euro-American system has on their lives. But my hardest struggle has been to admit and honor their daily, constant work when this means correction of *my* ignorance, resistance to *my* prejudice. Then I have to struggle to remember that I don't rule the world with my thoughts and actions like some judge in a tilt-back chair; and that by listening to criticism, not talking back but listening, I may learn how I might have been acting or thinking like one of the old powers that be.

For me, to be quite exact, honoring this work means saying that I began to reexamine my relation as a white woman to safety, white men, and Black people, after I told as a joke, a ludicrous event, the story of the Klan marching in my hometown, and a Black woman who was a fellow teacher said abruptly to me, "Why are you laughing? It isn't funny." And I began to reexamine my relation to the first people who lived in this country because a Shawnee woman, with family origins in the South, criticized my *use* of the Choctaw people's experience as a parallel to the experience of the white women of my family; she asked, "Who of your relatives did what to who of mine?" I started to examine my grasp of the complexities of my anti-Semitism when I spoke angrily about the disrespect of Arab male students, from Saudi Arabia and Kuwait, toward me as a female teacher, while also saying I resented their loudness, their groupiness, the money that enabled them to take over our financially shaky Black college, while my Black students, men and women, were working night jobs to survive, and the Jewish woman, my lover, who was listening to all this said quietly, "You are just being anti-Arab."

And when a month ago, I walked into my corner grocery, DC Supermarket, 8th and F streets, NE, with a branch of budding forsythia in my hand, and the owners, men and women I had termed vaguely to myself as "Oriental," became excited, made me spell *forsythia*, wrote it in Korean characters on a piece of scratch paper so they would remember the name in English; and said it was a flower from their country, *their* country, pronouncing the name in Korean carefully for my untrained ears; and then I had to think again about what I understood about what was "mine" and what was "somebody else's," what I didn't understand about immigration and capitalism and how I had taken without thinking, like picking a flower, the work and culture of Asian folk, without even being able to distinguish between the many different people.

As I've worked at stripping away layer after layer of my false identity, notion of skin, blood, heart based in racism and anti-Semitism, another way I've tried to regain my self-respect, to keep from feeling completely naked and ashamed of who it is I am, is to look at what I have carried with me from my culture that could help me in the process. As I have learned about the actual history and present of my culture, I didn't stop loving my family or my home, but it was hard to figure out what from there I could be proud and grateful to have, since much of what I *had* learned had been based on false pride. Yet buried under the layers, I discovered some strengths:

I found a sense of connection to history, people, and place, through my family's rootedness in the South; and a comparative and skeptical way of thinking, through my Presbyterian variety of Protestantism, which emphasized doubt and analysis. I saw that I had been using these skills all along as I tried to figure out my personal responsibility in a racist and anti-Semitic culture.

I found that my mother had given me hope, through the constancy of her regard for her mother and sisters and women friends, and through her stubbornness in the undertaking and completing of work. I found that my father had given me his manners, the "Pratts' beautiful manners," which could demonstrate respectfulness of others, if I paid attention; and he had given me the memory of his sorrow and pain, disclosing to me his heart that still felt the wrong, that, somehow, my heart had learned from his.

In my looking I also discovered a tradition of white Christian-raised women in the South, who had worked actively for social justice since at least 1849, the year a white woman in Bucktown, Maryland, hid Harriet Tubman during her escape from slavery, in her house on the Underground Railroad.[45] From the 1840s to the 1860s, Sarah and Angelina Grimke of South Carolina, living in the North, had organized both for the abolition of slavery and for women's rights, linking the two struggles. Angelina wrote:

> True, we have not felt the slaveholder's lash; true, we have not had our hands manacled, but our *hearts* have been crushed. . . . I want to be identified with the negro; until he gets his rights, we shall never have ours.[46]

In 1836 in her *Appeal to the Christian Women of the Southern States*, she said:

> I know you do not make the laws, but . . . if you really suppose you can do
> nothing to overthrow slavery, you are greatly mistaken. . . . 1st. You can
> read on this subject. 2d. You can pray over this subject. 3d. You can speak on
> this subject. 4th. You can act on this subject. . . .[47]

When copies of the *Appeal* reached Charleston, the sisters' hometown, the
papers were publicly burned, like other abolitionist literature, by the postmaster;
the police notified the Grimkes' mother that they would prevent Angelina from
ever entering the city again. In a letter to her family to explain her and her
sister's writings, Angelina said:

> It cost us more agony of soul to write these testimonies than any thing we ever
> did. . . . We wrote them to show the awful havock which arbitrary power
> makes in human hearts and to incite a holy indignation against an institution
> which degrades the *oppressor* as well as the oppressed.[48]

From the 1920s to the 1940s, Jessie Daniel Ames of Texas led an antilynching
campaign, gathering women like herself into the Association of Southern
Women for the Prevention of Lynching. By the early 1940s, the ASWPL
included over 109 women's organizations, auxiliaries of major Protestant denominations and national and regional federations of Jewish women, with a
total membership of over four million. The women used a variety of methods to
stop the violence done by the men who were of their kin or their social group,
including: investigative reporting for the collection and publication of facts
about lynching locally; attempts to change white news reporting of lynchings
toward a less sensational and inflammatory treatment; signature campaigns to
get written pledges from white sheriffs and other law enforcement officers to
prevent lynchings; publication in their communities of the names of white
"peace officers" who gave up prisoners to lynch mobs; mobilization of local peer
pressure in the white community with face-to-face or over-the-phone confrontation with white men by the women; and direct intervention by the women to
persuade a mob to stop its violence, including one ASWPL woman in Alabama
who stopped the lynching of the Black man accused of raping her seven-year-old
daughter.[49] The association repudiated the "myth of mob chivalry"; its statement of purpose said ". . . the claim of the lynchers [is] that they were acting
solely in the defense of womanhood. . . . we dare not longer permit this claim
to pass unchallenged nor allow those bent upon personal revenge and savagery
to commit acts of violence and lawlessness in the name of women."[50]

Lillian Smith of Georgia, who traced her political roots to the ASWPL, was
an eloquent novelist, essayist, and speaker against the forces of segregation from
the 1940s to the 1960s; in addition, she edited with Paula Snelling, the
magazine *South Today*, and ran a summer camp for girls where she raised social
issues like racism and nuclear war by having her campers create dramatic

enactments of the struggles between justice and injustice as they saw it in their daily lives. She is the woman who wrote in "Putting away Childish Things":

> Men who kill, riot, use foul words in the name of race will kill, riot, use foul words in the name of anything that safely provides outlet for their hate and frustrations. . . . They are the "bad" people. And we? We are the people who dream the good dreams and let the "bad" people turn them into night- mares. . . . we need ourselves to become *human*. . . . when we reserve this humanity of ours, this precious quality of love, of tenderness, of imaginative identification, for people only of our skin color (or our family, our class), we have split our lives. . . .[51]

In the 1940s Nelle Morton of Tennessee was also actively organizing interra- cial college chapters of the Fellowship of Southern Churchmen in the South specifically to protest anti-Semitic and Klan activity, and Southern interracial summer camps for Black, white, Arab, and Asian students.[52] During the same time Anne Braden from Alabama was moving from being a reporter on the 1945 trial of Willie McGee into a lifetime of activist work; she is the woman who has said:

> I believe that no white woman reared in the South—or perhaps anywhere in this racist country—can find freedom as a woman until she deals in her own consciousness with the question of race. We grow up little girls—absorbing a hundred stereotypes about ourselves and our role in life, our secondary position, our destiny to be a helpmate to a man or men. But we also grow up white—absorbing the stereotypes of race, the picture of ourselves as somehow privileged because of the color of our skin. The two mythologies become intertwined, and there is no way to free ourselves from one without dealing with the other.[53]

And in the late 1950s and early 1960s young Southern women came out of their church experience to work in the civil rights movement, and later in the women's liberation movement: Sandra "Casey" Cason and Dorothy Dawson from Texas, Sue Thrasher and Cathy Cade from Tennessee.[54] In my looking I found all these women who had come before me, whose presence proved to me that change is possible, and whose lives urged me toward action.

I have learned that as the process of shaping a negative self-identity is long, so the process of change is long, and since the unjust world is duplicated again every day, in large and small, so I must try to recreate, every day, a new self striving for a new just world. What do we *do* to create this new self? Lillian Smith said: do *something*, to overcome our "basic ambivalence of feelings," by which we move through our way of life "like some half-dead thing, doing as little harm (and as little good) as possible, playing around the edges of great life issues."[55]

There *are* lists of "Things To Do"; Smith published one herself in 1943.[56] We can learn something from such a list, but most of it is common sense: we already know that work against anti-Semitism and racism can range from stopping offensive jokes, to letters to the editor, to educational workshops, to changing the law, to writing poetry, to demonstrations in the street, to a restructuring of the economy. But because knowing what to do in a situation that you suspect may be racist or anti-Semitic, even knowing that the situation *is*, involves judgement and ethics and feelings in the heart of a new kind than we were raised with, then we will only be able to act effectively if we gather up, not just information, but the threads of life that connect us to others.

Notes

1. Barbara Deming, *We Are All Part of One Another*, ed. Jane Meyerding (Philadelphia: New Society Publishers, 1984), 326. Other works by Barbara Deming that have helped me include *Prison Notes* (New York: Grossman, 1966); *Revolution and Equilibrium* (New York: Grossman, 1971); *We Cannot Live without Our Lives* (New York: Grossman/Viking, 1974); and *Remembering Who We Are* (Pagoda Publications, 1981).
2. Deming, "Confronting One's Own Oppression," in *We Are All Part of One Another*, 237.
3. Patsy Sims, *The Klan* (New York: Stein and Day, 1978), 108–9.
4. Susan Laurence Davis, *Authentic History of the Ku Klux Klan, 1865–1877* (New York: S. L. Davis, 1924), 121.
5. Mrs. S. E. F. (Laura Martin) Rose, *The Ku Klux Klan or Invisible Empire* (n.p., 1913), 22.
6. John Stewart, *KKK Menace: The Cross against People* (Durham, N.C.: John Stewart, 1980), 30.
7. Works by Charles Waddell Chesnutt include *The House behind the Cedars* (1900), set in Fayetteville; *The Marrow of Tradition* (1901) set in Wilmington; and *The Colonel's Dream* (1905).
8. Eli Evans, *The Provincials: A Personal History of Jews in the South* (New York: Atheneum, 1980), 73, 79–84.
9. Carson McCullers published *Reflections in a Golden Eye* in 1941.
10. Bertha Harris's *Lover* was published in 1976 (Plainfield, Vt.: Daughters, Inc.). More information and creative discussion of Southern lesbian writers can be found in Mab Segrest's "Lines I Dare to Write: Lesbian Writing in the South," in *Southern Exposure* 9, no. 2 (1981).
11. Bettina Aptheker, "Abolitionism, Woman's Rights and the Battle over the Fifteenth Amendment," in *Woman's Legacy: Essays on Race, Sex, and Class in American History* (Amherst: University of Massachusetts Press, 1982), 32.
12. Ida B. Wells-Barnett, *Crusade for Justice*, ed. Alfreda M. Duster (Chicago: University of Chicago Press, 1970), 230.
13. Lillian Smith, *The Winner Names the Age*, ed. Michelle Cliff (New York: W.W. Norton, 1978), 154.
14. Aptheker, *Women's Legacy*, 50.

15. Joanna Russ, *How to Suppress Women's Writing* (Austin: University of Texas Press, 1983), 137.
16. "Death Suspects 16 to 60," Fayetteville (N.C.) *Observer*, November 6, 1979, A1.
17. "Klan / Nazi Defendants Claim Self-Defense," (Durham) *North Carolina Anvil*, October 31, 1980, 10.
18. Ida B. Wells-Barnett, *On Lynchings: A Red Record*, reprint (New York: Arno Press, 1969).
19. Will Durant, *The Age of Faith: A History of Medieval Civilization* (New York: Simon and Schuster, 1950), 591–92.
20. Rose, *The Ku Klux Klan or Invisible Empire*, 1.
21. *Papers Read at the Meeting of Grand Dragons, Knights of the Ku Klux Klan* (Asheville, N.C.: July 1923), 136.
22. Sims, *The Klan* 243.
23. Jerry Thompson, "My Life with the Klan," special report from the (Nashville) *Tennessean*, December 1, 1980, 1, 14.
24. "The 'New' Klan: White Racism in the 1980's," special report from the (Nashville) *Tennessean* (n.d.), 31.
25. Gerda Lerner, "The Rape of Black Women as a Weapon of Terror," in *Black Women in White America* (New York: Vintage, 1972), 173–93.
26. *The Chronological History of the Negro in America* (New York: New American Library, 1969).
27. Leonard Dinnerstein, *The Leo Frank Case* (New York: Columbia University Press, 1968), 19, 51, 71, 119, 132, 150.
28. *Testimony Taken by the Joint Select Committee to Inquire into the Conditions of Affairs in the Late Insurrectionary States* (Washington, D.C.: 1972), vols. 8–10.
29. Henry P. Fry, *The Modern Ku Klux Klan* (Boston: Small and Maynard, 1922), 189, 191.
30. Anthony P. Dunbar, *Against the Grain: Southern Radicals and Prophets, 1929–1959* (Charlottesville: University Press of Virginia, 1981), 230, 241.
31. Letter from Mary Weidler, American Civil Liberties Union of Alabama, Birmingham, September 26, 1979.
32. "Klan at IWY," *Do It Now: Newspaper of the National Organization for Women*, September / October 1977, 5.
33. E. Holland, conversation about National Anti-Klan Network organizing in North Carolina, Washington, D.C., April 30, 1984.
34. "U.S. 'Is Too Great for Small Dreams,'" *Washington Post*, January 26, 1984, A 16–17.
35. Letter from the Moral Majority, Inc., February 9, 1984.
36. "More Abortion Clinics Firebombed," *off our backs* (May 1984), 3.
37. "Green Light to Get Reds," *The Guardian* (April 25, 1984), 18.
38. "Less for Kids," *off our backs* (April 1984), 6.
39. "Chief Sees Migration, Not Mining, as Public Worry," *New York Times* (April 16, 1984), A7.
40. Cynthia Ozick, "Cultural Impression," in *Art and Ardor: Essays* (New York: Knopf, 1983).
41. Mary Boykin Chesnutt, *A Diary from Dixie* (Boston: Houghton Mifflin, 1949), 148–49.
42. Constance McLaughlin Green, *The Secret City: A History of Race Relations in the Nation's Capital* (Princeton, N.J.: Princeton University Press, 1967), 15.

43. Charlotte Baum, Paula Hyman, and Sonya Michel, *The Jewish Woman in America* (New York: New American Library, 1975), 140–41.

44. *This Bridge Called My Back* has an extensive bibliography of writing by and about women of color; it is now reprinted and available from Kitchen Table: Women of Color Press, P.O. Box 1753, Rockefeller Center Station, New York City, N.Y. 10185. *Cuentos* and *Home Girls* are also published by and available from Kitchen Press. *A Gathering of Spirit* can be ordered from *Sinister Wisdom*, P.O. Box 1023, Rockland, Maine 04841. *Third Woman* was published in 1980 by Houghton Mifflin; *Nice Jewish Girls* has been reprinted by The Crossing Press, Trumansburg, N.Y. Specific books by the authors I named which have helped me are: Leslie Marmon Silko's novel, *Ceremony* (New York: New American Library, 1977); Joy Harjo's poems, *She Had Some Horses* (New York: Thunder's Mouth Press, 1983); Toni Morrison's *The Bluest Eye* (New York: Holt, Rinehart, 1970) and *Song of Solomon* (New York: Knopf, 1977); Alice Walker's novel, *The Third Life of Grange Copeland* (New York: Harcourt Brace Jovanovich, 1970), stories, *You Can't Keep A Good Woman Down* (New York: Harcourt Brace Jovanovich, 1982), and essays, *In Search of Our Mothers' Gardens* (New York: Harcourt Brace Jovanovich, 1984); Audre Lorde's essays, *Sister Outsider* (Trumansburg, N.Y.: The Crossing Press, 1984); Muriel Rukeyser's poems, a collected edition by McGraw-Hill in 1982; Ruth Seid's (Jo Sinclair) novel *Wasteland* (New York: Harper, 1946); and Anzia Yezierska's autobiography, *Red Ribbon on a White Horse* (New York: Persea, 1950).

45. Aptheker, *Women's Legacy*, 35.

46. Gerda Lerner, *The Grimke Sisters from South Carolina* (New York: Schocken, 1971), 353.

47. Ibid., 139.

48. Ibid., 267.

49. Jacquelyn Dowd Hall, *Revolt against Chivalry: Jessie Daniel Ames and the Women's Campaign against Lynching* (New York: Columbia University Press, 1979), 175, 223–53.

50. Jessie Daniel Ames, *The Changing Character of Lynching, 1931–1941* (Atlanta: Commission on Interracial Cooperation, 1942), 64.

51. Lillian Smith, in *From the Mountain: Selections from . . . South Today*, ed. Helen White and Redding S. Suggs, Jr. (Memphis: Memphis State University Press, 1972), 131, 136–37.

52. Dunbar, *Against the Grain*, 230.

53. Anne Braden, *Free Thomas Wanley: A Letter to White Southern Women* (Louisville: Southern Conference Educational Fund, 1972).

54. Evans, *The Provincials*, 33–36.

55. Smith, "Addressed to Intelligent White Southerners," in *From the Mountain*, 116–17.

56. Ibid., 116–131.

INDEX